'Magnificently lively, detailed and bold, a real revolution in how we think about the development of medieval art and architecture. But it also does a fine and timely job of unsettling all kinds of assumptions about mutually impenetrable and isolated civilisations.'

— Rowan Williams, former Archbishop of Canterbury

'Once again, Diana Darke forces us to open our eyes and see the wealth of outside influences on Europe's architecture. With an often-startling originality she brings to life the charm and elegance that Islam brought to soften the northern vigour of Romanesque and Gothic.'

— Simon Jenkins, *Guardian* columnist, and author of *A Short History of Europe*

'A thrilling detective story that begins with a zigzag and ends with a radical reappraisal of our religious past. Whenever you visit a church or cathedral, take this book; you will learn a new way to read religious buildings, and a new way to think about Islam's place in Europe.'

— Edward Stourton, BBC Radio 4

'In this truly beautiful book, Diana Darke masterfully explores and unveils the much-ignored Islamic contribution to European architectural heritage. It is fascinating, enlightening and also educating to all those who see only stark gaps between civilisations.'

— Mustafa Akyol, Senior Fellow on Islam and Modernity, Cato Institute, and author of *Reopening Muslim Minds: A Return to Reason, Freedom, and Tolerance*

'Learned but lively, Islamesque invites us to look again at medieval European architecture, demonstrating beyond doubt that the spirit, techniques and crafts of Islam inspired many of its most glorious expressions.'

— Tim Winter, Lecturer in Islamic Studies, University of Cambridge

'A guide to some of the most remarkable buildings in Europe, *Islamesque* persuasively argues that the innovative techniques and motifs of Romanesque architecture can only be explained by wealthy Christian patrons employing architects and craftsmen from formerly Muslim Spain and Sicily.'

— Julia Bray, Emerita Abdulaziz Saud AlBabtain Laudian Professor of Arabic, University of Oxford

'It's rare to read a historical account of architecture where bias is eliminated and prejudice overcome. Diana Darke does just that, writing out of love and respect for places and peoples. In times of severe division, she dedicatedly turns the compass towards the true essence of civilisations: human cooperation.'

— Marwa Al-Sabouni, architect, public speaker, and author of *Building for Hope* and *The Battle for Home*

ISLAMESQUE

DIANA DARKE

Islamesque

The Forgotten Craftsmen Who Built Europe's Medieval Monuments

HURST & COMPANY, LONDON

First published in the United Kingdom in 2024 by
C. Hurst & Co. (Publishers) Ltd.,
New Wing, Somerset House, Strand, London WC2R 1LA

Distributed in the United States, Canada and Latin America by
Oxford University Press, 198 Madison Avenue, New York, NY 10016,
United States of America.

A Cataloguing-in-Publication data record for this book
is available from the British Library.

ISBN: 9781805260974

This book is printed using paper from registered sustainable
and managed sources.

www.hurstpublishers.com

Printed and bound in Great Britain by Bell and Bain Ltd, Glasgow

CONTENTS

PREFACE

This book is dedicated to the forgotten craftsmen of the Middle Ages who have bequeathed us a unique architectural legacy. Our great cathedrals of the Romanesque and Gothic eras stand as testimony to the immense skill of these people, to their knowledge of complex geometric vaulting, honed and perfected over centuries of earlier experimentation. But they also serve as elegant reflections of their collective aesthetic and their sheer love of ornamentation. Their signature styles are not just written all over the surfaces of these buildings, but are simultaneously deeply embedded within their structures, often disguised as decorative elements.

We in Europe and the British Isles are the fortunate inheritors of this legacy, the essential springboard which shaped all future pan-European architecture. We claim it as our own, born of our own brilliance, but it is time to create a new word for the twenty-first century, *Islamesque*, in recognition that what we have hitherto dubbed 'Romanesque' owes its sudden genesis not to classical Rome, but to master craftsmen schooled in the Islamic tradition.

INTRODUCTION

What is meant by 'Romanesque'? Expert opinions vary, yet 'Romanesque' has become a catch-all identifier, grouping buildings as early as the fifth and as late as the thirteenth century into one convenient category. Aspects of this style that could not readily be explained were either dismissed as aberrations or just ignored.

In the language of European art historians, 'Romanesque' is the name given to the architectural style that is said to have emerged across France, Italy, Germany and England after the so-called Dark Ages, as a precursor to glorious 'Gothic'. Their logic is that with the fall of Rome in 476 CE, major building projects in Western Europe came to a standstill, lacking both patrons and funds, and the stagnation—cultural, intellectual and economic—lasted till the arrival of Charlemagne (Charles the Great). Declaring himself the new Holy Roman Emperor, Charlemagne succeeded, by power of the sword, in taking over the Western Roman Empire as his realm. His half-century-long reign (768–814) is seen as sparking a cultural and intellectual renaissance, but the architectural contributions from the Islamic world to this renaissance are rarely explored.

More recent research, however, has shown that even Charlemagne, from his capital in Aachen, and the Abbasid caliph Haroun al-Rashid in Baghdad courted each other's favour through the regular exchange of luxury gifts, for the simple pragmatic reason that they shared two common enemies, the Byzantines and the Umayyads. The Byzantine emperor was a threat to Charlemagne in his ambitions to rule the whole of Christendom, while the Umayyad caliph in Córdoba was a challenger to Baghdad's claim to rule the Islamic world. Their different religions were irrelevant, trumped by geopolitical considerations. Such relationships between Muslims and Christians were common at all levels, based on mutual interest. Alliances fluctuated and alignments were complex, in accordance with the changing times, but underneath all the political manoeuvrings, there was far more cultural and commercial interaction than is often realised. One Andalusian travelling through the Levant at the time of the Crusades wrote: 'There is complete understanding between the two sides, and equity is respected. The men of war pursue their war, but the people remain at peace.'[1]

The mindset that Rome must be the source of all early Christian architecture was a particularly strong conviction in the nineteenth century, when the term 'Romanesque' was first coined by a scholarly French aristocrat, Charles-Alexis-Adrien Duhérissier de Gerville (1769–1853). In correspondence with a like-minded friend, he called it 'the debased Roman' style that preceded Gothic in the eleventh and twelfth centuries. De Gerville went on to become one of the very first architectural historians in France. 'Romanesque' as an architectural term then entered the European lexicon in a way that has remained unquestioned ever since.

In similar vein, one of the most distinguished British architects of his generation, Sir Thomas Graham Jackson (1835–1924), expressed an opinion typical of his age when he wrote that Roman architecture was admirably fitted:

> to become the parent of all the styles of modern Europe… it is the only ancient style with which the modern architect need trouble himself. The styles of Egypt, Assyria, Persia, India and China, admirable as they are in their several ways, are alien to our temperament, and have no direct bearing on our modern use… the circumstances amid which they arose and by which they were shaped are so different from our own that they teach us no other lesson, and for the practical architect they are dead.[2]

In his two-volume work on Romanesque and Byzantine architecture, a classic of its time, he also dismisses Hellenic art, the 'frigid and desperately dull' styles of ancient Greece, calling them 'as dead as Assyrian' for the British architect. 'It is with the architecture of Rome that we first begin to feel at home', he writes, 'because in it we find the seeds of all subsequent architectural growth during the dark and middle ages, the period of the Renaissance, and down even to our present day.'[3]

According to that European viewpoint, the earliest place where Romanesque suddenly 'appears' was in Lombardy, northern Italy, from where it spread into southern France and northern Spain, and across the Alps into Switzerland and Germany. From southern France the style was then identified moving north, heavily influenced by the Benedictine churches along the Santiago de Compostela pilgrimage route, and crossing the Channel with the Normans in the wake of their 1066 conquest of England.

No architectural style just 'appears' magically out of nowhere. All the key innovations attributed to Romanesque—new vaulting techniques, the use of decorative frames, interlace and ornamental devices like blind arcades, Lombard bands, blind arches, lesenes, Venetian dentil and the use of fantastical beasts and foliage in sculpture—can be traced back to their origins, and all of these without exception lead us eastwards. Christianity is, after all, an Eastern religion, born, like the other two great monotheistic religions of Judaism and Islam, in the East under the influence of many earlier cultures.

In reality, as will be shown in this book, the components of Romanesque were inevitable manifestations of cultural, intellectual and economic links between the Western European and the Islamic worlds throughout the ninth, tenth and eleventh centuries, and specifically were driven by the expertise required to construct these buildings. This expertise did not exist anywhere in Europe within the indigenous population, but where it did exist was in the skills of craftsmen working in the Islamic world, in particular stonemasons and carpenters. These master craftsmen came into Europe, initially to Italy via Sicily, and then Spain and northwards, through a variety of means. Some were hired directly, some came voluntarily to where there was work and others were brought forcibly as a result of conquest. Along with their skills, they brought an Islamic heritage which manifested itself in a multitude of design details which they incorporated into the buildings. These details provide the clues to the real influences and origins of what is termed 'Romanesque' but could perhaps more properly be called 'Islamesque'.

Such a thought is of course controversial, revolutionary even, overturning decades, even centuries of what has long been the received wisdom. But I have no doubt as to the value of such a study. In today's world of shrinking horizons and narrow nationalisms it is more important than ever to understand how closely interwoven the world's cultures are and how much we owe to each other, even though we may be from different races and religions. In the case of Europe and the Islamic world this is especially true, given the undercurrents of Islamophobia that are all too prevalent across Europe at the time of writing. Much that Europe learnt from the Islamic world in earlier centuries is intangible, like scientific and mathematical knowledge, but buildings are real. The evidence is there for all to see, once it is explained and the eye is trained.

My quest began with zigzags, credited as a Norman invention, a motif that appeared in decorative frames round medieval doors and windows in Britain soon after the Norman conquest of 1066. But what began as a book exploring the secret history of zigzags quickly expanded into something much bigger. Beyond the zigzags, multiple unexpected discoveries started to emerge from the shadows of these Romanesque buildings, as if they themselves wished to dispel the longstanding mysteries surrounding the identities of their craftsmen creators.

Many have marvelled at the leap forward in scientific understanding that the medieval European cathedrals represented. French author Paul Lacroix summed up the challenge well, writing:

> What immensity and depth of mathematical calculations; what knowledge of geometry, statics, and optics; what experience and skill in execution must have been possessed by the architects and builders in hewing, carving, and fitting the stones, in raising them to great heights, in constructing enormous towers and gigantic belfries, in forming the many arches, some heavy and massive, others light and airy, in combining and neutralising the thrust of these arches which interlace and hide each other up to the very summit of the edifice—all as if the most complicated science had humbly made herself the servant of art, placing no obstacle in the way of its free development.[4]

But science does not work like that. No new technology arrives ready-made, off the shelf. When, after fifty years of work on wind turbines, Andrew Garrad won the 2024 Queen Elizabeth Prize, nicknamed 'the Nobel of engineering', he spoke of how mathematical rigour underlies every new discovery. 'Mathematical modelling has to be extensive', he said, 'and thorough in advance, so that you are sure it is going to work before you start building.'[5] This is the kind of rigour that the early architects of medieval cathedrals possessed, their skills inherited across the generations from centuries of experimentation and experience.

In this architectural odyssey I have sought to bring together many strands that have not, to my knowledge, been studied together before, weaving them into a cross-cultural tapestry that I hope will enrich architectural appreciation. Academics have looked at single strands, often for decades, and this book builds upon their previous painstaking work, taking it further to make important multidisciplinary 'bigger picture' connections.

My research has led me to travel thousands of miles, visiting hundreds of Romanesque buildings scattered across England, Wales, France, Germany, Spain, Italy and Sicily, not to mention scores of sites across North Africa, Jordan, Palestine, Israel, Lebanon, Syria and Turkey. From tiny village churches like Kilpeck in rural Herefordshire to huge ruined abbeys like Jumièges on the Seine, from vast cathedrals like Speyer, towering over the Rhine, to remote and intimate monasteries like Saint-Martin-du-Canigou in the eastern Pyrenees, one thing has struck me time and again. All these buildings we in Europe label 'Romanesque' are deeply influenced by vaulting techniques and ornamental details I have seen across the Islamic world, a fact that seems largely unacknowledged. The thousands of 'Romanesque' monuments across Europe bear witness to the varied and eclectic sources from which they derived their inspiration—hardly restricted to Rome. It is as if our Eurocentric standpoint can only conceive of indigenous origins for all new styles and inventions that appear on European soil. When it comes to how we comprehend artistic and architectural creations, there is a tendency, a need even, to put them in boxes, in categories. But the reality is that influences do not stop at neat borders, be they geographical or otherwise, however much modern nationalists might wish it so.

* * *

The notion that the monks themselves were the craftsmen of their churches has been long debunked. 'All the great authorities', wrote Cambridge medievalist G. G. Coulton in 1953, 'from Viollet-le-Duc onwards, recognize that the builders of these cathedrals were laymen.'[6] At the Abbey of Saint-Savin-sur-Gartempe, sometimes referred to as the 'Romanesque Sistine Chapel', and a UNESCO World Heritage Site since 1983, even the on-site guide tells of how the magnificent twelfth-century painted murals covering the church were not the work of the monks at the abbey but a team of professionals—itinerant artisans about whom nothing is recorded except that they came, completed the work and left, presumably moving on to their next commission. The figural scenes from the Bible lead people to assume the artists must have been Christian, but it became increasingly clear to me that such assumptions were misplaced.

It is important to explain here that 'Islamic' does not necessarily mean 'Muslim'. 'Islamic' refers to the culture of countries governed by Muslim rulers. A building constructed in territory under Islamic rule is therefore called 'Islamic', though the people who built it may have been Muslims, Christians or Jews, or any combination of the three, each according to their specialism. The same applies in reverse, when talking about buildings constructed in lands under Christian rule, except that the word 'Christian', conveniently, applies to both the culture and the people. Christian architecture may therefore likewise have been built by Christians, Muslims or Jews, or any combination of all three, each according to their skills.

The sources at our disposal in studying the medieval Muslim communities in Europe are overwhelmingly Christian in provenance and voice. These Muslims left almost no literature recording their lives, and Christians took virtually no interest in the internal workings of their subject Muslim societies before the late 1200s. It is also evident from the work of scholars like Thomas Glick and Brian Catlos, American academics focusing on Muslim Spain, that many Muslims had the capacity to 'pass' as Christians, since they were bilingual and the men (in Sicily, sometimes the women too) tended to dress in ways that were indistinguishable from those of Christians. Muslims and Arabised Christians were therefore hard to tell apart, especially in Spain and in Sicily, both of which had been under Islamic rule for centuries. On the Iberian Peninsula, whilst speaking Arabic among themselves, Muslims also spoke Spanish fluently. They straddled cultures, even using different personal names in different contexts and for different audiences. As Catlos explains, 'They lived as an integrated part of a world circumscribed by Latinate institutions and marked by the Christian solar calendar with its saints' days and Christian feasts, whilst retaining their language and culture.'[7]

In Sicily under the Norman kings (1130–98), conquered after nearly three centuries of Arab rule, the Arabic calendar was kept, as were Arabic coins with Kufic script. There was widespread Greek/Arabic bilingualism, and the word 'Arab' could refer to Muslims, ex-Muslims and Arabic speakers of Christian, Jewish or Muslim backgrounds, just as the word 'Greek' or 'Byzantine' (*Rumi*, in Arabic, meaning 'of Rome') often included Arab Christians of the Eastern Church as well as local Sicilian Christians. Court records show how Christians called Muhammad, Abdullah, Ahmad and Ali lived alongside Muslims with Greek names, further blurred by references to individuals like 'Roger, who was once called Ahmad', and intermarriage, where a boy would take his father's religion and a girl her mother's, without the children's names necessarily following religious conventions.[8]

As the respected French art historian Jean Bony points out, once documentary information becomes a little more extensive from *c.*1200–50 onwards, 'the names of the most important architects appear increasingly often'.[9] Their names in the Latin sources always appear to be Christian, like William of Sens, yet that does not necessarily mean that they were Christians. Prior to that, the architects had been nameless, simply anonymous 'masters'.

* * *

The term 'Romanesque' is now firmly embedded in the European psyche, in the same way that the term 'Gothic' has taken hold, despite its first outing as a pejorative architectural term in the mid-1500s, meaning 'the barbaric style of the Germanic Goths'. In the view of Christopher Wren (1632–1723), widely regarded as Britain's greatest architect, Gothic should rightly have been called 'Saracen', as I explore in my book *Stealing from the Saracens* (2020). The word 'Saracen' has now dropped out of common usage, but in Wren's day it was the standard term used to describe Arab Muslims, the people against whom the Crusaders had fought in the Holy Land from 1095 onwards. It derives from the Arabic root *saraqa*, meaning to steal, and the clear implication is that Arab Muslims were seen as looters and thieves. All the Christian sources in medieval times use that same terminology, which is why it crops up regularly in this book, especially in quotes. In further terminology changes, 'Gothic', up till the sixteenth century, had simply been called 'French work' (Latin *opus francigenum*), because the Île de France was credited with suddenly giving miraculous birth to the style in 1144 at Abbot Suger's Basilica of Saint-Denis in northern Paris.

Romanesque has no such equivalent time or place of birth. Its origins are so unclear that art historians are at odds on its beginning. Its endpoint, on the other hand, is widely agreed to be *c.*1200–50, the date required for its seamless transition into Gothic. This very vagueness speaks volumes about how little the style is understood.

While Europe, following the fall of Rome, stagnated, the star of the Islamic world was rising, first in Damascus then in Baghdad, where it enjoyed its Golden Age from 750 till 1258. Nowhere in medieval Latin Christendom could match the sophistication of cities like Damascus, Baghdad, Cairo, Kairouan and Córdoba. In London and Paris all but the elites languished in squalor and disease, while the citizens of Islamic cities enjoyed free schools and libraries, running water, efficient drainage systems, daily rubbish collection and street lighting. Innovations that arrived in Europe at this time came from the far more advanced Islamic world, be it in town planning, science, mathematics, medicine, music, philosophy, engineering or architecture.

The European narrative generally credits the Italian merchant cities of Venice, Genoa, Pisa and Amalfi with driving the so-called 'commercial revolution' of medieval Europe that began in the eleventh century. But the Mediterranean, far from being a blank space waiting to be filled by the Italians, had already been dominated for two centuries, from 969 to 1171, by the Fatimids of Egypt, a Shi'i dynasty named after Fatima, the Prophet Muhammad's daughter. The Fatimid caliphs controlled the most complex and stable economy in the Mediterranean, ruled by a single dynasty. Only China could claim anything similar for such a long period. Nowhere in Latin Christendom, riven by its feuding aristocrats, even came close.

By the year 1000, al-Andalus, as Islamic Spain was known, usually translated as Andalusia, was becoming politically fragmented, already on the decline from its eighth-, ninth- and tenth-century heyday, but its cultural achievements and scientific superiority were never lost. They simply transferred to the service of the new Christian rulers and patrons, who were seeking the top craftsmen to build their monasteries, churches and palaces. Throughout the eleventh, twelfth, thirteenth, fourteenth and even fifteenth centuries, these craftsmen used their advanced technical know-how for Catholic monarchs like Alfonso I, Peter IV, and Ferdinand and Isabella, on prestige projects like al-Jaferia, the former Arab palace of the emir of Zaragoza.

On Muslim Sicily in the 1130s Arab masons crafted the stone of the Cappella Palatina, Roger II's private chapel, into decorative patterns of a sophistication and quality not seen by Norman eyes before. Byzantine artisans created the fabulous mosaics, while top Fatimid craftsmen, carpenters and artists alike were summoned from Cairo to magic the *muqarnas* wooden vaulted ceiling with staggering virtuosity, based around a motif of eight-pointed stars enclosing eight-petalled flowers. These elite craftsmen covered every surface with multicoloured paintings of enigmatic beasts and playful humans dancing, singing and drinking. Roger immersed himself in Fatimid customs, spoke Arabic and copied the lifestyle of an Arab ruler, living in exotic, richly decorated residences surrounded with lush gardens, fountains and lakes. His locally made red and gold coronation mantle was woven by Arab Muslims in his own workshops and fashioned from the silk of the local mulberry trees the Arabs had introduced. It was embroidered with the explicit symbolism of paired lions attacking paired camels, either side of a stylised palm tree. It carries an inscription in Arabic and the Islamic Hijra date of 528 (1133/34).

Small wonder, then, that the skills of Islamic craftsmen, be they masons, sculptors, carpenters or painters, are clear to see all over the contemporary Romanesque monuments of Europe. The British Museum's recent major exhibitions *Legion: Life in the Roman Army* (February to June 2024) and *Silk Roads* (September 2024 to February 2025) aimed to show, through objects, how multicultural and connected communities were across the continents. In some ways this book seeks to do the same for medieval Europe and the Islamic world, but through buildings instead of objects. Unlike objects, buildings do not move. Only the craftsmen move.

PART ONE

CLUES AND CRAFTSMEN

1

THE ZIGZAG CLUE

Zigzags have been the key that unlocked for me, in surprising and unexpected ways, the secrets of Romanesque architecture. The first time I became aware of them as a decorative motif was in my Ottoman house in Damascus, where they ran, three of them in parallel, horizontally around the walls of my courtyard. They did not seem random, yet no one I asked among my Syrian architect friends was able to tell me what they meant. I had always believed they must have had a purpose, but somehow that meaning had been lost. They had been deliberately chosen, after all, not just to decorate my own courtyard house, but Ottoman courtyard houses all over Damascus.

Throughout the restoration project of the house, from 2005 till 2008, the zigzags looked down on me, guarding their mysterious secret, and my two years of study at London's School of Oriental and African Studies completing an MA in Islamic Art and Architecture in 2009 brought me no closer to solving the puzzle.

Then in 2020 I watched a TV documentary called *The Secret History of Writing*.[1] In the opening scene the presenter was climbing up a bare mountainside led by her guide. They were heading to a remote ancient Egyptian turquoise mine in the Sinai Peninsula protected by a Temple of Hathor, Lady of the Turquoise, a site I recognised straightaway from my four years living in Egypt, from 1987 to 1991, as a favourite destination for weekend camping trips from Cairo. Known locally as *Serabit al-Khadim* (meaning 'Stelae of the Servant'), it perches high on a dramatic plateau, reachable only on foot via a stiff 400-metre ascent.

What I did not recognise, however, was what the presenter focused on next—a series of rock-cut markings on the stones near the temple. These now famous 'Sinaitic inscriptions', dated to 1850 BCE, were what had been identified by scholars as the very earliest example of human phonetic script,

1.1: The ancient Egyptian hieroglyph for water, a horizontal zigzag, as it appears (four times) on a stela at the Temple of Hathor, built high in the Sinai mountains *c.* sixteenth century BCE, at the pharaonic turquoise mines known locally as *Serabit al-Khadim*, Egypt.

the world's earliest pictographic-consonantal alphabet of twenty-two glyphs, from which all subsequent phonetic alphabets, including the Arabic, Greek and Roman, were derived.

It was christened 'proto-Sinaitic' or 'proto-Canaanite' by academics who deduced that it had been the scribbling of migrant Canaanites from the Levant working in the turquoise mine. Some of the same pictorial hieroglyphs of the ancient Egyptians had been used, and the hieroglyph for 'water' was represented by a wavy zigzag line.

It was my eureka moment.

The zigzag lines flowing round my courtyard walls represented water, but that knowledge had somehow been lost across the centuries, disconnected from its origins. I excitedly contacted the Syrian architect friend living in my

Damascus house, asking him to send me a photo of how the zigzags began and ended at my *iwan*, the open arch onto the courtyard. His photo made explicit something I had somehow failed to notice before, despite all my earlier reveries in that courtyard. The zigzags began on the left side of the *iwan* arch by bubbling up from a round circle, clearly intended to represent a spring. They then ran round the remaining walls before disappearing into infinity on the right-hand side of the arch. The symbolism was clear. Not only did water flow round my house, into the next house and so on and on into infinity, exactly as the water systems of Damascus had done since Aramean times from their sources in the mountains of Lebanon, but metaphorically, it also represented the bounty of God as he refreshed each house with his cool running water, the source of all living things. *Ja'alna min al-ma' kull shay hayy* runs the Quran quote (Sura 21, verse 30), meaning 'We made from water every living thing.' Water is mentioned sixty-three times in the Quran, always in the context of creating life.

That wavy zigzag line has passed into our alphabet as the sound 'M', since all words for 'water' in Canaanite, Hebrew and modern Arabic begin with the letter 'm' (*ma'*, *mayya* etc); in Arabic script, the letter 'M' is a small squiggle in the middle of a word, and in Latin script our letter 'M' is like a miniature zigzag.

1.2: The trio of zigzags that run as a symbol of water, emerging from a round circle representing a spring, that decorate the walls of my courtyard house in Damascus, also seen in many other Ottoman courtyard houses in the Syrian capital.

Once alerted to the zigzag motif as a pattern representing water, I started to notice it everywhere, especially on churches and cathedrals that were labelled 'Norman', as Romanesque is known in Britain. This was the moment when I began to wonder what this term 'Romanesque' really meant. Was the zigzag a solitary case of appropriation or was it the tip of the iceberg? Might other features widely deemed typical of European Romanesque be likewise derived from far beyond Rome and Europe, without acknowledgement, indeed probably without awareness of long-forgotten origins?

From the Fatimids to the Normans

Starting from that zigzag epiphany, I began to trace the zigzag through the temples and tombs of successive Egyptian dynasties, through the churches and monasteries of their Coptic descendants, and into the decorative repertoire of the earliest Islamic dynasty, the Syrian Umayyads, where it bursts out in dramatic fashion on the facade of Mshatta, a desert winter palace of the eighth century. The palace still stands today as a ruin beside the perimeter fence of Jordan's Queen Alia International Airport, but its stunning zigzag facade was shipped to Berlin as a gift from the Ottoman Sultan Abdul Hamid II in 1903 to Kaiser Wilhelm II in gratitude for the German role in the construction of the Hejaz railway. When Berlin's Pergamon Museum reopens in 2027, it will be on display once again within what is scheduled to become the largest museum of Islamic art in the world. Its complex blend of geometry and natural motifs is typical of Syrian Umayyad art, brimming with the effusive energy of nature. The Umayyads displayed consummate skill with irrigation systems at all their desert palaces. Accustomed as they were to arid environments, water management was essential to their survival. The zigzag pattern that dominates the carved limestone facade of Mshatta surely represents the life-giving water that flows through the lush vegetation where sculpted beasts and birds are intertwined in the foliage. The great art historian K. A. C. Creswell (1879–1974), in his seminal work *Early Muslim Architecture*, observes that in the centre of each of the twenty zigzags is a different rosette: some are hexagons, some octagons, and each has a different kernel, demonstrating the remarkable richness of Umayyad stonemasonry skills.

The zigzag also appears in Abbasid patterns in Mesopotamia, but reached its zenith under the Fatimid caliphs at al-Qahira (Arabic 'the Victorious'), modern-day Cairo, the capital they founded in Egypt in 973. Among all the dynasties that ruled the Islamic world during the medieval period, the Fatimids (909–1171) were arguably the most active in their patronage of the arts and the most distinctive in their style. A highly energetic sect of Ismaili Shia Muslims (the only Shia Muslims to have a living, hereditary imam, known as the Aga Khan), they appeared in the Syrian desert in direct challenge to the orthodoxy of the earlier Sunni Umayyad and Abbasid caliphates. For over 200 years, they dominated trade in the Mediterranean, extending their reign over much of North Africa. For our zigzag purposes, however, the most important fact to focus on is that they were contemporary with the Normans—and indeed with the era of so-called Romanesque.

The great wealth of the Fatimids derived from the life-giving waters of the Nile and their extensive commercial ties with Europe, India and East Asia, which allowed them to spend lavishly not only on grandiose building projects but also on sponsoring the production of top-quality textiles, ceramics, carved wood, ivory and rock crystal. Relatively few of their architectural achievements in Cairo have survived—just a handful of mosques like al-Azhar and al-Aqmar. Zigzags feature prominently in what does remain, in mosque arches and domes, and were then carried over into Mamluk architecture, as at Cairo's Mosque of Baybars, and on into Ottoman architecture, as in the

1.3: The dramatic zigzag as a continuous motif representing water flowing through abundant vegetation, carved on the limestone facade of the eighth-century Umayyad caliph's palace of Mshatta. Originally in the desert near what is today Amman airport in Jordan, it is now at Berlin's Pergamon Museum.

public drinking fountain-cum-Quran school of Katkhuda in the famous heart of Old Cairo, *Bayn al-Qasrayn*, 'Between the two [Fatimid] Palaces'.

Only fragments of these magnificent Fatimid palaces remain, but many luxury items made under Fatimid rule have thankfully survived the test of time and are scattered across museums round the world. Both London's British Museum and the Victoria and Albert Museum boast their share, as does the Louvre in Paris. Some, like rock crystal ewers, are credited with magical powers, and often found their way into the treasuries of European cathedrals, abbeys and basilicas. Saint-Denis in Paris holds one such object, gifted to Theobald the Great by Roger II of Sicily on the occasion of his son's marriage to Theobald's daughter, then later given to Abbot Suger, regent of France during the Second Crusade, in an example of how precious objects passed between elites across cultures in highly influential ways. The motifs carved on these translucent ewers were often fantastical birds, beasts like lions and twisting tendrils so typical of Romanesque architecture, as seen on the Mshatta facade centuries earlier.

As if all this were not enough, my zigzag voyage of discovery was then further turbo-charged by two visits to Sicily in 2022, leading to more revelations about Romanesque.

Fatimid and Norman fates had first intertwined in the Emirate of Sicily (827–1091), when Egypt was majority Christian and Sicily majority Muslim. The Normans invaded Sicily and southern Italy as mercenaries fighting for the Byzantines, but then cast off their paymasters and conquered the island for themselves. Starting piecemeal from 999 onwards, they took many decades to complete the conquest and establish the County of Sicily in 1071, followed by the Kingdom of Sicily in 1130. After the violence of the initial conquests, both the Muslim and Christian communities were pluralistic and inclusive, overlapping culturally at all levels. Noblemen, merchants, masons, craftsmen and pilgrims of all faiths moved freely between Fatimid and Norman spheres of influence.

Even so, I was still taken aback, especially in Palermo, to be confronted with zigzags in such profusion and in positions of such prominence in so many Norman buildings. The Normans kept the capital Palermo, first founded by the Fatimids, as their own capital, adapting and incorporating the extant Arab palaces and refashioning Fatimid mosques into churches. According to tenth-century Arab geographer Ibn Hawqal, Palermo had 300 neighbourhood mosques in addition to its main mosque.[2] Of the refashioned buildings, nine were acknowledged by UNESCO in 2015 as worthy of a group World Heritage Site listing. Citing what it calls 'Arab-Norman' Palermo of the era of the Norman Kingdom of Sicily (1130–94) as an 'outstanding example of stylistic synthesis', the UNESCO description states that this collection of buildings 'bears witness to a particular political and cultural condition characterized by the fruitful coexistence of people of different origins (Muslim, Byzantine, Latin, Jewish, Lombard, and French)'. This interchange, it continues, 'generated a conscious and unique combination of elements derived from the architectural and artistic techniques of Byzantine, Islamic, and Western traditions'.[3] This acknowledgement of Islamic influence comes better late than never, though in my view it unfairly credits Byzantine, Islamic and Western traditions equally, when the real innovations—in stonemasonry skills, ribbed vaulting techniques and decorative repertoire—were overwhelmingly Islamic.

It is recorded that the Normans destroyed many Arab towns and buildings on the island initially, but since the population of the island was majority Muslim, after the initial conquest they needed the cooperation of the indigenous people to stay in power. They therefore maintained good relations with them, incorporating Muslims at high levels of government and employing Muslim craftsmen to build their hybrid Arab-Norman palaces and churches, whose Arab styles they evidently admired and found aesthetically pleasing.

As for zigzags, none occur in Byzantine or Western decorative architecture anywhere on European soil before Sicily. Their most prominent appearance comes in Roger II's Throne Room within the Norman palace at Palermo, where they form the foundation of the composition in a key mosaic symbolising royalty and fertility—a set of red and green zigzags under the feet of two confronted lions, facing each other and raising their paws to the central date palm laden with fruit.

At the Benedictine cloister of Monreale Cathedral (*c.*1172–1200) on the outskirts of Palermo, the striking column fountain in the cloister courtyard is deeply incised with zigzags, as are some of the surrounding columns. The arches of the cloister itself are all decorated with them, alongside wild creatures embroiled in the foliage of the carved capitals.

At La Zisa, also on Palermo's outskirts, the Arab Room marble fountain served as the model for the Arab Hall at Leighton House, London home of Lord Frederic Leighton (1830–1896), a Victorian painter and sculptor. The fountain is carved with zigzags on the surface where the water runs, as indeed are most public fountains (Arabic *salsabil*) across the Islamic world.

Palermo Cathedral (1184), built on the site of the city's main Fatimid mosque, is also heavily decorated with zigzags and other features of Islamic architecture, as are Norman tombs in Palermo cemeteries like Sant'Orsola,

1.4: Zigzags representing water decorate the slender columns that surround the fountain in the cloister of Monreale Cathedral, originally part of a Benedictine monastery on the outskirts of Palermo, commissioned by the Norman king William II of Sicily (r.1166–89).

so much so that it is easy to forget these are not Islamic graveyards but Christian ones. All the architectural evidence suggests that zigzags entered into Norman culture in Sicily.

Throughout the twelfth century the Normans then brought both these styles and quite probably the craftsmen back to France, and began to build structures like the Benedictine and Cluniac Vézelay Abbey (1120) on the pilgrim route to Santiago de Compostela. Recognised by UNESCO as a World Heritage Site as early as 1979, Vézelay is widely deemed a triumph of Burgundian Romanesque, while its zigzag arches and rib vaulting remain unrecognised as Sicilian Islamic borrowings. The rib vaulting, which requires a far more advanced understanding of geometry than was present in Europe at that time, then begins to appear in France's early Gothic cathedrals, abbeys and basilicas like Saint-Denis (1135–44), Sens (1135/40) and Senlis (1151).

Particularly ironic, in the light of such Islamic sophistication, is the famous lintel of the Vézelay portal which portrays the 'heathens', namely the 'godless' Arabs and Turks, as physically backward and grotesque, with pig snouts, elephantine ears and other deformities. Bernard of Clairvaux, founder of the stricter Cistercian branch of the Benedictines, preached in favour of the Second Crusade at Vézelay in 1146, and the deliberate dehumanisation of the non-Christian 'enemy' in this way, more political than religious, was consistent with Pope Urban II's call in 1095 for the First Crusade, as a mission to capture the Holy Land and 'exterminate this vile race'.[4]

Zigzags and other Arab elements also passed into European architecture through Italian cities like Amalfi, another major trading partner of Fatimid Cairo. The Holy Roman Emperor Conrad II ordered the construction of what was then the Western Christian world's largest ever church in Speyer (1030–83), overlooking the Rhine. Along with the cathedral of Santiago de Compostela (1075), Cluny Abbey (1085) and Durham Cathedral (1093), it was one of the most ambitious projects of its time. Zigzags feature copiously in the decoration round Speyer's arches, on the ribs of the vaulting at Santiago de Compostela and, above all, at Durham.

Zigzags arrived in England with the Norman invasion of 1066 and were first seen at Durham Cathedral, which I now dub 'the English zigzag capital', built between 1093 and 1133. It was the UK's first cathedral to be inscribed on UNESCO's list of World Heritage Sites, internationally recognised as a Romanesque masterpiece. The clerk of works at Durham told Andrew Ziminski, author of *The Stonemason*, during the latter's apprenticeship course, an oral tradition that Moorish masons, brought as prisoners from the Holy Land after the First Crusade of 1095, had first imported the new quadripartite vaulting technology to northeast England.[5] As well as their vaulting techniques, their decorative repertoire came too. Why else do zigzags occur here for the first time in England and in such profusion? Prince-Bishop of Durham, William de St-Calais, the Norman knight/monk in charge of the cathedral construction, is also said to have brought with him from France Muslim masons captured on campaign in Sicily. Beyond zigzags, the sudden simultaneous appearance of fantastical beasts, arabesques and geometric patterns in so-called Romanesque buildings across England at this time clearly points to the Arab Fatimid influences acquired by the Normans in Sicily.

As I walked from Durham Cathedral to the railway station, my zigzag-obsessed eye noticed stylised zigzags on a manhole cover. Zigzags, it seems, far from being restricted to a narrow Romanesque world, have entered the mainstream...[6]

1.5: Zigzags deeply carved into the columns of the nave in Durham Cathedral, originally part of a Benedictine priory, commissioned by the Norman Bishop of Durham. The cathedral was recognised as far ahead of its time, with advanced use of ribbed vaults and pointed arches, constructed at speed in 1093–6.

2

FANTASTICAL BEASTS, FRAMES, FOLIAGE AND FACES

Exploring the Ancient Archetypes

Ancient peoples' early choices of decoration shed light on their attempts to comprehend the world around them. Once we are connected to this deeper past, we can grasp how archetypal patterns—like zigzags—have been passed down through buildings as part of our cultural heritage. What we think of today as 'national' styles can thus be better appreciated as the hybrid, multi-influenced architectural achievements that they are.

Fantastical Creatures

A major feature of Romanesque architecture is the sudden proliferation of fantastical creatures popping out of the foliage carved all over stone doorways, capitals and arches, especially in cloisters. Theatrical dragons started to appear, along with exotic griffins, winged lions, monkeys, elephants, camels, hippos, rams, ostriches, cranes, pelicans, eagles and peacocks in contorted postures, often in pairs, wrestling with each other or in stylised postures either confronted (facing each other) or addorsed (back to back), not only in church sculpture but also on reliquaries, lamps, floor tiles and even embroidered onto priests' vestments. Sometimes they were hybrid, half horse, half goat, part serpent, part fish, sometimes with many heads on one body or many bodies on one head.

The popularity of these creatures famously drew the censure of the influential Benedictine abbot, mystic, co-founder of the Knights Templar and later saint, Bernard of Clairvaux (1090–1153), who, in a letter written *c.*1125, railed against this use of animals in church sculpture. 'What business', he exclaims indignantly, 'have those ridiculous monstrosities, those creatures of wonderfully deformed beauty and beautiful deformity, before the eyes of studious friars in the courts of cloisters? What mean those filthy apes, those fierce lions, those monstrous centaurs, those half-men, those spotted tigers, those fighting soldiers and horn-blowing hunters?'[1]

His distaste for such excesses led him to break away from the Benedictines to help found a new order, the Cistercians, whose abbeys were notable for their much plainer, unadorned architecture, largely free from animal or figural sculpture. 'O God!' he bemoans, 'if one is not ashamed of these puerilities, why does one not at least spare the expense?'

So why did the Church condone such costly carving and why did all those fantastical creatures suddenly appear in the Romanesque period, generally defined as between 1000 and 1250? The usual answer is to cite popular illustrated texts known as the medieval bestiaries, along with a few references to medieval illuminated manuscripts. Rarely does anyone query where the medieval bestiaries themselves came from, or why they suddenly became popular, let alone the mystery of the hybrid human-beasts and their antics. We know from the eleventh/twelfth-century image of a Fatimid hare on display in New York's Metropolitan Museum of Art at the time of writing that there is a lost Fatimid bestiary called 'The Speech of the Wild Animals'. Sometimes scholars look back to Aesop's Fables (written between 620 and 564 BCE) as a primary source, and while these are certainly well known to modern European readers, the reality is that Greek was not widely read in medieval times, neither were the fables imbued with religious significance in the way that the medieval bestiaries were by the Church, seeking to justify their sudden prominence in the churches. More importantly, such Christian interpretations of the creatures ignore the role of the much earlier Near Eastern and Egyptian fables, which, once their purpose and playfulness is fully understood, help decode these enigmatic Romanesque capitals as far more secular than sacred.

Aesop himself was assumed to have been a freed slave living in Greece *c.*600 BCE, perpetuating the oral storytelling tradition, and the Fables were only collated and written down several centuries later. They were turned into verse by Babrius, a Roman living in Syria in the early third century CE, who even acknowledged the earlier antecedents, writing:

> The fable, O son of Emperor Alexander (Severus), Is an invention of the ancient Syrians (Assyrians) Who were ruled in former days by Ninus and Belus. They say that wise Aesop was the first to tell them To the Greeks, and Cybissus to tell them To the Libyans as well.[2]

The earliest fables found in the ancient Near East and Egypt tend to feature two animals having an argument or debate. One is recognisably higher up the hierarchy, while the other is in an inferior social position. They each boast about their virtues and downplay their rival. The debate is then settled by an authority figure or deity, who usually rules in favour of the underdog. There is nothing inherently religious in these fables.

Depictions of animals behaving like humans had a long history in the Mesopotamian and Egyptian traditions, stretching back to about 3000 BCE, and have frequently been interpreted as social satires. During the Egyptian New Kingdom (*c.*1550–1080 BCE) the village of Deir el-Medina, located on the west bank of the Nile opposite Luxor, offers very important clues as it was home to the artisans who worked on the royal tombs of the Valley of the Kings, the top craftsmen of their day, salaried staff, who were well paid by their pharaonic masters. The original ancient name of the village was *Set maat*, Place of Truth, and the craftsmen were known as 'servants of the Place of Truth'. Thanks to the dedicated work over several decades of a team led by a French Egyptologist,[3] thousands of papyri and ostraca (potsherds) were excavated and analysed, to give a remarkable picture of community life in the ancient world across a 400-year period. This showed how the artisans, a mix of Egyptians, Nubians and Asiatics, were employed as stone-cutters, plasterers and painters and were organised into two groups, a method still used right up to the Middle Ages for building work, with one group working on the left, the other on the right side of the building.

The Deir el-Medina workers were evidently literate, and their jobs were highly prized and passed down through their families. Among the finds were many humorous depictions of animals, some of which were clearly intended as social satire because of the blatant role reversal—an apparent outlet for the servants' views on their masters. Armies of mice, for example, are shown in chariots storming a castle full of cats, in a scene mimicking those depicted on ancient Egyptian wall paintings where the king in his chariot is attacking his enemies in battle. The mice succeed, and subsequent scenes show the mice in the castle being waited on by the cats, who have now become the servants. The mice are generally shown fully dressed while the cats are shown naked: more role reversal, as servants were usually shown naked.[4] There are also groups of animal musicians, like fully dressed canines. Assyrian stone-carved reliefs in the British Museum show how music was integral to societies as early as the ninth to the seventh centuries BCE in ancient Mesopotamia, an important part of religious and secular ceremonies and banquets. Examples feature in these reliefs of ancient stringed instruments we would recognise as types of lute, harp and lyre, along with wind instruments such as flutes and pipes and percussion instruments like drums, cymbals, bells and rattles. These subjects went on to become common motifs in Middle Eastern art, passing from the Egyptian Copts to the Syrian Umayyads, who then brought them into Spain (see Chapter 3).

Kalila war-Dimna *Animal Fables*

Not well known in European art history circles is the fact that the Islamic world had its own books of illustrated animal fables well before the medieval bestiaries, very much part of Muslim culture and widely enjoyed and appreciated for their humour and didactic teachings. Such was the reputation of these fables that the first book commissioned for translation from the Arabic by Alfonso the Wise, King of Castile, León and Galicia from 1252 to 1284, was precisely such a book, in the knowledge that it contained stories where the animals instruct the ruler in how to govern effectively. *Kalila wa-Dimna*, originally translated into Persian in the sixth century, then into Arabic in the eighth century from the Sanskrit original of the second century BCE, is considered a masterpiece of world literature. Alfonso also requested the translation of Arabic works on astral magic, astrology and alchemy, keen to learn what was deemed to be the secret knowledge of the once-powerful Arab caliphs.

Kalila and Dimna are the two jackal narrators and protagonists, with lessons for kings. The lion is the king, with a faithful ox as his servant. Muslim masons would have been very familiar with these animal fables as part of their cultural tradition, another example of how deeply embedded knowledge within the Islamic world only reached Latin Christian elites as late as the thirteenth century. This was the era when much knowledge passed across into Christian guilds, from which Muslims were then excluded. The Arabic fables were known to have been illustrated as early as the tenth century by the Fatimids of Egypt, who enjoyed figural and animal representation in their art, even nudes.[5]

The Fatimids were heavily influenced in their art and architecture by earlier Iranian cultures. French historian and scholar of Islamic art Georges Marçais (1876–1962), who specialised in the architecture of North Africa, saw what he called 'the undeniable Iranian character' of the animals and people that occur in the tiles excavated in the Islamic palaces of Tunisia and Algeria. The same creatures occur in the palaces of the Norman kings and in the churches of Palermo. Marçais's highly respected publications are still considered among the standard works on this subject. The sculpture, he asserts, of our cathedrals and cloisters:

2.1: Manuscript illustrating the animal fables known as *Kalila wa-Dimna*, humorous tales where the animals instruct the ruler on how to govern, first translated into Arabic from the Sanskrit original in the eighth century, and familiar to Muslim culture long before the medieval bestiaries appeared in Latin Christendom.

> is also inspired from the same source, copied from precious silks or ivories which merchants or pilgrims brought back to France, the lions and griffins carved by our Romanesque sculptors which affirm the Iranian Islamic influence. In our churches of the Auvergne or Poitou or in the Fatimid palaces of Egypt, these decorative images have the same character, purely ornamental. They are never accurate animals from nature. They are stylised. Their details are never naturalistic. Bird plumage becomes *rinceau*, the tail of a lion ends in a fleuron. Man and hunter, drinker, musician, incorporating geometric or floral arabesque.[6]

Another borrowing from Iran was the Fatimid use of paired animals, confronting each other or addorsed, especially with raised wings, representing power and religion in Sassanian art. The Umayyad craftsmen in the workshops of Madinat al-Zahra, the caliphal palace-city just outside Córdoba, also used the same paired motifs, as seen in the ivory pyxis (a cylindrical cosmetics box with separate lid), dated to 968, engraved with the name of the caliph's son, al-Mughira, now in the Islamic collection of the Louvre. Again, the message from father to son was not religious, but more political, about the realities of power and rivalry. A creation of magnificent craftsmanship, the pair of lions attacking the pair of bulls, set within an eight-lobed medallion, would have been well understood and might even have been given partly in humour, as a nod to the struggles that would inevitably come his son's way as leader. The pyxis carving is also a superb example of the beaded interlace which the artist used to bind all the medallions together, as discussed in the coming pages.

Humour and Superstition

The kind of humour first seen at Deir al-Medina continues through the centuries, no matter what the religion of the ruling class, especially in Egypt, and can be seen again in the seventh/eighth-century tempera drawing on the limestone wall of a monk's cell at the Monastery of Apollo at Bawit, 300 kilometres south of Cairo in the Nile Valley, where three mice are petitioning a cat for peace, one of them holding up a white flag of truce.

At Canterbury Cathedral (1070) fantastical animal musicians appear for the first time on English soil, in the capitals of the crypt and St Gabriel's Chapel in the late eleventh century. They include a curly-horned standing ram playing a fiddle, and a straight-horned shaggy beast blowing into a wind instrument while a friendly dragon tries to distract him by tugging at his sleeve. At Bristol Cathedral (1140) too, the capitals have animal musicians: a ram playing a viol and a monkey with a wind instrument. Rams were viewed as symbols of fertility in ancient Sumerian culture.

Christian interpretations of such scenes attempt to see them as the triumph of good over evil, where, for example, a basilisk (meaning 'little king' in Greek) represents the devil, who will kill the heedless sinner with his venom. It is, however, extremely unlikely that the monks asked the sculptors to create these creatures with such interpretations in mind; far more likely that the craftsmen, deeply imbued with knowledge of these archetypal animal fables, enjoyed the fun of creating these creatures. Maybe it was their way of poking fun at their masters. If they were ever aware of the convoluted symbolism their masters strove to apply to these fantastical creations, they would no doubt have found it even more amusing.

2.2: Exceptionally skilfully carved humorous capital in the crypt of Canterbury Cathedral (late eleventh century), where zoomorphic animal musicians appear on English soil for the first time, to the puzzlement of English clergy who sought religious meanings in them.

The mason responsible for the Canterbury crypt carvings with dragons and other beasts entangled in foliage, and anthropomorphised animals, had exceptional talent. Nothing is known about his identity, but his work is so unlike anything else in the country that it is assumed he must have come from abroad, carrying knowledge of such motifs and creatures in his head, rather than copying them from manuscripts, as some have theorised.

In the southern main entrance porch of Canterbury Cathedral is a lion's head with its tongue sticking out, described by one guidebook as 'a gesture of holiness'.[7] From its location, it is very clearly nothing of the sort, but simply a lion trying to look fierce to frighten off evil spirits. This Canterbury lion bears a distinct resemblance to the Egyptian god Bes, likewise seen as a protector from evil, and also depicted with his tongue sticking out, as on the Dendera Temple.

Lions were already extinct in Europe in the Middle Ages, but not in the Middle East, where they were often kept as pets at the royal court, as in Fatimid Cairo, for example, in the tenth and eleventh centuries. Carvings of lions or other felines were very common in medieval times, probably more so than any other animal. In ancient archetypes, as at the Babylonian Gate of Ishtar, built under King Nebuchadnezzar II (r.604–562 BCE), the biblical conqueror of Jerusalem, lions, bulls and dragons appear as representations of the chief Babylonian gods, Ishtar, Haddad and Marduk, protecting the city.

2.3: The Babylonian Gate of Ishtar, built in the sixth century BCE, is crowned with merlon crenellations and framed by a distinctive frieze of white beads (see pages 32–35). It is covered in stylised lions, bulls and dragons representing the chief Babylonian deities.

A similar lion's head, sticking its tongue out in a rather unconvincing attempt to look fierce, can also be seen in Speyer, Germany, in the centre of the arched entrance to a medieval house in the old quarter of the city at No. 25 Heerdstrasse. At St Bartholomew the Great (founded 1123) in Smithfield, London, one of England's most atmospheric Romanesque churches, a cat is carved high up in the transept, again as a guardian talisman to protect the holy space from evil.

Another creature with antecedents going right back to ancient Egyptian art is the hare, generally seen as a symbol of good luck, fertility and prosperity. It was continued via Coptic art into Fatimid art, where it was taken up as a motif with enthusiasm, often in interlacing roundels carved onto wood or stone as architectural friezes.

In the nave of Wells Cathedral (1175) there are animals and hybrid animal-humans, such as a bird with a serpentine tail and a crowned human head. They are not part of a story—each one is separate and individual—but the Christian interpretation strove to see, for example, the stork as a prudent servant of God who, by eating a frog, was pursuing evil spirits. Medieval culture was highly superstitious, and in the largely illiterate society of Latin Christendom, such explanations from learned clergy would have appealed to gullible minds.

Beakheads

So-called 'beakheads', another decorative sculpted motif seen as characteristic of Romanesque and Norman architecture, and which first appeared in England in 1121 at Reading Abbey, and slightly earlier in the twelfth century in France and in Spain, would have appealed to that same mindset.

How They Were Used in the Middle East

Beakheads are likely to have derived from the eagle-headed divine creatures found in both ancient Egyptian and Assyrian sculpture reliefs, performing the same function in ancient cultures as they did in Romanesque times, namely, as guardians of a sacred space. They are not always birds, however, and I recently came across what I now believe may even be their true origin, a stylised ibex frieze of eight recurring heads belonging to an eighth/seventh-century BCE Sabean (ancient Yemeni) temple, now on display in the Louvre. The Sabean sculpture that we can see in museums around the world shows a preference for the regular repetition of a single element, often with frontal representations of the head, almost abstract, with no attempt at a naturalistic depiction.

When the whole ibex is shown it is always in profile, standing or crouching with oversize horns, set in repeating frames, making for a very distinctive decorative style, which must have had a long gestation in the second millennium BCE, since the ibex is the creature most strongly linked to the sacred imagery and aesthetic tastes of the ancient inhabitants of South Arabia. The two main gods of Saba are known by the epithet 'god of ibexes', and the horns are associated with divine protection.[8]

Sometimes the snout appears to curve round the frame, like the beakhead on a Romanesque arch. It could well have been misinterpreted as a bird, when it should have been an ibex.

The ibex is still seen to this day as a symbol of national identity by Yemenis, representing many positive attributes of the quick and nimble mountainous Yemeni people. It was the prey of Arabian leopards, wolves, jackals, foxes, eagles and vultures, and was used in many ancient Middle Eastern cultures, often depicted in hunt scenes, where beyond its literal meaning it was thought to suggest spiritual concepts like resurrection, and seasonal cycles like rain and drought, life and death. It also represented fertility. In the ancient artwork of Mesopotamia, Iran, Arabia and the Horn of Africa, going as far back as the fourth millennium BCE, it is often depicted as a pair of animals, flank-

2.4: A delicately carved third-century fantastical griffin with raised wings, found at the royal palace of Shabwa, where the Yemeni Sabean civilisation of the Hadramaut in southern Arabia had a long tradition of stoneworking and sculpture.

ing a sacred tree or Tree of Life. The ancient Assyrians brought bronze artwork with the motif to Olympia in Greece. The Sabeans (1200 BCE–275 CE), unlike the Mesopotamians, had a long tradition of stoneworking and sculpture, as is evident from this delicately carved winged griffin capital from the royal palace of Shabwa, dated by stratigraphic context to the third century BCE, on display in Yemen's National Museum in Aden.

The Sabeans were the oldest and most important of the early Arabian civilisations, centred in today's Yemen, whose wealth, fertility and prosperity was based round the frankincense and myrrh trade and agriculture fed by the massive ninth-century BCE Marib Dam, parts of which are still impressively extant.

The Queen of Saba is familiar to us through the biblical story of the Queen of Sheba and her visit to King Solomon in Jerusalem. The Sabeans were also the original creators of the distinctive Yemeni multistorey tower houses, decorated with white plaster zigzag friezes and elaborate window grilles in stylised plant forms. They are mentioned three times in the Quran as believers in God, like the Christians and the Jews, and even the bursting of the dam is mentioned.

How They Were Transferred into Europe

The fact that the beakheads made their first appearance on European soil in Spain is telling, as the Iberian ibex, still found in mountainous areas of Spain and in the Pyrenees, was plentiful in medieval times, appearing widely in Islamic art of the Córdoba Caliphate. From northern Spain the beakhead motif spread to western France and north to Bayeux, from where it crossed the Channel to appear in settings like the arches of entrance portals to churches, as at the church of St Mary and St David at Kilpeck in Herefordshire (*c.*1140); St Mary the Virgin, Iffley, in Oxfordshire (*c.*1160), or on the facades of castles, as at Norwich. They appear in localised clusters—on fourteen buildings around Oxford, for instance, and a whole grouping in villages round Bayeux and another in villages of the Saintonge region—which suggests that they were the creation of specific itinerant sculpture artists or workshops who brought the styles in from Spain in the early twelfth century. Romanesque art historians have always found them baffling, unable to pinpoint any specific earlier motif, even wondering if they are just a variant of the zigzag (also called a 'chevron'). Sometimes they have simply been described as 'inventions of the medieval mind… impossible to classify objectively'.[9]

Small wonder, then, that these top masons would have continued to work with the animal and figural traditions they were used to, and may even have derived some satisfaction from being able to carve fantastical creatures that their masters were unfamiliar with. Why else would Bernard of Clairvaux rant and rail so about the sudden appearance of the creatures, if they had always been part of the Christian imagery of the Church?

Paired animals feature again in exquisitely carved rock crystal ewers made in the late tenth century from a single block for the Fatimid caliphs, with fantastical birds, beasts and twisting tendrils. The bodies of the animals are decorated with the distinctive bead-like dots whose origins are explored in the following pages. A few of these Fatimid luxury rock crystal items have survived and found their way into cathedral treasuries in Europe, where they were repurposed and given religious significance as reliquaries for precious saints' bones and such like. One in the British Museum was said to contain a hair of the Virgin Mary. Another is in the treasury of St Mark's Basilica in Venice, while another was in the possession of Abbot Suger at Saint-Denis. Creatures like peacocks in Iranian culture were thought to ward off evil spirits and to act as protective talismans for their owner. Cats and dragons were other favourites, their protective qualities often repurposed in church settings. At the tiny Lullington church of All Saints in Somerset (*c.*1150) for example, the font is carved with a ring of four cats' heads, all sprouting foliage in Islamic style. Above, a Latin inscription translates as 'In this holy bowl sins are washed from the soul'—another example of how clergy found ways to appropriate Islamic motifs to reinforce their own messages. Cat-masks with two strands of foliage entering their ears and exiting their mouths appear quite commonly in Romanesque church sculpture. At Lincoln Cathedral the font, made of precious Tournai marble, has fantastical winged beasts, Assyrian-style, usually positioned at temple entrances as guardians of the site.

The ancient archetype of a beast eating its own tail, as seen at Kilpeck Church in Herefordshire (see Chapter 11), was called *ouroboros* in ancient Greek, meaning 'tail-eating', but the first known image appears in ancient Egyptian iconography on one of the shrines enclosing the sarcophagus of Tutankhamun of ancient Egypt, thought to represent an eternal cycle of life, death and rebirth, the beginning and the end of time. Also in the Tutankhamun tomb, it was found in the 'Enigmatic Book of the Netherworld', an ancient Egyptian funerary text describing the union of Ra with Osiris. From the ancient Egyptian usage, it also passed into Roman magic talismans and then into Islamic alchemy, in a tenth-century copy of a work called *All is One* by Cleopatra the Alchemist.

Beaded/Pearled Frames and Interlace

It is hard to overstate the importance of the distinctive frame made up of round beads within parallel bands that we have already noted in the pyxis of al-Mughira, running continuously and seamlessly like interlace round all the medallions, stitching the whole ensemble together into a marvellous unity. It is a key Islamic decorative device that begins to appear in Romanesque capitals in the early eleventh century, shortly after the Córdoba Caliphate disintegrated in 1031. It also features as a frame, in both this pyxis and another ivory pyxis, also made in the workshops of Madinat al-Zahra, and likewise showing Iranian influence. Known as the Pyxis of Zamora, it is now on display at the National Archaeological Museum in Madrid, dated by an inscription to 964 and dedicated to the caliph's concubine. Covered in delicately carved peacocks and gazelles, intricately interwoven with foliage and scrolling continuous interlace, its message again is in no way religious, but simply a token of his love and esteem. The same beading occurs within the Kufic lettering of the inscription, while a frame of knotted interlace weaves round the recurring eight-lobed medallions that decorate the magnificent ivory casket known as the Leyre Casket, named after the Leyre monastery where it was repurposed as a reliquary. Made in the caliphal workshops of Madinat-al-Zahra, it is dated to 1004 and shows twenty-one scenes of courtly entertainment, together

2.5: The delicately carved ivory Leyre Casket made in the caliphal workshops of Madinat al-Zahra in 1004 has a frame of knotted interlace round eight-lobed medallions showing typical scenes of courtly entertainment, with paired lions, gazelles, eagles and a unicorn, all entwined in a vegetal and floral paradise.

with paired lions, gazelles, eagles and a unicorn, entwined in a vegetal and floral paradise: a pinnacle of Islamic craftmanship.

It is fascinating to track this pearled/beaded frame as it begins to appear in Romanesque sculpture, especially in capitals, becoming a signature device for the artist. Again and again it will appear throughout this book and be highlighted, because it is in these underlying elements, which form the framework to any work of art, that the clues are to be found. When an artist begins a new commission, he starts by setting out his framework to give his piece its overall structure, to define its borders, be it on stone, wood, ivory or any other surface. One thing I observed early on in my research was that Islamic artists favoured working with frames, and the type of frame they favoured most of all was this beading. This is why it was chosen to frame the title roundel on the cover of this book.

In looking for the origins of this motif I first noticed it at Berlin's Pergamon Museum, where it framed the arch of the famous sixth-century BCE Gate of Ishtar, with white round flowers used instead of pearls. Then I saw it at the British Museum, used as a beaded frame in Sassanian sculptures of winged *senmurvs* (*simurghs*), creatures with the head of a dog, lion's paws and a bird's tail—an ancient Iranian fantastical beast known for its service to men as a distributor of seeds. The Sassanian Palace at Ctesiphon on the banks of the Tigris (30 kilometres southeast of Baghdad) was the capital and administrative centre of the Sassanian Empire (224–651) until it was captured by Muslim armies in 637. I also noticed it in slightly later Byzantine mosaics, not as a frame, but highlighting the edges of haloes of saints or crowns of emperors, where it most likely represents precious glittering white pearls. Occasional appearances also feature in Coptic art, as in the beaded framed lozenges that appear in the sanctuary of the sixth-century Red Monastery in Sohag, Egypt.

Pearls are mentioned six times in the Quran (*c.*610–32), always in connection with paradise gardens, where descriptions are given of people wearing silk garments and bracelets of gold and pearls. After that it appears for the first time in an Islamic context in the Umayyad mosaics in the Dome of the Rock (*c.*690) in Jerusalem, and then in the Damascus Umayyad Mosque (completed 715), where it is used, for the first time in Islamic art that I have been able to establish, as a pearl frame. From the Dome of the Rock onwards, the first iconic piece of architecture built by the Umayyads to declare their new caliphate, the beaded frame becomes a hallmark of Islamic art. Mosaic work was always a specialism of Byzantine artists, but now they were commissioned by the Umayyad caliph al-Walid I to carry out these mosque mosaics. Their new subject matter, determined by the new masters, was visions of Paradise, with fantasised trees, gardens, palaces and rivers.

By the tenth century, when the Byzantine mosaicists were sent for again, to decorate the new mihrab (the niche indicating the direction of prayer towards Mecca inside a mosque) of al-Hakam II at the Córdoba Mezquita, the pearled border no longer appears in the mosaics, but only in the stucco carving framing the arch, work that would have been carried out by Muslim artists since stucco work was a Muslim specialism. Gold and pearls are also the two precious materials most mentioned in the Cairo Geniza documents (a cache of medieval manuscript fragments rediscovered in the Ben Ezra Synagogue in Old Cairo in 1896), showing how much they were valued too under the contemporary Fatimids, who likewise favoured the use of the pearled border in their art. The Fatimid mihrab added to Cairo's Ibn Tulun Mosque is framed by a pearled border, as is the Fatimid minbar (the pulpit beside the mihrab from where the imam gave the Friday sermon) in Hebron's Ibrahimi Mosque, the oldest surviving minbar with geometric decoration. Even the world map from the Fatimid *Book of Curiosities* now held at the Bodleian Library bears the tell-tale dots.

In Muslim Spain it was now the turn of the top Muslim craftsmen, like those who had carved the ivory boxes for the Córdoba Caliph, to create new works for new Christian masters. At Santiago de Compostela the reconstructed rose window is decorated with continuous bands of interweaving pearled interlace. The same Islamic motifs are seen recurring in new contexts, as in the monasteries and abbeys that now needed to be built as the lands of northern Spain were gradually recaptured by the Christians. There is no shortage of irony in a situation where, thanks to a change in the political realities on the ground, the new Christian overlords, wealthy from booty and taxes extracted from their conquered Muslim enemies, now employed the top Muslim craftsmen to work for them at their new monasteries, founded to cement their religious authority over the newly conquered territory.

At St Peter's Church in the Oxfordshire village of Charney Bassett, a Romanesque semicircular tympanum (the decorated space in the arch above a doorway) in the chancel shows a figure flanked by two winged griffins, his arms round their necks. Local historians wonder if it represents Alexander being transported to heaven on his Celestial Journey, a myth common in the Near East, but once again, the striking element is the tell-tale beaded frame that encloses the image, the hallmark of Islamic work from both Fatimid Egypt and Umayyad Spain, seen so often on Romanesque sculpture across Europe. The human features are in the typical naive style seen in the Umayyad palaces of Syria, and the costumes and postures are also naive, almost child-like, ornamental, not realistic.

The crypt capitals in Canterbury Cathedral also bear cat-masks, sometimes called Green Men, sprouting tell-tale Islamic beaded interlace foliage from their mouths, often weaving continuously round all four sides of the capital. The carving style of these early capitals with their deeply cut bevelled curving stems is very typical of Fatimid Islamic decoration. Developed from earlier Egyptian Christian Coptic and Muslim Tulunid styles, Fatimid carving evolved to become much more complex, using figural motifs more frequently and experimenting with deeper, sharper incisions and creating increasingly elaborate abstract forms.

Foliage

Medieval carvings of Romanesque leaves were often in idealistic patterns, not imitations of true-to-life nature. The usual practice was to carve stiff leaves, resembling geometric forms, a stylisation that was typical of Islamic art and that can be traced back, like the zigzag, to its origins in ancient Egypt.

Georges Marçais, who originally trained as a painter and engraver, was one of the first to understand these characteristics of Islamic art. After visiting his brother in Algeria, where he saw Islamic buildings for the first time, Marçais decided to enter academia, becoming Professor of Islamic Art and Architecture at Algiers University during the French occupation. His groundbreaking books on the architecture of the western Islamic world of North Africa (the Maghreb, including the Berber culture) and Andalusia are still considered among the standard works in their field. His artistic background gave him a deep feeling for the complexity of the Islamic buildings he studied, along with special insights into the Islamic aesthetic. He understood that the Islamic craftsman felt no need to recreate any real plant, so his acanthus leaf might, for example, look more like a palm leaf. He also saw the archetypal influences on Islamic art, recognising its debt to ancient Egyptian, Assyrian, Hellenistic and Iranian Sassanian styles. Motifs like the pine cone, for example, were continued from the Assyrian repertoire, where it was widely used to represent fertility. He contrasted the Islamic approach, where the Quran can be written but there is no illustration of the judgement, with the Christian religious tradition, in which 'prophets and saints, cherubs and personages of the drama occupy all the space, imposing themselves in a tumultuous order, congregating in the portals and porches of cathedrals, to tell the faithful what awaits them in the formidable judgement at the tympanum'.[10]

'Islam', he wrote, 'does not have such lessons to teach, and anyway, did not believe these means are the way to divulge them.'[11] In mosques the Muslim master craftsman concentrated his decorative attentions on the entrance portal, the mihrab and the minbar. Marçais noticed how the designs go back to Mesopotamian motifs which convey the necessary thoughts about life, death and the omnipotence of God. 'The theologian does not intervene, unlike in our Christian art', he observed, and noted how the Muslim decorator, as early as the tenth century in the Córdoba Mezquita, used keystone sculptures where each one was different, in a complete disregard for classical symmetry. Even so, he could see that the whole building adhered to an underlying geometric rigour, based not on the rectilinear classical tradition but on the curvilinear representation of infinity.[12] This, he concluded, is how Islamic art and architecture developed the arabesque, a continuous rhythmic running motif, infinitely extendable. Adopted from cultures the Arabs had taken over during the early Islamic conquests, it was their own stylised version of long-established earlier Sassanian and Byzantine naturalistic plant-based scrolling patterns that had always stayed within the given space.

2.6: Delicately carved arabesque stonework in the Damascus Umayyad Mosque (715) that scrolls endlessly with no beginning or end, always abstract, not mimicking a particular plant species and often not botanically possible.

Heavily abstract, the scrolling foliage is never attempting to mimic a particular plant species; in fact, leaf forms known as 'half-palmettes' often spring sideways from the stem in a way that is botanically impossible. The arabesque first appears in Umayyad Syria on the facade of the eighth-century Mshatta desert palace and the wooden ceilings of Jerusalem's al-Aqsa Mosque, and then moves west with the Umayyads to Spain later that century. The same thing happened with the zigzag, traceable back to the ancient Egyptian hieroglyph for water, then adopted by Islamic art to represent flowing water and used as a continuous decorative frame round arches or panels, carved into stone, stucco or wood in prestige buildings like palaces and mosques.

Stiff Leaf

The origin of the Romanesque style of capital known as 'stiff leaf' is traceable back to ancient Egypt, where stylised papyrus, palm and lotus plants were used as decorative symbolic capitals on temples to represent the divine creation and rebirth of the natural world. Why would it suddenly have appeared in the eleventh and twelfth centuries unless it was brought in by the new craftsmen? In the Nile Delta, dense papyrus thickets were found in the marshes, so papyrus was used in Egyptian art as the heraldic plant of Lower (northern) Egypt, while the lotus or water lily represented Upper (southern) Egypt. According to ancient Egyptian cosmology, the world was created when the first god stood on a mound that emerged from limitless and undifferentiated darkness and water, in a mythical echo of the moment each year when the land began to reappear from beneath the annual floodwaters of the Nile. Papyrus marshes were therefore seen as fecund, fertile regions that contained the germs of creation, and the temple columns in the form of papyrus plants, bound together stiffly, represented the primeval marsh and the magic moment when the land was reborn, equated with the creation of the world. The walls of tombs often showed ritual hunts that took place in the papyrus thickets, teeming with wild birds, fish and dangerous creatures like hippos and crocodiles. The meaning was always to illustrate the symbolic defeat over this untamed chaos and to confirm the maintenance of order.

Figural Paintings and Eight-pointed Stars

Far less well known than these decorations of stylised plant-form arabesques was a whole tradition of figural painting, both of humans and of animals, in the early centuries of Islam. This was first seen under the Umayyads in their eighth-century desert palaces like Qusayr Amra, where courtly scenes of hunting, wrestling, craftsmen working, musicians, singers and naked bathing are depicted in frescoes on the interior walls, showing the caliph in the company of kings of other empires, including the Byzantine emperor, the Iranian Sassanian shah and Roderic, King of Visigothic Spain (d. 711 CE). So important are these examples of early Islamic art and architecture that Qusayr Amra and its frescoes, dated 723–43, were designated one of Jordan's six UNESCO World Heritage Sites in 1985. The inside dome of the caldarium depicts the first known representation of heaven on a hemispherical surface, with the constellations and figures of the zodiac.

Painting in the Baghdad School style, encouraged during the Islamic Golden Age under the Abbasids, continued this artistic tradition. Each face is different, highly expressive and clearly an individual, with different gestures and movements, quite unlike the stylised sameness so typical of Byzantine icon art, where the same faces stare out from the same beseeching eyes.

2.7: Bear playing a lute, framed within a lozenge shape, one of many similar images found on the walls of the bathhouse of the Umayyad desert palace Qusayr Amra (723–43), still in situ, Jordan.

Marçais noticed how Byzantine art also used geometric decor, but that Muslim art distinguished itself by its use of polygons, often in starred shapes, especially the eight-pointed star. In Assyrian stone reliefs at the British Museum, the eight-pointed star can already be seen in use as one of the symbols of the goddess of war, Ishtar, along with the crescent moon and the lion. In Islamic art it first figured on the ninth-century wall paintings in the Abbasid caliph's Samarra palace (Iraq), and by the twelfth century the eight-pointed star had spread across the Islamic world, seen in mihrabs and minbars from Egypt and the Maghreb all the way to Andalusia. Muslim masons must then have carried it into church architecture, as it begins to appear in striking form, often in continuous roundels, in abbey churches like Moissac and Conques in France, both well-known stops on the pilgrimage route to Santiago de Compostela and controlled by the powerful Benedictines, who could afford to pay for the top craftsmen.

The Random Element

There are many examples in Fatimid art showing that drawings were not used in advance to plan out work. With continuous scrolling this kind of spontaneous approach did not matter, as the motif would always fill the space, but when it came to inscriptions such an approach was less successful. In the case of the Fatimid mihrab carved in stucco in the Ibn Tulun Mosque in Cairo, for example, the sculptor ran out of space and the letters had to be squashed inelegantly into a corner. This kind of characteristic and approach shows itself again in medieval buildings in Europe, where symmetry is lost, not considered important, as seen, for example, on the facade of Lessay Abbey (*c.*1095—twice rebuilt, but consistently respecting the original arrangements) in Normandy, where the windows are not placed at regular intervals, nor are they even the same size and shape—another clue that Muslim masons were involved in the original construction. It is perhaps a relevant reflection of this tendency that in the Arabic language concepts like symmetry and consistency are difficult to translate using just one word. Such words as do exist, like *tawaazun* and *tanaasuq*, emphasise an underlying sense of harmony, rhythm and balance, all of which are considered more important than straightforward symmetry.

Ornamental Mouldings and Radiating Faces

Decorative mouldings started to appear in the eleventh century running round Romanesque church portals, known as archivolts or voussures, to highlight the inner curves of the stone arches. Sometimes they are very simple, with just three recessed and ornamented bands; at other times they are very complex with as many as fourteen, as at the monastery of Santa Maria de Sigena in Aragon (1183).

Sometimes they feature geometric patterns like zigzags; at other times they carry human figures and animals. They were first seen at the ancient Mesopotamian caravan city of Hatra in today's northern Iraq, only discovered in the twentieth century, where radiating busts of gods, men and animals decorate the arches of the vast temple *iwan* (the open courtyard arch) complex. Like Palmyra and Doura Europos, Hatra, capital of the kingdom of Hatra, ruled by Arab princes, was a rich trading entrepôt between the Mediterranean and the powerful Parthian kingdom in the second century. Its remarkable collection of over 300 sculptures show very little Roman influence and are mainly Middle Eastern in their style, clothing and jewellery.

Their temples and associated deities reveal syncretic blends of Mesopotamian traditions and iconography that are millennia old, like the sun god Shamash (Arabic *shams* means sun), sometimes with Graeco-Roman overlaps. When the area fell under the rule of the Islamic State of Iraq and Syria (ISIS) in 2015, a lot of the larger statues were defaced and damaged, but many managed miraculously to survive. The study of Hatra's civilisation is still in its infancy, but the Arab Umayyads adopted this type of archivolt ornamentation with gusto and used similar busts prolifically in the carved stucco and stonework of their eighth-century desert palaces like Khirbat al-Mafjar near Jericho in Palestine.

It is highly significant that decorated archivolts first started to appear at church entrances in France and Spain during the Reconquista, as if the style was introduced from Spain. They became widespread during the eleventh century, but largely ended by the early thirteenth century, dates that fit with the increasing migration northwards of sculptors and masons into Latin Christendom that followed the gradual collapse of the Córdoba Caliphate from the early 1000s onwards. The idea of the figures taking on religious significance seems to have been adopted, and also of using them to tell stories. The use of drapery on the statues was another similarity with the statues at Hatra.

All these elements of what we today call Romanesque—carvings of fantastical creatures in our churches and cathedrals; exotic stylised foliage running continuously in abstract forms, never realistic or even botanically possible; and faces appearing in archivolts, were way beyond the imagination and technical skill set of Europeans at that time. They arrived on European soil in the eleventh and twelfth centuries via the Islamic world and its highly skilled craftsmen, as the coming chapters set out to prove.

2.8: Carved stone statue of a military commander from the wealthy second-century caravan city of Hatra (today's northern Iraq), ruled by Arab princes, where archivolts in temples and palaces featured human figures and animals, an ornamentation that was then adopted by the first Islamic dynasty, the Arab Umayyads of Syria (661–750).

3

COPTIC AND FATIMID FORERUNNERS

The strong connections between the indigenous Christian Copts of Egypt and the esoteric Muslim Fatimids are perhaps most clearly embodied in the facade of Cairo's Coptic Museum, which, in homage to the Fatimids, is an almost exact replica of the stunning 1125 facade of al-Aqmar Mosque. So similar are the two buildings that the first-time visitor to the Coptic Museum is likely to do a double take, till they learn that the Coptic Museum frontage dates to 1910 and that the choice to mimic the facade of al-Aqmar Mosque was a conscious decision, in order to reflect how the Copts, and Coptic craftsmen in particular, had thrived under the Muslim dynasty of the Fatimids.

The impressive facade was recreated in fine limestone by an Italian architect, commissioned by the Comité de Conservation des Monuments de l'Art Arabe, an organisation set up in 1881 as part of the Ministry of *Awqaf* (Charitable Religious Endowments) by the Khedive Tawfiq to preserve Islamic and Coptic monuments in Egypt. The sunburst arch motif in the centre above the door is especially striking and had something of a revival in the late nineteenth and early twentieth centuries as a symbol of Cairo, even chosen to crown the entrance portal of the Royal Automobile Club in Downtown Cairo.

In the late 1980s many historic buildings in the heart of Old Cairo were partially submerged, suffering from chronic neglect of the sewage system, only reachable along rickety planks. Today, the drainage issues have been resolved and the monuments have all been well restored, not just by the Comité, but, in the case of the Fatimid buildings, also by the enthusiastic Bohra community of India, a branch of the spiritual descendants of the Fatimids.

Under Fatimid rule (969–1171) there was comparative tolerance of the Copts and they occupied many important positions in the Fatimid government. Both Coptic churches and Islamic mosques recycled a great deal of

3.1: Facade of al-Aqmar Mosque (1125) in Old Cairo, one of the few Fatimid mosques to have survived, and whose decorative repertoire shows how closely aligned Coptic and Fatimid styles were.

earlier stonework from ancient Egyptian temples, in a way that was evidently seen as acceptable by both religions.

From about 1000 onwards, any classical influence in Egyptian churches disappeared, and Islamic influence became especially marked in ornamental church design. Many examples are still extant, such as in the twelfth-century painted ceiling of the Old Church of St Anthony's Monastery, a day's drive southeast of Cairo, or in the beautifully carved eleventh- to thirteenth-century wooden screens in the churches of the four surviving Coptic monasteries of the Wadi Natrun (at that time called the Scetes desert), a valley off today's Cairo-Alexandria Desert Road. In the magnificent high wooden doors of Deir al-Suryan, the Monastery of the Syriacs (adherents of the Orthodox Syriac Church) today under the Patriarchate of Alexandria and All Africa, the techniques and patterns of inlaid ebony, ivory and bone have, as specialist in Coptic art Gertrud van Loon explains, 'undeniably been influenced by Islamic decorative designs but naturally combined with Christian images'.[1] They were commissioned by the Abbot Moses of Nisibis in the first half of the tenth century, with saints, crosses and geometrical motifs. Age-old motifs like carnivores attacking ruminants, usually a lion attacking an antelope, and fruits like pomegranates representing fertility were used by both religions. As a result, van Loon concludes, 'without the architectural setting and presence of Christian elements like a cross, it would be impossible during the Fatimid period to distinguish between a screen made for a Muslim or a Christian building.'[2]

A similar testimony to the interaction between the Coptic and the Islamic art of that era is the sanctuary screen made of sycamore and cedar which was removed from Cairo's church of St Barbara to the Coptic Museum. It has forty-five panels elaborately carved in fine relief with human figures, fabulous animals, riders on galloping horses, gazelles and musical ceremonies. In the famous Hanging Church in Cairo the signature Islamic beading was used extensively in the woodwork frames. The same thing applies in literature and illuminated manuscripts, where styles and designs were shared by Muslims and Christians. Coptic literature flourished from the fourth to the ninth century, with the Arabisation and Islamisation of Egypt occurring only gradually over hundreds of years. From the tenth century onwards, Copts began to translate their religious texts into Arabic, and by the thirteenth century Coptic was no longer a living language, used only among clerical elites, having been completely replaced by Arabic. Today it only remains in use as the liturgical language of the Coptic Church. By the late 1200s Coptic religious texts used Kufic script and Islamic-style decoration with elaborate floral and geometric patterns, often in the blue and gold that was typical of contemporary Islamic religious texts.[3] For anyone not able to read the Arabic, the Coptic and the Islamic manuscripts would have been indistinguishable.

The Copts, who today account for around 15 per cent of the Egyptian population, are the direct descendants of the ancient Egyptians, and this inheritance is exhibited in their early monasteries, like the fifth-century White and Red monasteries at Sohag in the Nile Valley, where features from ancient Egyptian architecture can be clearly identified. Their exteriors look like Egyptian temples and their facades are topped with a cavetto cornice, featuring waterspouts reminiscent of pharaonic temple prototypes. Coptic art and architecture always exhibited a special kind of aesthetic by virtue of this pharaonic inheritance.

In 2012 the interior sanctuary of the Red Monastery was restored in glorious technicolour, giving a very clear idea of the Coptic decorative repertoire, which included zigzags, stylised scrolling foliage, braiding and knotwork—

3.2: Interior of the fifth-century Coptic Red Monastery, Sohag, Upper Egypt, after the 2012 restoration, showing how the Copts continued the use of bright colours, zigzags, braiding and knotwork, elements that were taken back to Ireland by Irish monks and used in Celtic decorative designs.

clear influences on Celtic decorative patterns that were taken back to Ireland by the early Irish monks.

The Role of the Coptic Church in European Monasticism

All Christian monasticism stems, either directly or indirectly, from the Egyptian Desert Fathers, early Christian hermits who lived in remote areas of the Roman province of Egypt, from around the third century CE.

St Anthony, also known as Anthony the Great (251–356), was the first, living to the astonishing age of 105, and his monastery in the mountainous Eastern Desert is still active and open to the public. By the late fifth century, hundreds of monasteries and thousands of hermits' caves had been established. In 356 the Patriarch of Alexandria wrote the influential *Life of Anthony*, a text which introduced Egyptian monasticism to the West, and led a succession of European figures like St Jerome, St John Cassian and St Benedict of Nursia to visit Egypt. So many Irish monks travelled to Egypt that a guidebook was written for them, a copy of which still survives in the Bibliothèque Nationale in Paris.

The cult of the Virgin Mary was well established early on in Egypt, even before the Council of Ephesus in 431 which declared Mary to be the Mother of God. The cult was especially popular in monasteries, with many named after Mary, and every city or town had a sanctuary devoted to her. Egyptian artists and craftsmen depicted versions of the Virgin in every medium, from textiles and manuscripts to sculptures and wall paintings, from the Nativity to her death and assumption. The hems of her robes often bore pseudo-Kufic inscriptions. Most commonly of all she was shown enthroned with the Christ child, either as a young mother suckling her child, on the model of the pharaonic images of the goddess Isis with her son Horus, or as the Mother of God in full regal majesty, seated frontally and serving as a throne for Christ. Old Testament themes occur in Coptic textile design, wall paintings and sculpture, with fourth-century murals depicting Adam and Eve, Noah's Ark, Abraham's Sacrifice of Isaac, the Exodus, Jonah and the Whale, Daniel in the Lion's Den and the Three Hebrews in the Fiery Furnace. Other common Old Testament subjects are David and Goliath, Jacob's Dream and Moses receiving the Tablets of the Law. All are scenes that subsequently feature repeatedly in Romanesque sculpture.

The theme most frequently encountered in Coptic art, however, is that of Christ in Majesty, commonly painted in niches and monks' cells. Many examples have been identified by scholars connecting ancient Egyptian to Christian art, especially relating to eschatology, death and judgement. The Christ in Majesty has been likened to the so-called 'Osiris pose', where the Egyptian god of the dead is shown standing with a crook and a flail over his shoulders, held so that they form a 'V' shape on the chest, a form that is copied for the Judging Christ on several Irish crosses. The image seems to have been quite well known in Europe, as over sixty statuettes of Osiris have been found in medieval Gaul.[4] The weighing of souls is another subject that had a long history in ancient Egypt, as depicted on the walls of tombs and in the Book of the

extraordinary achievement unparalleled in Islamic history, a logistical triumph that underscored the Fatimid mastery of administration and planning even before they established themselves in Egypt'.[7]

The Fatimids were also keen not only to employ the talents of their indigenous craftsmen, many of whom were Arabised Christians, the Copts, but also to bring in skills from elsewhere, such as fellow Ismaili sympathisers from Basra in southern Iraq, whose expertise as potters and painters was legendary, together with Syriac and Armenian Christian stonemasons, whose sophisticated constructions can still be seen in the three remaining Fatimid gates of Cairo, Bab al-Nasr, Bab al-Futuh and Bab Zuwayla. Iranian Sassanian and Byzantine designs and styles were absorbed and refashioned into many exceptional buildings and works of art, the like of which had not been seen before in the Islamic world, let alone in Europe.

Just as Muslims inherited the artistic and architectural traditions of Rome, Byzantium and the Iranian Sassanians, synthesising their designs into new forms of complexity, so too was Byzantine art in turn strongly influenced by Islamic art from the eighth century onwards. As a highly abstract and fully developed Islamic style emerged, Byzantine artists adapted Islamic motifs for their own use, even using Islamic ornamentation in their illuminated gospels.[8]

Orthodox Islam, as represented by the Abbasids in Baghdad and by the Umayyads in Córdoba, saw the rulers of the rival Fatimid dynasty in Cairo as heretics, calling them 'Batiniyya', from the Arabic *baatin*, meaning inner or esoteric. The caliph claimed to be divinely guided, the prophesied Islamic Messiah, the *Mahdi*. According to the Fatimid world view, the Quran was to be interpreted allegorically and religious truth could be discerned only by the discovery of inner meaning. Under their highly secretive system of initiation a novice entered their world of esoteric doctrines, a process which involved seven to nine graded stages till he reached the level of Grand Master. Workers and artisans were organised into guilds with ceremonial rituals which, according to the *Encyclopaedia of Islam*, are thought to have reached the West and influenced the formation of European guilds and Freemasonry.[9] This is not a rabbit hole I wish to go down, but I cannot help noticing the coincidence of timing, in that Freemasonry in Europe begins to appear in the fourteenth century. By that time the skills of Muslim masons would have largely finished passing over to Christian contemporaries, who then kept these closely guarded trade secrets to themselves, to ensure their craft monopoly and the exclusion of all rivals. The same thing happened when the Venetians stole the Damascus glassmaking techniques after Tamerlane's sack of the city in 1401, then assiduously protected their new monopoly on the island of Murano.

Much Fatimid architecture today has been lost, either destroyed or built over by subsequent Sunni rulers, keen to obliterate all traces of what they saw as a heretical Shi'i dynasty. The two main Cairo palace complexes, the Eastern and the Western, were built in the late tenth century at the heart of the walled city, in an area that still today is known as *Bayn al-Qasrayn* (Arabic 'Between the two Palaces'), even though almost nothing of them remains.

What does remain, however, are contemporary accounts of these two enormous caliphal palaces which describe that there were 1,000 watchmen—500 mounted, 500 on foot—with 12,000 hired servants as well as many women and slave girls. The exterior walls, like the facades of all subsequent Fatimid and Ayyubid buildings, were decorated with blind arcades, a decorative design adopted from the Sassanians, whose sophisticated palace at Ctesiphon provided the model after it was first captured by Muslim armies in 637. The houses inside the Fatimid palace walls were described as 'like mountains', many with seven storeys and some even with fourteen. Height, it seems, was not a problem for Fatimid builders, and a reliable source described how there was a roof garden on top of one seven-storey house where the tenant raised a calf, which was used to turn a waterwheel to lift water from a well to irrigate orange trees, bananas, flowers and herbs planted on the roof.[10] Even today, Cairenes routinely keep livestock—chickens, sheep and cattle—on the roofs of tall blocks of flats, feeding the larger animals till they are fat enough for slaughter, a much more cost-effective source of meat than relying on the local butcher.

No Fatimid furniture has survived and come down to us, and just a few fragments of interior architecture have been found, specifically, carved wooden friezes of superb craftmanship, dated to the early eleventh century, most of which are on display in Cairo's Museum of Islamic Art. The majority are wooden panels several metres long, with narrow borders of geometric or arabesque interlace, enclosing a frieze of alternating lobed and barbed octagons and hexagons (as found on the later Wells Cathedral floor tiles). Each octagon typically contains a single human or animal figure, while each hexagon contains a pair of figures engaged in courtly activities like hunting, dancing, music-making or drinking. Archetypal scenes of the banquet and the hunt alternate with effigies of eagles, birds (sometimes human-headed), hares or gazelles. Pairs of animals, confronted or addorsed, especially peacocks and lions, are common, and traces of colour—gold, blue and red—show that they were originally brightly painted. 'Timeless and spaceless, priority is given to concept over representation of things observed',[11] says Fatimid expert Assadullah Souren Melikian-Chirvani, Research Director of the Aga

Khan Trust for Culture. All these themes and their treatments are the antecedents of the Romanesque carving found soon after in European churches and abbeys, and even in the Bayeux Tapestry, where the hunt and animals feature prominently, especially in the framing borders.

The Louvre, Paris, has an exceptionally beautiful piece of carpentry thought to have once formed part of the palace doors, consisting of a panel of carved roundels enclosing a horned antelope and a man entwined in the arabesque foliage, with the characteristic pearled beading on the frame of the roundels. Complex interlacing bands in patterns continue a tradition that goes back to Umayyad design known from architectural panels and floor mosaics, notably those excavated at Khirbat al-Mafjar near Jericho, Palestine. Interlacing roundels are also found on early Iranian bronzeware.

Unlike the previous Abbasid abstract designs, Egyptian artists under the Fatimids showed an unusual predilection for representation of both human and animal forms, generally in a free and relaxed style.[12] Jonathan Bloom is convinced that the craftsmen did not work from drawings or patterns but worked directly in their chosen medium, be it ceramics, metalware, textiles, carved ivory, carved crystal and goldwork, and in secular architectural decoration. No figural art is known in religious settings like mosques or shrines, but the Fatimids clearly enjoyed it in secular settings, and even held a documented painting competition, where one artist painted a dancing girl coming out of the wall and another painted a dancing girl going into a wall. Trompe l'oeil painting was especially favoured. The reason for this Egyptian love can almost certainly be traced back to Coptic and ancient Egyptian precedents where wall painting in funerary settings was ubiquitous.

One of the main crafts to be revived under the Fatimids was stonemasonry for public buildings, often erected at great speed. The craftsmen with the requisite skills for this level of sophisticated decorative stonework are thought to have been brought in from Greater Syria, where limestone was abundant and stonemasonry was literally as old as the hills. Some may have been Byzantine Christians, some Ismaili Muslims; it does not matter which, as the Fatimids with their vast wealth would have brought in whoever was at the top of their profession. Bloom observes that artisans throughout the Fatimid period, 'whatever their own confessional affiliation—were willing to work for whatever patrons were available in whatever style they requested, as long as they were paid'.[13]

Jerusalem, itself part of Greater Syria at that time, was also a known centre for stonemasonry. When restoring my Damascus house in 2005, I employed Muslim refugee Palestinian stonemasons (displaced by the creation of Israel), as my Syrian Sunni architect had assured me they were the best—a fact that illustrates how deeply rooted such traditions remain across the centuries. In Cairo, the first time Syrian stonemasonry skills are evident is at al-Hakim Mosque, completed in 1013. It is clear that the stonemasons were not Copts, because the beautiful bands of arabesques and the elegant geometric interlace that can still (despite the sometimes garish restoration by the Bohra sect) be seen in the carved blocks of the minaret tower shafts and the entrance portal are quite unlike the stone decoration found in their local contemporary churches. By the end of the Fatimid Caliphate, stone had become the preferred medium for the facades of all public buildings and these skills were incrementally perfected. The surviving mosques show beautifully worked decoration in stucco and stone.

The facade of al-Aqmar Mosque in Cairo is the most spectacular example, where many of the Coptic features can be seen carried over into Islamic architectural decorative patterns. It is perhaps the most beautiful ensemble of Fatimid stonework to survive, and the whole mosque was built in three years, from 1122 to 1125. The meaning of this facade is not understood, but it has been suggested that the three main elaborate blind arches represent Ali, Hassan and Hussain, the key figures in Shia Islam, and the entire composition of seven blind niches recalls the first seven imams of the Ismaili line. The Quran itself has seven verses mentioning that there are seven heavens. The controlled extravagance of the ornamental patterns gives the facade a life of its own, almost as if it is detached from the structure.

A few architectural marble slabs have been retrieved from later Cairene mosques, such as the reused slab found in the mosque of the Mamluk Sultan Barquq. It was found upside down, redeployed as part of the floor paving, its connection to an unknown earlier Fatimid building deliberately hidden. All the surviving slabs are framed in vegetal scrolls, like a stylised tree crowned by a fleur-de-lys or sometimes a trefoil half-palmette, in the tendrils or branches of which animals like peacocks, eagles, deer and fish are entangled. They are on display in Cairo's Museum of Islamic Art.

The Fatimids, unsurprisingly, given their interest in astrology and cosmology, favoured stellar decoration with strapwork star motifs that appear in many forms of Fatimid art. Eight-petalled interlaced rosettes were a particular favourite, patterns that then also emerge a few decades later in European Romanesque cathedrals, along with rows of eight-pointed stars, as on the lintel at Conques Abbey.

Another architectural feature much favoured by the Fatimids, and which then appears in subsequent Romanesque architecture on European soil, is the

3.3: Engaged columns with papyrus-shaped capitals as seen at the ancient Egyptian third-millennium BCE funerary complex of Djoser in Saqqara, Egypt.

engaged column (where the column is part-embedded in the wall and part-protruding). Traceable all the way back to the ancient Egyptians, where it can be clearly seen in Djoser's funerary complex at Saqqara, it passed down through the Copts into local Egyptian architecture, where it is first seen in an Islamic context in the mihrab of the highly influential Ibn Tulun Mosque, before passing into Fatimid architecture.

The famous al-Azhar Mosque was erected in little more than a year and completed in 972, though instead of stone it used brick, hidden behind carved facades of magnificent stucco plaster decoration carved with lush vegetal designs. It is the oldest Fatimid structure to survive in Egypt, built with an arcaded courtyard. In surviving stucco, stone and woodwork, the deeply chiselled style known as 'bevelled' was used in arabesques, introduced from Iraq during the Tulunid period.

Many Coptic churches were restored during the Fatimid period, but there was one unexplained, atypical incident in 1009 when the eccentric caliph al-Hakim ordered the Holy Sepulchre in Jerusalem to be destroyed. Jesus was venerated as a prophet by Muslims and some accounts even mention a small mosque that had been built inside the Holy Sepulchre as early as the tenth century. The church had already been severely damaged by fire in 938 and there was certainly Fatimid looting later that century, but even so, scholars like Bloom agree that this event was taken much more seriously in Latin Christendom than it was by Byzantine Christians in the region itself. The church was in fact never fully destroyed, and a few years later in 1033, al-Hakim's successor, the caliph al-Zahir, gave the Byzantine emperor permission to reconstruct it.[14] Fatimid restorations to the mosaic work in Jerusalem in both the Dome of the Rock and al-Aqsa Mosque also took place during al-Zahir's reign, and the consensus is that a corps of top Byzantine craftsmen would have been brought in.

In the twelfth century the Fatimids also renovated the small mosque inside St Catherine's Monastery in the Sinai, originally erected as a conciliatory gesture by the monks during the rise of Islam in the seventh century. The mosque is still used to pray in by the local Bedouin population. The wooden minbar shows the typical Fatimid carving with bevelled arabesques and interlaced geometric patterns.

Fatimid Art and Humour

A characteristic feature of Fatimid art, perhaps little known and appreciated, is its deep-rooted sense of humour. Living creatures are often depicted, be they animals or humans, with sardonic smiles or in comic poses, as if relishing a sense of the absurd and poking fun at authority figures. One example is the ruler depicted as the Royal Hunter, seated on his horse and holding a falcon on his left wrist tied by a short retaining strap, a motif that can be traced back to third-century CE Sassanian Iranian monumental stone bas-reliefs in Iran, many of which can still be visited today. A Fatimid golden lustre bowl in the Cairo Museum of Islamic Art carries this motif and has been dated to the early eleventh century. The solemn pose is then satirised by the rider's facial expression, a quizzical eyebrow raised and an ironic smile.[15]

Royal symbols were also objects of ridicule, such as the winged lion, associated with royalty from the earliest times in the Middle East, or the winged eagle-headed beast referred to as a griffin in Western art history. The griffin is an imperial symbol much used in Sassanian Iran, as was a bird of prey with spread-out wings pointed downwards, a heraldic posture sometimes used to support the king's throne platform in early Islamic Iran. On eleventh-century golden lustre bowls in the Cairo Museum of Islamic Art both animals are shown in comic, bizarre poses, the griffin prancing—very sure of itself—the lion appearing to stalk its prey, but failing to see the hare drawn above it. The images appear light-hearted and have something of a cartoonist's drollery

3.4: A Fatimid golden lustreware bowl in the Cairo Museum of Islamic Art shows the Fatimid tradition of poking fun at the ruler. It depicts him in the solemn pose of Royal Hunter on his horse, with falcon on his wrist, but satirised by his own facial expression, his quizzical eyebrow raised, with an ironic smile.

about them,[16] the same light-hearted feel already noted in the Canterbury crypt musicians, sculpted just a decade or two later (see Chapter 2). Very often the scenes are timeless and spaceless, with no background setting except possibly a highly stylised tree, something that also brings to mind the statues on Wells Cathedral's West Front Resurrection Tier, where Arabic position numerals were found (see Chapters 5 and 11).

Thematic images like the Labours of the Months were often shown (a cycle of twelve images where each depicts an activity, such as pruning trees in March, or a man carrying a basket slung over his back after harvesting grapes in September) as well as scenes of duelling, with two men brandishing sticks above their heads in a dramatic gesture, their clothing indicating their elevated social status. In another image, two well-dressed contestants in a cockfight restrain their birds while glaring at each other theatrically, again in an almost cartoon-like style. The design of the palmettes and the use of a cross with four widening arms were other commonly used designs that signal Iranian influence. Astrological themes were often depicted; so, for example, the two human-headed birds, turning round and glaring at each other, usually described as 'harpies', represent the zodiac sign of Gemini, symbols seen on bronzeware in Iran till the thirteenth century and on eleventh-century bowls displayed in Cairo's Museum of Islamic Art. Sets of twelve bowls each depicting one of the signs of the zodiac were used in royal banquets in Iran and presumably in Near Eastern Arabised lands. They symbolised human destiny through the rotation round the fixed point of planet Earth. All such motifs then appear a few years later in Romanesque sculpture.

There is a sense of individualism in Fatimid art that may reflect the diverse human fabric of Egyptian society, something that may also explain the great variety in sculptural works found in eleventh- and twelfth-century Spain. In Egypt there were urban Greeks in Cairo and Alexandria, communities that were first established in the wake of Alexander the Great's conquest in the fourth century BCE. In addition to the Muslims who controlled political power and dominated numerically in the cities, there were the native Egyptian Copts (descendants of the ancient Egypt of the pharoahs) who were converted to Christianity early on by St Mark, creating their own separate Coptic Church well before Byzantine rule. There was a smaller but important Jewish community, linguistically Arabised like the Muslim majority, well connected to the outside world through their commercial activities, as well as a significant minority that formed an Armenian colony.

The Fatimid ruling establishment was exceptionally receptive to these multiple strands of influence and did not attempt to restrict them to any one centralised style. This degree of range and variety makes it very difficult, if not impossible, to determine the faith of the craftsmen, even in the case of the fragment known as the 'Jesus icon', on display at the Museum of Islamic Art in Cairo, with the unmistakeable head of Christ in Majesty originally enclosed in a roundel. His full frontal bearded and moustachioed face looks directly out of the dish fragment with big staring eyes and small lips. His halo rings his head with three arms of a cross splaying out behind it. There is none of the flippancy or mockery found in the other images.

Other creations of the Fatimid craftsmen, so fragile that less than ten complete items remain, were the exquisite rock crystal objects, carved from single blocks of the semi-precious stone, all of them inscribed with the honorific names of the Fatimid caliphs. Most are to be found today in medieval church treasuries and royal collections in Western Europe, with Cairo's Museum of Islamic Art having acquired its specimens on the international art market. The ones that ended up in Western European churches and monasteries are thought to have passed to Europe via Crusaders in the Holy Land who acquired them after the Fatimid palaces were looted.

The earliest piece, a ewer, is preserved in the treasury of St Mark's Basilica, Venice, and names al-Aziz (975–96), the first Fatimid caliph whose reign began in Egypt. The same flippancy and sense of humour comes across clearly in the subject matter, two lions, symbols of monarchy in the Middle East from early antiquity onwards. They sit on their hind legs on either side of a formalised split half-palmette, their expressions snarling, with a tuft like a human eyebrow topping their beady eye and their tails curled up. Another jug, today in the Palazzo Pitti in Florence, is carved with a pair of confronted ducks on either side of a split palmette, and another is today in the Louvre, having been taken from the Treasury of Saint-Denis during the French Revolution, and another, initially labelled 'Byzantine', was acquired in 1883 by the South Kensington Museum (later renamed the Victoria and Albert). Much Iranian Sassanian influence has been noted in the paired animals, but again, it is impossible to specify the religion or ethnicity of the craftsmen who created these exquisite works of art.[17]

Fatimid luxury textiles also ended up in Europe, like the so-called 'Veil of St Anne', dated by a Kufic inscription to 1096/7, now in Apt Cathedral in Provence where it is venerated as a relic of the Virgin's mother. Common textile designs were pairs of griffins and foxes with tracery of fine scrolling vines bearing leaves and palmettes. Latin Crusaders, after their capture of Jerusalem in 1099, also imitated late Fatimid gold dinars. In Europe they had only minted silver coins.[18]

Very little Fatimid brass or silverware still exists, which is curious since it is clear from contemporary chroniclers that many monumental items like incense burners and oil-lamp containers existed that were so big they did not fit through the mosque doors, so one door had to be taken down, then put back after they had been carried through. It is also clear that much lavish silverware was used at Fatimid banquets, all of which was presumably melted down and possibly converted into coinage. Both the architecture and the precious objects were subjected to furious anti-Ismaili destruction in 1171 at the time of the toppling of the Fatimids. Saladin, the Sunni Muslim leader during the Third Crusade and later sultan of Egypt and Syria, annihilated much of the material legacy of the Fatimids in his zeal to restore Sunni orthodoxy and Abbasid suzerainty to Egypt. Only mosques were protected by their religious status.

The Fatimids were known to have used paper rather than papyrus or parchment by the tenth century, an invention brought in from China where it had first been produced a thousand years earlier. It then entered Europe via the Islamic world in the eleventh century. Of the hundreds of thousands of books known to have been highly valued in the Fatimid libraries, only tiny fragments remain, scattered all round the world, including in Dublin's Chester Beatty library, where two surviving folios of the famous Blue Quran (950) are held, coloured with precious lapis lazuli, gold and silver.

Fatimid book illustration is known to have existed from various sources, but nothing, sadly, survives. When the Fatimid dynasty fell in 1171, the caliph's library in Cairo contained an estimated 1.7 million books, many of which Saladin sold.[19] Others were destroyed. The same was true in Islamic Spain, where only one manuscript is known to have survived from the 400,000 in the caliph al-Hakam's library.

All manuscripts of the Fatimid period that might have had paintings to accompany the text have been lost, which is why the scenes depicted on the wooden carved panels are so important as indicators of what the art of book painting probably looked like. Arab sources make it clear that wall paintings loomed large in the architecture of Fatimid Egypt, but only fragments of stucco wall decoration have so far been found, the result of a chance dig at a Cairo *hammam* (bathhouse), now on display in the city's Museum of Islamic Art. Dated to the eleventh century, it shows a haloed turbaned figure in a red patterned robe holding a beaker of wine, framed in the tell-tale black-and-white beading. That same white beading is used to frame the frescoes by the unknown artists at the French abbey church of Saint-Savin-sur-Gartempe (see Chapter 10). The best approximation to what Fatimid painting would have looked like is today to be found outside Egypt, in Norman Sicily, conquered after centuries of Arab rule. The paintings on the ceiling of Roger II's Cappella Palatina, dated to the mid-twelfth century, are likewise framed with white beading, but also show clear Iranian influence in the figures (see Chapter 6). Even Iranian themes are depicted, like the mythical king Zal being lifted up as an infant by the mythical bird, the *simurgh*, an episode from the tenth-century Shah-Nameh, Book of Kings. The central figure of the ruler presiding over a wine banquet, probably the most famous image in the ceiling, is shown wearing an Iranian crown and flanked by two court dignitaries.

The tradition of making fun of the ruler, seen in the Fatimid objects discussed above, also continues in Sicily, where the *Kalila wa-Dimna* manuscripts of the eighth century, written in Arabic by the Iranian writer Ibn al-Muqaffa, are the inspiration for the collection of exemplary stories completed in 1159

The remains of over seventy-five Islamic palaces have been found across Libya, Tunisia, Algeria, Morocco, Spain, Portugal and Italy, and studied by scholars like Felix Arnold, who has shown that the new Muslim rulers strove to introduce the architecture of first the Umayyads, then the Abbasids to their newly conquered lands.[24] That said, it does not automatically follow that Islamic buildings were built by Muslims. They could equally have been built by Christians, following the Muslim styles their new masters wanted, but they would still be called 'Islamic' because they were produced under Islamic rule.

After fast-paced expansion from the Arabian Peninsula, the Islamic armies had expelled the Byzantine Empire from North Africa by 711. Local Berber tribes converted to Islam and joined them. They then reached the Atlantic, crossed the Strait of Gibraltar and extended Islamic rule into Western Europe. The speed of conquest was such that the caliphs had to outsource the governorship of North Africa to local Arab dynasties, and of these the most successful were the Aghlabid emirs. Deputised on behalf of the Abbasid Caliphate in Baghdad to subdue rebellious parts of North Africa, the Aghlabids paid tribute to Baghdad, but were essentially independent. Culturally, however, they were akin to the Abbasids, beneficiaries of their knowledge and scientific advances, as the sophisticated vaulting techniques used in their fortresses (*ribats*) at Monastir and Sousse testify. They ruled from their capital of Kairouan in today's Tunisia from 801 till 909, when they were displaced by the Fatimids, both in North Africa and in Sicily.

The importance of the new Aghlabid capital of Kairouan cannot be overstated. At its peak between the ninth and eleventh centuries, Kairouan was one of the greatest cities of Islamic civilisation. Located in the middle of a wide open plain among extensive olive groves, its Old City, the *madina*, is still among the best-preserved Islamic urban centres of medieval times. Little remains of the governor's palace today, but the Great Kairouan Mosque, at the heart of the city, is in continuous use, still serving as both a place of prayer and as a university teaching Islamic sciences, endowed with a huge library.

The features of the mosque that would today be recognised as Romanesque, but predating Romanesque by two centuries, are legion: blind arches and arcades, twinned columns on its courtyard arches (as in European cloisters), decorative zigzags, lobed (also known as cusped) windows in a circular frame like rose windows and barrel vaults. It has several domes, the largest of which rises over the mihrab and dates to 836. One of the oldest in the western Islamic world, it is an octagonal drum on a square base, supported on

3.6: The earliest known example of the squinch, a means of supporting a dome on a square base, seen at the Sassanian Palace of Ardashir in Firuzabad, Iran, built in 224 CE. Still in situ.

3.7: The ninth-century Aghlabid dome above the mihrab at the Great Mosque of Kairouan, today's Tunisia, an octagonal drum supported on a square base by squinches.

squinches. These are small, discreet arch supports in the four corners of a square or rectangle that support the interior of a dome, transforming it visually into an octagon when viewed from inside. The earliest known squinch still standing can today be seen in Iran, at the Sassanian Palace of Ardashir in Firuzabad, dating to 224 CE.

The mosque's minaret, also dated to 836, is the oldest still standing in the world, and served as a model for North Africa and for Andalusia. Its ninth-century minbar still boasts its original woodwork, a masterpiece of Islamic carpentry with a wealth of vegetal and geometric patterns derived from earlier Umayyad and Abbasid designs, including pine cones, vine leaves, eight-pointed stars, diamonds and squares. The exterior walls are strengthened with extremely powerful buttressing. In the course of restoration work in 1935, brightly coloured painted ceilings were discovered, dating to the mid-eleventh century. Red is the dominant colour, with scrolling vegetal arabesques, based around a recurring motif of the eight-pointed star in square panels, each of which uses a different design.

Also in Kairouan, but in the Mosque of the Three Doors (dated by its inscription to 866), another key feature that would later appear in Romanesque architecture can be clearly seen in the decorative corbelling, where each corbel bears a different vegetal design, without repetition.

This remarkable Aghlabid structure was built by a private patron, possibly a merchant from Andalusia, and boasts one of the earliest surviving examples in Islamic architecture of a richly decorated external facade. The arches rest on recycled ancient columns engaged into the wall.

Even earlier than the Kairouan Mosque, the Fort (*ribat*) of Sousse in today's Tunisia was built in 821, and also has structural and ornamental features which would later become characteristic of Romanesque architecture, notably the roof crenellations and the feature known in Europe as 'Venetian dentil', a decorative continuous arcade running round the top of the walls.

Above the gate is a small chamber used as a mosque, whose dome, supported on squinches, is the oldest such dome in Africa. A rare inscription dated to 821 above the doorway of the *ribat*'s cylindrical tower credits the emir's freed slave and *mawla*, named as Masrur al-Khadim (the Servant Masrur), with the construction. The Arabic word *mawla* in this context can mean a non-Arab convert to Islam, which would apply to a Turk or an Iranian as well as to a European; it is impossible to know which, since first names like this were generally changed to Arab ones. *Masrur* means 'happy' or 'pleased' in Arabic. The oldest surviving Islamic monumental inscription in Tunisia, this too provides evidence that it was common for men to be captured or

3.8: The Aghlabid Mosque of the Three Doors in Kairouan (866) is one of the earliest surviving examples of a richly decorated external facade in Islamic architecture, with decorative corbelling where each corbel is different, without repetition. Its high recessed arches rest on engaged columns and its minaret has crenellations and *ajimez* windows.

enslaved for their skills. In this case, the slave was rewarded with his freedom, though the relationship between slave and master in the Islamic world was overall very different to that in Latin Christendom. Islam encouraged the freeing of slaves as a beneficial act, and slaves often rose to high positions in government, becoming trusted advisers to their masters. The most famous case was that of Jawhar the Sicilian, who, after serving in the Fatimid army, rose to become a Fatimid general, conquered Egypt and founded the city of Cairo as the capital of his Fatimid master's empire.[25]

Slaves were among the commodities traded by all sides, both Christian and Muslim, across the Mediterranean. The Italian merchant maritime cities, like Naples, Amalfi and Venice, and the Aghlabids both used Black (Arabic *'abid*, meaning servants) and white (Arabic *saqaliba*, meaning Slavs) people as palace attendants and soldiers. Originating outside the Frankish and Byzantine empires, mainly from Central Asia and the Balkans, the slaves were in high demand. The Arabs referred to Europeans as *Rumi*, meaning Greek Orthodox Byzantines from the empire of Rome, or *Rum*, and *Rumi* commercial activities in North Africa during the eleventh century 'were so numerous, and their purchases so great, that they could drive up the prices of commodities to very high levels'.[26] They were first-rate customers for the goods sold in the Arab markets of North Africa and Sicily.

The Great Mosque of Sousse, built alongside the *ribat* and completed in 851, has tall blind arches decorating the niche of its mihrab. Once again, an inscription records that its construction was supervised by a freed slave and *mawla* of the emir, named as the Servant Mudam, meaning 'enduring' or 'persevering' in Arabic. The prayer hall is covered with rubble stone vaults instead of the usual flat wooden ceiling. The dome in front of the mihrab has an octagonal drum with scalloped squinches and carved floral decoration. Below the dome in the tympanum of the supporting arches on either side is a striking checkerboard pattern made up of lozenges filled with rosettes and other floral motifs, decorative styles that appear over a century later in Europe's Romanesque churches.

Mahdia: The First Fatimid Capital

Other key influential buildings of *Ifriqiya* (Arabic for Africa), as the region was known, belonged to the Fatimid dynasty that followed the Aghlabids in 909. Challenging the orthodoxy of the Sunni caliphates in Córdoba and Baghdad, the Shi'i Fatimids founded Mahdia (in present-day Tunisia) as their capital, named after the Mahdi, the divinely guided imam who was their caliph. As Shia Muslims they believed in the hereditary principle of succession, and therefore regarded Ali, the Prophet Muhammad's cousin and son-in-law, as the first caliph (Arabic *khalifa*, 'successor'). Though later named by others 'Fatimids' after Fatima, Muhammad's daughter (he had no sons who outlived him), they in fact called themselves *al-dawla al-alawiya*, meaning 'the State based on Ali'.

The Great Mosque of Mahdia, begun in 916, follows the typical layout of a large courtyard surrounded by open arcades on four sides like a cloister, an arrangement that was typical of mosques in North Africa and closely follows the earlier ninth-century layout of the Great Kairouan Mosque. The monumental portal and its galleried portico projecting forward from the walls have survived from the original tenth-century structure, the same style of projecting entrance that was later used in Cairo at the Fatimid al-Azhar Mosque. The remainder is a careful reconstruction by archaeologists based on their findings, so is thought to be a faithful representation. Georges Marçais was the first to document the structure, much of which had originally been clad in marble, stripped and taken as booty to Italy in a raid carried out by a Pisan-Genoese fleet in 1087. The church of San Sisto in Pisa is thought to have been the beneficiary of the marble. The church also boasts other Islamic trophies like an Arabic tombstone and Islamic ceramic dishes (known in Italian as *bacini*) of the tenth and eleventh centuries, quite commonly found on the exterior walls of local Italian churches of the period. Pisan churches alone boast over 1,800 such *bacini*.[27] It is also striking that the architecture of Pisa Cathedral and the Leaning Tower uses the same tall blind niches and blind

3.9: The monumental portal of the Great Mosque of Mahdia (916), first capital of the Fatimids, successors to the Aghlabids, in today's Tunisia, showing the porch with its tall blind arches, the same as those that appear on European cathedrals like Pisa a century or so later.

arcades as the architecture of the Mahdia Mosque's original tenth-century entrance portico. The same use of narrow blind niches was found in the mihrab, now reconstructed, echoing the ones on the entrance portal.

Similarities have also been noted between the eleventh-century groin vaults (where two barrel vaults cross, also known as cross vaults) in the Mahdia Mosque portico ceiling and the subsequent groin vaults at Cluny and Autun (France) and Monte Cassino and Sant'Angelo in Formis (Italy), all Benedictine abbeys, which suggests not just that a transfer of styles took place between the Fatimid capital and Europe, but also a transfer of manpower, probably as captives, since the local expertise did not exist so early.

The dome above the mihrab resting on pendentives also predated by centuries the Romanesque churches in France which introduced similar domes, as at the twelfth-century churches of Cahors, Souillac and Loches. Pendentives were originally a Byzantine technique, first seen fully formed at the sixth-century Hagia Sophia in Constantinople, where the weight of the dome is

3.10: The Ribat of Sousse, today's Tunisia, built in 821 under the Aghlabids, even earlier than the Kairouan Mosque, showing the roof crenellations and arcaded frieze known as 'Venetian dentil' that appear in European cathedrals some two centuries later.

transferred to the four corners of the square supporting base by four semicircular arches.

When the Fatimids left their two royal cities of Mahdia and al-Mansuriya and transferred their capital to Cairo, they left their realm of *Ifriqiya* in the hands of the Zirids, a Berber tribe. The Fatimid caliph sent them architects, workers and materials to build their capital Ashir, in gratitude for their role in helping put down a local insurgency, and specifically sent them 'an architect more able than the others of *Ifriqiya*',[28] proving once again that when it came to prestige projects, top craftsmen were brought in. Everyone recognised that the local builders would not have been up to the job.

Another Berber tribe, the Bani Hammad, set themselves up as rivals to the Zirids, trading out of the port of Béjaïa. Their prosperous dynasty lasted 150 years until 1152. Skilled agriculturalists and builders, the Bani Hammad

3.11: The blind-arched tower minaret at Qal'at Bani Hammad in today's north-central Algeria, the most imposing remnant of the royal city built in 1007 by the Berber Bani Hammad tribe, whose dynasty lasted until 1152. Its features can be seen in many later mosque and church towers across Europe.

produced an architectural masterpiece, today a UNESCO World Heritage Site, that can still be seen in the Hodna Mountains of modern north-central Algeria: a royal city built in 1007 called Qal'at Bani Hammad, meaning the Castle of the Hammad Tribe. Originally surrounded by 7 kilometres of city walls, it had commercial and artisanal districts, magnificent gardens and many palatial complexes like the Palace of Health and the Palace of the Star. The most striking element of the royal city to remain is the square minaret tower of its Great Mosque, with its tall blind niches and overlapping arcades, still standing in three vertical registers.

4

SARACEN CRAFTSMEN ACROSS EUROPE

Architectural styles change very gradually, taking many generations to evolve. No huge shift just happens overnight, unless of course it is brought in from elsewhere, by foreign craftsmen. The two places in Europe which are generally ignored for the purposes of Romanesque, but which I would argue are the most significant of all, are Muslim Spain and Sicily. These are where I will begin my story, and demonstrate how the styles that are seen there, and which themselves originated further east under Islamic influences, then found their way into Europe and into its great cathedrals.

The world of construction and decorative crafts was dominated by Muslims in early medieval Europe, and modern research is bringing to light more and more evidence showing how these Muslim communities thrived, their skills in high demand, as well-paid and well-respected members of society, whilst living under new Christian masters. Across Latin Christendom, not just in the Iberian Peninsula, Sicily and southern Italy, but also, perhaps surprisingly, in France and in Germany, many of those whose skills were still sought after chose to stay in Europe, not as slaves but as free agents. As well as craftsmen, these people ranged from farmers and agricultural workers to highly educated medics, often in fields like surgery and obstetrics. Muslim midwives served in the royal families of Castile and Navarre till as late as the fourteenth and fifteenth centuries.[1]

In Spain and Portugal

The obvious place to begin is Spain's highly influential Great Mosque of Córdoba, first built in 785–6 as the spiritual heart of the Umayyad capital, and modelled on the Great Mosque of Damascus. Even today it is still referred to locally as the Córdoba Mezquita (Spanish for mosque), despite its conversion into a Catholic cathedral in 1236 when the armies of Castile captured it during what was known as the 'Reconquista', the Christian reconquest of the Iberian Peninsula. As the premier building of the Emirate (and later Caliphate) of Córdoba for several hundred years, the mosque saw every form of advanced technical innovation used in its construction, especially in the ribbed vaulting of the domes. Displayed on its rear wall are over 700 masons' marks dating from the tenth-century extensions under al-Hakam II and al-Mansur (Almanzor), when the Umayyad Caliphate of Córdoba was at its peak. Attempts have been made, as part of the 'de-Islamisation' of the Mezquita made over the years by the Catholic *Cabildo* (town council) in charge of the building, to present the masons' marks as the work of Christians, using all sorts of arguments which have since been conclusively disproved.[2] Most of the marks are in fact simply the names of the individual masons written in Arabic script, which show that the masons were literate and capable of writing their own names in cursive, flowing, continuous Arabic script, while most masons' marks in Romanesque buildings in England, even two centuries later, were based on simple straight lines, only much later progressing to basic capital letters like 'T', 'W' and 'P'.

When the Umayyad prince Abd al-Rahman was exiled from Damascus and his native Syria in 750, establishing a new Umayyad dynasty in Andalusia, he put out the call to all Umayyad sympathisers to come and help him build a new Syria in Spain. As a result, artists and craftsmen flocked to Spain from Syria and other Umayyad realms, bringing with them Syrian building techniques, styles and decorative motifs.

In his nostalgia for his Syrian homeland, Abd al-Rahman introduced to Spain plants like the pomegranate and the date palm, features which then found their way for the first time into the decorative patterns of stonework, woodwork, ceramics and textiles across Europe. Technological innovations from Syria like the waterwheel and other advanced irrigation techniques were also brought to Spain, where local Christians were able to learn from them. The Cistercians, in particular, whose strict non-meat diet led them to develop fish-farming, acquired knowledge about complex hydraulic engineering techniques from the many Muslim vassals they employed at their monasteries.[3]

Evidently the knowledge was not always retained, as in 1275 the property owners and residents of one city (Orihuela) were ordered 'to clean and repair the drainage ditches and the large and small irrigation canals... so that the water might flow without impediment just as it had flowed in the time of the Moors'.[4] Water mills were recorded as being built by Muslims for Christian masters throughout the eleventh century. Under the Islamic principles of

4.1: These cursive masons' marks from the tenth-century extension to the Córdoba Mezquita were found during a restoration and are now on display near the mihrab. Their marks are mostly their own names written in Arabic, showing they were literate many centuries before their European counterparts.

irrigation, water was collective property tied to the land, with collective responsibility to maintain the hydraulic system. The Christians, however, imposed a feudal style of ownership where half the water was taken by the Church and other elites, with the remaining half for everyone else. When the Abbey of Santa María la Real de las Huelgas, a well-endowed monastery of Cistercian nuns near Burgos, and favoured venue for royal Castilian weddings (including that of Edward I of England to Eleanor of Castile in 1254), took way more than its share, there were riots and protests.[5] The wood used to build water mills was plentiful in Spain at that time, and as in Damascus, where poplar trunks were the preferred choice for construction due to their length and straightness,[6] the Umayyads in Spain imported the same Syrian techniques. Arabic numerals, known in the east since the eighth century, arrived in Spain in the ninth century and were used by all Arab Muslims.

When the Christian armies began retaking Iberia from Muslim control, Christian kings like Alfonso VI of Castile gave vast sums to the French Benedictine monastery of Cluny. These, ironically, were the same funds, derived from Muslim tribute taxes, that helped to finance the great works of Spanish Romanesque and in turn helped local Muslim artisan industries to thrive. The new churches needed not only new architects, masons and craftsmen, but also finely worked cloth, glass, wood and luxury ivory products, all of which were Andalusian in origin.

Mozarabs

According to American academic Thomas Glick's groundbreaking work, *Islamic and Christian Spain in the Early Middle Ages* (2005), very little research has been done on the social organisation of the Mozarabs (Arabised Christians who had lived for centuries in Spain under Islamic rule). Their cultural role in monasteries of Mozarabic foundation was downplayed due to generally negative views of them held by the Catholic Church. The level of ignorance was such that as late as the nineteenth century European Catholics believed that the Muslims of Iberia were ethnically Spanish rather than of Arab origin.[7] By the end of the tenth century it was estimated that 50 per cent of Christians in Iberia had converted to Islam and taken on Arab customs, culture and knowledge. Large Muslim cities like Toledo, Córdoba, Zaragoza and Seville had separate Mozarab enclaves. The word itself comes from the Arabic *musta'rab*, meaning 'Arabised', and was used in Christian sources from the eleventh century onwards, but not by the Muslims themselves. They used the word *nasara*, meaning 'Nazarenes', to describe the Christians living under their rule.

Mudéjars

The word *mudéjar* in Castilian Spanish is often translated as 'one permitted to remain' (after the Reconquista), though the Arabic, *mudajjan*, means 'subjugated' or 'tamed'—clearly derogatory as it is usually applied to domesticated animals, especially poultry. The Mudéjar elite consisted mainly of middling to wealthy local families of craftsmen who served as royally appointed functionaries. Their industrial and craft activities (such as soap-making, cloth manufacture, carpentry or construction) provided them with the capital and connections required to obtain official positions. They often used Romance surnames derived from the Arabic name of their trade, such as *al-najjar*, carpenter, which was Spanishised as Anajar or Amajar. These trades then stayed within families as they were passed down through the generations. All descendants of the Iberian Peninsula's Mudéjares were finally ordered to leave by Felipe III of Spain in 1609, so that by 1615 Islam had essentially disappeared from Western Europe, not to reappear till the twentieth century.[8]

Muslim Society under the Christians from 1050

In the pioneering study by Brian Catlos, Professor of Religious Studies at the University of Colorado, *Muslims of Medieval Latin Christendom* (2014), it becomes clear that Muslims and their communities (always referred to as Saracens in contemporary texts) thrived for over 500 years in medieval Europe, even after the Reconquista. The reason for their success, as Catlos proves through his research, was because they remained actively integrated within the larger Christian and Jewish societies in which they lived.

This may run counter to today's perceptions, because we in Europe have been brought up with the rhetoric of the Reconquista as promulgated by the clergy and nobles inspired by the culture of Burgundy and the north of France, thanks to their twelfth-century construction of the twin images of El Cid as a religious warrior and of St James as Matamoros, the Moor-killer. But far from being a binary struggle between Christendom and the Muslim world, the history of the Iberian Peninsula was, as Catlos explains, 'a battle for peninsular hegemony among a shifting array of Christian and Muslim powers, each of which pursued its own agendas and chose its allies and enemies with little regard to religious identity'.[9]

There was never a neat frontier, and the divisions between Christian and Muslim principalities were subtle and imprecise, with porous boundaries. Their elites intermarried and their politics were deeply entangled. They traded with each other and raided each other, fought alongside each other and against each other, as Catlos explains. Christians began to reconquer Muslim territory as early as the tenth century, but by then the Mozarabs, though still Christian (with Eastern elements in their liturgy and practices and thus seen as second-class Christians by the Catholic rulers), had adopted Arabic language and culture and were in positions of authority in both Muslim and Christian principalities, acting as conduits for mutually beneficial collaboration. Atrocities like massacres, forced conversions and mass deportations tended to be carried out by recently arrived outside actors or transient non-natives, like the Normans after the fall of Barbastro in northeast Spain in 1064, when they broke the surrender pact and shipped large numbers of Muslims back to France, including skilled masons and craftsmen with technical skills unknown north of the Alps and the Pyrenees at that time.[10]

There was little forced conversion among those living alongside each other. The population remained overwhelmingly Muslim with small native Mozarab and Jewish populations. The Christians arrived gradually, and the consecration of what had once been congregational mosques as Christian churches often took more than a decade after the conquest of the Muslim towns. Under typical agreements, boundaries were agreed about how to divide the towns or cities, and the usual practice, as in the case of Murcia, was that the Christians took the fortress/citadel along with the main congregational mosque beside it, while the Muslims were allowed to keep their other smaller mosques, about ten of them in the case of Murcia. At Murcia it is documented that the Muslims protested at the Christians taking their main mosque, saying it was in their agreement that they be allowed to keep it, but the Christians told them they had misunderstood the agreement and that it was 'not fitting' that they should be woken up in the middle of the night by the Muslim call to prayer just below their walls.[11] Christian monasteries and noblemen were gradually granted Muslim-occupied lands, but the Muslim population stayed on, maintaining the existing networks of agricultural and craft production, but now with the new Christian neighbours as customers and suppliers. This remained the pattern across the peninsula throughout the centuries as the bulk of the territory came under Christian rule between 1050 and 1350.

Over a number of decades, the mosques which had initially served as churches for the Christian conquerors were either wholly or partially demolished and replaced with purpose-built churches in basilica style. The bulk of this building work, not just the design and engineering, but also the decoration, was carried out by Muslim workers and craftsmen. This is the style that came to be known as Mudéjar. Whether this happened because local Christians admired Arab-Islamic aesthetics and artisanal skill, or because they saw it as a manifestation of Christian domination over Islam, the fact remains that the Mudéjares helped establish and extend Christianity in this region. As Catlos puts it:

> Local Muslims built and decorated the churches their Christian lords and neighbours worshipped in. Whatever complex and perhaps self-contradictory reaction this may have elicited among both Christians and Muslims, church construction served as one of the motors of *mudéjar* prosperity and integration. Moreover, Muslims were not called on to do this because they were cheap and readily available labour. The accounts we have of the payment and employment of these artisans show that they were well-paid and highly esteemed... The origin of *mudéjar* society cannot be understood simply in terms of religious identity. Ethnicity, class and local conditions were also powerful factors.[12]

Muslim engineers, craftsmen and workers continued to dominate the building trade well into the fourteenth century. The positions of royal master builders and carpenters in Aragon, Navarre and Valencia were often held by Mudéjares, who enjoyed both prosperity and prestige, such as Çalema Alatili, a master engineer (*magister geniorum*) of Lérida who worked on projects for Pere the Great, including his royal palace in Tarazona; and Abrafim Bellido of Zaragoza, entrepreneur and merchant, who served as a master builder in Valencia in the 1290s.[13]

Local conditions varied, but in every case, Muslims were regarded as a legitimate and permanent feature of these societies. There was little or no religious violence, marginalisation or oppression except in areas where Muslims were actively engaged in political and military resistance to Christian rule. The revolts that raged in Valencia and Andalusia in the second half of the twelfth century had remarkably little impact on Christian–Muslim relations in Aragon, Navarre, Catalonia, Castile and León. The Church—or at least the papacy—was not best pleased with this state of affairs, and in 1205 Pope Innocent III remarked of Alfonso VIII that 'by his conduct it would appear that he loved the mosque and the synagogue more than the Church'.[14]

The Muslims who chose to stay included farmers and agricultural workers but also substantial numbers of craftsmen and artisans, particularly in the fields of construction, carpentry, decorative crafts, metalworking, especially in arms and armour, soap-making and high-end tailoring. In 1309 in Tudela alone there were nineteen Mudéjar carpentry shops, twenty-three smiths, twenty-six shoe-makers, fourteen straw weavers and six barbers, serving a network of Christian clients, which meant they were integrated into the local economy. This is the reason why Muslims in these lands continued to dominate these economic sectors for centuries.

The construction of the castle of Alandroal in Portugal is recorded, thanks to an on-site inscription, as the work of a Moor named Galvao in 1298, in the employ of a Christian master. In 1368, Charles le Mauvais (the Bad) of Navarre granted to the Mudéjares of Toledo a remission of half their taxes for three years for their technical assistance during his wars, especially in fortification and engineering.[15]

While many Muslims were integrated into the predominantly Christian societies, many were also expelled, or forced to convert, during and after the Reconquista all the way through to the seventeenth century. As for the Jews, the Catholic monarchs expelled them all in 1492. Muslim masons and carpenters in Córdoba, after its capture in 1236 by the Christians, were compelled to work on religious buildings for a specified period every year in return for exemption from taxes. This active integration within the larger Christian and Jewish societies in which they lived only started to change when their skills were slowly acquired by Christians working alongside them, a process that was largely completed by 1600.

The buildings were no longer 'Muslim' in style, but the skill of the craftsmen was such that they could turn their hand to churches or palaces for their

Christian overlords, whilst still employing the same repertoire of techniques and decorative styles, albeit on different subject matter. In Aragon, Navarre and Valencia the positions of royal master masons and carpenters were often held by free Muslims living under Christian rule, testimony to the good working relationships that generally existed between the Christian overlords and their most highly skilled Muslim subjects.

When the Córdoba Caliphate collapsed into civil war in the early eleventh century, Muslim masons, still at the top of their trade, moved to work for wealthy Christian employers like bishops and abbots on new commissions at churches and monasteries. From this point onwards, they would have stopped using their own names written in Arabic script, as their new paymasters would neither have been able to read nor identify them, making payment problematic. They therefore had to adopt new signs, and the most sophisticated of the masons chose the most complex signs, like five-pointed stars,

4.2: Ninth-century carved capital from the Córdoba Mezquita decorated with Islamic pearl beading in the frame and stylised plants like papyrus. These features go on to form the basis for the so-called 'stiff leaf' capitals that begin to appear in European early medieval cathedrals.

trefoils, quatrefoils or other plant-based motifs, the very ones which we find in highly developed Romanesque buildings across Europe.

The masons also brought with them their sophisticated repertoire of motifs, transferring them from Muslim to Christian contexts. One important example can be seen in a ninth-century Muslim carving from a capital at the Córdoba Mezquita, where the mason uses stylised plants like papyrus, which go on to form the basis for so-called 'stiff-leaf' Romanesque capitals and all their future elaborations. The capital also features the signature Arab frame running along the top, in the form of the typical continuous pearl beading, which we will see again and again taken over into Romanesque carving.

The Saint-Génis-des-Fontaines Lintel

Hugely important and influential, this earliest known architectural sculpture of the Apocalyptic Christ in Majesty became the much-imitated model that then began to grace the portals of Catalan churches from the early eleventh century onwards, becoming a standard feature of church entrances and facades all over Europe by the twelfth century. The lintel sits above the entrance to the Benedictine abbey church of Saint-Génis-des-Fontaines, in what was originally part of historic Catalonia, today the French department of Pyrénées-Orientales, close to the Spanish border. Carved in white marble from nearby Céret, the lintel represents a continuation of the image of the seated bearded caliph within a frame as seen in the tenth-century Umayyad palace of Madinat al-Zahra, itself a continuation of the archetypal Middle Eastern image of the enthroned ruler.

Dated by an inscription to 1019/20, it is the first known example of a Christ in Majesty figure at the entrance to a church. The Christ figure, the angels, the Apostles, and the arches that frame all the figures are in turn framed by that same signature pearl beading. It is a major clue that we will see repeatedly in Romanesque carving, taken over into Christian buildings all over Europe. It is also the earliest example of Islamic beading in a Christian context.

The inscription on the lintel is in Latin, the language of the new masters, but the deeply cut bevelled foliage of the arabesque frieze and the *mandorla* (almond-shaped oval) framing of the seated and haloed figure of a bearded Christ indicate that the mason must have been schooled in the Córdoba tradition. The fingers of all the figures are large and spatula-like; the folds on their garments shown as stiff incisions. Of the six smaller figures, some are bearded, some beardless; all are disproportionate, with encircled protruding eyes and over-large heads, comparable to Fatimid figures as seen on the ceiling of the Cappella Palatina, which in turn adopted influences from earlier Coptic fig-

4.3: The lintel at the entrance to the Benedictine abbey church of Saint-Génis-des-Fontaines, dated by an inscription to 1019–20, showing the earliest known sculpture of Christ in Majesty, set in a horseshoe arcade framed with pearl beading. Located in historic Catalonia, today the French department of Pyrénées-Orientales, close to the Spanish border.

ural representation. All share an otherworldly absence of realism, an abstract quality characteristic of Islamic art.

How it Ended

The Muslim domination of the building and decorative trades on the Iberian Peninsula and in Sicily, southern Italy and other areas of Europe continued right up into the fourteenth and fifteenth centuries. Muslim master masons and artisans worked on the renovations of al-Jaferia (the former Hudid palace in Zaragoza), on Antipope Papa Luna's building projects in Zaragoza, Peñiscola and Calatayud, and on churches and secular buildings throughout the Crown of Aragon. The family-oriented organisation of ateliers and the low conversion rate helped keep technical knowledge and special skills specific to the community.

In the Kingdom of Navarre there was a similar landscape. The leading Muslim families came from professional backgrounds—like engineers and physicians—and craft backgrounds like carpenters, smiths, shoemakers and tailors. The kings were keen to exploit Muslim know-how and Carlos II (1349–87) sent the royal carpenter, Çalema Çaragoçano, to recruit a wool dyer, a washer and a carder, and ordered him to inspect the structure and functioning of watermills in Aragon so that he could construct similar ones back in Navarre. Muslim engineers like Zalema Alpuliente, 'master of works of the castles of La Ribera', constructed and maintained the kingdom's fortresses, while Muslims served as physicians, vets, grooms, falconers and envoys for the royal family and for bishops, and as armourers and goldsmiths to the royal court.[16] In 1371 the master engineer Mahoma de Burgos settled in Tudela in the pay of Queen Jeanne de Valois.[17] In Castile-León Muslims dominated the building trades and decorative crafts, while Muslim physicians were very popular among the Christian elite, since Islamic medical science was far superior to Latin medicine till at least the late Middle Ages.

Castilian monarchs embraced 'Moorish' styles of decoration, architecture and dress, even after Mudéjar styles were largely out of fashion. Pedro the Cruel, for example, commissioned a series of buildings in the most exuberant Islamicate styles, such as the Alcázar in Seville with its pseudo-Nasrid Patio de las Doncellas and the elaborately renovated Mudéjar-style palace at Tordesillas, which became a Clarissan convent after Pedro's death.

Muslim slaves with special knowledge and skills were particularly prized and valuable. Catlos cites the example of how Valencian silk merchant Guillermus Straery promised to manumit his slave Mahomet Abendenu after twelve years of service, if the latter would teach him his secret techniques for silk-dyeing and then promise to refrain from practising them himself once he was free.[18]

In spite of laws which expressly aimed to segregate and discriminate against Muslims, in practice a range of sources from the late fourteenth century, including notarial registers, municipal records, land transfer and loan documents, chancery documents, royal account books and trial records, show that Muslims continued to construct mosques, worship publicly, openly practise forbidden professions such as medicine, dress and pose as Christians and travel with or without permission. All of this, Catlos concludes, 'reflects a fundamental disconnect between legislation and the socio-economic realities in the Middle Ages'.[19]

In Sicily

As in the Iberian Peninsula, so too in Sicily Muslims exercised a near monopoly in building trades, including stone sculpture, brickwork, carpentry, stucco carving, plastering and engineering. Muslim master builders were in charge of the construction of palaces, castles and fortifications.

We also know that Roger II, after his campaign in North Africa to conquer more Islamic lands, took Bône (today's Annaba) in modern Algeria in 1153 and brought back thousands of Muslim prisoners. The sources do not specify why he did this but, given that it was expensive and logistically difficult to transport large numbers of people from one territory to another, especially when it involved sea journeys, he must have had good reason. One logical explanation is that he identified amongst the population of Bône people with skills which were superior to those he had back in Sicily in his own country, and he therefore transported them back to have them embellish his own buildings and teach their skills to his own population. That the workforce employed on the Norman buildings in Sicily must have been highly skilled is proved by the remarkable speed with which monuments were erected, often within one year.

In France

Some Muslims, as already discussed, were brought into Europe from their own lands, willingly or otherwise, often by Crusaders returning from the Holy Land. Even Richard the Lionheart, who spent most of his life outside England either on Crusade or in Normandy, is recorded as employing 'Saracens' at Domfront and in the nearby forest of Le Passeis, according to the Norman Exchequer records of 1195.[20] Medievalist John Gillingham tells us that 'he appears not to have worried about the scandal or fear that might have been caused by the employment of Muslims in Western Europe'.[21] In 1196, near the end of his life, Richard built Château Gaillard, his favourite castle, overlooking the Seine between Rouen and Paris, using many features taken from Islamic architecture. It is striking when walking round Les Andelys, the town at the foot of the castle where his workers would have lived, how many features the houses still have with Islamic echoes—two-tone stonework, multiple arches, winding narrow streets casting shade and giving privacy, and so on. Château Gaillard itself was completed very fast, in just two years, with no mention of the master mason's identity. Construction speed is another hallmark of Islamic architecture. Craftsmen at the top of their game worked swiftly and efficiently.

Richard's small group of adult male Muslims must have been brought into his retinue for a reason, but the records only state that they were provided with appropriate clothing, and that one, called 'Gibelin le Sarrasin', received some funds, '50 s.', to purchase a horse.[22]

As in Britain, written evidence of the involvement of Saracen masons on medieval Christian constructions in France is sparse, though it is clear enough from the buildings themselves. However, a handful of documented instances do exist, as in Gascony at the Château des Quat'Sos, with its four round

4.4: The round-towered Château des Quat'Sos in Gascony, France, documented in a chronicle as built by 'Saracens' with such strong foundations and unfamiliar workmanship 'that the buildings of our time cannot be compared to it.'

towers, one at each corner. In the fourteenth century, the English attempted to take it from the French, but a chronicle states 'they did little mischief, for the castle was very high, and built of a hard stone. It was erected a long time since by the Saracens, who laid the foundations so strong, and with such curious workmanship, that the buildings of our time cannot be compared to it.'[23] Finding their machines had no effect on the walls, the English resorted to mines instead.

In Avignon, even as late as the fifteenth century, Papa Luna (1328–1423), the Antipope Benedict XIII, owned Muslim slaves and was a patron of Muslim artists and artisans, contracting Muslim architects and carpenters to build and furnish his palaces and churches.[24] A nobleman from Aragon who had studied law at the University of Montpellier, he was elected pope in 1394 at the age of sixty-six and lived to the age of ninety-four. This was at the time of the so-called Western Schism, where a rival pope, hence 'Antipope', was elected at Avignon in opposition to the Pope at Rome. He was initially recognised by France, Scotland, Sicily, Castile, Aragon and Navarre. Today the Palais des Papes, or Papal Palace, in Avignon, with its distinctive Islamic high blind arches, is a UNESCO World Heritage Site and considered one of the largest and most important medieval Gothic buildings in Europe.

As the fifteenth century progressed, however, economic recession and competition, religious reactionism, papal Crusade rhetoric and civil disorder in France gradually undermined Christian–Muslim relations, stoking the perception of Muslims as disloyal.

In the Latin Kingdoms of the Holy Land

When the Crusaders ('pilgrims', Latin *peregrini*, as they called themselves, Arabic *bilghriyyin*) arrived in Syria and Palestine they found what Catlos calls a 'dizzingly diverse' society,[25] far more complex than that of either Sicily or Spain. In many areas that they conquered, Muslims were only a part of the population, often in a minority, especially south of Acre and Jerusalem and west of the Dead Sea, where the countryside was overwhelmingly populated by Arabised Syriac Orthodox Christians. There were many concentrations of Melkite Orthodox Christians, Armenian Orthodox and Maronite Christians around Mount Lebanon. There were also notable Jewish communities, though much of the Jewish population of the Galilee had converted to Islam and integrated with the Muslims in the preceding centuries. As for the Muslim community itself, as well as the Sunni orthodox majority, there were also Shi'is as a consequence of Fatimid domination and missionising. On top of that, the coastal mountains were havens for a number of secretive heterodox

4.5: The Papal Palace in Avignon, France, was commissioned by the Antipope, nicknamed Papa Luna (1328–1423), who contracted Muslim architects and carpenters to build and furnish his palaces and churches with their distinctive Islamic high blind pointed arches.

sects including the Alawis (the sect of the ruling al-Assad family in today's Syria), the Druze and the Assassins, none of which recognised the legitimacy of either the Fatimid or the Abbasid caliphates, and one of which—the Assassins—was 'explicitly revolutionary'.[26]

The lack of Muslim solidarity in the face of the First Crusade (1096–9), so often cited by European historians, was therefore hardly surprising, given the environment of multilayered ethnic, cultural, linguistic and religious identities that formed the so-called Holy Land. It was never the neat Christian–Muslim binary that we like to imagine. Neither were the Franks (Arabic *al-Ifranj*), as the Muslims referred to the Crusaders, a coherent or unified group. Rather they were competing factions of foreign warrior families. Those from Provence, Lorraine and northern France who made up the bulk of the forces were split by rival bonds of regional origin, family and vassalage. The Norman bloc was in fact southern Italian, led by Bohemond of Taranto (Prince of Antioch, 1089–1111), whose father had conquered Islamic Palermo in 1072. Pisa, Genoa and Venice had been raiding and trading with Muslim lands for generations.

The confusing scenario in which the Crusaders found themselves might explain the fact that here, in the Holy Land itself, they barely appropriated any Islamic artistic architectural styles in the way Europeans had done so enthusiastically in Spain and in Sicily. Catlos speculates that this was perhaps a consequence of a heightened sense of ethno-cultural opposition and a sense of vulnerability, a reflection of their insecurity in this challenging environment, that they never felt sufficiently sure of themselves and their permanence in this new territory. All they took back was the pointed arch, which they had in any event already encountered via Muslim craftsmen in Europe, and Muslim slaves with skills, who were very valuable.[27]

During and after the establishment of the Latin Crusader Kingdoms (1098–1291), some Muslims moved north or east into other Islamic-ruled lands, but most local Muslims continued to live in their homeland, albeit subject to new masters, even though Latin rule was often oppressive, arbitrary and violent. Ascalon, the Fatimids' sprawling military centre and strategic port, was finally taken by the Crusaders in 1153. Antioch, as a cosmopolitan place of encounter for Latins, Byzantines, Armenians, Syriac Christians and Muslims, boasted the most regionally integrated society within the Latin kingdoms, most of which were

> united only in their determination to preserve their own status above that of all the subject peoples. The highly fragmented and internally competitive character of the Latin elite, the absence of a pre-established political order and institu-

> tions, and the transitive nature of the Crusade experience (whereby pilgrims visited, fought and returned home), meant that the kingdom of Jerusalem offered both challenges and opportunities for its Muslim subjects.[28]

Pragmatism was often the key to integration and mutual interest, but the ruling Latin Frankish Christian elite definitely saw themselves as superior to the indigenous Eastern Orthodox Christians.

Islamic Guilds

Craft guilds were a deeply rooted aspect of medieval Muslim society, and the first documented mention of Islamic guilds comes in the tenth century when the Fatimids, in their capital of Cairo, awarded the artisan class special privileges. This gave them great prosperity, which in turn helped stimulate the commercial revolution that took place under Fatimid rule.[29] Cairo guilds even had their own form of unemployment and sickness benefit in which all members participated. Unlike European guilds, Islamic guilds were interconfessional, with Muslims, Jews and Christians admitted on equal terms, sharing a deep-rooted ideology and a moral and ethical code which was taught to all novices. They were also often closely aligned with Sufi or Dervish Brotherhoods, with whom they shared a system of passing through stages from apprentice to master, in both craft training and moral instruction. There were elaborate rules, along with signs and gestures of recognition, a point of similarity with European Freemasonry that has long been noted.[30] The Austrian scholar Joseph von Hammer (1774–1856) regarded the whole of the European guild system as being derived from Islam. Quality of production was paramount and closely supervised by the master craftsman, and the mantra often repeated in Europe that Muslims deliberately put a flaw in their work 'because only God is perfect' is an absurdity. The penalty for bad craftsmanship was temporary exclusion.

In the medieval Kingdom of Navarre, which straddled the Pyrenees into both modern France and Spain, Muslim-dominated trades like silverwork, carpentry, leather work, soap-making, ceramic manufacture and construction depended on techniques that could be appropriated and imitated over time and were therefore subject to mounting Christian competition, especially as the economy was progressively Christianised, with Church authorities controlling commissions. One amusing case is recorded in 1479, where the canons of the cathedral of Tarazona issued a formal act of excommunication against their Muslim architect Ali Daracano, whom they had commissioned to rebuild their bell tower.[31] In all these sectors Muslims faced the challenge of preserving their proprietary knowledge in the face of deliberate attempts by Christian craftsmen to appropriate their techniques. The Muslim resistance to conversion, the continuing use of Arabic within the community, and the family-oriented nature of business all helped to keep their skills ring-fenced, but gradually, aided by frequent capture of skilled Muslim slaves, the balance began to tip in favour of the Christians. By the end of the 1400s, therefore, Muslims had gradually lost their dominance of a number of crafts, including silk, paper and ceramics, as Christians developed parallel industries. The Christians incrementally learnt Muslim skills and then established Christian guilds which actively lobbied against their Muslim competitors.[32] One interesting exception is recorded in the early sixteenth century: an all-Muslim confraternity of construction workers in Zaragoza, dominated by the Galí dynasty (from Castile and Aragon) of master builders and carpenters, with high-level commissions including castles, palaces, elite homes and churches.

Signed Work and Identity

It is striking in Romanesque buildings that almost no signatures have been found and the identities of the master builders and craftsmen remain unknown. This may have been simply because the bishops and abbots did not wish to highlight anyone other than themselves, but it may also be because signed work by Muslim craftsmen was rare even in the Muslim world. Leo Mayer, Professor of Islamic Studies at Haifa University, devoted the final years of his life to compiling lists of Islamic craftsmen—architects, woodcarvers and metalworkers—and found that fewer than 8 per cent of works were signed by their makers.[33] He travelled extensively to collect his material and wrote about the difficulties which beset his task—the scarcity of local daily chronicles, the lack of personal diaries, guild accounts and contemporary treatises on technical matters and (with the laudable exception of Ottoman Turkey) the lack of properly kept archives. As a result, he said, the history of Islamic architects would remain up to a point anonymous, but he hoped that his roll list would serve as a foundation for future work, so that the unsigned work of these and other masters could eventually be identified.[34] He noted one tenth-century architect and geometrician at the Umayyad Court of Córdoba, called Maslama bin Abdullah, but said his buildings were not mentioned.

Masterminding the Design

When major Islamic buildings like mosques or palaces are studied, researchers generally find that the organisation of spaces and volumes conforms to a geometric order that incorporates even the tiniest of ornamental details, exactly as is subsequently found in Romanesque buildings. Such an organisation, where the whole and the parts are in direct correspondence with each other, speaks of one mastermind behind a building's conception, and the kind of knowledge of constructional detail and experience that the European patron, be he king, bishop, abbot or nobleman, simply could not possibly have known or even aspired to. Abbots and bishops would certainly have taken an interest in the construction of their new churches, giving instructions on the dimensions they wanted, and making sure their own images occurred somewhere prominent within the decorative schema—in mosaics, carved stone statues or stained glass; but they could not possibly have had sufficient knowledge of complex geometry to come up with such advanced designs on their own.

In Romanesque Europe, the only known pre-existing building that exhibited such complex geometry applied in architecture, both in plan and elevation, was the Great Mosque at Córdoba, colloquially the Mezquita. It anticipated in a particularly daring way a theory of structural equilibrium that can be recognised in subsequent Romanesque and Gothic buildings like Laon Cathedral.[35] Its equilibrium of forces was achieved through the revolutionary use of the pointed arch, which enabled a building to adapt to any span and any height, leading to greater elasticity and flexibility in construction, and to the infinite varieties of vault that followed, and the disappearance of the old-fashioned barrel vault.

This is precisely the evolution we then witness first in Romanesque cathedrals and abbeys and later in Gothic cathedrals across Europe. Jean Bony (1908–1995), academic and historian of Romanesque and Gothic architecture, detected this new urge for 'ordered spaciousness'[36] where the vaulting enables a rhythmic pattern of bays to run from the roof arches to the ground through increasingly reinforced yet decorated piers. He also notes 'the brittle thinness of shafts and moldings, and the principle of destruction of all solid surfaces'.[37] Such characteristics—the rhythm of repetition and what is known as 'the continuous order', and the dislike of leaving wall surfaces undecorated (what is known as *horror vacui*)—lie at the core of Islamic architecture. The tenth-century Brethren of Purity (Ikhwan al-Safa), an Iraq-based grouping of mystic philosophers who included craftsmen in their ranks, devoted a whole epistle of their famous *Encyclopedia* to the subject of ratio and proportion, illustrating how 'geometry provides the fundamental basis of every artform', and 'the most harmonious of constructions [buildings]' are those that are 'informed by the best of proportions'.[38]

It was clearly a key area where the expertise of Islamic craftsmen exerted a strong influence on medieval European architecture, an influence that translated into buildings that were coherently planned by a single mastermind, a fact that is often remarked upon by art historians marvelling at the unity of conception on display in Romanesque buildings. British art historian Kenneth Clark (1903–1983), in his landmark *Civilisation* TV series, stands in France's twelfth-century Vézelay Abbey and comments:

> I can think of no other Romanesque interior that has this quality of lightness, this feeling of Divine Reason. And it seems inevitable that the Romanesque should here merge into a beautiful early Gothic… We don't know the name of the architect of Vézelay, nor of the highly individual sculptors at Moissac and Toulouse, and this used to be taken as a proof of Christian humility in the artists, or, alternatively, a sign of his low status. I think it was just an accident.[39]

The evidence, however, suggests that it was no accident. A further discovery which Clark, in his 1969 series, would not have known about was the astronomical alignment of the nave, which in 1976 was found to cast a series of light pools in a straight line down the exact centre of the nave as the sunlight at the summer solstice entered the high clerestory windows.

Such knowledge was very familiar to the Islamic world, where Ibn al-Haytham's *Book of Optics* (*Kitab al-Manazir*), completed in 1021, explained theories of visual perception and how light was transmitted, and the aesthetics of colour and proportion, which heavily influenced philosopher, theologian and scientist Bishop Robert Grosseteste (1168–1253) at Lincoln Cathedral (see Chapter 11).

Labour was extremely well organised in the Islamic construction world, with stone craftsmen, for example, divided into numerous subcategories, like quarrymen, rough hewers, cutters, sculptors and assemblers. The same applied to craftsmen working with plaster, brick and ceramics. This high degree of specialisation made it possible for them both to achieve a very advanced level of technical ability and to work at speed. Such a system had to be coordinated by the overall master—the *muhandis*, a kind of engineer-geometrician—and it also demanded a certain unity and consensus on aesthetic rules.[40] A master craftsman would have been well trained on the job, first working his way up as an apprentice within his specialisation, such as a stucco expert, mason or carpenter. One factor that may well have been instrumental in the development of this organisational capability was the astonishingly fast spread of Islam in the seventh century over a wide area. Regions that had formerly been separated by linguistic division were now

4.6: Behind the almost mystical harmony of the nave at Vézelay Abbey in Burgundy, France, lies the rigour of Islamic geometry and optics, whereby its astronomical alignment casts a series of light pools down the exact centre at the summer solstice, knowledge that was very familiar to the Islamic world, through Ibn al-Haytham's *Book of Optics* (*Kitab al-Manazir*, 1021).

united by the widespread diffusion and use of Arabic, the common language of both religion and science. Construction experts could therefore move easily from one site to another, as a vast array of new building projects were initiated by different patrons in centres of learning like Damascus, Baghdad and Cairo, spreading out across North Africa, and then onto the European mainland in Sicily, southern Italy and Spain.

These economic realities made teams of Muslim craftsmen highly mobile, a mobility that could be triggered not just by the new projects of new rulers offering the highest rates of pay, but also by political upheaval. This is what happened in the centuries of turbulence in Muslim Spain when the Córdoba Caliphate was disintegrating from 1009 onwards, and the military campaigns waged against it by the northern European Christian kings gradually gained ground in what they called the Reconquista. Some engineers and craftsmen might find themselves part of a refugee population fleeing war, or be taken prisoner as valuable booty and transported to different regions to serve new and unfamiliar masters. Others, especially the most expert, were well treated and well paid.

Muslim craftsmen had already been experimenting with advanced building practices based on their knowledge of geometry for two centuries on European soil before they were called upon to apply their skills to Christian churches. The evidence is embedded in the buildings themselves and must take precedence over such textual sources as may or may not exist, and which, even when they do, are invariably written to reflect well on the founder and therefore cannot be taken as accurate records. Medieval chronicles proliferated from the twelfth century onwards and fabrication of history became something of an industry in Latin Christendom, nowhere more so, perhaps, than at Chartres,[41] whose famous relic, the Sancta Camisa (the Virgin's Birthing Robe), needed historical authentication. Sanctioned versions of history even appear in the stained glass, notably in the Charlemagne Window (c.1210), where Charlemagne is shown killing the Saracen king in the Holy Land—where he never went—and defeating the Saracens in Spain—the only battle he ever lost.

Recent studies of masons' marks at Santiago de Compostela offer further proof that the building was the product of an overall mastermind. One study notes: 'The general aspect of constructive regularity within the cathedral is characterised by a stringent architectonical system which is used throughout the whole church and determined by strict rules of dimensions and proportions.'[42] The author likewise observes, 'This manifest consistency in design is in a way preparatory to the gothic building methods we find about a century later in France',[43] but without making the connection back to the geometric forerunners in Muslim Spain, above all at the Córdoba Mezquita.

Reputations spread, and those at the top of their profession went to wherever they could earn the best living, which inevitably meant the royal courts or the most senior clergy.

5

SARACEN CRAFTSMEN IN BRITAIN

When we look to identify the builders, the anonymous 'masters' of Romanesque architecture, across Europe and Britain, the written sources are notoriously scant. Most of the evidence for their identity is generally embedded within the buildings themselves, but there are also a handful of cases where the people also get a mention or where they have left marks of a different kind.

Lalys

One of these is named Lalys, a mason whose arrival in Britain with a returning Crusader knight is recorded in a Welsh chronicle. The knight in question, who died after 1142, is Sir Richard de Grenville, one of the Twelve Knights of Glamorgan who had taken part in the Norman conquest of Wales, for which he was rewarded with the lordship of Neath. The chronicle is the *Gwentian Chronicle*, or *Brut Aberpergwm*, which states that Richard, towards the end of his life, undertook a pilgrimage to Jerusalem and brought back 'from the land of Canaan' a man named Lalys who was 'well-versed in the science of architecture, who erected monasteries, castles and churches'. He is credited with the construction of Neath Abbey in 1129, notable for its elegant early pointed arches and vaulting. A Grenville family pedigree dated 1639 confirms the story. The Welsh nobles of Glamorgan were known to be fascinated by their genealogies, but usually this consisted in fabricating stories to do with their own personal claims of kinship and lineage in order to boost their status.[1] A story about bringing back a Saracen captive does not fit within that kind of narrative and may even have been seen as detrimental to the de Grenville family, so there is no reason to doubt the chronicle's veracity.

Further corroboration lies in the fact that the parish of Laleston, now in the county borough of Bridgend, 16 kilometres from Neath, is named after

Lalys. *The National Gazetteer of Great Britain and Ireland* of 1868 states that the parish, comprising the hamlets of Upper and Lower Laleston, 'was given by Richard de Granville to "Lalys", who built Neath Abbey... The church, dedicated to St Illtyd, has an ancient tower, built by Lalys... Laleston House is the principal residence.'

The name 'Lalys' is evidently an anglicisation of his original Arabic name, possibly 'al-Aziz'. Aziz is a common man's name in the Middle East, used by both Muslims and Christians, derived from the Aramaic root meaning both 'great, powerful' and 'dear, precious, darling'. When used with the Arabic definite article *al*, it is also one of the ninety-nine names of Allah, and could even have been a nickname, 'the great one', a reference to his high skill. Local people giving nicknames to foreigners who live among them, or names they can more easily pronounce, has long been a common practice in all countries, indeed still is.

The *Topographical Dictionary of Wales*, originally published by S. Lewis in 1849, records the same information under the entry 'Laleston':

> This parish derives its name from Lalys, a native of Palestine, and an eminent architect, whom Richard de Granville brought over with him on his return from the Holy Land, and employed to build the abbey of Neath in this county. As a reward for the ability which he displayed in his erection of that magnificent structure, Richard bestowed on him this manor, to which Lalys gave his name, and on which he resided, until, after erecting several churches and castles in the principality, he was appointed architect to Henry I, and removed to London... The church, dedicated to St. Illtyd, is a spacious and venerable structure, the tower of which was built by Lalys.

His appointment as the king's architect speaks volumes for his exceptional ability and technical expertise, the like of which was new to Britain.

The story of Lalys seems to echo others in mainland Europe, especially in Spain where it seems that Muslim slaves of powerful Christian owners often enjoyed more prestige and real power than a free but poor Christian, and even a better lifestyle, if their skills merited it. After their masters died, they often came to form part of the former master's network of patronage and dependence.[2]

Ulmar and the Paynim

Another named individual is 'Ulmar the mason', mentioned in Eric Fernie's *Architecture of Norman England* as a serf given to the priory of Castle Acre in Norfolk to help with the building in the late eleventh century.[3] In the on-site guidebook at Castle Acre, however, the said Ulmar is described as 'a mason from Acre', likely to have been brought back from 'the Holy Land', where stonemasonry skills among Palestinians were extremely high quality and the art of crafting the local limestone into excellent building material had been perfected across the centuries. Castle Acre Priory stands today in ruins, but the superb stonework of its imposing west front still has echoes of the mighty arch and blind arcades of the ancient city of Ctesiphon (near present-day Baghdad), transported to the Norfolk countryside, where it now serves as a favoured backdrop for filmsets and weddings.

5.1: The West Front at Castle Acre Priory, Norfolk, England, with its tall blind arcades, pointed and interlocking arches, is recorded as built by 'Ulmar', a mason from Acre in the 'Holy Land', probably brought to England for his skills by a returning Crusader at the end of the eleventh century.

Small numbers of Muslim slaves were brought home by returning Crusaders—or even by clergy, pilgrims and functionaries who had spent time in the Latin Mediterranean—but records of such individuals are very rare. They appear only by chance, like the 'Ethiopian' named Bartholomew, 'formerly a Saracen', who ran away from his master in 1259; or a 'Mahumet' who was found to be living in late-thirteenth-century Wiltshire. Any slaves or captives who found themselves in northern Europe would most likely have come as converts, having been baptised as a formality by traffickers, or as apostates.[4]

There are other cases which are hard to prove, but which, taken collectively, amount to more than just legend, and are likely to have at least some truth behind them. One such is the case of the Saracens of Biddulph Moor in Staffordshire, named 'Moor' because of the dark complexion of its inhabitants, with its highly unusual church of St Chad, built *c.*1150, the oldest building in Stafford.

A feature on St Chad was written in 2014 on the BBC website, under the heading: 'Ornate carvings thought to be made by stonemasons from the Middle East peek at you from every corner of St Chad's Church in Stafford.'[5] The local priest, who believed the masons would have been allowed considerable creative freedom, also thought that the elaborate carvings in the main part of the church, where richly decorated patterns and figures cover almost every archway and pillar, were the work of a group of stonemasons from the Middle East who were brought back to England during the Crusades. One of the main archways is completely covered in sculptures of owls with crossed wings, with many carvings of serpents around the pillars said to represent the local Lord Orm, founder of the church. As well as a Green Man or two with beaded foliage streaming from their mouths, there are strange carvings of beakheads and bare-chested figures wearing short skirts and wristbands, animal faces and human forms thought to be Syro-Phoenician or Egyptian in origin. One human figure is thought to be based on the Babylonian goddess Ishtar, with symbols of death and rebirth.

The first appearance in print of the Biddulph Moor story was in John Sleigh's *A History of the Ancient Parish of Leek* in 1862, where he states:

> One of the Lords of Biddulph, a Knight Crusader, is reputed to have brought over in his train from the Holy Land a Paynim [a now archaic word meaning 'pagan' or 'non Christian', expecially used of Muslims] whom he made Bailiff on his estate, and from whose marriage with an English woman the present race of 'Biddle Moor men' is traditionally said to have sprung. Probably this infusion of Saracenic blood may account for their nomadic and somewhat bellicose propensities.[6]

The term 'bailiff' at this time was similar to a provost at a monastery, someone charged with worldly administration and the law—a highly trusted position. The story is expanded further in the 2012 book *Staffordshire Folk Tales*, a record of oral traditions by local 'Journey Man' Johnny Gillett, who describes how Orm had brought back a band of Saracen stonemasons, thinking they would be useful, since 'many people from that region of the world had a high reputation for their stonework', and Orm 'had it in mind to build a church in nearby Stafford that would be dedicated to St Chad'. It continues:

> And so these Muslim craftsmen began work on this Christian place of worship. It was not unusual for such things to happen across Christendom in those days. What room did those Saracens have for argument anyway? Much like the Moors put to work on the chapels in southern Spain, Orm's Saracens set to work climbing up and down ladders, and chipping away to create a unique church in Staffordshire.[7]

He goes on to explain that Lord Orm gave them residence in Biddulph Moor in a temporary camp, and that one of the men, their leader, could speak perfect English. He was known as 'the Paynim', and over the course of the journey back from the Holy Land, a friendship and respect had begun to grow between the two men, such that Orm made him his bailiff.

When the church was finished, it was described as 'like a building plucked out of Palestine to be placed in the middle of England… like nothing else in the region'. Particularly striking, Gillett says, were the heads carved into the arch and the unusually angular beasts surrounding the entrance which looked down on all who entered. The brickwork had geometric patterns typical of Islamic stonework, but the most interesting carvings were to be found on the capitals, which seemed to be of lions or dogs. These, Gillett claims, were in fact *simurghs*, mythical creatures 'part lion, part phoenix, said to symbolise the wisdom of God'. He says that the Saracen masons also worked on the font, incorporating monkeys and lions, and four huge pomegranates, opening up to make the bowl: 'It was certainly unlike any other font known to Lord Orm.'[8]

The Paynim supervised the work and developed a reputation as a diligent and fair man who kept comprehensive records. At some point Orm introduced him to another of his bailiffs who had a daughter, and soon a marriage was arranged, which resulted in the birth of a son. The Paynim, now absorbed into the new community, chose to name his son Richard, after the king. The other Saracen stonemasons soon found wives too and became part of the local community, living up on Biddulph Moor; a distinct group of people 'recognised for their unique nature for many years and centuries thereafter'.[9] The descendants of the Saracen bailiff's family became known as the Bailey family, and the graveyard has many Richard Baileys buried there. The local church of St Lawrence in Biddulph has a series of stone coffin lids, on each of which is a carved cross and sword, arranged round its outer walls, thought to belong to Crusader knights.

Another intriguing case is the unusual 1980 novel *A Month in the Country*, by J. L. Carr, which was made into a film in 1987 starring Colin Firth and Kenneth Branagh. At the end of a month spent restoring a medieval mural in a remote Yorkshire church, the climax comes when the restorer, played in the film by Firth, suddenly realises that the artist who painted this exceptionally high-quality original mural must have been a Muslim who fell to his death from the scaffolding just before completing the work. This, he concludes, is the only possible explanation for why the entire mural is superbly executed except for the bottom right-hand corner, which is painted by a much inferior hand, probably a local assistant, depicting a man falling. Branagh's character, an archaeologist, simultaneously finds a skeleton assumed to be the dead artist, because he is wearing an Islamic crescent moon necklace and is buried in unconsecrated ground just beyond the graveyard.

Carr is said to have based his novels on real events, so given the striking nature of the story, he must have come across something that suggested to him that a Muslim was working as an artist in an English church in medieval times, producing an exceptional mural. Of course, the real person who is recorded falling from scaffolding is William of Sens, the architect brought over from France in 1174 to rebuild Canterbury Cathedral after a fire had destroyed its Romanesque choir and its magnificent painted wooden ceiling. He was the first person to introduce stone six-part ribbed vaulting to England in 1177. Nothing beyond his name is known of him, but we have to wonder where and from whom he learnt his exceptional construction skills. The church records say that he was replaced by an architect known only as William the Englishman, who followed the same plans, perhaps showing that William of Sens's skills by that stage had been successfully passed on to a protégé. The remainder of the craftsmen working would have remained the same, so there would have been a great deal of continuity anyway. The important thing was for the church to be able to record that an Englishman had now taken charge.

Arabic Numerals Carved in Wood

My research took a new turn, a zigzag even, when I was alerted to Arabic numerals, normally hidden from public sight, carved into the roof timber beams in Salisbury Cathedral. The Arabic numerals had only come to light as accidental discoveries during dendrochronology (tree-dating) investigations sponsored by English Heritage, research aimed at fixing the age of the original trees used in construction and thereby giving an accurate date for the building.

My quest for evidence now had a new focus, and several locations I could explore, thanks to the information compiled by Professor Dan Miles, the Oxford dendrochronologist who had conducted the Salisbury Cathedral tree-dating exercise in 2002. According to Miles, most examples of the Arabic numerals are concentrated in prestige buildings of the thirteenth and fourteenth centuries, such as cathedrals, bishops' palaces and manor houses in Somerset and Wiltshire. Among those buildings is West Court Farm at Shalbourne, now run as a bed and breakfast. Their Savernake oak roof timbers were dated by dendrochronology to 1316, and by happy chance I was able to spend a night there. No Arabist had ever looked at their numerals, and that evening and the following morning, to benefit from both natural and artificial light, I clambered into the loft armed with a torch and a camera to inspect the Arabic numerals carved into the beams as assembly markers. The resident pigeon was indignant, but what I found convinced me even more that these numerals were the work of Arabs, from the facility with which they were carved and above all the spontaneity. There was nothing laborious about them in a way that might have suggested they were newly learnt. In recent studies at Santiago de Compostela looking into the masons' marks, it is observed that they were carved 'freehand', without the use of templates, and therefore differ slightly from each other, in the same way that a signature on paper varies a little.[10] Who other than people for whom this was their native script would have been able to do that, centuries before Arabic numerals were in general use in England?

It was exactly the same at Wells when I arranged to visit the loft of the Priory of St John, now a private home, which also has Arabic numerals carved into its roof timbers, dated to 1314/15 by a dendrochronology report. Once again, the sheer quality of the timberwork and the carpentry skill, combined with the ease and flair with which the numbers were carved, all pointed to two things—that the craftsmen who made this exceptional roof were at the top of their game, further proven by the fact that the roof had not needed any repair in the seven centuries of its life, and that they were likely to have been Arabs. It cannot have been pure coincidence that the roof timbers at Salisbury Cathedral with their Arabic numerals were likewise dated to 1315/16 by the English Heritage dendrochronology report. I saw photos of these, but was unable to see them at first hand as they are no longer accessible, high up out

5.2: Cursive freehand Arabic numerals carved as assembly markers by the original carpenters in the roof timbers of West Court Farm, a manor house in Wiltshire, England. The numerals were dated by dendrochronology to 1316. In situ.

of view above the stone vaults of the cathedral roof. The carpenters were almost certainly the same team of men, travelling from one prestige job to the next according to their commissions. One other building in Wells appeared in Dan Miles's table of Arabic numerals used as carpentry assembly marks, and that was the King's Head Inn on the High Street, where dendrochronology had dated the roof timbers to 1318/19. I went into the pub to enquire, but the ceiling is so high up, at second-floor level, that the numerals cannot be seen with the naked eye from below, and the current owner was not even aware of their existence. What was striking, however, was that even from that distance, the sheer quality of the complex craftsmanship was apparent, as a magnificent piece of carpentry.

On 14 December 2003, *The Times* published an article by their archaeology correspondent, Norman Hammond, about precisely that astonishing dendrochronology report first conducted on Salisbury Cathedral's exceptionally fine roof timbers, among the oldest in the country. It began by declaring that

Salisbury Cathedral, 'that epitome of Englishness immortalised by Constable's paintings', had a roof built of Irish oak and 'may well have been assembled by French craftsmen'. It described how the report conducted by the Oxford Dendrochronology Laboratory had shown that the timbers were dated to oaks felled in the spring of 1222 from virgin forest south of Dublin, a wood recognisably distinct from 'cultivated' English oaks. Some were over 300 years old by the time they were felled. 'The quality was superb', Dan Miles is quoted as saying in the article, 'far in excess of what was needed for the job.' The trees were wanted urgently, as the masons 'were racing ahead raising the walls of the cathedral, but the carpenters were running out of timbers'. The roof in the North Nave Triforium where the Arabic numerals were found is described by Miles, who had seen many a cathedral timber roof over the course of his lifetime, as 'the most splendid medieval lean-to-roof in any English cathedral... the jewel in the crown of all the Salisbury roofs... and one of the finest surviving medieval roofs in the country.'[11]

The Times went on to say that the finding in the Salisbury roof timbers was unexpected, since 'it had been generally supposed that common craftsmen did not know how to read, let alone understand Arabic numerals'. Their use was not universal even in Shakespeare's day, only becoming widespread in the early 1600s. Yet the Salisbury Cathedral roof was built in 1224, more than three and a half centuries earlier. The article quotes Dan Miles as saying: 'The master carpenters working on Salisbury's roofs were clearly educated people with a thorough knowledge of continental mathematics centuries before this knowledge was commonplace in Britain.' Therefore, the article concludes, they must have come over from France, as if France was somehow miraculously three and a half centuries ahead of England!

The great authority on carpenters' marks, Arnold Pacey, notes that the overwhelming majority of carpenters' assembly marks continued to be in Roman numerals till as late as the sixteenth century. At Ancient High House in Stafford, for example, a building dated by dendrochronology to 1594, the carpenter used Roman numerals in most of the building, then changed to Arabic numerals when the number counts were too high for him to carry on using the unwieldy Roman numerals in the elaborate structure.[12] Pacey notes that carpenters even seemed to prefer using complex systems of adding tags, loops and circles to the Roman numerals in order to distinguish one sequence from another, rather than using the unfamiliar Arabic numerals. One possible reason for this, he speculates, might have been the practical consideration that Roman numerals were easier to mark, since they only involved making straight lines, whereas the curved shapes of Arabic numerals were harder to inscribe.[13] The tool required to make such curved shapes in wood, a race-knife (a two-pronged fork with one prong acting as the fixed compass point while the other was a small sharply curved blade with which to gouge a curved line in timber, inevitably having to run against the grain) is not documented as existing in England till the mid- to late 1300s at the earliest, and in practice was not in widespread use till the late fifteenth and early sixteenth centuries.[14] This is a full century later than its use for carving the Arabic numerals in Salisbury. The far more logical explanation, therefore, but one that no one seems to want to consider, is that the craftsmen, far from being French, were Arabs, or at any rate trained within the Islamic world, and that they brought their own tools with them, as all craftsmen would.

Another obvious point is that both Arabic script and Arabic numerals are essentially cursive, unlike Latin and Roman numerals which are entirely formed from straight lines. These basic differences show clearly too in the masons' marks, where it is striking that Latin Christians and European Christians to this day show a preference for masons' marks formed from straight lines, like 'Z', 'T' and 'W', or just combinations of shapes formed from straight lines. When a cursive masons' mark is seen, therefore, formed from curves like the trefoil or the quatrefoil, maybe it is not illogical to speculate that the mason may have been an Arab, since it is so unusual in the European medieval context. The curve was harder to make in both wood and stone, and the trefoil in particular appears in Romanesque buildings like Rochester and Wells cathedrals, but then disappears from the fourteenth century onwards, when it is again striking that masons' marks seem to be almost exclusively formed from straight lines once more. It may just be coincidence, but it does tally with the possibility that the Freemasons and Christian guilds that appeared from the fourteenth century onwards began to exclude Muslim masons at this point, essentially froze them out, after first learning their skills from them. Another striking coincidence is that the pearl-beaded framing so prominent in Romanesque buildings from 1000 onwards also disappears in the fourteenth century, as if the Muslims using this signature framing on their work also began to disappear around this time. It is interesting to note that in the stained glass at Lincoln Cathedral, the beading is not present in the fourteenth-century glass, but is brought back in the nineteenth-century glass, as if the Victorian craftsmen understood that the beaded framing was present in the earliest glass, so they chose to mimic it, in an attempt to give the new glass an older, more authentic feel.

Arabic Numerals Carved on the West Front Sculpture of Wells Cathedral

The only Arabic assembly numerals in Britain found so far carved on stone, as opposed to wood, were discovered during a nineteenth-century restoration of the sculptures of the famous West Front of Wells Cathedral (1235–42). As with the Arabic numerals found at Salisbury, this was an accidental discovery and was duly recorded in the *Proceedings of the Somersetshire Archaeological and Natural History Society* of 1888 (abbreviated hereafter to *Somerset Proceedings*). Charles Cockerell, Professor of Architecture at London's Royal Academy, writing in 1851 before the Arabic numerals were discovered, begins his study of the iconography of the West Front by commenting that no one can behold the sculptures 'without wonder and admiration' and that 'the most cursory observation of the learned eye recognises at once a grand design and order'.[15] The thrust of his study is to make a case for the native genius of the Anglo-Saxons who, in his view, created the sculptures. The Reverend Percy Dearmer, writing in 1898, ten years after the Arabic numerals came to light, praises the statuary as 'the finest collection of medieval sculpture to be found in England' and describes the figures themselves as 'finer than any others in this country… almost as beautiful as the greatest masterpieces in Italy or France'. He mentions the Arabic numerals found on some of the sculptures in what is known as the 'Resurrection Tier' (the sixth and highest row of sculptures) on the northern part of the front, taking it as 'fairly conclusive proof that the workers were Italians, and very likely from Pisa itself',[16] because, he explains, Arabic numerals were used in Italy long before they were in England, having been introduced by Fibonacci of Pisa in 1202.

Whilst it is true that Fibonacci, also known as Leonardo of Pisa, published his *Liber Abaci* in Italy in 1202, in which he explained the Arabic numbering system he had learnt in what is today Algeria, modern scholars are firmly of the view that only a very small number of highly trained scientists and possibly mathematicians in academic circles actually used these Arabic numbers in the thirteenth century, even in Italy. There was general resistance to the adoption of something so new and so different among the conservative-minded population at large across Europe. 'The old familiar Roman numerals were clung to', Dearmer writes, 'only finally being abandoned once the modern fashions of the Renaissance took hold and a new mindset was established.'[17] Arabic numerals appear for the first time in the Wells accounting books, known as the 'Cathedral Fabric Book' (where expenditure on building works was recorded), for the year 1587–8, and it is hard to believe that craftsmen would have been more numerate than accounting clerks.[18]

5.3: The West Front of Wells Cathedral, where Arabic position marker numerals were found carved at the base of the stone statues of the Resurrection (Sixth) Tier by the original sculptors in the 1240s, but not understood by the later English fitters and therefore erected in the wrong niches.

Writing in 1992, American academic John W. Durham concluded that the general adoption of Arabic numerals by European bookkeepers occurred at least 500 years after their introduction to the scholarly world, and that this was because academic mathematics had little influence on the practice of accountancy. In 2020 Raffaele Danna established that Arabic numerals spread slowly from Italy, especially Pisa, to the rest of the European continent, only reaching widespread diffusion at the end of the sixteenth century, and that England and the Low Countries 'stand out as the latecomers in this innovations cycle'.[19]

The original *Somerset Proceedings* of 1888 have now been archived on the internet, freely available to all. They include a 'Memorandum relative to the Arabic Numerals found on certain of the carved groups in the West Front of Wells Cathedral' by a 'Mr Irvine', who explains that the use of Arabic numerals on the West Front was discovered by the late E. B. Ferrey, Cathedral Architect, while making his survey of the front for its repair. Irvine provides a table of the numbers as they occur on 33 of the 150 figures that run across the sculptured front of the Resurrection Tier. Each sculpture, as he explains, 'no doubt originally had a number, such number being invariably cut in the parts [of the sculpture] representing the earth, out of which the dead are emerging. North of the centre of front the Arabic numerals are used; south of such central line, Roman numerals only.' As the table itself shows, many numbers are missing.[20]

This is the point where most previous studies have run out of steam, but given the immense importance of this unique clue, I was determined to follow the evidence to the furthest possible extent. With the help of the Wells Cathedral archivist, Veronica Howe, and Jerry Sampson's book on the West Front, I have been able to reach what I believe to be completely new and original conclusions (see also Chapter 11).

Among the handwritten notes the Wells archivist was able to dig out for me were those of Mr Irvine, the only person beyond Mr Ferrey, the Cathedral Architect, to see these stone blocks at first hand. Irvine observes that strict sequencing had been lost, with some Arabic numerals repeated, and 'One Roman numeral had wandered among the Arabic ones.' He is puzzled by why numbers as high as seventy-nine are found, given that 'such a number of groups [of sculptures] would have been greater than the number of niches on one-half of front.' As to the subject matter of these Arabic-numbered groups, he observes that they were naked figures, and that 'the only earthly adornment retained by the rising figures was the retention by kings and queens of crowns, and of mitres by bishops. The monumental slabs which the figures are seen pushing aside, were in every case *plain*, without *cross* or other ornament on them' (original italics).

All these facts taken together make it highly likely that the Arabic numbering system was part of the original stonework and ran all the way across the West Front, not just on the north half. As Irvine himself remarks in his 'Memorandum', the numerals 'were clearly intended to guide the builders as they removed the sculptures from the stone-mason's yard to the Front. It is natural to suppose that these sculptures were in their places when Bishop Jocelin dedicated the Cathedral, in 1239, after the completion of his work.'[21]

Some months later, the Wells archivist sent me notes made by the late great cathedral historian Linzee Sparrow Colchester (1914–1989), giving his own views on the Arabic numerals found on the West Front during restoration. He writes that the Roman numbering sequence was in perfect order from I to XXXII, but that the Arabic numbering sequence had 'not the least semblance of order'.

This made him wonder whether the stones had been removed again on a subsequent occasion when the numbering was not observed or heeded. 'It has been suggested', he writes, 'that the figures South of the centre were removed and numbered *c.*1380 when the Harewell Tower was built, and the figures North of the centre *c.*1430 when the Bubwith Tower was built. But even this date', he ponders, 'seems too early for the use of Arabic numerals by masons.'

The idea that Arab masons may have worked on the original structure, using their own numbering system, is not entertained by any of these men, yet it is the only scenario that would explain why the numerals were missing from some stones due to decay or age; why those that bore the Arabic numerals did not bear a cross; and why they got jumbled and out of sequence in later restorations by non-Arab builders who could not understand them. It is entirely plausible, therefore, that there was a separate workshop of Arab masons. Local talent would simply not have been up to the job, as Dearmer rightly remarks, when he speculates that they may have been Italians, commenting, 'Pleasant as it would be to our national pride, we can hardly believe that Englishmen produced what seems to be the earliest example of such magnificent and varied sculpture in north-western Europe.'[22] What he cannot credit, however, is the possibility that such superior carving might have been the work of skilled Arab masons, using their own numbering system, even though he too admits that Arabic numerals 'did not become common in England till the sixteenth century'.[23]

The clinching proof that the masons must have been Arabs, using their own familiar numbers, comes in the book by Jerry Sampson, the man who devoted his life to studying the great West Front at Wells and was closely involved in the restoration programme of 1974–86. He found from his research that the work of the skilled sculptors was outpacing the construction work on the West Front itself. The niches were therefore not ready to receive the figures, which would explain why they needed to be marked up with placement numerals so they could be put in place later by the fixers. None of the other figures on the entire West Front had any position numeral markings, Sampson established, since none were found on any of the sculptures taken down from the rest of the building during the twelve-year restoration. This, he concludes, means that position numerals must have been unnecessary elsewhere, because the other statues were put into their niches immediately on completion. Those that were fitted into their niches straight away were 'an excellent fit'.[24] He also proved that 'if the Arabic-numbered sculptures are returned to their proposed original positions, the whole distribution of the Dundry blocks in the resurrection tier falls within two tight bands, one to the north and one to the south', which shows that the top masons using Arabic numerals were working on both sides of the centre.[25] Dundry was the expensive fine-grained stone reserved for the top masons' work, brought in from a quarry near Bristol, as opposed to the cheaper Doulting stone from the local quarry.

Sampson writes:

> If we accept that the Arabic numerals were the cultural property of the sculpture workshop in the thirteenth century, then there is nothing more likely than that when they were laid off *c.*1243 their secret went with them... the fixers who were charged with installing the northern resurrection groups were left with incomprehensible hieroglyphs as their guide.[26]

The reason these skilled masons were laid off in 1243 was due to a lack of finance following Bishop Jocelin's death in 1242. Jocelin had been in charge of the cathedral, but when he died it was claimed by the rival canons of Wells and Bath. Suddenly the money that had been allocated to completing the West Front sculpture had to be diverted to fund the huge litigation costs of a lengthy court case in Rome at the papal curia. It took fifteen years to settle, by which time the sculptors, who might initially have expected to be called back to complete the work, had long since departed. Such a team of top-notch masons was always in demand, so would simply have been summoned to the next high-end commission. The speculation is that they moved on to Glastonbury Abbey, where the quality of the sculpture testifies to the presence of a first-class team of sculptors. Work at Wells did not resume till 1286, at the Chapter House complex, so the sculpture of the West Front gable and the South Tower was abandoned. It was not restarted and completed till the fifteenth century.

Adelard of Bath

On one of my many visits to Wells I was told a different story (a clear case of wishful thinking) by one of the cathedral's volunteer guides about how the Arabic numerals came to be on the West Front statues. It was based around the influence of Adelard of Bath, another example of a determination to find English origins for the Arabic numerals at all costs; but it does not bear scrutiny. Known as a transmitter of Arabic science—notably algebra, geometry, alchemy and mathematics—to England, Adelard's biography is incomplete. The main source for his life is his own writings, but he is thought to have been born *c.*1080 in Bath and then to have travelled extensively, first in France, then moving on to Sicily and southern Italy around 1116, both of which were under Norman rule at that time. He addresses his nephew: 'We agreed that I would investigate the learning of the Arabs to the best of my ability; you on your part would master the unstable doctrines of the French.'[27] In the decades following the First Crusade, the Arabs and their culture were seen as very exotic and romantic, representing the new and unexplored world of Islam. In Sicily Adelard would for the first time have come into contact with the Arab culture that the Normans had adopted under their king Roger II, and it is also where, according to the received wisdom, Adelard is thought to have learnt Arabic well enough to translate many scientific texts from the Arabic into Latin, notably Euclid's Elements, the original version of which had been lost in the West, but had survived only in Arabic translations from the Greek.

Nowhere, however, does Adelard himself claim that he could read Arabic. Modern historians like Margaret Gibson, writing in Charles Burnett's edited volume on Adelard of Bath, question Adelard's authorship of the Latin translation of al-Khwarizmi's astronomical tables, since there are 'mistakes in the Arabic of a magnitude that even a non-Arabist can comprehend'.[28] It is also puzzling that in Adelard's treatise on falconry there is no mention of Arabic influence, yet in his travels in southern Italy it seems hardly credible that he would have been unaware of the development of the Arabic practice of falconry, knowledge which was first introduced to the Norman counts and kings of Sicily by Arabs.[29]

Adelard returned to the West Country in 1126, over a century before the Arabic numerals appeared at Wells, and died there *c.*1142. The theory told to me by the cathedral guide was that Adelard's scientific knowledge of geometry, algebra, alchemy and mathematics somehow passed to a man named Elias of Dereham, a friend of Adam Lock, the man named as the second master mason at Wells, who, according to this version of events, then taught his masons to use Arabic numerals. Elias was a gifted administrator and clerk of works at Wells till 1222, who died *c.*1245, about a century later than Adelard of Bath.

This account is not credible for two reasons. Firstly, Adelard does not show any knowledge of, or desire to use, Arabic numerals in any of his works, and recent scholarship has shown that the early-twelfth-century text *Liber ysagogarum*, one of the earliest works to introduce Arabic numerals to the West, is most unlikely to have been written by Adelard since its Latin style is very different to his.[30] Secondly, if Adelard had been responsible for teaching the use of Arabic numerals to masons, how is it that Roman numerals still remained the overwhelmingly more used numbering system? Teaching a largely illiterate group of craftsmen such a radically different system when the old Roman system had served them perfectly well for centuries seems implausible. How would the new system have benefited them, given that the Arabic numerals were harder to make, being mainly curved, free-flowing shapes, rather than the straight simple lines of the Roman numerals they were used to? Given the timing, surely it was far more likely that the masons were in fact Arabs, brought back by returning Crusaders, using their own familiar numbering system.

The Wells Cathedral Fabric Book shows that the single biggest cost in cathedral building was not the stone, which was readily and cheaply available from local quarries, but the cost of skilled labour. It was reckoned that a fully qualified mason, a freemason, earned about £7 to £10 a year. Based on the number of masons' marks found in the cathedral, it has been calculated that up to twenty masons were employed on the building at any given time, therefore costing in the region of £150 a year. At Rochester Cathedral, experts have arrived at the same figure of about twenty masons at any one time, moving from one section of the cathedral to the next, based on careful analysis of the masons' marks. Bishop Grandison of Exeter was able to afford thirty masons a year in his rebuilding of Exeter Cathedral, because he inherited the land and property of his brother, a count in Savoy, who died without issue. The only person who could afford greater expenditure was the king himself.

Masons' labour costs might be another very understandable reason why Crusaders would bring back 'Saracen prisoners'. Despite the expenditure involved in transporting such people, along with their board and lodging for the entirety of the long return journey, the Crusader knights must have thought it worthwhile, especially if these men had skills which were either unavailable or else extremely rare and expensive back home. The likelihood is that such skilled craftsmen would also have been ordered to bring their tools with them, be they masons or carpenters, which were also recognised as superior to English ones.

If we imagine a comparable situation in today's world, where a wealthy couple want to build a luxury house for themselves, how would they go about it? They would certainly not go to their local builder, who would only manage a run-of-the-mill job. They would make sure to get hold of the very best workmen, with the highest skills, even if they had to be brought from abroad, even though that would obviously cost a great deal more. An off-the-shelf kitchen is not a patch on a top-quality bespoke kitchen—a fact that shows in the price. If you can afford the best, you go for the best, and it shows in the end result.

Masons' Marks

Unlike assembly marks in Roman or Arabic numerals which were simply to ensure the correct pieces of timber or stone were installed in the correct places, masons' marks were personal to the individual mason and served to identify his work. The earliest masons' marks so far discovered in England are in Westminster Hall, the oldest part of the Houses of Parliament, erected for William II (William Rufus) in 1097, and in Norwich Cathedral, dating to 1119. Art historians generally agree that these masons were likely to have been imported by the Normans, hence the common assumption that they were French, especially given that they also brought in their own Caen stone for their prestige projects. From studying the masons' marks at Westminster, Rochester, Wells, York, Gisborough Priory in North Yorkshire and Canterbury, and comparing them with ones found in northern Spain, notably at Santiago de Compostela, the destination of the pilgrimage controlled by the Norman Benedictines, and at Vézelay, a major French starting point for Santiago, I have been able to draw some interesting comparisons. The five-pointed star occurs across all the sites, a complex geometric masons' mark that has been traced all the way back to the Great Pyramid at Giza dating to 2500 BCE, much used in the Islamic world and found multiple times in the Córdoba Mezquita. The trefoil, an elaborately curved mark that must have been made using a compass to form the three-petalled flower, is the most interesting, occurring across all the sites in the parts of the building where highly skilled stonework is found, easy to miss as it is often only faintly inscribed. In Santiago there are also quatrefoil signs, like four-leafed clovers, in the same locations, suggesting that the geometric sophistication was greater in those parts of the cathedral. In the Córdoba Mezquita there are examples of phytomorphic (plant-based) marks, many of which are known to be archetypal ancient Egyptian representations of the divine, like the half-open lotus flower. It is logical to assume that the simpler masons' marks belonged to the common-or-garden masons, while the complex, sophisticated ones, which were harder to make in the first place, using curves and/or geometry, belonged to the more skilled masons, the top team. What all experts agree on, however, is that the most sophisticated sculpture, like carved capitals, has never been found to carry a single mason's mark, and the assumption is that this was because the master sculptor's work was unique and well known so there was no need to mark it, unlike the so-called 'bankers' marks', where masons marked their work in order to be paid. The bankers' marks tend to be far simpler and in the parts of the building where less complex, bulk construction was required, like the nave walls.

Masons are often described in contemporary medieval documentation as 'temperamental, untrustworthy, duplicitous and frequently working to their own creative agendas rather than the visions of their patrons'.[31] Art historian

Matthew Reeve writes that at Wells the sculpture itself provides compelling evidence of how the Wells atelier must have been a dynamic group of high-quality sculptors, and indeed the central inspiration for what has come to be known as 'the West Country School of Masons', whose influence has been detected across the region. Scholars concur that given the lack of biblical imagery or New Testament subject matter in the Wells capitals, they must have been the product of the imaginations of the sculptors themselves, not dictated by the religious patrons. This confirms the extent to which the masons acted independently and did not follow a programme laid down for them by their masters. At Wells, as Reeve explains, 'the capitals especially stand as a curious one-off in English medieval art: in their remarkable dynamism and plasticity, and in their ornamentation of the main body of a cathedral church, there is no ready parallel for them in all of English Gothic architecture'.[32]

Some experts have queried why there should be this apparent disconnect at Wells between the rather random 'Romanesque'-style carving on the nave capitals and the early Gothic design, and have attempted to come up with all sorts of convoluted explanations, while simultaneously commenting on the quality of the stonework and its unique vitality and iconography. They have looked at the development of imagery, technique and even style in the nave capitals, saying that it implies a process of constant experimentation and improvisation, with more restrained foliage in the eastern sections of the late 1170s and early 1180s, then becoming more and more complex as it moves in a westerly direction. Remarks have been made about the way the sculpture seems to grow organically from the pillars themselves in successive stages from east to west, increasingly questioning the earlier stiff-leaf design and pushing the boundaries of reality well beyond what could be botanically possible. The subject matter of the animals is considered, with meanings looked for in the pairs of birds and fantastical beasts, these enquiries eventually concluding that they must be creations of the sculptor, and were not based on any instructions from the patron.

All these dilemmas and apparent contradictions would be resolved if these commentators could accept that the masons were not only brought in from abroad but had also been schooled in an Islamic tradition of decoration and possessed, as craftsmen at the top of their game, the ability to create a cohesive organic space as one unified construction. They stuck to the subject matter in the carving that they were familiar with in settings from southern France and northern Spain, exactly the same subject matter as in the capitals at the monasteries of Saint-Michel-de-Cuixà, Saint-Martin-du-Canigou, Santa

Maria de Ripoll and Santo Domingo de Silos in Greater Catalonia (see Chapter 8); the same as in the cloisters of Moissac in southern France (see Chapter 10); and the same as in the cloisters of Monreale and Cefalù in Sicily, all of them Benedictine, all of them known to have been built by local Arab Muslim masons (see Chapter 6). The names of the highly talented Wells masons remain unknown. Indeed, as Reeve comments:

> [t]he origin of the Wells workshop constitutes one of the great unknowns of artistic production in the early Gothic period. The Wells sculpture seems to emerge from an atelier fully formed and comfortable with the medium of the stone capital and the range of imagery employed in the 1180s.[33]

In the twelfth-century French and Spanish monasteries, a common subject matter on painted ceilings and in decorative sculpture was scenes of normal everyday life and the Labours of the Months, often enclosed in roundels, just as they had been in Fatimid decorative carving a century earlier. Pictures of carpenters making the ceiling can be seen at al-Jaferia Palace in Zaragoza, and frescoes of craftsmen even appear in the eighth-century Umayyad baths of Qusayr Amra in today's Jordan. As such, they are familiar forerunners to a number of the Wells capitals in the nave and western transepts which feature images of peasant labourers wool-combing and spinning, a leather worker, butchers and even a mason carrying a block of stone and an axe.

The seven Old Testament prophets who appear at Wells cannot all be identified, and commentators puzzle over what the source of the images might have been, saying 'the Wells prophets do not appear to have derived from any typical collection of Old Testament imagery, but rather represent instead a collection of both the major and minor prophets taken at random... remarkable for their sheer diversity of imagery'.[34] As usual, all the explanations sought by Romanesque art historians do not extend their horizons beyond Europe, or even beyond England.

Ipswich Man

One final case I wish to focus on is that of the so-called 'Ipswich Man', since his identity has been scientifically researched by a BBC Two TV documentary, the first episode in a series called *History Cold Case*, broadcast in 2010. The five-strong *Cold Case* team followed clues from a thirteenth-century skeleton found buried in a Franciscan friary graveyard near Ipswich. His DNA showed him to be from the North African coast, approximately modern Tunisia, and the belt buckle buried with him suggested he was not a friar, as friars only wore rope belts tied at the waist.

The team established that the friary had been built in the thirteenth century by a Norman noble and landowner named Lord Robert de Tiptoft (d.1298), who had accompanied Lord Edward, the future Edward I (Longshanks) of England on his Crusade, sometimes called the Ninth (and final) Crusade, to the Holy Land in 1270. Dr Adrian Bell, who was then a historian at Reading University, was given the task of unearthing links between the friary and de Tiptoft, and discovered, by looking through John Weever's *Ancient Funeral Monuments* (1631),[35] the first full-length book dedicated to the study of English church monuments and epitaphs, that de Tiptoft himself was buried, along with his wife, Eva, in the same friary graveyard as the Tunisian man. The text also records that de Tiptoft stopped at Tunis on his way back from the Holy Land, along with Prince Edward and King Louis IX of France (Louis the Saint), who was renowned for his zeal in converting Muslims to Christianity.

I contacted Adrian Bell about the programme, and he kindly gave me a few more sources that he and a colleague had unearthed during their research. One chronicle records: 'Louis bought many slaves and Saracens with his own money and had them baptised and provided for.'[36] Another added that some of the Saracens were already baptised when they were sent to France before the king's own departure from Acre.[37] There was also an entry for payments made from the royal accounts to these converts, or *baptizati*, in France.[38]

An entire book dedicated to Louis the Saint's converts from Islam came out in 2019,[39] explaining that as many as 1,500 *baptizati* received stipends from the royal accounts from 1253 till as late as 1305, by which time the first generation of adult converts would have died and the second generation have been largely assimilated. Most were settled across a range of northern French towns, to facilitate their smooth absorption into the majority Catholic population and to ensure their acquisition of French language skills. Intermarriage was encouraged. The book cites examples of such individuals, like Johan Sarrasin, listed as a policeman in Paris in 1309, and Gobert Sarraceni, a tax collector for the French Crown in the late thirteenth and early fourteenth centuries, to show how later generations became integrated into established social and economic structures, becoming thoroughly Christian and French, with only their names 'Sarrasin' and 'Sarraceni' betraying their Arab origins. It appears that attitudes were surprisingly tolerant: 'There was no perceived disconnect between being a Muslim in Egypt and looking like a northern European Christian',[40] concludes the author. Even after conversion the epithet 'Sarrasin' was kept, with the most ironic instance perhaps being the case of John Sarrazin (John the Saracen), the Benedictine monk whose excellent translation of pseudo-Dionysius's *The Celestial Hierarchy* for the Abbot Suger at Saint-Denis is credited with providing the spark which inspired Suger's philosophy of divine light, the supposed trigger for the birth of Gothic architecture. But as Romanesque art historian Thomas Jackson helpfully opines, 'it is not likely that any amateur, however accomplished, should be the author of a fresh constructional movement in architecture. The suggestion must have come from some practical master mason, the real architect of the building.'[41]

Professor Bell also established that the Norman noble Robert de Tiptoft was recorded in the Pipe Roll (an annual financial audit of government expenditure maintained by the Norman Exchequer) as being accompanied on Crusade by six English knights, each of whom was paid the sum of 100 marks for their service. A grand total of 225 English knights are recorded as being paid for going on Crusade that year, according to the Pipe Roll. In an entry for 1272 in the *Flores Historiarum* (a collection of thirteenth-century Latin chronicles put together by English medieval historians), Bell also found mention of a number of nobles, including the Norman knight Thomas de Clare, a companion of de Tiptoft on Crusade, bringing back 'four captive Saracens' to London.

It is therefore highly likely, the *Cold Case* scientists deduce, that the Tunisian could have been baptised and brought back as a convert by Crusader knights, or else brought back as a slave or prisoner. Why would they do this? The only plausible reason is that he, like many others, had skills which were so useful and rare back home that it was considered worthwhile paying for his keep on this long journey back to England. He then lived and died at the friary and ended up buried there alongside the friars. A modern-day Grey Friar, Brother Philippe, was interviewed by one of the *Cold Case* team to try to get the bottom of how such a burial on hallowed ground might have been authorised, and in answer to their question Brother Philippe produced a letter from no less a figure than Pope Innocent IV, dated 1250, giving the friars the privilege of being able to bury the friars 'and those of their family' in the friary graveyard. Brother Philippe interpreted this to mean that the friars were given special dispensation by the Pope to bury any non-Christians who worked in support of them, as part of their community, alongside them in their graveyard.

We will never know whether this cover-all phrase 'and those of their family' was deliberate or not, used by the friars or by the Pope disingenuously. What we do know, however, from other recorded cases—in monastery archives in twelfth-century northern Spain, for example—is that Muslim masons lived alongside monks as lay members of their community in places like Santo Domingo de Silos, building the church and the cloisters (see

Chapter 8). No information about their burial arrangements has been unearthed, as yet.

At the end of the *Cold Case* documentary, the lead scientist, Professor Sue Black, then head of Britain's top unit for forensic analysis, part of the University of Dundee's Centre for Anatomy and Human Identification, puts the find in context, saying:

> we have evidence of African individuals in this country from Roman times, and certainly from medieval times, and by Tudor times we know that Queen Elizabeth I is saying we have too many North African individuals in this country, we need to send them back... How do you go from a small number of individuals in a community, to such a point that you've got the monarchy saying this is too much, we have to be able to stop this happening? There's no doubt this hasn't been researched and I think it should. If nothing else, what we've done is to say 'Here's one! We've found it, excuse me! Start with this one!'

In researching the evidence presented in this book, I too have often felt like a forensic investigator, following one clue after another, never knowing where the path would lead, delving into musty attics looking for Arabic numerals, straining my eyes squinting at medieval tracing floors for signs of the use of different tools, examining artworks with a magnifying glass to detect tell-tale motifs, unearthing books at the London Library that have never been taken out before, and tracking down from their obscure bibliographies academic articles that would have taken their authors many years to put together.

Professor Black ends by summing up the situation this way:

> We have scientifically identified beyond all reasonable doubt, which is all any court in the land will ask of us, that this individual is of African ancestry. We are absolutely certain of his ethnicity and that is rare, very, very rare. In terms of human history and migration patterns, this is terribly, terribly important.[42]

PART TWO

ISLAMESQUE ARCHITECTURE ACROSS EUROPE

6.1: Arabic inscription on a column in the nave of Santa Maria dell'Ammiraglio (1143), a church that still follows the Eastern Orthodox rite of its founder George of Antioch, admiral to Roger II. Framed by a pair of scrolling arabesque bands, the script uses the foliate style that was favoured by the Fatimids in the eleventh and twelfth centuries, where the lettering ends in leaf-like terminals, a design later copied in Norman decorative settings. Palermo, Sicily.

6

SICILY

The Arab-Norman Synthesis

Sicily holds the key to unlocking the secrets of Romanesque architecture in Europe, since so many decorative features first enter the Norman repertoire on the island, all of them Arab and Islamic in origin. Zigzags are the most obvious one, featuring heavily in all the major monuments built under Norman rule, notably Roger II's royal chapel, the Cappella Palatina (1130–40), in Palermo; the cathedral at Monreale with its dramatic zigzag fountain column in the cloister (1172); the La Zisa palace zigzags on the Arab Room marble fountain; and Palermo Cathedral itself, covered in zigzags (1184–5).

In no other European location, not even in Andalusian Spain, was there such a thorough mingling of Arab and Norman peoples and cultures. Although the Normans wrought much destruction on the island during its conquest, they maintained good relations with the majority Muslim population, incorporating them at high levels of government and employing their craftsmen to build their hybrid Arab-Norman palaces and churches. Christians were outnumbered two-to-one by Muslims at the outset.[1]

Sicily was always a melting pot of Mediterranean cultures, but its greatest period of wealth and prosperity came with the arrival of the Arabs from North Africa, whose coast was barely 150 kilometres away. For two and a half centuries before the Normans arrived, the island was ruled by a succession of caliphs, and Palermo, the capital, grew into one of the largest and wealthiest cities in Europe. The Emirate of Sicily (827–1091) was a milieu where commercial partnerships between Muslims, Jews and Christians were common, as testified by the Cairo Geniza documents.[2] The Arabs reorganised agriculture through efficient terracing, water management and land reforms, building a series of magnificent castles, palaces and mosques across the island, almost all of which the Normans destroyed. As Count Roger de Hauteville in 1093 wrote: 'Who, seeing the huge and widespread destruction of the castles and cities of the Muslims, and observing the vast destruction of their palaces, built with such great skill... could not consider this to be a great and manifold disaster and an incalculable loss.'[3]

The Normans were great opportunists. Having first come to Sicily as mercenaries in the service of the Byzantines and the Lombards, they then took over the island themselves, keeping Palermo as their capital. The celebratory tone of the Norman chronicles speaks of a rapid conquest, where the people living on the island were oppressed by the infidels and wished to make Roger de Hauteville their ruler. In practice very little is known, apart from the initial landings in 1061, about the subsequent stages of the invasion, except that the Arab capital Palermo was forced to capitulate in 1072 after several months of siege, and that between 1077 and 1086 the Normans arrived again with a more substantial fleet to renew their campaign, which finally succeeded in 1091, after thirty years of hard fighting. William of Apulia, a Lombard chronicler[4] of the conquest writing in the 1090s, records that Palermo in the late eleventh century was 'a city hostile to God... enslaved by demons', and that Roger

> did not harm anyone, even though they were all pagans. He treated all those he conquered with fairness. And with glory to God he shattered the foundations of the impious temple: in place of the mosque he built a church to the Virgin Mary. And the temple of Mahomet and the devil, transformed into a sanctuary of God, became a portal to heaven for the righteous.[5]

Palermo Cathedral, the building he is referring to, replaced the premier mosque of Sicily, and no Norman building on the island gives us more clues about the Muslim workforce employed there than this cathedral. Under the Norman narrative, the buildings erected under their rule in the late eleventh and twelfth centuries were their own creations, yet the buildings themselves tell a very different story. Virtually all the monuments, the cathedrals, the churches, the palaces and the castles built under the Normans were Arab in the sense that the craftsmen were Arab, sometimes imported from Egypt and North Africa, sometimes local, but always using their own Islamic styles and traditional skills.

Recognition of this inconvenient evidence has been slow in coming. It took UNESCO till 2015 to inscribe on its World Heritage list what it calls 'Arab-Norman Palermo and the Cathedral Churches of Cefalù and Monreale', dating from the era of the Norman Kingdom of Sicily (1130–94). Collectively, the nine buildings on the list are an example of what UNESCO calls 'a social-cultural syncretism between Western, Islamic and Byzantine cultures on the island which gave rise to new concepts of space, structure and decoration. They also bear testimony to the fruitful coexistence of people of different origins and religions (Muslim, Byzantine, Latin, Jewish, Lombard and French).'[6]

In the wake of the UNESCO listing, a whole spate of publications has appeared in recent years, many in Italian only, but sometimes translated into English or French, written by Italian scholars, detailing the buildings and their characteristics. The Palermo Tourist Office even hands out a free 272-page paperback called *Arab Norman Itinerary*, produced by UNESCO itself, which covers not only the nine most important monuments but also a further thirteen structures, mostly churches and palaces, scattered around Palermo and its environs. All of them feature zigzags in abundance, especially round the arches of portals and windows. Even Norman tombs and cemeteries use Arab architecture, making them feel more like Muslim cemeteries than Christian ones.

Of these twenty-two monuments, only two have survived from the Arab period, both of which date from Fatimid rule: the Baths of Cefalà Diana located in remote hills southeast of Palermo, and the Palace and Park of La Favvara (also known as Maredolce), discreetly tucked away among what are today some of Palermo's poorest suburbs.

Water Systems

To illustrate how fully Arab these styles were, the best place to start will be these two surviving Fatimid buildings, so that their features can then be directly compared with their Arab-Norman successors. What both structures share is a complete mastery of sophisticated water systems, way in advance of anything the Normans would have seen elsewhere.

The Baths of Cefalà Diana are unique as the only Islamic thermal complex in Sicily, on the site of natural hot springs, recorded as still being in use up till the 1920s, when they fell into disrepair. Today they have been authentically restored to their original layout and reopened to the public, not for use as baths, but to learn about the history of the site and its backstory. Inside, as well as the vaulting and the pointed arches, there are other telling details, like the arched geometric lace-like window at the far end, and the design of the red sandstone capitals, identical to those in the courtyard of al-Azhar in Cairo, completed in 972.

The original Arabic name of the remarkable fortified palace of La Favvara means 'water source', and once more, the site was chosen for the abundant

6.2: Interior of the restored tenth-century Fatimid Baths of Cefalà Diana built with vaulting and pointed arches around hot water springs in the hills inland from Palermo, Sicily. Such complex mastery of water systems was also used to transform Sicily's irrigation and agricultural productivity.

spring on the slopes of Monte Grifone which fed the lake that surrounded it on three sides. Despite the unsightly illegal buildings that still abut parts of the complex today, the beauty of the location is clear to see, between the sea and Monte Grifone. It was originally the country residence of the emir Ja'far, surrounded by lush gardens, but was then taken over and rebuilt by Roger II in 1150 on pre-existing structures of the Islamic age dating to the tenth or eleventh century.

Designed round an open quadrangle with a shaded vaulted portico whose dimensions and style are similar to those of the courtyard of al-Azhar Mosque in Cairo, the exterior has typical Fatimid high blind arches decorating the tall defensive walls, while the interior has both a quadripartite vaulted ceiling and a tall Arabic domed tower, resting on squinches. Benjamin of Tudela, a Jewish traveller from Spain visiting in 1171, described how the lake was full of many different varieties of fish, and how the king (Roger II) often sailed small boats on the lake 'with his women'. The palace garden was thought to be modelled on the Arab-Iranian style of paradise garden.

The North African palace architecture of Qal'at Bani Hammad, built in 1007, with luxuriant gardens and large artificial lakes where nautical games were held, heralds a similar arrangement at the later Norman palaces of La Favvara, La Zisa and La Cuba in Palermo.[7] Ingenious hydraulic systems captured spring water to supply the Norman palaces of Sicily, a skill imported to the island from Fatimid North Africa, copying the Islamic love of fountains and the sound of running water, designed as places of rest and recreation to evoke the Islamic Paradise. The best preserved of these can still be seen at La Zisa (begun in 1165 by Arab craftsmen), on the outskirts of Palermo, in the throne room of the Norman king, where he sat like an Arab ruler while water flowed out of the wall and onto a zigzag-patterned marble slab, then out into an artificial basin in front of the palace. All the ornamental elements—like the blind niches and arcades reflecting the continuous frieze of the Venetian dentil and the polylobed arches—were not only carried over from the North African palaces into the Norman palaces of Sicily, but also into the church architecture of Palermo.

The Normans, like the Arabs before them, used these palaces as hunting lodges and summer retreats, and the gardens and orchards round the city that thrived thanks to plentiful water were known as *Conca d'Oro* (the Golden Conch Shell) by Palermo residents.[8] The network of irrigation tunnels built by the Arabs below Palermo is so extensive it has not yet been fully explored. The Palazzo Reale, or Royal Palace (also known as the Palazzo dei Normanni, or the Palace of the Norman Kings), stands on the same site as the Arabic *qasr* (fortified palace) of the Muslim emirs, still known today as the *Cassaro*, from the original Arabic.

North African Influences

All the palaces and summer residences built in Sicily under the Normans show strong influences from North Africa, with Fatimid-Zirid styles and designs. These attributes show in both secular and religious structures, such as pointed arches with upraised piers (i.e. square supports for arches, held up on groupings of slender columns either side of a doorway), Kufic inscriptions and upraised cupolas. The design in stone-inlaid floors and panels, the animal and floral motifs, the stalactite honeycomb vaults (Arabic *muqarnas*) and the general floor plans all betray this influence. For example, the pointed arch, corbelling and stalactites of the Cappella Palatina (royal chapel of the Normans), La Zisa and other Norman structures closely resemble the Great Mosque of Tlemcen and the buildings of Qal'at Bani Hammad in Algeria.[9]

The upraised domes of the churches of San Cataldo, San Giovanni degli Eremiti (St John of the Hermits) and Santa Maria dell'Ammiraglio (St Maria of the Admiral, known as La Martorana), all built under Norman rule, show common elements of design with those found in North Africa and Spain. The general forms of these churches are indicative of North African styles, as are their designs and motifs. The floral patterns and various geometric designs as well as the animal depictions have almost exact equivalents in structures found in what the Arabs called *Ifriqiya*. The inscriptions carved into their stonework and woodwork all indicate a common source with the Fatimids and, in some cases, an Egyptian inspiration.

The use of a dome (Arabic *qubba*) on four pillars, like the Cubula in Palermo, originated in North Africa, and its use in Sicily is one of the earliest examples.[10]

Speed and Efficiency of Islamic Construction

After they had demolished most of the pre-existing Arab architecture on the island, what the Normans ordered to be built in its stead, using the same indigenous Muslim engineers, masons and craftsmen whose families in earlier generations had built the original structures, unsurprisingly turned out, as seen at La Favvara, to be far more 'Arab' than 'Norman'. The Normans were clearly in awe of the superior construction skills they found in the local Muslim workforce and embraced their techniques and styles wholeheartedly.

It is a known and recorded characteristic of Fatimid architecture that cities and buildings were constructed very fast. The great Tunisian historian and philosopher Ibn Khaldun tells us that the Hammadid city of Béjaïa on the coast of modern Algeria, and its great Palace of the Pearl, were built in a single year, from 1067 to 1068. It had close trading ties with Pisa in the eleventh century, which is also relevant for the features that start to appear in Pisan 'Romanesque', such as zigzags and blind-arcaded facades.

European art historians instinctively tended to credit the Normans with the new architectural style that emerged on Sicily, but the art of building on Sicily at that time was almost exclusively the preserve of Islamic or Islamised craftsmen. This is demonstrated by the quality of the architecture itself, even though the Latin Christian sources did not acknowledge the Muslim paternity of their churches in any of their literature, presumably because of racial and religious aversion,[11] or possibly because it did not matter to them.

Professor Giuseppe Bellafiore, Dean of Architectural History at the University of Palermo, began to redress this balance, writing in 1976:

> the purely Norman element in Arabo-Norman architecture is less than the name might suggest. The Norman rulers had the tact and the foresight to accept, and even like, what they found. The strength and efficiency of the Norman administration derived from its policy of deliberate flexibility toward the existing Muslim order on the island. Thus culture in general, and artistic tradition in particular, owed little to the Normans' own land of origin.[12]

Bellafiore also explains that the methods of construction and the formal characteristics typical of Palermo architecture remained unchanged for decades after the Norman period, still deeply rooted in the traditions of Muslim Sicily, as the stylised motifs of vegetation, geometrical figures and shell-shaped niches, blind arches, corbels, merlons, twisting and zigzag columns, zigzag-decorated arches, slender shafts or columns, and so on, are all drawn from the repertoire of Islamic Sicily. Even the motif of the grotesque and caricatured human figure itself had been present in Sicily earlier, with 'the Saracens painting or sculpturing the human figure ever since the time of Roger'.[13]

In his forensic and comprehensive study of Palermo Cathedral (1184–5), Bellafiore proves conclusively that it is 'a monument which represents the apex of the artistic creativeness of the Norman period in Sicily and, therefore, the highest and most comprehensive text of Fatimite architecture in Sicily'.[14] He poses an interesting question: how is it this huge cathedral was built in a single year, when north European cathedrals of the same period took far longer, often decades? The answer, he concludes, is first and foremost because it was conceived 'with an architectural coherence that could only have been the hallmark of a fully evolved style at the height of its artistic achievement', a coherence that is obscured today by the subsequent Gothic, Baroque and Neoclassical additions. The other factors that would have helped with the speed were the excellent nearby quarries, the ready availability of construction funds from the Royal Treasury, and a large quantity of reusable material from the earlier church-mosque. The speed of construction of the Córdoba Mezquita in Umayyad Spain a full four centuries earlier, but likewise in one year, from 785 to 786, is explicable for the same reasons, in that case recycling material from the earlier Visigothic church.

6.3: Despite the many additions made in later centuries, much of the original twelft-century fabric of Palermo Cathedral is still visible, especially around the exterior of the eastern apse and at the upper roof levels, where it shows typical Islamic craftsmanship.

The construction of every major church in Sicily built during the Norman period was completed remarkably quickly. The Cappella Palatina took just one year from 1131 to 1132 and La Martorana from 1142 to 1143. Monreale Cathedral, completed between 1174 and 1176, was also extremely fast. Secular projects too were completed quickly, like the *sollazzo* (pleasure palace) of La Zisa, conceived as a summer residence for the Norman kings, where they lived like their predecessors the Arab emirs, enjoying music, courtly entertainment and hunting in the extensive gardens, known as the *Genoardo*, from the Arabic *Jannat al-Ard*, meaning Earthly Paradise. Cefalù Cathedral was the only known exception, begun in 1131 by Arab craftsmen, but not completed till 1240, due to later workforce problems. Pointed arches were used in these cathedrals a few years before they miraculously 'appeared' at Abbot Suger's Basilica of Saint-Denis, completed in 1144.

Another reason which must have helped with the speed of construction of all these Arab-Norman buildings was that Palermo, as well as enjoying its own skilled local Muslim workforce, also benefited from massive waves of immigration from North Africa due to wars and famines during the twelfth century. Among these immigrants would have been Islamic artists and artisans of advanced culture and great experience. Medieval Egyptian historian al-Nuwayri (Novairo) wrote that in 1147–8, when the short-lived Norman Kingdom of Africa was established (1148–60), 'a great number of inhabitants left the country [North Africa] and most of them came to Sicily'.[15] Roger II is also recorded as capturing much of the population of the island of Djerba, which must have included craftsmen, and transporting them back to Sicily. Arab sources mention that a large part of the Sanhaja (one of the largest Berber tribal confederations) also fled from North Africa after the destruction of Qal'a, in the years between 1152 and 1163, together with a number of Bani Hammad chiefs.[16]

These calamities were not the only cause of mass immigration from North Africa to Sicily. When the coast of North Africa was under Norman domination, a regular slave trade with Sicily permitted a constant flow of men and materials into the island. Arab historian al-Muqaddasi states that Mahdia was an open market for Sicily, and that King Roger, after the conquest of Bône in 1153, had sent an enormous number of Muslim prisoners to Sicily.[17] Given the intense building programmes of Roger and the Williams, it would be logical to assume that many of these would have been skilled artists and artisans who boosted the workforce, just as some 250 years later the Mongols under Tamerlane would deplete Damascus of its top craftsmen and transport them to Samarkand to help build monuments testifying to Tamerlane's own glory.

Georges Marçais described the architecture of Norman Sicily as 'the last, fully mature fruit of an artistic culture based on a complete understanding of the means of expression inherent to the Fatimite artistic world, which had assimilated its various components from African and Middle Eastern sources'.[18] During this period, as Bellafiore also confirms:

> Sicily does not belong to the nascent world of European art, the uncertain means of expression of which was the result of growing pains, but to the Islamic Mediterranean world. On the contrary—a fact often denied by scholars—it was this world, of which Sicily was an inseparable part, that irradiated towards Europe those impulses which were to become the fundamental yeast of its own art.[19]

The Fatimid Roots of Palermo Cathedral

Based on his detailed research, Bellafiore is convinced that, though the organic unity of the architecture of Palermo Cathedral was 'definitely laid down',

> the figurative and decorative side of the work was left to the free fancy and imagination of the artists responsible for the grandiose ornamental texture on the walls, so reminiscent of enormous carpets, and so akin to the contemporary Islamic art of weaving...[20]
>
> ...
>
> for, indeed, in this art the laws of symmetry did not rationalise the language of ornamental patterns to the point of mortifying it, but allowed it to retain the distinction of being unique. This subtle contradiction of symmetry and uniqueness was fundamentally typical of the clear and logical Oriental and Islamic world in which the cathedral was so deeply rooted.[21]

This point, observed by Bellafiore to be at the core of Islamic art and architecture, is something that becomes apparent time and again in Romanesque cathedrals across Europe, something that, after many years of exposure, it is possible to develop a feel for, as the eye becomes trained and learns to sense these fundamental differences between the classical and the Islamic approach.

The eastern end of the cathedral, free from later additions, is where the original quality and style of the Arab workmanship can still be seen most clearly. The arches of the apse are decorated in the highly sophisticated black lava inlay known as *intarsia*, the painstaking labour of expert stonemasons, collectively producing a play on light which has its origins and stylistic kinship in North African Fatimid architecture.[22] In addition to the complex interlaced blind arcading, the stone *intarsia* decoration demonstrates an extraordinary variety of themes, with blind arches, little rosettes and stylised animals, as in the double-headed eagle, symbol of the Church of Palermo. It almost looks as if the inlaid decoration has been woven into the stone, like embroidery or tapestry, very similar to that found in the Palace of Ziri in Ashir, in today's Algeria, built in 947 by Ziri, a Berber supporter of the Fatimids and founder of the Zirid dynasty. The palace is thought to have been modelled on that of the Fatimid caliph in Mahdia. It also exemplifies what is possibly the dominant theme of Islamic art, namely, the desire to cover all available surfaces with ornamentation, something that we will see again inside many other Romanesque buildings, such as the nave of Bayeux Cathedral and the Chapter House in Bristol.

At Palermo Cathedral today, none of the wooden ceilings are still extant because they were destroyed by tampering in the late eighteenth century, and there is no pictorial record of what they looked like. There is, however, much information from literary sources, such as descriptions in contemporary records of *c.*1185 of how the Norman church was entirely roofed in timber, together with geometric, epigraphic and floral motifs and sacred images, with sapphire blue and gold the dominant colours.[23] The roof was described as 'fashioned in the shape of the bottom of a ship', in other words it was keel-shaped, the typical Fatimid shape, 'all of good workmanship and painted with images of saints, both male and female, and angels and various ornaments which render it gracious'.[24]

As Bellafiore notes, historians who are only familiar with Christian artistic cultures measure Sicilian examples against them, then draw strange and improbably ideal relationships between Norman Sicily and the most diverse and only vaguely identified European regions. He proves that many Norman Sicilian churches reproduced ground plans very similar to those of both secular and religious Muslim buildings, and concludes that the origin of the ground plan of certain centric churches like Santa Maria dell'Ammiraglio, San Giovanni degli Eremiti, San Cataldo and Santa Maria Maddalena in Palermo, for example, all of which have the spatial and structural features of centric churches, should not be directly attributed to Byzantine church models. Rather, they are much closer in both time and geography to the secular Fatimid architecture of Sicily and North Africa, as well as to the mosque and tomb architecture of Fatimid Egypt, like al-Juyushi Mosque in Cairo (1085) and tombs like Sayyida Ruqayya (1133) in al-Qarafa, Cairo's Southern Cemetery. In other words, the culture that gave rise to the Norman Sicilian centric churches was Muslim, even if there may in the past have been some Byzantine influence. San Giovanni degli Eremiti, built by order of Roger II and at his expense between 1142 and 1148, is built from blocks of squared volcanic rock, with walls so smooth that the overall structure has been described as 'flawless, with a purity of form that refers to the geometric symbolism of Fatimid culture'.[25]

Bellafiore explains how all Fatimid architecture 'showed a marked propensity for a central or centralising structural organism which had in the *qubba*, that is, the cubic and domed volumetric element, its real or conceptual fundamental nucleus'.[26] The Cappella Palatina sanctuary likewise is centralised under the dome: 'One might say that the Cappella Palatina embodies in miniature the basic idea behind all the great churches built under Norman sovereignty.'[27] In the basilican churches of the early Christian period, the best

6.4: The upraised red domes of San Cataldo, built *c.*1160 in central Palermo, are directly modelled on North African Fatimid mosque domes, as are the recessed blind arches that decorate its walls.

viewpoint for taking in the whole church is always at the entrance, not in the choir or the centre of the sanctuary. Based on such detailed analysis, Bellefiore concludes, 'We are completely in the sphere of Muslim aesthetic values and of Fatimite art in particular.'[28] In the longitudinal churches in Sicily, like the cathedrals at Palermo and Monreale, each ground plan is different, so was never following a set layout, but was always centred on the choir:

> The architects evidently adopt very fluid ichnographic schemes, in most cases offering unique, autonomous and never-to-be repeated solutions. One gets the impression that the directives for the construction, which must surely have been laid down by the superior political or ecclesiastical authority, were only generically binding. It is therefore unthinkable that their source of inspiration was wholly Western, stemming from the Cassino-Latin and the Cluniac-Northern schools, as certain modern scholars have sustained.[29]

The same characteristics can be seen in North African Fatimid buildings, including Zirid and Hammadid, specifically in the Palace of Ziri at Ashir and the Palace of al-Manar, the Dar al-Bahr and the Qasr as-Salam at Qal'a, all of which group round a central space even in buildings without a strictly square ground plan.[30] The same thing appears in the Great Mosque of Damascus, longitudinal in design, and at that of Kairouan, where it is the space in front of the mihrab that is solemnised by a dome and by special architectural features.[31]

The interiors of both religious and secular buildings built during the Norman reign were covered in a layer of chalky stucco, as found at La Zisa, at Palermo Cathedral and in the Palazzo Reale itself. Stucco had been the preferred material for decorative carving in Islamic art and architecture going right back to Umayyad days in the eighth century, and was heavily used in Umayyad palaces. These walls reflected the coloured light from the stained-glass windows, the vivid colouring of the wooden ceilings, and the colourful marble floors. As Bellafiore explains, the essence of the building was that

> it was a Church to be lingered in, not to await the advent of some awe-inspiring omnipotence, invisible and alien, but in a marvelling transport of the senses and particularly of the eyes. The architecture of the Norman period was certainly one in which chromatic values, mature fruit of a long and profound experience of Middle Eastern origin, were essential components.[32]

Idries Trevathan, in his PhD-turned-book on the use of colour and light in Islamic art, tells us that recent technical analyses on a variety of Islamic architectural decorative works support the thesis that Muslim craftsmen deliberately sought to create 'sensations of light' by using reflective materials in stucco such as gypsum, powdered marble and eggshell. He even finds evidence that they were aware of the science of optics and the importance of luminosity to the aesthetics of colour.[33]

Bellafiore, when describing the interior of Palermo Cathedral, remarks:

> we are far from being inside one of those contemporary Northern churches where the light plays on tones of a single range of colour; it would be more proper to say that we are in one of those Muslim edifices, sacred or profane, where stuccoes, interior decoration, and above all painted ceilings, were designed to stimulate the participation of the senses, or to put it otherwise, evoked the divine as a sublimation of those senses. It should be added that Palermo Cathedral, in stressing chromatic values, follows the trend of late twelfth century Muslim architecture, which embraced the whole Mediterranean basin from Spain to Egypt.[34]

Palermo Cathedral as Church-Fortress

The spiritual component was not the only one in the cathedral. There was also the political one, with its many-sided aspects—military, executive and ruling—which were so vital in the days when conflicts of power were frequently settled by force. Palermo Cathedral was erected against the backdrop of complex politico-religious requirements and ideals (a state of affairs similar to Canterbury and Durham cathedrals for the Norman conquerors). The Sicilian cathedrals of Troina (*c.*1078–80), Mazara (*c.*1086–93) and Catania (1086–90) were also fortresses. Catania especially, with its massive system of towers—two on the main facade and two at the ends of the transept, all with staircases leading to upper levels—still exhibits this strongly fortified character. The passageways and circuits for the rounds ensured mobility and useful footways for the soldiers, in the shelter of the battlements of the apses, and used to run without interruption round the whole perimeter of the church—these were brought to light in their entirety in the restorations of 1957–9.[35]

Cefalù Cathedral (1131) was likewise planned as a church-fortress, as is clear from its outer fabric, still original, with its towers and battlements. Its

6.5: The fortress-church of Cefalù Cathedral with its towers and battlements was begun in 1131 by Arab craftsmen using pointed arches and recessed *ajimez* windows, but took until 1240 to complete, due to later workforce issues.

block-like imposing architecture of a tower-edifice is similar to the *manar* (watchtower) of the Zirids from which it is descended.[36]

Monreale Cathedral, the immediate predecessor of Palermo Cathedral, is also a fortress-church, with its massive towers and upper passageways round the circuit of the battlements. The ensemble with the archiepiscopal and royal palaces and monastery formed a fortified citadel. Palermo Cathedral benefited from all this previous experience in the construction of church-fortresses and represents the pinnacle of that experience. Its system of overhead passages in all their complexity is a masterpiece of engineering and planning. The Muslim architects were sufficiently confident and versatile in their craft that they could transfer their own experience and architectonic 'language' to typological schemes alien to their tradition and apply it to the cathedrals they now built for their new Norman masters. They had learnt the art of fortress-building from examples in both Moorish and Fatimid areas. The most important cities founded by the Fatimids—Mahdia in 916, the first Ashir in 935, Sabra al-Mansuriya (near Kairouan) in 947, Cairo in 969, the second Ashir in 974 or 977–78, Qal'a in 1007 and Béjaïa in 1067—were all fortified and the princely palaces they contained were like keep strongholds.[37] This fortified character is then evident in Romanesque abbeys and cathedrals across Europe, like Mont Saint-Michel, Jumièges and Speyer.

The towers defended the entrances, especially the main one. Sicilian architects had no shortage of Fatimid models: al-Sqifa al-Kahla gate at Mahdia, Bab al-Bahr at Béjaïa, and the three Fatimid gates of Cairo—Bab al-Nasr, Bab al-Futuh (1087) and Bab Zuwayla (1092). The great tower of Palermo Cathedral is clearly the work of Muslim craftsmen and engineers, as is demonstrated both by the type of wall masonry, consisting of regular courses of small, squared stones, and by the fact that it is filled with inert material, a widely used technique in Islamic fortifications since the earliest times.[38]

Mosaics and Paintings: The Cappella Palatina

The only painted ceiling in Sicily to survive today is inside King Roger's Cappella Palatina (Palace Chapel), built between 1132 and 1140, part of the Palazzo Reale. It represents the largest ensemble of monumental painting still extant anywhere in the medieval Muslim world, and one of the most extensive in twelfth-century Europe. The timber roofs in the cathedrals of Messina and Monreale only have a few visible trusses left. Both the ceiling of the Cappella Palatina and that of Messina Cathedral have as their central motif the eight-pointed star obtained by superimposing one square on top of another.

The eight-pointed star holds immense cultural and religious significance across many cultures, but was particularly favoured by Islamic artists, to symbolise celestial entities like the moon, sun, planets, stars and comets. The Cappella Palatina stars are bordered by a ribbon which intertwines to form cross-shaped spaces. Inside these and the stars, seashell motifs are hollowed out to resemble the petals of a flower in delicate tones of yellow, blue and white, while human and animal figures are included as well as plants.

These patterns follow a time-honoured local tradition of North African and Fatimid origin, with motifs of interweaving ribbons, the eight-pointed star combined with the symmetrical cross, the hollowed-out seashell, vine shoots and animal figures. The same motifs appear at Qal'at Bani Hammad, in certain plaster corner pendentives of the eleventh-century Dar al-Bahr, and in the ceilings of the Great Mosque of Kairouan, which date back to the same period as the Zirid emir al-Mu'izz (r.1016–62), a vassal of the Fatimids. Georges Marçais also notes that the stellar polygons obtained by the interlacing of continuous ribbons were a favourite motif among Fatimid artists of the Maghreb and in Fatimid Egypt.[39] The Arab Sicilian poet Ibn Hamdis (b.1056) describes the Palace of al-Mansuriya (1088–1104) at Béjaïa as 'full of all the animals of the chase and… plays of light with the sun… which prevented the light from pouring into the interior in one headlong rush'.[40] Béjaïa was the Hammadid dynasty capital (on today's Algerian coast) and was closely tied through trade to the Italian city of Pisa.

There is perhaps no one who has devoted more of his career to studying the Cappella Palatina, and specifically its wooden ceiling, than Jeremy Johns (b.1954), Professor of the Art and Archaeology of the Islamic Mediterranean at Oxford University. He was able to benefit from the restoration of the 18-metre-high ceiling that was carried out from 2005 till 2009. Thanks to the scaffolding, this was the first time that art historians had the chance to examine the craftsmanship and paintings, neither of which are ordinarily visible to the naked eye.

From this opportunity, he concluded that the team of craftsmen were Muslim artists who probably trained in Fatimid Egypt before being summoned to Palermo by the new Norman king, Roger II, and that the overwhelming majority of the scenes depicting human figures are directly drawn from the traditional cycle of Islamic palace architecture,[41] where the ruler is shown in his court, drinking, hunting and being entertained by wrestlers, musicians and dancers, scenes that had been typical since the ninth century in the Abbasid palaces of Baghdad and Samarra. The fantastical animals and birds—griffins, dragons, sphinxes, lions, elephants, giraffes, bears, gazelles, snakes, eagles, peacocks and hares—belong to the typical Fatimid tradition, often in confronting or addorsed pairs. Less than 10 per cent depict scenes from the Christian tradition, and Johns assumes that these would have been specifically commissioned by the Norman patron or his agents. Every image is separate, not linked into a narrative story, and each one is framed by pearled beading in a huge variety of shapes; again, each one is different.

He was also able to deduce conclusively that, contrary to previous suggestions, the ceiling was always part of the chapel construction, specifically designed for the space, in conjunction with the other works on the mosaics, because the wooden brackets from which the ceiling is suspended, together with the ventilation slits between the ceiling and the roof, were built into the original wall masonry of the nave. He also deduced that the carpenters and

6.6: Detail of a female lute player painted by a Fatimid artist on the wooden ceiling of the Cappella Palatina, *c.*1140, framed with the same pearl beading that surrounds every image on the ceiling. Such scenes of courtly entertainment are then seen on the sculpture of European cathedrals.

6.7: Fatimid painted image of two flute players on the wooden ceiling of the Cappella Palatina (*c.*1140) flanking a wall fountain with a lion's head and zigzags carved into the surface where the water runs down. The Islamic pearl-beaded frame encloses the whole ensemble.

painters must have worked together as a single coordinated team, since the massive stalactite pendants in the centre were painted on the ground then hoisted into place afterwards. It calls to mind the same method that was still being used much later for the West Front sculptures of Wells Cathedral in 1243, except that there the sculptors completed the sculptures in the ground workshop, marking them up with Arabic numerals for the fixers, but then moved on to their next commission when the money dried up, before the statues were put in their niches. As a result, the Norman/Anglo-Saxon fixers put the statues in the wrong niches since they were unable to read the Arabic numerals, putting them in randomly as best they could, a process which necessitated all sorts of complex adjustments to the niches (see Chapter 5).

No such headache in Palermo, where royal funds flowed freely to facilitate the construction work taking place at remarkable speed. The extremely high level of skill required for the successful execution of the ceiling makes it obvious that this was not the first experimental work of a group of novices, but of an experienced workshop of itinerant specialist carpenters and painters at the top of their game, who had clearly carried out similar commissions for other wealthy clients across the Mediterranean world. The religion of the patron would have been irrelevant, just as it would be today. As long as the patron paid accordingly, the team would carry out the commission to the highest possible level, with the perfectionism characteristic of all great artists. The fact that this is the only example of their work that survives, Johns concludes, can only be because all other examples have been lost through wars or fires; though he speculates that after completing the Palermo ceiling, the team might have sailed off to Constantinople where they built a similar *muqarnas* vaulted painted ceiling for the twelfth-century palace of the Moukhroutas, long since destroyed, but known from descriptions to have likewise portrayed scenes from the Islamic courtly tradition. Johns tells us that only fragments of similar work remain from Coptic churches, from a palace in Murcia, Spain, and from the palaces of Qal'at Bani Hammad, all dating to the eleventh and twelfth centuries.

Johns makes the common-sense point that before 1130 there had been no royal court on Sicily for nearly ninety years, meaning that 'an indigenous workshop expert in the construction and decoration of palace ceilings could not have survived unemployed and without court patronage for three generations only to reappear at the height of its powers after Roger's coronation'.[42] This is exactly my argument with both Romanesque and Gothic architecture, namely, that every time a new sophisticated feature or technique appears to 'pop out' fully formed, like some kind of Virgin birth, it cannot have come from a local source. Common sense dictates that this is simply not possible, especially in medieval times when architectural styles evolved and developed very slowly.

Johns argues that Roger II imported many craftsmen from all over the Mediterranean to build his capital in Palermo, and certainly it is recorded that he brought expert Christian mosaicists from Constantinople, always recognised as the foremost centre of mosaic work together with Antioch in Syria, just as the caliph Abd al-Rahman III in Córdoba had likewise summoned mosaicists from Constantinople to decorate the mihrab of his extension to the Córdoba Mezquita. Mosaic work was always recognised as a Byzantine skill, and the first time Christian mosaicists worked for new Muslim masters was at the Dome of the Rock (*c.*690) in Jerusalem.

It was normal practice for the ruler to get the top people for his prestige building projects, and Sicily was no exception. Johns mentions that sculptors were imported from the Italian mainland and southern France, but given the timing—the 1130s and 1140s—the likelihood is that skilled stone workers would not have been native Italians or Frenchmen but Arabs living in Italy or France who were now working for Christian masters following the collapse of the Córdoba Caliphate, where the construction industry was dominated by Arabs well into the thirteenth century.

The top team of carpenters and painters who created the ceiling at the Cappella Palatina evidently did not train any local artisans whilst on Sicily, for later structures like Cefalù Cathedral are not as refined; there are no *muqarnas* (the most complex and hardest kind of decorative vaulting to perfect, and therefore almost never found in European settings), no Arabic inscriptions, the courtly figures are no longer holding drinking cups but crosses, and the royal eagles and bulls become symbols of the Evangelists. It is as if the local artists tried to copy the Cappella Palatina ceiling but lacked the requisite expertise.

Of the handful of images that depict Christian models—like David playing his harp or David and his scribe—there are small clues that the Muslim artist was not familiar with the material. The instrument depicted, for example, could not have existed as represented, as it would not have been capable of making any sound. It is as if, Johns speculates, the Muslim artists were instructed to insert these subjects because the patron wanted them to complement the Solomonic themes in the mosaics in the chapel sanctuary. He sees nothing Romanesque in the paintings either and wonders if the artists were shown images from illuminated manuscripts to serve as their models. The same thing happens in the Wells West Front, where a sculptor carves Noah and the Ark showing the ark as a clinker boat, but with the planks overlapping the wrong way, as if the artist is unfamiliar with northern European clinker boats or clapboard houses and therefore gets it wrong when shown a two-dimensional sketch to copy.

The other Christian images which appear in the ceiling are an image of Daniel seated between two lions and a man on horseback slaying a dragon. The image of the Royal Lion Strangler or the Master of Beasts was common in the twelfth century within the Islamic world, familiar from Near Eastern prototypes, so transposing it to the Christian story of Daniel in the Lion's Den was a simple step. In the Islamic tradition the lions have their mouths open to lick Daniel.

There are four images in the ceiling of a horseman slaying a dragon, each in its own panel. The dragon is always serpentine, covered in scales, but its head is fox-like with pointed ears, not unlike the Norman beakhead. The Muslim artists struggled with the knight's armour and military cloak, as unfamiliar apparel to them, but they still managed to translate the image as a whole into their own stylistic idiom. In other words, there is nothing specifically Christian about these images. Most mounted dragon slayers represented by Muslim artists from the mid-twelfth century onwards were shown transfixing the dragon with a spear rather than a sword. In depictions of Samson and the Lion, the Fatimid lion as it appeared on standards was always shown moving from right to left, tail and right paw raised, exactly the same posture that is then taken into heraldic blazons by Crusader knights returning from the Holy Land in the twelfth century, when the concept of heraldry first emerges in Europe.[43] Images of a lion-rider or a griffin-rider were familiar to Muslim artists from earlier archetypes in Sassanian sculpture.

Roger II's chief minister and admiral from 1126 to 1151, George of Antioch, was likely, according to Johns, to have been an Armenian born in Antioch in ancient Syria, but trained in Zirid *Ifriqiya* before defecting to Norman Sicily. He is thought to have been largely responsible for Roger's Arabic *Diwan* (administrative council), and in his own church known as La Martorana, or Santa Maria dell'Ammiraglio, a mosaic depicts Roger's divine coronation by Christ.

Johns speculates that the Fatimid artists would have left Cairo during a time of dynastic crisis and social unrest. In that sense they would have been migrant workers looking for new commissions abroad. The Fatimid peak in art and architecture was reached around 1060 and was sustained till the 1120s, but thereafter sources of patronage would have started to disappear, a date that ties in well with the apparently sudden appearance of Romanesque monuments across Latin Europe. Other top-level Fatimid crafts like carved ivory and rock crystal also stopped being produced at around the same time, so artists seeking new work would have had to become itinerant and find their fortunes abroad.

Out of such chaos and turbulence, artistic creativity can often find surprising stimulus, and in my view, this is the creativity that then starts to appear in early Romanesque sculpture, where the skills of top-level craftsmen are challenged to produce something new for new masters with different ideas and requirements to those of their former masters. For those at the top of their game, such adjustments were manageable. They could alter their repertoire where required and produce something from within their knowledge, albeit adjusted to fit the new specifications. Some Islamic scenes, for example, like the seated ruler drinking wine from a goblet, flanked by two attendants, could easily have been used by Muslim artists as the basis for a portrayal of

6.8: The mosaic-covered dome of the Greek Orthodox church of La Martorana (*c.*1143) in central Palermo is supported on four squinches and an Arabic inscription runs round its base. Its exterior architecture also shows many features of Islamic workmanship.

the Last Supper in a Christian setting, since scenes of court banqueting occur frequently in Fatimid art.

Sicily would have been a stepping stone, enabling these talented Muslim artisans to enter Europe and to work on high-level projects. Their reputations would have spread, and through word of mouth they would have been summoned to their next commission, be it in mainland Italy, France, Germany or England.

Ernst J. Grube, German historian of Islamic art and the first curator of the Islamic collection at New York's Metropolitan Museum, who worked with

Jeremy Johns studying the painted ceiling of the Cappella Palatina, was one of the world's leading authorities on Islamic art and marvelled at the 'astonishing common ground' between the iconography of the medieval Muslim world and the iconography of the western medieval Romanesque world, observing that a full study would no doubt lead to 'astonishing results'.[44]

On the floor of the Cappella Palatina there is magnificent marble work known as *opus sectile* (cut work), sometimes also called 'Cosmatesque' after the Italian Cosmati family of the thirteenth century who claim to have invented the style, even though the intricate geometric patterns are clearly Islamic in design. According to Johns, the floor was made by artisans from Campania in southern Italy in accordance with the Byzantine tradition and Muslim craftsmen using Islamic geometric designs. Other examples in Palermo occur in the interlacing, angular geometric ornament of the pavement of the church of San Cataldo (1154), in the columns and ceilings of the baldachins for the tombs of Roger II and his daughter in Palermo Cathedral (1150), and in the mosaic columns of the Monreale cloister (1172). This use of *opus sectile* then spread to church floors across Europe, used especially to demarcate the holiest areas like the chancel. The most notable example outside Italy is in London's Westminster Abbey in front of the High Altar. Commissioned by Henry III and laid in 1268, it marks the spot where the monarchs of England have been crowned for the last 700 years (see Chapter 11).

The wall mosaics in the Throne Room of Roger within the *Jawharia* (Jewel) Tower of the Palazzo Reale are another unique synthesis of Byzantine techniques, with mythological hunting scenes and royal creatures like lions and leopards in confronted pairs flanking a palm tree. Such images derived originally from Iranian Sassanian and Mesopotamian art, and then evolved through contact with the Islamic world, particularly in Muslim Spain and in Seljuk Anatolia. The Normans would never have seen a lion, extinct in Europe since the fourth century, when the Romans bemoaned that they could no longer find them for their 'beast-shows'. It would have been like a mythical beast to them, famous for its ancient representation as the king of the beasts.

The Pisan Tower next to the *Jawharia* has the proportions of a typical Norman fortified *donjon* keep, but the exterior wall decoration, with its interplay of blind arches, niches and mouldings, as Johns observes, 'bears the unmistakeable stamp of Fatimid architecture'.[45] The same exterior decoration of blind arcades can be seen in the Norman keep of Norwich Castle, and in nearby Castle Rising and Castle Acre, a Cluniac priory. The ground plan of the Pisan Tower is the same as the Qasr al-Manar at Qal'at Bani Hammad, and its 'volumetric concept recalls Zirid architecture'.[46]

6.9: The pleasure palace of La Zisa on the outskirts of Palermo was built *c.*1165, the best preserved of the Arab-Norman hunting lodges, surrounded by lush gardens and rich in water features like lakes and fountains.

The use of clusters of columns, either four or paired, moderate in height and diameter, was frequently found in Fatimid architecture. The practice was taken on in the architecture of Norman Sicily, notably at the Cappella Palatina and La Zisa, similar to the way they are used at al-Azhar and al-Hakim mosques in Cairo. The system of the mihrab with a bay in front is constantly found enriched by columns in Fatimid mosques and in North African and Egyptian Fatimid art. Exactly the same pattern was adopted for the apses of Sicilian churches. Unlike Graeco-Roman architecture, the columns were never a dominant feature; instead, they widened the appearance of the aisles horizontally to beyond their actual dimensions, almost creating the impression of a multicolumned or hypostyle hall. There was also no difference, as Bellafiore's study observes, in the essential artistic concepts behind the Islamic architecture of Norman Sicily, between religious buildings like Monreale Cathedral and the Church of the Magione, and the secular ones like La Zisa palace and the Throne Room of Roger II.

Another entirely new feature occurs in the mosaics at Monreale. As Bellafiore notes, although the mosaicists themselves came from Byzantium to complete the project, the schema of the mosaics, completely covering all the architectural surfaces and extending to nearly 7,000 square metres, spreads out and multiplies in an all-embracing way that gives the impression of being enveloped by a garden in Paradise, almost like a dream or a moment of rapture, typical of Islamic architecture. That same sensation is experienced in the cloister, with its highly decorated capitals supported by columns often embellished with thousands of gold and multicoloured tesserae, not to mention the small jewel-like courtyard round the zigzag-columned fountain which recalls the intimacy of the Muslim gardens and royal palaces of Palermo, where peace and solace from worldly concerns could be sought.

As is characteristic of Islamic art, there is no attempt at symmetry in the astonishing variety of the capitals with their many elegant sculptures. At both Monreale and Palermo cathedrals, typical Fatimid traditions are found in the decorative roundels containing geometrical roses, stars, crosses and interwoven bands; eight-pointed stars with alternating acute and round points; and animals in combat, with interweaving ribbons, chevrons and zigzags[47]—all features which subsequently carry over into Romanesque art and architecture.

The sculpted figurative motifs (especially in the likeness of human masks) that frequently appear on the exterior of the Norman churches in Sicily also have precedents in certain tenth- and eleventh-century North African and Egyptian buildings, such as the cats' heads in the Palace of Ziri at Ashir, and at Qal'at Bani Hammad, where quite similar heads were found on the minaret of the mosque. The human figure was not taboo in Fatimid art, as can be seen in a number of sculptures from Mahdia, now kept in the Bardo Museum of Tunis, and from Fatimid paintings on walls or on ceramics.[48]

Muslim–Christian Relations in Sicily

During the course of their rule the Norman kings encouraged the large-scale immigration of Latin Christian settlers from mainland Italy, so that by the end of the twelfth century the Latin Christian population far exceeded the Muslim, leading to anti-Muslim sentiment. To avoid civil unrest, Holy Roman Emperor Frederick II (1194–1250), an avid patron of the arts and sciences, relocated tens of thousands of his loyal Muslim Sicilian subjects to Lucera on the Italian mainland, whilst continuing to employ them in his personal retinue and in his armies against the papacy, in the same way that Fatimid rulers had promoted loyal Christian subjects within their armies.

Recent scholarship is finally starting to look more closely at the highly formative Muslim period of Sicily's history. The primary historical focus hitherto has been into political and military struggles—the 'outer-skin of history', as Palermo-born archaeologist Ferdinando Maurici describes it—while the social, economic, ethnic and cultural changes, 'the deeper currents that proceed at a generally slower pace',[49] have often been overlooked, even though it is these which ultimately tell us so much more about how life was lived in real communities, not just in political elites. It is tempting to think in terms of neat boundaries between historical periods, when everything changed just because the ruler changed, but the reality was different, as daily life for most continued much as before, albeit under new masters. Cultural identity is a constantly evolving thing, not fixed in time, and Sicily was always a bridge between Europe and the Muslim world.

Roger enjoyed friendly and diplomatic relations with the Fatimid court in Egypt, as the use of Fatimid craftsmen in the Cappella Palatina ceiling demonstrated. Credit is invariably given to the Normans for their enlightened and tolerant attitude towards the mixed population they inherited, but the reality is that their numbers on arrival were small, and if they were going to succeed in their ambition to rule the island they needed the help and cooperation of the existing Arab administrators. Their tolerance was based on self-interest, and they recognised that the pre-existing Arab system of statecraft, learning, architecture, agriculture and science inherited from Sicily's Islamic past was without exception superior to and more advanced than their own. Small wonder that they adopted it so wholeheartedly. Arab administrators employed in the Norman court played a very important role in twelfth-century Sicily, with many of the structures and practices of fiscal administration based on those of Fatimid Egypt.

These 'Palace Saracens' as they were called, eunuchs who had ostensibly been converted to Christianity but who remained covert Muslims, would have been well placed to arrange for Muslim craftsmen to work on Norman building projects, both inside Sicily and beyond. They adopted Latin or Frankish baptismal names, like Philip (the name of Roger's favourite), Martin, Peter and Richard, and were permitted after 1148 to be buried in land belonging to Benedictine monasteries, alongside palace staff. In the context of Sicily and southern Italy, those with Christian names could never be assumed to be Christians, just as those with Arab names were not automatically Muslims. In the town of Corleone for example, inland from Palermo, there were Christians called Muhammad, Abdullah, Ahmad and Ali, living alongside Muslims with Greek names, who could pass for Sicilian Christians.[50] Under the Muslim Emirate of Sicily in the ninth and tenth centuries many Christians converted, and marriage to Christians was allowed as long as the male offspring followed the father and became Muslim and the female offspring became Christian like the mother. Under the Norman kingdom the incentives for high-ranking Muslims to convert were considerable, and donation records in Greek show how 'Roger who was once called Ahmad, gave three estates to the archbishop-elect of the church of Palermo, lands conceded to Roger/Ahmad by his godfather, Count Roger II.' Many such cases of being rewarded with land in return for conversion are recorded.[51]

According to an eye-witness account of 1184 by Arab historian Ibn Jubayr, the Christian women too were indistinguishable from the Muslims. He saw them on their way to church to celebrate Christmas, speaking Arabic, dressed in gold silks and colourful veils and 'bearing all the finery of Muslim women in their attire, henna and perfume'.[52]

It is in Palermo that the most beautiful and magnificent examples of architecture are concentrated. Ibn Jubayr was utterly enthralled, writing in his chronicle: 'It is a city full of marvels, with buildings similar to those of Córdoba, built of limestone. There are so many mosques that they are impossible to count. Most of them also serve as schools. The eye is dazzled by all this splendour.'[53] This image of learning fits with the fact that the man chosen to lead the expedition from North Africa against Sicily was not a warrior, but a respected judge and scholar from the city of Kairouan. His speech rallying his men ended with the words:

> I have been given this appointment because of my achievements with the pen, not the sword. I urge you all to spare no effort, no fatigue, in searching out wisdom and learning! Seek it out and store it up, add to it, and persevere through all difficulties, and you will be assured of a place both in this life, and in the life to come![54]

Though Palermo, as the Arab and Norman capital, is the best endowed with Islamic-style buildings, other Sicilian cities and towns also have some interesting examples. In the heart of Messina, always a Christian stronghold even in Arab times, close to the waterfront, there are still two buildings with unmistakeable Islamic influence. The cathedral, built under Norman rule and consecrated in 1197, was almost entirely destroyed, first by the devastating earthquake of 1908 and then in 1943 during the Allied invasion of Sicily, when incendiary bombs were dropped by the British. Today's cathedral is a twentieth-century reconstruction of the original, but judged to be an accurate representation, based on earlier descriptions.

Just a few yards away is another church, Santissima Annunziata dei Catalani, also built under the Normans in 1150–1200, which miraculously survived both the earthquake and the bombing. As a result, it sits at the original twelfth-century ground level, 3 metres lower than today's buildings. Built on top of a temple to Neptune, Roman god of the sea, its marble columns and capitals were recycled into its arches, making an interesting blend of classical and Islamic.

Its two-tone exterior in black basalt and white limestone is strikingly Fatimid in decor, with multiple blind arcades, zigzag friezes galore and eight-pointed stars in roundels set within the curve of each of the arches. Every eight-pointed star is different, apparently random in its pattern and design. It is a good example of the total disregard for symmetry, which is a consistent hallmark of Islamic architecture, always seeking to imitate nature, where nothing is perfectly symmetrical and no two leaves are the same. Yet underlying the apparent randomness is the precision of geometry, applied throughout. In that way, the building is seen as a reflection of God. He creates what appears to be random, with every type of difference and variation, yet exerts a deep underlying control and order on his creations.

According to the 'Norman Sicily Project'[55] which surveys Norman monuments constructed on the island in the late eleventh and twelfth centuries, there were a total of forty-seven monasteries on the island. Four of the most important—Lipari-Patti, Catania, San Giovanni degli Eremiti and Monreale—were Benedictine foundations, the Benedictine order being the one most favoured by the Normans, and it is unlikely to be coincidence that it is in the Benedictine monasteries of Italy, France, Spain, Germany and Britain that Romanesque features can first be identified.

Roger gave the existing monasteries large donations and founded new ones, while trying to keep a delicate balance between the Byzantine Greek Orthodox clergy and the appointment of new Roman Catholic bishops. He was keen to take on a new role as protector of Christianity on the island, obtaining the right to carry a shepherd's crook and to wear the ring and robe that were symbols of imperial majesty. The popes, on the other hand, had long been wary of the growing Norman power in southern Italy, and in 1127 the Pope even preached a Crusade against Roger.

Now that the Arab-Muslim past of Sicily is beginning to be better understood and studied, more and more people are also beginning to realise the huge impact which their intellectual and scientific legacy had, first on southern Italy and from there on the whole of Europe. Roger II continued the Arab tradition of tolerance towards other religions, bringing together scholars from both East and West to create a court of flourishing intellectual freedom that was the envy of the world. The cultural exchanges that took place were instrumental in waking Europe up from its so-called 'Dark Ages' and in stimulating the rise of the Renaissance. The kingdom not only preserved its top Muslim professional and cultural elites at least till the mid-twelfth century, but also continued to attract Muslim scholars, literary figures, artists and craftsmen from the Islamic world. As a centre for the translation of scientific works, Palermo was second only to Toledo in Spain. Many of the Arabic texts translated in Sicily—covering subjects like astronomy, medicine, philosophy and mathematics—contained miniature pictures, not as gratuitous embellishments but as a visual clarification of the text, stylistically indebted to illustrated Arabic books of the tenth century, forming key links between artistic and scientific depiction and proving that Arab artists were always capable of figural and animal representation. Sicily and southern Italy played key roles in laying the foundations on which later academic and architectural advances would be built and which stimulated the flourishing of science, literature, art and architecture in Renaissance and early modern Europe.

By 1250 the majority of the Muslims on Sicily had either converted to Christianity or been expelled, just as they were from Spain and Portugal in the years after the 1492 Reconquista by the Catholic monarchs Ferdinand and Isabella. The Arab presence on the island, however, never completely disappeared. Indeed, it lives on in the population, as recent genetic studies have revealed that most Sicilians have Arab blood, as exemplified in their Y chromosome.[56] The Maltese, too, may be directly descended from Islamic Sicily, and the Maltese language is thought to be the Siculo-Arabic spoken in Sicily, still surviving today.

7.1: A sphinx guarding the main portal on the west facade of Ruvo Cathedral, Apulia. The decorative carving on the portal makes extensive use of palmettes, interlacing roundels, friezes of fantastical beasts and beaded interlace. The head between the sphinx's legs is said by local people to be that of a 'Saracen'.

7

ITALIAN ISLAMESQUE

The earliest place where Romanesque is widely agreed by European art historians to have 'appeared' is in Lombardy, northern Italy, in spite of the evidence which shows how so many Romanesque features can be seen earlier in Sicily (see Chapter 6). From Lombardy, it is correctly seen as spreading into northern Spain and southern France and across the Alps into Switzerland and Germany. From southern France the style is then identified as moving northwards, heavily influenced by the Benedictine churches along the Santiago de Compostela pilgrimage route, and then from northern France into England, brought across the Channel with the Norman conquest in 1066.

But how do art historians explain why the style appeared in Lombardy? The Lombards (Latin *Longobardi*, meaning 'Longbeards') were a Germanic tribe, and did not suddenly arrive in northern Italy with a ready-made architectural tradition of their own. Whatever became labelled subsequently as Lombard architecture was not their own invention but acquired from antecedents within Italy, most of them derived from Islamic sources. Not only that, but mounting evidence shows that the masons and sculptors who created these distinctive styles were Arabs, probably Muslims.

The medieval Italian city states—like Amalfi, Naples, Pisa, Genoa and Venice—traded extensively with the Islamic world between 1000 and 1250 and were deeply influenced by the high sophistication of the luxury items they encountered from centres like Damascus, Baghdad, Cairo and North Africa. Perhaps the most obvious Islamic style recognisable to a Western eye, often occurring as a backdrop ornamentation in such items, is now called 'Arabesque', originally derived from the Italian word *arabesco*, a term first coined in the sixteenth century. Two other terms, 'Moresque' (from 'Moorish') and 'Grotesque', were used almost interchangeably with Arabesque in European art history circles till as late as the nineteenth century. An

English–French dictionary from 1611 defines Moresque as 'a rude or anticke painting, or carving, wherin the feet and tayles of beasts, &c, are intermingled with, or made to resemble, a kind of wild leaves, &c'.[1] Merriam-Webster's dictionary defines grotesque as 'a style of decorative art characterized by fanciful or fantastic human and animal forms often interwoven with foliage or similar figures that may distort the natural into absurdity, ugliness, or caricature'. Sometimes Arabesque was also used interchangeably with 'interlace' or 'scroll' decoration because the pattern repeats endlessly, without beginning or end; or else with 'strapwork' because it uses ribbon-like forms often interwoven in geometric motifs.

The 'Comacini Masters'

One of the commonly cited theories among art historians to explain the sudden emergence of Romanesque on Lombard soil is based around the so-called 'Comacini masters', early medieval stonemasons who took their name from the tiny Isola Comacina, the only island in Lake Como, northern Italy. There they were said to live in isolation, guarding their secret skills. They were described as an extraordinary group of talented craftsmen, sculptors who represented the remnants of an unbroken tradition of secret stonemasonry directly linked to Rome. Their knowledge and expertise were said to have been passed down through guild-like brotherhoods joined together for mutual protection. Some even claim them as the original 'freemasons' from whom the Freemasonry movement derived its mysterious practices[2] (see Chapter 4). These masons from Como and the Lombard capital Pavia are then credited with spreading their remarkable style across to Languedoc and the Iberian Peninsula, into western France and England, over the Alps to central and southern Germany, and even as far afield as Sweden. Quite why these secretive masons waited so long, all those centuries since the fall of Rome, to reveal their skills, is not explained.

So what did this Lombard style consist of? Its elaborate sculptural decoration appears on pulpits, portals and capitals, and is characterised as 'a world peopled by fabulous and horrid beings, animated by linear and geometric decorations, usually interlaced, and by coarsely worked figural representations'.[3] The Comacini masters were said to have been influenced in their use of interlace by Lombard metalwork, but interlace and geometric designs had already reached the Italian decorative arts as a result of contact with the Islamic world, as can be proved through multiple luxury Islamic items like ceramics, ivories and metalware, that are now in museums round the world. The metalworking sculpture workshops of Córdoba, for example, at their peak in the tenth century, were known for producing a distinctive style of zoomorphic Hispano-Islamic metal sculpture like the Monzon lion now in the Louvre, with stylised features, open gaping mouths and playful, almost humorous, facial expressions.[4] An overlap with subsequent zoomorphic styles of Romanesque sculpture seems clear, while interlacing knot designs, together with elaborate geometric patterns, also entered Italian decorative arts via contact with the Islamic world.[5]

More Islamic influences, full of charming naivety, that recall the carved caricatures of Romanesque architecture can be seen in the Arabic manuscript illustrations of adventure stories like the eleventh- to early-twelfth-century *Maqamat* of al-Hariri and the eighth-century *Kalila wa-Dimna* fables.[6]

In the earliest examples from Lombardy and especially from the Como and Pavia area, dating to the late eleventh and early twelfth centuries, the full, smooth forms of the animals have reminded some sharp-eyed observers of incense burners from the Arab tradition, and the sunken, flattened vegetal reliefs which decorate the facades are also reminiscent of Abbasid-style carved-out and flatter abstract designs like scrolling palmettes. The same rich decoration on the capitals and their abaci (the flat supporting slabs directly above them) can be seen in the highly elaborate and ornamental Umayyad, Abbasid and Fatimid sculpture found across Syria, Iraq and Egypt, similarities which hint at the identity of these mysterious Comacini masters.

Within Italy, many examples are often cited of this 'Como-Pavian' sculpture, all dateable to the late eleventh and early twelfth centuries. They include the reliefs of Sant'Abbondio, San Fedele and Santa Margherita in Como; Sant'Ambrogio (St Ambrose) in Milan; the crypt capitals of Modena Cathedral (completed 1106) and San Savino in Piacenza (consecrated 1170); the nave capitals of Parma Cathedral (*c.*1120); the crypt capitals in San Michele Maggiore in Pavia, whose dome is carried on Islamic-style squinches; and the Torre della Ghirlandina, the five-storey bell tower of Modena Cathedral, highly decorated with interlacing arcades, Venetian dentil and Lombard bands.

The Basilica of San Giulio, on the island of the same name in Lake Orta, despite many later Baroque overlays still has unusual early-twelfth-century features in the carvings of its pulpit, resting on four green marble columns, each one different and featuring a variety of capitals depicting animals locked in combat, such as two clawed monsters attacking a deer and a griffin biting a crocodile. The animals' bodies are often marked with rows of decorative holes made by use of the trepan, a tool to bore holes in stone.

Coincidentally the birthplace of William of Volpiano, the abbot charged with construction of famous Benedictine abbeys like Mont Saint-Michel and

7.2: The western facade of San Michele Maggiore (completed 1130) in Pavia is seen as the prototype for many Lombard churches, decorated with 'Lombard bands' beneath the roofline, and *ajimez* mullioned windows. Its dome is supported by Islamic squinches.

Fécamp, the basilica also has groin vaulting in its nave and aisles, an unusual octagonal lantern and a bell tower with Lombard bands and *ajimez* (double arched windows separated by a slender column, sometimes also called mullioned windows; from Arabic *ash-shammis* meaning 'exposed to the sun'). They were characteristic of Arab architecture, common in Islamic and Mozarab buildings, as are the circular windows centred above them. All these features date to the twelfth century.

The bell tower is very similar to that of the Benedictine Abbey of Fruttuaria, also founded by William of Volpiano, north of Turin, an abbey that became so

7.3: The tall twelfth-century bell tower at San Guilio on an island in Lake Orta, northwest Italy, has elegant *ajimez* mullioned windows, while the basilica has an octagonal lantern and groin vaulting in its nave and aisles.

wealthy and powerful in the twelfth century that it minted its own coins and owned eighty-five churches in Italy, along with other possessions across Germany and Austria. William was later made a saint, and his likeness is thought to be depicted in the twelfth-century pulpit carving at San Giulio.

There are also many examples of this so-called Lombard style of the Comacini master masons in central and southern Italy, likewise appearing in the late eleventh century, then spreading more widely in the twelfth and thirteenth centuries. In addition to the Comacini masters, a second group of masons has also been identified, referred to as the 'Campionesi masters', taking their name from Campione, an Italian enclave on the shores of Lake Lugano, surrounded by Switzerland, less than 30 kilometres due west of Isola Comacina.

The so-called Lombard tradition developed around 1130–40 and has a certain freedom, showing the mature execution that only comes from many generations of experience and expertise. Italian art historian Joselita Raspi Serra describes it as

> rich in contrasts of light and shadow which emphasize the thick and full modelling of form... Devoid of symmetry and of any static quality, it assails the churches both outside and inside, peopling them with swollen monsters inspired by Moslem bronzes and winged animals reminiscent of Sassanian fabrics, fusing motifs inspired by the early medieval period with others originating in Coptic reliefs and sixth-century ivories in a vital ensemble which, with respect to Milanese sculptures, demonstrates a maturity of expression.[7]

She observes these same features in the decoration of churches in western France, concluding that 'It would not be at all surprising if Como-Lombard stonemasters, especially those operating in Pavia around 1130, had influenced the sculptors of western France.'[8] She marvels at the vastness of the diffusion of the style across such a wide area and at such speed. The sculptors were thought to have travelled in closely knit bands all around Europe, which is almost certainly true, except that, rather than roaming freely like itinerant craftsmen, they were more likely to have been summoned or even taken from commission to commission by their Christian overlords, be they Norman noblemen, Benedictine abbots or churchmen.

From the churches of western France, like Notre-Dame la Grande and Saint-Hilaire in Poitiers, Saintes, Angoulême and Aulnay, all of which date between 1125 and 1150, Serra is convinced, as am I, that the Normans brought the styles (and of course the masons capable of executing them) into France (from Italy and Sicily) and then across the Channel to England. This theory challenges the viewpoint persistently put forward by Polish art historian George Zarnecki that the origin of the motifs used in sculpture like that found in Canterbury Cathedral crypt and at Ely Cathedral must have been from the north, from Celtic or Scandinavian sources.

The 'Lombard Romanesque'

The chief characteristic of so-called 'Lombard Romanesque' was a type of external decoration on the facades of buildings, predominantly churches, that took the form of rhythmic rows of ornamental blind arcades. These were duly called 'Lombard bands', rows of round blind arches with no structural function or purpose, since the arches were not open as windows, but purely serving as decorative features on exterior and, less often, interior walls. The fashion for blind arcades spread from Lombardy across the Alps, where the cathedrals of Speyer, Mainz and Worms have galleried apses of the Lombard type.

Some have suggested early Byzantine buildings like the fifth-century Mausoleum of Galla Placidia in Ravenna as the inspiration for blind arcades, but Byzantine influence on the art and architecture of Italy began to weaken from the eighth century onwards as the political and religious connection between Italy and the Eastern Empire, with its capital in Constantinople, was severed. In 726 the Byzantine emperor Leo forbade the worship of images and ordered all icons to be destroyed, leaving icon artists washed up and suddenly unemployed. Many no doubt migrated westwards to Italy, but their style is unlikely to have changed, with the same identical expressionless faces,

7.4: The minaret of the Great Mosque of Kairouan, in today's Tunisia, built by the Aghlabids in the ninth century, using decorative blind arches and buttressing on its outer walls.

quite unlike the varied facial expressions of Arab art, already discussed in earlier chapters, where each person is clearly an individual.

Far more likely in terms of immediate influences for the blind arches and arcades, in my view, via pre-existing structures that were closer in both time and style than Ravenna, is the Great Mosque in Kairouan, where the world's oldest surviving minaret dates from the eighth and ninth centuries and has rows of blind arches on its exterior, as well as more rows of blind arches beneath its ninth-century ribbed dome, and where its main entrance is crowned by a blind arcade.

Late-tenth-century mosques in Toledo, converted to churches in the twelfth century, are more examples, all of them closer in style and time than Ravenna. The origin of the blind arch and arcade was without question certainly well east of Rome, as the very first known example still stands at Ctesiphon on the Tigris river, southeast of Baghdad in today's Iraq, royal capital of both the Parthian and the Sassanian empires for over 800 years. The facades flanking the famous arched gateway to the Sassanian capital from 226 to 637 still carry dramatic rows of blind arcades as their ornamentation.

7.5: The likely origin of blind arches and blind arcades can still be seen in the arched gateway to Ctesiphon, third-century capital of the Sassanian empire on the Tigris in modern Iraq.

This is where the Romans and Byzantines would have first encountered them, as too did the first Muslim armies when they conquered Iran in 651. Due to the geographical proximity and continuation of styles, the device was incorporated early on into Islamic architecture as a favourite decorative feature, especially popular under the Fatimids and widely used in mosques across their territories in both North Africa and Sicily throughout the ninth, tenth and eleventh centuries.

Sicily is where the Lombards are most likely to have observed the decorative blind arcade known as the 'Lombard band' as a dominant decorative style, since even though their empire in Italy was wiped out in 774 by Charlemagne, King of the Franks, they remained as colonists in southern Italy and Sicily. The Norman kings of Sicily encouraged immigration to Sicily by granting lands and privileges to their own people from Normandy, Provence and Brittany and from Lombardy, a process of 'Latinisation' to strengthen the 'Latin stock'. In today's language it would be called social engineering to alter the population balance, since the newcomer Latin Christians were a minority on the island compared to the majority Arab Muslims and the pre-existing Greek Orthodox population. The Norman mercenary Robert Guiscard de Hauteville (1015–1085), a key figure in the Norman conquest of southern Italy and Sicily, divorced his Norman wife and married a 'six Anglo-Saxon feet tall' Lombard princess, the formidable Sikelgaita, who fought alongside him in battle and gave him a son, Roger Borsa, who became the effective ruler of southern Italy from 1085 till his death in 1111. The bulk of the Lombards arrived in Sicily between 1090 and 1120, and together with the Norman ruling class were responsible for transforming it from a Muslim/Greek Christian island into a Latin kingdom. Migration from northern Italy continued till the end of the thirteenth century. William of Apulia, chronicler of the Norman conquest of Sicily, is thought to have been a Lombard, because his treatment of the Lombard characters involved in the conquest is far more sympathetic than that of the other chroniclers of Norman history.[9]

Another element generally designated 'Lombard' but in practice found much earlier on mosques in North Africa and introduced to Sicily and Italy from the Islamic world is the 'lesene', also known as a pilaster strip, a vertical buttressing device that was both structural in reinforcing the outer walls or corners of towers and decorative in breaking up the surface of the exterior wall on churches and castles into segmented sections. Like the Lombard band, it spread across into northern Spain, north into Rhineland Germany and into France and England.

Vaulting and Venetian Dentil

The cities of Lombardy in the twelfth century—like Pavia, Cremona, Lodi and Como—were in a constant state of rivalry and war with each other, but even as buildings were destroyed, they were rebuilt ever more elaborately as part of that rivalry. In Milan the only church to escape destruction by Holy Roman Emperor Frederick Barbarossa in 1160 was Sant'Ambrogio (St Ambrose). The nave dates from 1128 and the rib vaults from 1140. Thomas Graham Jackson, in his 1913 book on Byzantine and Romanesque architecture, tells us that 'It remains perhaps the earliest example of a completely vaulted church in Italy.'[10] Its atrium also survives, sometimes called the 'paradise' in early churches, with a garden and fountain, more echoes of Islamic design, as too are the squinch arches rising into a slow octagon, pierced with windows to light the space below where the altar is positioned. The sculpture on the capitals of the atrium and nave have been dated to the eleventh century and show rams, griffins, bears and eagles, while the door jambs and lintel are carved with interlacing patterns of foliage in which even Jackson sees 'scarcely any memory of classic art'.[11] He claims that Lombard architecture 'has much affinity with our own Norman Romanesque, which indeed may claim descent from it through the School of Burgundy'[12]—a rather apt observation since it illustrates he has correctly identified the similarities between Lombard and Norman building styles.

Another major decorative characteristic of what art historians have dubbed Lombard, or 'First Romanesque', is the arcaded border known as 'Venetian dentil', sometimes also called 'billet moulding', which runs as a wall frieze just below the roof. It features as one of the most distinctive ornamental motifs in Venetian medieval palace architecture and became the commonest way of defining window panels and arches in Venetian Gothic palaces. Victorian art critic John Ruskin was eloquent in its praise: 'Nothing was ever, nor could ever be invented, fitter for its purpose, or more easily cut... most truly deserving of the name of the "Venetian Dentil".'[13]

Christopher Wren cited St Mark's Basilica (San Marco) in Venice as an example of a 'Saracen' building, and even Jackson writes:

> One may perhaps, without being too fanciful, trace an oriental feeling in Venetian architecture from first to last: in the ogee arches of the windows and doors; in the strange Arabian-looking tester over the pulpit at Grado; in the picturesque decoration with inlaid plaques of the Palazzo Dario. These are all features peculiar to Venice and the countries over which she ruled, and seem to show that she always looked east rather than west.[14]

Venetian dentil is seen in the Basilica of Santi Pietro e Paolo in Agliate near Monza, considered the first Lombard Romanesque church, dating to 875, but this is predated by the Aghlabid Ribat of Sousse of 821, where it occurs all round the exterior and gateway.

Like the blind arch and blind arcade, its origins lie well beyond Rome, and one of the first, oft-cited, examples is in the Hagia Sophia in Constantinople of 537. But apart from the Byzantine influence, it should be remembered that in the ninth and tenth centuries the Byzantine Empire was fading, and the Islamic world was the real power in the Mediterranean region, with the Umayyads in control of all of today's Spain and Portugal, in what was called al-Andalus, and the Aghlabids in North Africa from their capital Kairouan and the Fatimids in Sicily and in Egypt. Theirs was the dominant culture, with a far greater sophistication than could be found in Latin or Eastern Christendom at that time in all fields, architecture included, specifically when it came to vaulting techniques and geometrical knowledge, not to mention stonemasonry, woodcarving and stucco work, all of which were part of the repertoire of their cultural heritage and deeply embedded.

7.6: Considered to be the first church of 'Lombard Romanesque', the Basilica of Santi Pietro e Paolo in Agliate (875) near Monza has 'Venetian dentil' like earlier North African *ribats* (fortresses) and mosques, with *ajimez* windows and polychrome patterning on its bell tower.

Within the great monuments of the Islamic world, the so-called Venetian dentil frieze can be found in abundance, not just in the Ribat of Sousse, but also in the Kairouan Great Mosque and the decorative patterns of its minaret, the oldest in the world, still standing and dating from the eighth and ninth centuries. It is also found in the Fatimid gates of Cairo, Bab al-Nasr and Bab al-Futuh (1087), and the likely source of inspiration too for the exterior apse of San Fedele in Como, where it runs in two bands in a slightly more exaggerated form above and below the two-tone arches of the galleried apses.

As well as blind arcades, lesenes and Venetian dentil, other recognised key features of Lombard Romanesque are tall bell towers, domes on octagons,

7.7: The apse at the Basilica di San Fedele in Como, northern Italy, is decorated with the Venetian dentil frieze already seen in the North African mosques like Kairouan, with typical Islamic two-tone stonework in its galleried arcade.

high arches at ground level, stucco ornamental carving, crude figures, triforia, *ajimez* and interlace, all of which can be shown to have antecedents in the Islamic world.

Hybrid Mosque-Churches

The minaret of Kairouan's Great Mosque is the prototype for all the minarets of the western Islamic world, serving as a model throughout North Africa and Andalusia. In its massive, majestic form and austere decoration it is likely to have also served as the model for early Lombard Romanesque bell towers like those at Lucca, just as it did for the tall bell towers of early Romanesque churches in Catalonia, northern Spain, like Sant Climent de Taüll.

In Pavia, the Lombard capital, San Michele Maggiore is the prototype for all other Pavian churches. Its octagonal dome at the crossing of nave and transept is a 30-metre-tall asymmetrical structure supported on squinches, and reportedly the earliest example of this form in Lombardy, completed in 1130. Seen as typical of the Lombard Romanesque style, it exactly copies Islamic octagonal domes on squinches. At the Kairouan Mosque, for example, there are several such domes, the largest of which is over the mihrab. This Kairouan dome is one of the oldest and most remarkable domes in the western Islamic world, built *c.*836. San Michele Maggiore's other Islamic-influenced features are mullioned *ajimez* windows (five double and one single), geometric designs and bas reliefs with human and animal fantastical figures.

In southern Italy many twelfth-century basilicas imitate the common practice in mosques of positioning a dome directly in front of the mihrab, tangent to the rear *qibla* wall, as seen, for instance, in al-Hakim Mosque in Cairo (990) and the Great Mosques of Sfax (849) and Sousse (850–1).

The masons adapted the Islamic mihrab to be the bema (the Orthodox version of a chancel, where the clergy sat, in front of the altar) of an Orthodox church, thereby joining two diverse traditions to make something unique. Where they followed specific Byzantine ecclesiastical architecture, it was because of essential liturgical and symbolic requirements for the Orthodox rite. However, the detailing of individual components such as the transitional vaults and domes indicate that the masters and skilled artisans translated these Byzantine elements into the language of Islamic architecture.

All the church domes use squinches, and although squinches occasionally appear in Middle Byzantine churches, they were invariably supported at eight rather than four points, as in the Katholikon at Hosios Loukas (*c.*1011) in central Greece. In contrast, the domes in the Islamic buildings of North Africa

7.8: The porticoed entrance to the Fatimid al-Hakim Mosque (990–1013) in Cairo, Egypt, is crowned with merlon crenellations and decorated with tall blind arches inset with lozenge patterns, a model used by many later Italian churches.

and Egypt consistently use squinches and are supported at just four points. Not only that, but the specific design of the squinches in these basilicas, outlined with multiple projecting arches, as in San Giovanni Vecchio and Santa Maria de Tridetti in Staiti, Reggio Calabria, evoke those in the Qauat al Qubba in Sousse (late tenth to early eleventh centuries), and the compound semicircular squinches in Santa Maria at Mili (near Messina) are very close to those in both the Great Mosque at El Kef (eleventh century) and the Mosque of Bled al-Hadhar at Tozeur (1027–30). These squinches are so close to Islamic prototypes as to suggest that they represent a tradition ultimately based on the translation of the forms of Islamic North Africa into the brick construction of southern Italy and Sicily.

These church sanctuaries are entirely vaulted and feature domes above a bema supported on tall transitional vaults and/or drums that rise high above the other spaces. Pointed rather than round arches are used in the larger structural spaces, such as between the bema and the nave. The exterior brickwork uses decorative volcanic black stone inlay (*intarsia*), as seen on the eastern apse of Palermo Cathedral, to give a contrasting polychromatic light and dark effect, as well as vertical reinforcing pilasters, in the same way as is typical in Islamic construction in North Africa, whose coast is barely 150 kilometres away.

Rural churches built between 1091 and 1130 in the Val Demone region of Sicily and in Calabria (at the southern tip of mainland Italy) owe a particular debt to the Muslim architecture of North Africa in their planning, their detailing and sometimes even their symbolic content.[15] The most striking aspect of these churches is the degree of freedom with which their builders experimented, incorporating Islamic forms and features into buildings intended for Orthodox Christian worship. This synthesis was most unlikely to have been a deliberate policy of the Norman patrons. It was simply a reflection of the mixed workforce on the ground whose creativity had translated Islamic forms and aesthetics into an indigenous construction, the result of a century and a half of Muslim rule on Sicily and in southern Italy before the Norman conquest. It is precisely this ability of Muslim or Islamicised builders to work within Christian environments for Christian overlords that we then see all over northern Spain, France, Germany and England. The signs are there, if the buildings themselves are closely examined.

Another striking point of similarity between the Islamic and Romanesque architectural styles comes in the appearance of engaged colonettes with inset niches used at the corners of the apses. The use of engaged columns becomes a characteristic of the Romanesque, but similar details are ubiquitously found in mihrabs in Muslim North Africa, such as the Great Mosque of Kairouan, built in 862–3.[16] The Islamic aesthetic also becomes evident in the pure geometric volumes of the exteriors of the churches. At Santa Maria at Mili, for example, the octagonal drum and smooth cupola resemble the mihrab dome of al-Hakim Mosque in Cairo (990), and the squared drum and hemispherical cupola at Santi Pietro e Paolo at Itala (Messina) resemble the domes of the Great Mosque of Sfax (early tenth to eleventh centuries) and the entry gate of the Great Mosque of Mahdia (founded 916). Multiple recesses surround the arches of the cupola of the Great Mosque of Tunis (864) and dog-tooth friezes are used in the minaret of the Great Mosque of Sfax. Finally, interlaced arcading, one of the most distinctive motifs decorating this group of churches, must have entered the architecture of southern Italy through Islamic connections to Muslim Spain, where it appears for the first time in the portals of the tenth-century Córdoba Mezquita.

This group of churches in Calabria was put on the UNESCO Tentative List in 2006 for their Byzantine heritage, a heritage broken by the Lombards in

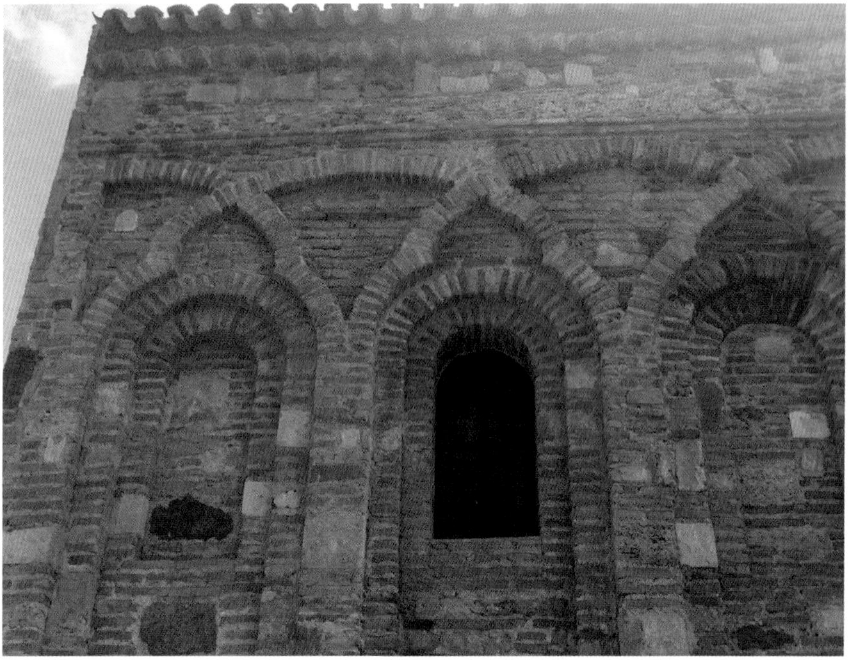

7.9: Delicate Islamic interlaced arcading, with pointed and recessed arches, is found in the decorative brickwork of many churches in southern Italy and Sicily, as here in Santi Pietro e Paolo at Itala, Messina.

the ninth century,[17] with no mention of the Islamic influence that came from the centuries of earlier Arab presence in southern Italy.

Pisa and Assisi

High blind arches at ground level, so typical of Islamic architecture, are perhaps most memorably seen at Pisa Cathedral, where the lozenge shapes decorating the exterior at ground level are also very distinctive. Construction began in 1063, funded by the spoils plundered from Palermo during the Pisan naval campaign, the same year as the reconstruction of St Mark's in Venice, symptomatic of the strong rivalry between the Italian maritime republics, vying with each other to produce the most beautiful and exotic place of worship. The polychrome marble exterior and the interior use of alternating black and white marble in the raised lancet arches, together with the elliptical dome, are all recognisably Islamic in style, with the spatial effect of the interior recalling the great mosques. The famous Pisa griffin perched on the roof is another trophy of military victory over the Muslims, possibly from the 1087 Mahdia campaign.

Pisa had itself been captured by the Arabs in 1005, but the Pisans then had 'repeated successes against the Saracens, from whom they conquered the island of Sardinia in 1025, and whose fleet they destroyed off Palermo in 1063, just one year before work on the cathedral began in 1084, capturing six great vessels of the enemy laden with merchandise'.[18] They could well have captured craftsmen during their military campaigns, which could help explain the many Islamic features of the cathedral and its campanile, the Leaning Tower, perhaps the ultimate in galleried arcading, begun in 1173. The considerable engineering challenges of the tower would have required a deep understanding of geometry (the famous lean is the result of subsidence, not flawed construction), while the delicate decorative motifs and intricate geometric patterns, along with the interplay of arches, columns and ornamental details, all bear the hallmarks of the typical elegant Islamic aesthetic. Before the erection of the remarkable ensemble of cathedral, campanile and baptistery on what is now known as the Piazza dei Miracoli (Square of Miracles), Pisa had not even had its own school of architecture and there was no local pre-existing tradition to which it can be traced.[19] The name generally cited as the originator of the cathedral's unique design was one Buscheto, about whose background nothing is known, though scholars concur that in his 'far-reaching unitary vision' he ranks as one of the greatest architects of the eleventh and twelfth centuries, and that his innovative style was 'extremely cultured'.[20]

It has also been noted that the original dome of Pisa Cathedral, which came to light during the post-Second World War restorations, was supported on squinches and slender pointed-arch windows, the same techniques that were used in the Fatimid architecture of Sicily and Egypt.[21] Grove's *Encyclopedia of Medieval Art and Architecture* also notes the cathedral's 'singular mixture of structural solutions and decorative elements', citing forerunners such as St Simeon's Basilica (*c*.490) in Syria for the centralised space of the ground plan, and Islamic buildings of the Maghreb and Spain, like the ninth-century Great Mosque of Kairouan and the tenth-century palace of Madinat al-Zahra in Córdoba, with their use of stilted (horseshoe) arches in the aisles, the pointed arch and the alternation of black and white voussoirs.[22]

Pisa's architecture had a huge influence on Italian Romanesque, inspiring many other building projects at Lucca and at Florence, where similar Islamic blind arcading, galleried apses, zigzag columns and polychrome facades were heavily featured, as at San Miniato al Monte, located on one of the highest

7.10: The elegant blind arcading of Pisa's Leaning Tower (1173) reflects the Islamic aesthetic, a style not seen in Pisa before its Arab conquests. The structural engineering would have required advanced geometrical knowledge typical of Islamic architecture. The tower's lean is the result of subsidence, not faulty construction.

hills in Florence, with its striking black-and-white geometrically patterned marble facade. The contrasting patterning continues inside, each lozenge within a black frame set against a white background, and also a black trefoil within a black frame, where the shape of the trefoil, clearly made by interlacing compass arcs, is exactly the same as the masons' mark already discussed, and is likely to indicate an Islamic workforce. The semicircular arches are also in alternate black and white masonry, as are the circular frames of the high

7.11: The tall blind arches at ground level of Pisa Cathedral and its Leaning Tower are decorated with lozenge patterns, modelled on those found in Fatimid mosques of North Africa.

oculus windows. The patterns are designed to run in flowing orders, like the continuous black frames running uninterrupted round all the clerestory window frames, and the wooden ceiling is painted with geometric patterns of red, green and black. Many of the geometric shapes enclose eight-petalled stylised flowers, and high up on the external facade, directly above the mosaic of Christ, is another eight-petalled flower or star pattern, set in black against a white background, in the centre of a continuous blind arcade made entirely from black and white marble. This use of frames, continuous orders, alternate colours and geometric shapes is new, suddenly appearing in Lombardy in a dramatic and innovative style, and all are hallmarks of Islamic architecture. The delicate scrolling arabesque of the *opus sectile* pavement depicting the signs of the zodiac is another clear indicator, as is the vaulting of the crypt.

Much of the San Miniato al Monte building project was funded by the wealthy Florentine cloth merchants' guild, who could certainly afford to use the finest materials and the best craftsmen. Their trade would have included luxury textiles from the Islamic world, so it is possible they could also have imported skilled craftsmen from Egypt or Syria to build and ornament the church. It adjoins a Benedictine monastery and is regularly described as one of the finest Romanesque structures in Tuscany.

In Umbria to the south of Tuscany stands one of the most evocative churches in Italy, rich in Islamic craftsmanship. The dramatic fortress-like Basilica of San Francesco, built into the hillside in Assisi just two years after

7.12: The delicate lace-like patterning of this *opus sectile* zodiac pavement in the Florentine church of San Miniato al Monte is typical of the many Islamic decorative styles taken over into Italian churches in the eleventh and twelfth centuries.

the saint's death in 1226, is a remarkable example of advanced engineering, built on tall blind arcades, one church on top of another, the complex vaulting seen as a synthesis of Romanesque and Gothic. The ornamental details include slender columns flanking the doorways, geometric tracery in the rose window, *ajimez* windows and doorways along with cusped pointed arches. The freestanding bell tower is decorated with lesenes and *ajimez* windows increasing in registers towards the top to lighten the stonework, a Middle Eastern anti-seismic device that withstood the severe earthquakes of 1997. In a much earlier but little-known episode of history, documented in a recent book,[23] St Francis himself, in an attempt to transcend conflict at a time of religious fervour and vilification of Islam throughout Christian Europe, ventured across enemy lines during the Fifth Crusade in 1219 to meet with the Sultan al-Malik al-Kamil in Egypt. The two men discussed war, peace and faith, and on Francis's return he proposed that members of his Order should live peaceably among the Muslims.

Use of Stucco

The long tradition of stucco carving goes right back to the ancient Egyptians, who used it as early as 1400 BCE in their tombs, though it was also especially favoured by the Iranian Parthians and Sassanians. When the Muslim armies conquered Mesopotamia and Iran in the seventh century, the tradition was assimilated into early Islamic architecture, where it then appeared in the carved and painted ornamentation of eighth-century Umayyad palaces like Khirbat al-Mafjar near Jericho. The favoured material for making stucco was high-quality gypsum which occurred naturally in the deserts of Syria and Iraq, and I still recall seeing my first raw gypsum sheets in the desert around al-Rusafa in Syria and being struck by its unusual sheen and appearance. It was often called 'the poor man's stone' since it was much easier to transport and to carve than stone.

Stucco carving remained popular under the Abbasids, who developed flatter, more abstract motifs in their palace decoration, and the techniques then moved west, first to Egypt, where they were brought to Cairo in the delicately carved vegetal patterns of the window grilles, arches and mihrabs of the Ibn Tulun Mosque. The Fatimids used it extensively in their mosque decoration, and the technique then reached its peak in Muslim Spain, with the cascading multilobed arcades of the eleventh-century al-Jaferia Palace in Zaragoza and the elaborately carved patterns of the Alhambra Palace in Granada, using typical star motifs and beaded interlace.

7.13: A carved stucco panel from the ninth-century Abbasid caliph's palace at Samarra, showing the typical Islamic aesthetic of interwoven cursive polygons, based round abstract plant life, eight-petalled flowers and pearl-beaded frames.

Via Fatimid channels the skill will have entered Sicily, from where it will have moved onto the Italian mainland and travelled north up into Lombardy. The tradition remained unbroken in the Islamic world, and indeed in the Coptic world, so the techniques are likely to have been reintroduced to Europe via Arab craftsmen, who were always recognised as masters in the field of stucco in the same way that Byzantine Greeks were recognised as masters in mosaic. The delicately carved chancel screens, or the fragments thereof, found in the eleventh- and twelfth-century churches of Calabria will therefore almost certainly have been carved by Arab artists, given their level of sophistication, as Muslims now working in a new environment for Christian masters in southern Italy. Later Baroque and Rococo architecture in Italy went on to make heavy use of stucco decoration in churches and palaces, becoming part of the Baroque concept of *bel composto*, the integration of the three classic arts of architecture, sculpture and painting.

Fragments of stucco panels taken from Santa Maria di Terreti (now in the National Archaeological Museum of Reggio Calabria) are thought to have formed part of a *transenna* (a chancel screen). They are decorated in a pronounced Islamic style, with panels featuring intersecting and beaded roundels, each of which contains two confronted animals, peacocks in the upper register and griffins feeding on a plant in the lower. There are remnants of colour and multiple pointed stars. Other churches in southern Italy also have rectangular stucco frames enclosing stylised beasts in profile, like dragons, griffins, lions and doves, interwoven with climbing arch patterns. This style of pairing using zoomorphic imagery together with ribbons of text is exactly like the marking often used in Islamic textiles to identify the royal owner and verify authenticity (like Roger's red silk coronation mantle) and known as *tiraz*, from the Iranian word for embroidery. Scholars agree that Muslim artists would have carved these exquisite stucco altar screens, since stucco carving had long been a hallmark of Islamic architecture and a vehicle for sophisticated expression in Islamic art.[24]

The Tempietto Longobardo, or Oratorio di Santa Maria in Valle, south of Venice, also shows Arab-Muslim links in technique and style of the stucco decoration, thought to have been added in the eleventh or twelfth century. They are the most famous medieval stucco sculptures in Western Europe, recognised by UNESCO as part of a World Heritage Site in 2011.[25]

Also at Cividale del Friuli is the font and baptistery of Callixtus, covered with interlacing patterns of knots and figures of birds and animals. Jackson considers the animals 'grossly barbarous'. He sees other stucco altar frontals,

7.14: The stucco carving at the so-called Tempietto Longobardo ('Lombard Temple'), north of Venice, the most famous medieval stucco sculpture in Europe, is framed by delicate eight-petalled flower friezes.

on the other hand, 'where the ornament is excellent, even beautiful, but the attempts at figures of men and animals are beneath criticism'.[26] The rather primitive and crude figures are reminiscent of those at the early Islamic palace of Khirbat al-Mafjar of *c.*750, so the assumption is that these particular Muslim artists were highly skilled in the geometric and vegetal motifs they were familiar with, but less confident in their representations of humans and animals.

Jackson comments that several sculptures of the same date and style can be found in Dalmatia, in particular a doorhead at Kotor (in today's Montenegro), dating from the early ninth century, which shows the same contrast in the execution of figure and ornament. It was erected by one 'Andreasci Saracenis', from which we know he must have been a 'Saracen'.[27]

Apulia, Campania and the Latin Valley (Lazio)

The Muslim artisans who worked on the churches in southern Italy, some of whom assisted in the production of figural reliefs, probably had no choice in the matter, as pro-Norman chroniclers refer frequently to the Muslim captives taken at various sieges and battles. After killing all the men at Judica in Sicily, Count Roger sent the women to Calabria to be sold. He used money raised in this way and from other booty to build or rebuild churches, just as, ironically, the Aghlabids had built their mosques in North Africa from the booty gained by the Islamic conquest of Sicily. History goes full circle, as the buildings of the newly enriched victors rise up, often using labour brought from the captured lands.

Roger I's enslavement of the women of Judica is well known, and an early skirmish at Butera, one of the strongest outposts of anti-Norman sentiment in Sicily, also ended with many captives in Roger's hands. Arabic sources lament that once Christians ruled the island, Saracens who survived shipwrecks off the coasts of Sicily were enslaved. What became of the captives is rarely divulged, although we know that Roger's brother, Robert Guiscard, included Saracens in one of his significant donations to the Benedictine monastery at Monte Cassino, some 130 kilometres southeast of Rome. Whether or how the monastery put the gifted captives to use is not known, though it is interesting to note that Monte Cassino, under its famous abbot Desiderius (1058–87) who went on to become Pope Victor III, oversaw a massive rebuilding programme in which pointed arches suddenly appeared in the abbey. Desiderius supported the Normans, unlike Pope Gregory VII, who repeatedly excommunicated Robert. In the complex power struggles to control southern Italy, the Pope was finally forced to recognise Robert's authority over the regions of Campania that he and his Norman armies had taken by force.

It is thanks to the movement of Arab craftsmen from Sicily onto the Italian mainland during the time of the Normans that so many buildings in Apulia (Puglia) and Campania still bear the hallmark Islamic signs. However, even well before the arrival of the Normans in southern Italy, there was already an Arab presence. Muslim armies, mainly from North Africa, made regular raids into the countryside in southern Italy from around 826, plundering villages and taking prisoners to be used as slaves within the Islamic Empire. In 846 they even sacked Old St Peter's Basilica (San Pietro) in Rome, an event which led Pope Leo IV to order the construction of the Leonine Walls enclosing the Vatican Hill for future protection. The walls were reinforced with forty-four strong towers, built between 848 and 852, using Saracen prisoners, who were set to work in chain gangs.

Saracinesco is a commune in the Metropolitan City of Rome, attested by an inscription, formed of Saracens who escaped and were trapped on its 900-metre rocky outcrop after the 846 raid on Rome. Even though they converted to Christianity, the population is still known for its distinct customs, costumes and 'exotic' good looks. Local names like Almanzor are common and the local mayor Giuseppe Dell'Ali acknowledges his Arab heritage with pride. The coat of arms is an image of two Saracens' heads overlooking a castle, and typical Arab characteristics have been noted in the buildings.

From around 850 onwards, Muslim armies started to settle in strategic areas to control trade within the territory. Their skills as agriculturalists, water engineers and craftsmen enabled them quickly to establish peaceful relations with the local inhabitants, and their military garrisons developed into residential neighbourhoods called *rabatane*, from the Arabic *ribat* meaning fortification. The most important of these still exists today at Tursi, some 250 kilometres southeast of Naples, where the Saracen legacy is apparent in the hilltop residential layout, the customs, food and even the dialect, in what is still known as the Rabatana. Tricarico, some 80 kilometres north of Tursi, and Pietrapertosa, just 40 kilometres south of Tricarico, were also Saracen settlements, as was Castelsaraceno, 70 kilometres west of Tursi.

Salerno, as a Mediterranean port exposed to myriad influences from Arab and Byzantine cultures, became the capital of Norman rule in southern Italy, already famous for its hospital, the Schola Medica Salernitana. The first of its kind in Western Europe, the hospital flourished particularly from the late eleventh century, after the arrival of Constantine the African, a learned Muslim merchant from Carthage who had travelled widely in

Egypt, Syria and Iran, reputedly as far as India, acquiring the most up-to-date medical knowledge of the time. Whilst lecturing in Salerno, at that time an independent principality of Lombardy ruling over most of southern Italy, before the Norman conquest, he translated medical encyclopaedias from Arabic into Latin.

Constantine also brought with him a great deal of experience of Muslim building techniques, gained from the Fatimids of North Africa. In Salerno he converted to Christianity, then retired to Monte Cassino Abbey for the final decades of his life, becoming a Benedictine monk and dying there in 1098, a decade after Desiderius (later Pope Victor III), with whom he must have been closely acquainted. The date of his arrival fits with the first appearance in Latin Christendom of the pointed arch at Monte Cassino, used in 1071 in the porch of the abbey and financed by the Italian merchants of Amalfi. The Schola Medica Salernitana revolutionised the whole of medical study in Europe, while also creating a generation of prominent medical teachers.

Hospital architecture in Europe was likewise revolutionised, with Muslim physicians like Constantine helping to establish scores of hospitals from the twelfth century onwards. Islamic hospitals, built round courtyards to encourage the movement of light and air, introduced new holistic care concepts such as the calming influence of music and running water, and were often surrounded by gardens and orchards in order for patients to benefit from the healing power of nature. Early hospitals of this type originated in eighth-century Baghdad, then spread via Cairo across North Africa into Muslim Sicily and Spain, usually attached to mosques. In Córdoba alone, the Andalusian capital, some fifty hospitals were built in the Islamic period. All treatment was free. These designs were then followed in Europe, where they were attached to monasteries. Crusaders had admired such institutions in the Holy Land, adopting similar systems, like the Knights Hospitaller, the Order of Knights of the Hospital of St John of Jerusalem, founded in the early twelfth century and headquartered in Jerusalem. Richard the Lionheart was even treated by Saladin's personal physician.

The cathedral at Salerno, completed 1085, has Islamic inflections in the lions placed next to the jambs that guard the entrance portal of the church, as well as in the star-shaped ornaments that decorate the interlaced arches of the belltower of 1140, recalling Algerian Islamic buildings like the Zirid palace of Ashir and Moroccan buildings like the Kutubiyya Mosque (1160–95) in Marrakesh. The tall and spacious double-arcaded cathedral courtyard has facades inlaid with black lava *intarsia* eight-pointed stars within roundels, and feels more like a mosque courtyard with its central basin fountain.

7.15: The mosque-like courtyard of Salerno Cathedral (1085), just south of Naples, uses Islamic polychrome decoration with volcanic *intarsia* inlay, tall high arches, a galleried upper arcade and medallions carrying eight-pointed stars.

Some 150 kilometres northeast of Salerno, the quality of the richly decorated stonework in the lovely cathedral of Troia can only have been the work of Muslim masons, with its eight-pointed stars, crescent moons, interlaced medallions and exotic fantastical beasts with raised wings. The rose window with its delicate stone-carved lattice grilles between the spokes, each of the eleven grilles with a different geometric pattern, is easily the most beautiful in Apulia.

The stone-carved relief known as George and the Dragon in Aversa Cathedral, just north of Naples, has a very distinctive abstract style, and is sometimes referred to as a 'medieval Picasso'. The dragon is more like an Assyrian lion, its body decorated with the characteristic circles within circles to represent the mane, while the bearded knight on horseback beneath the

7.16: The twelfth-century cathedrals of Apulia in southern Italy show many hallmarks of Islamic architecture, like this delicately carved geometric rose window at Troia, where every section is different, with no symmetry.

dragon calmly runs his sword through the creature without even looking at it. In its frontality it has echoes of the 2,000-year-old Palmyrene sculpture relief known as the Lion of al-Lat that was severely damaged by ISIS in 2015, but in its subject matter it recalls the seventh-century BCE Assyrian relief at the British Museum of the Lion Hunt of Ashurbanipal, described as a supreme masterpiece of Assyrian art, where the king finally confronts the lion directly, grasps it calmly by the neck and runs it through with his sword.

Canosa in Apulia was the favourite city of Bohemond de Hauteville, later Prince of Antioch, who had gone on the First Crusade and come back fascinated by all things oriental. He built his mausoleum next to the cathedral,

7.17: This stone-carved relief at Aversa Cathedral just north of Naples is so abstract it is sometimes called a 'medieval Picasso'. It is known as 'George and the Dragon', though the dragon is more like an Assyrian hunting scene, where the ruler, a bearded horseman in this case, calmly impales the huge lion, decorated with small circles seen on many Middle Eastern archetypes to represent animal manes.

where he was buried in 1111, with marble exterior facings decorated with blind arcades and a domed roof reminiscent of those he would have seen in Syria. The elaborately carved stone bishop's throne in the cathedral rests on a pair of elephants with pearled beading.

The shortlived Emirate of Bari (847–71) oversaw a period of economic prosperity, and its last emir, Sawdan (857–71), is recorded by a Hebrew chronicle as ruling wisely, being on good terms with resident Hebrew scholar

Abu Aaron, and embellishing the city with a mosque, palaces and public amenities like running water. Christian monastic chronicles, on the other hand, describe him as 'most impossible and wicked'. Bari Castle was rebuilt on the orders of Roger II by Arab workmen and Bari Cathedral boasts a fine capital in the shape of winged sphinxes decorated with tell-tale beading, while its exterior has tall blind arches, lesenes, Lombard bands and *ajimez* windows.

Nearby Bitonto Cathedral is modelled on that of Bari, its slender columns carrying zigzag and spiral carvings with elaborate animals on the capitals, and has a very fine griffin tile, now in the local museum, with raised wings, a foliate tail and a delicate beaded interlace frame.

7.18: Mosaic of a griffin in Bitonto Cathedral, Apulia, southern Italy, framed in a decorated roundel with beaded interlace. The fantastical beast is shown in typical Middle Eastern pose, foreleg and wing raised, with a heraldic-style foliated tail.

The main portal of Trani Cathedral (1159–86), 50 kilometres north of Bari on the east coast, shows strong Islamic influence in its arch of animal sculptures in interlacing roundels, some beaded framing and even carved elephants, their eyes with drilled pupils.

Ruvo Cathedral, one of Apulia's most outstanding Romanesque monuments of the twelfth century, has two griffins on its portal with stylised manes and body patterns reminiscent of Assyrian lions, and a rose window with an astonishing central geometric pattern formed of beaded interlace.

Exile to Lucera

The Lombard colonists on Sicily saw the influence of the Muslim and crypto-Muslim elite as a threat, a factor that probably helped to seal the Muslim fate. In 1224, to please Pope Honorious III, promoter of the Fifth Crusade, who feared the presence of Muslims so close to the papal state, Frederick II of Hohenstaufen (King of Sicily and later Holy Roman Emperor) ordered the remaining 20,000 Sicilian Muslims to be deported en masse to the hilltop settlement of Lucera (*Lucaera Saracenorum* or *Luğêrah*, as it was known in Arabic) in southern Italy, some 150 kilometres northeast of Naples. A further 40,000 were exiled to the surrounding region of Apulia. They were joined in 1249 by the Muslims of Malta. The Catholic clergy from that point on ran a deliberate and successful disinformation campaign to de-emphasise Malta's historic links with Africa and Islam, a strategy which created the rampant Islamophobia which has been a traditional feature of Malta and other southern European states and which lives on.[28] An ice-cream parlour in the central square still sells, among its many flavours, a dark chocolate variety labelled 'Il Saraceno'.

The Muslim colony in Lucera thrived for seventy-five years, and in the wording of the local tourist leaflet, 'its flowering was so remarkable that it was soon compared by contemporary travellers and Muslim historians to the Cordoba of the caliphs'. The inhabitants still paid taxes to Frederick and still served as loyal subjects in his army. His personal bodyguard was recruited exclusively from them, leading his enemies to nickname him 'the Sultan of Lucera'. Skilled carvers were mentioned as being amongst the Arabs deported to Lucera, and Frederick clearly put them to work building his remarkable hilltop octagonal Castel de Monte with its striking octagonal Arab-style bastion and complex bathrooms with running hot and cold water conduits, the like of which were unknown in Europe at that time. Its purpose seems to have been for pleasure far more than defence, in line with the king's known esoteric interests. He kept a harem and eunuchs there, hunted with falcons in the surrounding woods and even experimented with camel breeding. Frederick was hailed as *Stupor Mundi* (Wonder of the World) by his fans, or the Anti-Christ by his critics.

But in 1300 Lucera was seized by the count of Altamura, and its entire population was slaughtered, sold into slavery or exiled. Their mosques were demolished and replaced by churches. Christian soldiers and farmers were brought in from Burgundy and Provence and settled in the colony instead. It was the end of Muslim presence in medieval Italy, after more than four centuries. Only the wealthiest citizens and most valuable craftsmen were permitted to ransom themselves. King Charles II of Anjou, who had instigated the attack, used the funds raised from the slave sale to pay off a debt to the Bardi family. Muslims who were trained in the arts, including embroiderers, masons and woodworkers, were sent to Naples. Some who had initially been imprisoned in Barletta were freed by royal decree before making the trip. They were evidently considered valuable commodities, though what happened to them once they arrived is not known. In August 1300 Charles wrote to his courtier Giovanni Pipino de Barolo: 'What an offence to... [the Catholic] faith that Saracens flourish in Our kingdom, inhabitants to this day of Lucera. And We have always planned in Our heart to depopulate that city and move the Saracens out of it, so that it might be populated with Christians.'[29]

He did, however, allow 200 households of 'free Muslims' (*Saracenni libri*) to settle 30 kilometres north of Lucera, as he continued to find them useful to him.

8

SPANISH ISLAMESQUE

Northern Spain, together with Sicily and southern Italy, is where Muslim culture in medieval times merged with Latin Christendom, bequeathing a lasting cultural legacy, the result of its highly sophisticated and powerful presence on the Iberian Peninsula for nearly 800 years. It is one of the ironies of history that the Arab Umayyads, exiled from Damascus, did not 'invade' Spain in 711, as we are so often told, but were invited in by the Christian Visigoths (a Germanic tribespeople who had been living on the Iberian mainland for 300 years) to help them defeat a rival king. No one could have imagined that within twenty years the Muslim armies would reach northwestern France. When the Umayyad Caliphate of Córdoba began to disintegrate, it splintered over the course of the eleventh century into a patchwork of about twenty short-lived statelets. These in turn fell prey first to two Moroccan Berber dynasties, then to the rising Christian kingdoms in the north. It was this political turmoil that sowed the seeds for the transfer of skills from the advanced construction workforce of the Umayyads, over the course of the critical eleventh and twelfth centuries, into the buildings we now call Romanesque.

Naturally, I expected to find Islamic influence in a peninsula where Arabs had lived and ruled for so many centuries, but not necessarily to the same extent in these northern areas. After all, the Muslim armies had raided but never conquered Galicia or its capital, Santiago de Compostela, or northern Catalonia or much of the Duero Valley. By the time the Christian Reconquista was complete in 1492 many Muslims had already emigrated from Spain and Portugal and by 1610, when the Spanish Crown announced a series of edicts expelling them, another three million had left.

What I came to realise, however, from visiting a wide range of Romanesque churches and monasteries in northern Spain, was that all the turmoil in military history and change in rulers throughout this critical period, dramatic though it certainly would have been for those directly involved in the fighting, had surprisingly little effect on the everyday lives of ordinary people. Although the Muslims were now subject to new lords, new laws and taxes, their social habits, marriage practices, names, clothing, cuisine, religious observances, daily economy and artisanal expertise stayed essentially the same.

Not only that, but the various Christian kingdoms of the north—Castile, Aragon and Catalonia—were also in constant rivalry with one another during the eleventh century, regularly allying with Muslims against fellow Christians, just as Muslims frequently allied with Christians against fellow Muslims. The alliances of the Catalans and Aragonese with Muslims against their hated Castilian neighbours, and the alliances of Castilians with Muslim Seville against the Catalans, are clear examples.[1] In other words, the drivers of conflict were power struggles, not religious affiliation. Amidst all this turbulence, no matter who the rulers were, Muslim or Christian, buildings continued to be commissioned and the people who constructed them stayed largely the same, namely, those who were best qualified to do so. Indeed, I would argue, it was from the seeds of this crucial 200-year cross-fertilisation that the style we now call 'Romanesque' was born.

The status quo is succinctly summed up in a wall plaque in Spanish at the twelfth-century monastery of San Juan de Duero on the banks of the Duero in Soria, a town some 150 kilometres west of Zaragoza. Christians, Jews and Muslims, the plaque explains, all lived alongside each other, sometimes fighting each other, but always influencing each other. Their coexistence was complementary, because each group had different spheres of influence and action—and here is the interesting part. The Moors, it clarifies (the word used by Spanish Christians to denote Arab Muslims in Spain, in the same way that 'Saracen' was used to denote Arab Muslims across Italy, France, Germany and Britain), were the most skilled in agriculture and construction, the Jews took charge of commerce and moneylending, while the Christians were the knights and the serfs (*caballeros y villanos*). In other words, the Christians inhabited the upper and the lower echelons, providing the hierarchy in which everyone knew their place. The Muslims, Jews and Christians, the monastery plaque continues, retained their own traditions, customs and particular rules, though this coexistence did not mean equality, simply tolerance. It is the same hierarchy that is illustrated in the painting by Renaissance artist Il Sodoma (Giovanni Antonio Bazzi) on the cover of this book, in which St Benedict represents the Christian elite founding the monastery, a lowly monk does the basic trowel work, and a team of skilled 'Saracens' make the building rise from the ground.

What the Umayyad Arabs of Damascus brought to the Iberian Peninsula (for Portugal was also under their rule) from their homeland in the Levant was a level of knowledge in advanced irrigation methods and construction techniques that far exceeded that of the native Spanish population, so they always dominated in those two fields. The word *alarife* is still occasionally used today for an architect in modern Spanish, from the Arabic *al-aarif*, meaning 'the one who knows how', that is, someone who has practical knowledge based on experience, as opposed to intellectual or abstract knowledge, Arabic *al-aalim*, 'the one who knows philosophy or scholarly matters'. Unlike their contemporaries in Latin Christendom after the fall of Rome, those in the Islamic world had not lost the classic works of Greek and Roman scientists and mathematicians, but had translated them into Arabic, then mastered and developed that knowledge further for centuries, perfecting the geometry of vault construction at a time when Europeans had neither the knowledge nor the expertise to anywhere near that level.

Gradually, through coexistence in the Iberian Peninsula, even as the rulers changed from Muslim to Christian, the monastery libraries began to acquire and translate some of these Arabic texts and to learn from them. Literacy in Latin Christendom in the Middle Ages was concentrated in the hands of very few, essentially just the elite of the clergy and the aristocracy, but the literacy level among Muslims of all statuses was considerably higher than among their Christian contemporaries, thanks to the Quran schools which boys attended from the age of eight (sometimes as early as age six) till around the age of fourteen. Many Muslim craftsmen would therefore have enjoyed basic literacy and numeracy skills from an early age, as well as the practical skills of agriculture and construction acquired through generations of experience.

Catalonia

The style which art historians call 'First Romanesque' is generally agreed to have entered Spanish Catalonia from Lombardy in Italy, via southern France, first appearing through construction projects sponsored by the hugely energetic Benedictine Abbot Oliba (*c*.971–1046), a wealthy aristocrat. Today the monasteries of Catalonia, notably those of Ripoll and Poblet, and even those in modern-day France that are in historic Catalonia, like Saint-Michel-de-Cuixà and Saint-Martin-du-Canigou, are presented to the visitor as manifestations of the Catalan national identity, 'emblems' of Catalonia, its 'soul' even. Ripoll is called 'the cradle of Catalonia' while Poblet is hailed for its key role in the art, culture, history and spirituality of New Catalonia. Both monasteries have been slickly restored in recent years with hi-tech visitors' centres to project their narrative, in which Oliba's name is everywhere. He is termed 'the spiritual founder of Catalonia'.

In addition to his numerous building projects, Oliba was also a prolific writer, translating many Arabic manuscripts into Latin and thereby helping to revive knowledge that had been lost to eleventh-century Western Christian scholars. The Interpretation Centre at Ripoll omits any mention of the Arabic texts and speaks only of the Benedictine monks and their 'enormous capacity to spread the Christian faith, and their magnificent contributions to medieval science and literature', as if the monks did it all on their own. Oliba is recorded as encouraging monastery workshops (scriptoria) where such books were copied and illustrated.

Oliba was not the first such abbot, however. All Catalan monasteries in the tenth and eleventh centuries contained Arabic manuscripts from Muslim Spain, especially from Córdoba, the capital of the Umayyad Caliphate. Córdoba was recognised and acknowledged as the leading intellectual centre of Europe, and the library of Caliph al-Hakam II, by the year 1000, had 40,000 works covering mathematics, astronomy, physics, medicine and philosophy, when most monasteries had fewer than 400. Most of these Arabic texts had reached the caliph's library at Córdoba at least a century earlier from Baghdad, the great scientific centre in the East founded by the rival Abbasid Caliphate in the late eighth century during Islam's Golden Age. The court at Baghdad attracted top scientists from all over the world. Scholarly works were translated from Greek, Iranian and Sanskrit into Arabic, and the ideas contained in them were worked on and developed further over the next 200 years. The library was definitively destroyed by the Mongols in 1258 at the Siege of Baghdad, but the Abbasid craftsmen were captured and put to work on Mongol buildings instead. As ever, top craftsmen were valuable booty, their skills highly prized by ambitious rulers keen to immortalise their conquests through the finest buildings possible.

Before Oliba, a French-born scholar and teacher called Gerbert of Aurillac (*c.*946–1003) also studied at Ripoll before becoming Pope Sylvester II in 999. In his lifetime he was renowned as a monastic reformer and the most learned man in Christendom. This future pope, sometimes called the 'Scientist Pope', was of humble origins but grew to be the leading mathematician and scientist of his age thanks to the knowledge he acquired from his Arab Muslim teachers in Spain. Gerbert is said to have fled one night from a Cluniac monastery in Aurillac to Spain, where 'he lodged with a Saracen philosopher… to learn the science of the stars and others of this kind of art from the Saracens'.[2] He went on to endorse and promote the study of Moorish and Graeco-Roman mathematics and astronomy, reintroducing the abacus and the armillary sphere, lost to Latin Europe since the end of the Graeco-Roman era. He also developed a fascination for the Christian bishops and judges of Spain who seemed to mimic the great teachers of the Islamic *madrasas*, dressing and talking like Arabs and who had acquired their knowledge of mathematics and natural sciences through immersion in Muslim culture.

These Mozarab Christians under Islamic rule in Spain were permitted to follow their own religion, and exactly as happened in Damascus in the seventh century, where the Church of John the Baptist was shared by Muslims and Christians for nearly a century, the Umayyads in Córdoba shared the Visigothic church for many decades (from 710 till 785), till the ruler Abd al-Rahman bought the Christian part and turned it into the main mosque of his dynasty, still known in Spain as the Córdoba Mezquita. As in Damascus, the Christians were compensated with land for churches elsewhere. Over the course of the Catholic Reconquista, tens of thousands of mosques across the country were destroyed. The city of Córdoba alone is recorded as having had 3,000 mosques, of which only one remains today, the Mezquita itself.

The Islamic civilisation of Andalusia around the year 1000 was far more advanced than anything in Latin Christendom, which is why so many European scholars travelled to study at cultural centres like Córdoba and Toledo, sponsored by the caliphs. According to the twelfth-century English historian William of Malmesbury, the future Pope Sylvester II learned his computing skills and the Hindu-Arabic numeral system via a Muslim scholar from the prestigious university of al-Qarawiyyin in Fez, today's Morocco, which had close ties with the Umayyads of Córdoba at the time. Through the combined efforts of Muslims, Jews and Christians, Arabic manuscripts were translated into Latin. Many of these Christians were churchmen who would become Pope Sylvester II's lifelong friends. The Arabs, during their many centuries of dominance, intermingled and intermarried with local populations, creating a multicultural environment, while the coexistence of Arabic, Latin and local Romance vernaculars bred multilingualism.

Beyond churches, a few bridges also survive from Oliba's time, such as the Pont de la Cabreta in the foothills of the Pyrenees en route to Ripoll, the technology of which, with its excellently constructed arches and ability to follow the natural contours of the landscape, bears all the hallmarks of Islamic architecture. It is on the Oliba Route, a waymarked thematic trail, 200 kilometres long, linking key buildings promoting 'Catalan Romanesque'.

In the early eleventh century the only stonemasons and builders who were capable of such constructional masterpieces were those schooled under

Islamic culture, be they from Lombardy via Sicily or from Andalusia. They could have been Muslim or Christian, Mudéjar Muslims who chose to remain, Mozarab Arabised Christians or crypto-Muslim Moriscos; it does not matter which, since the styles they assimilated were in any case those of Arab Islamic culture. The fact that it has been noted that the Canigou cloister capitals bear a resemblance to the decorative features of the Kairouan Mosque gives us another clue, a link to an external, as opposed to a local, cultural influence.

From the tenth century onwards, Mudéjar slaves formed a considerable and important part of the property of the wealthy abbeys and were their principal craftsmen, usually living with the lay brothers and monks.[3] Likewise until the tenth century Mozarabs had lived peacefully among the Moors of medieval Spain, under the direct authority of a functionary appointed by them with the acquiescence of the local Moorish governor. They stayed voluntarily under Muslim rule, 'attracted by the higher cultural level to become more or less Arabicised, mixing with them'.[4] Following the military conflicts of the Reconquista, these Mozarabs began a gradual exodus to Christian kingdoms, settling mainly in the territory north of the Duero river, often in mountain regions, with León as the most important centre: 'These Mozarabs brought with them their building methods which, besides emulating the Moorish architecture they recalled, also constituted their own style.'[5]

The Pyrenean Monasteries

The Abbey of Saint-Michel-de-Cuixà, first founded in 878, sits at the foot of Mount Canigou, regarded as sacred by the Catalonians. Today the abbey forms one of the largest religious complexes in the south of France, in what was at the time northern Catalonia. Abbot Oliba had the crypt and the distinctive bell tower built before his death in 1046, while the cloister, built of pink marble from Villefranche, was added the following century from 1130 to 1140 by what the on-site abbey guidebook describes as 'a new generation of religious sculptors'. It goes on: 'The Cuixà school of sculpture produced brilliant work in all of Catalonia, both north and south of the Pyrenees, and particularly at Serrabona and in the cloister of Elne.' The quality of the sculpture in the capitals is exceptional. Even though only thirty-seven of the original sixty-three survived and were shipped to America by an American antique collector living in France, then bought by the Metropolitan Museum in New York where they are now on display at the Met Cloisters, good quality copies have been erected in situ.

Architecturally there are several elements at Saint-Michel-de-Cuixà where the Islamic influence is striking. On first arrival it is the tall rectangular bell

8.1: The Benedictine Pyrenean abbey of Saint-Michel-de-Cuixà in today's France used to be within historic Catalonia. Its tower displays many features taken from Islamic models, like the *ajimez* windows that multiply towards the top, its arcaded Lombard bands decoratively separating the storeys, and its lesenes simultaneously reinforcing and decorating its corners and walls.

tower that draws attention, with its arcaded Lombard bands running horizontally as decorative features to mark and highlight divisions in the floor levels, and its lesenes running in vertical bands from top to bottom, including at the corners, again as decorative additions to divide the space. At the lower levels there are just two single horseshoe arch windows per facade, but at the higher levels there are two pairs of narrow twin windows, known in Spanish as *ajimez*, from the Arabic, as explained earlier. Similar free-standing towers have already been seen in northern Italy and Sicily. As so often in Islamic architecture, what appears at first glance to be a decorative feature belies an underlying structural function. By making more window space incrementally towards to the top, fewer stones are needed so the load is lightened and the stability of the structure is improved. The model here is likely to have been the tower at Qal'at Bani Hammad.

The southern arcade of the Cuixà cloister is the earliest, where the decorative motifs of the capitals are linked to plant and zoomorphic styles—wide leaves spread out, eagles with outstretched wings, stocky monsters with enormous heads, their mouths open to devour their prey. Lions recur, either in a frieze or in groups of four animals, their heads joined at the corners, two by two. None of these capitals is in its original position, but even the later ones betray their origins by the iconography. In the western arcade, for example, one capital has a seated figure with oriental features holding in his hands the paws of an animal being devoured by a pair of lions on either side. Each capital is separate, distinct, not linked to any overarching narrative. Other sculptures have the characteristic Islamic drill-hole patterning made using a trepan.

The crypt, built *c.*1030–5, has vaulting the construction of which would only have been known to masons familiar with Islamic techniques. The ring-shaped space encircles a huge round central pillar that holds up a semi-barrel vault, like a palm tree with its spreading branches.

The tribune or raised gallery that was once at the western end of the church, where the important people sat during church services, has disappeared, though parts of the sculpture have been assembled and are on display in a side room, awaiting eventual full reconstruction. The only complete example of such a tribune can still be seen at the remote monastery of Serrabona, miraculously preserved in wild and beautiful oak forests some 30 kilometres east of Saint-Michel-de-Cuixà, built by the same school of twelfth-century master sculptors from the same pink Villefranche marble.

The pink Villefranche marble entrance to the Cuixà abbey church, originally part of the lost tribune gallery, is decorated with fine sculpture, its arch ringed with an arabesque ribbon decorated with a range of fantastical beasts, complemented by St Luke's bull and St Mark's lion set within the spandrels. The whole portal is crowned with an elaborate, carefully carved cornice and, as the abbey booklet observes, 'there is no empty space in this tight composition'—another known characteristic of the Arab *horror vacui* and love of decoration. New York's Metropolitan Museum, in its description of the characteristics of Islamic art, states that its dominant feature is maybe an almost obsessive desire to cover all surfaces with ornament. The door jambs are marked by life-size elongated statues of Sts Peter and Paul, the lateral surfaces of which are ornamented with an Islamic-style arabesque pattern of twisting, scrolling flora set within a frame.

Here, as so often, it is the frame that is the key. Quite apart from the fact that Islamic artists always liked to put sculptural motifs within a frame, it is also worth noting that a craftsman, of whatever religion or ethnicity, when given a commission by whatever patron or ruler to produce certain subjects

8.2: The sculpted tribune in the remote Pyrenean priory of Serrabona, carved from pink Villefranche marble in the twelfth century, is the most complete in Europe, displaying the zoomorphic fantastical creatures that were brought into Catalonia from Middle Eastern archetypes.

in the carving, would instinctively begin by setting the background framework to his work before embarking on the carving of the scene itself. It is in this background framework that the artist or sculptor reveals the archetypes he draws on, the deeply embedded traditions of which he is a part. That is why endlessly scrolling arabesques and the pearl-beaded interlace and frames are such clear indicators of Muslim masons at work. The on-site guidebook tells us that the walls used to have geometric coloured decoration.

Close to Saint-Michel-de-Cuixà, perched 1,100 metres up on Mount Canigou, is the Benedictine monastery of Saint-Martin-du-Canigou, which also bears many of the hallmarks of Islamic architecture. Only reachable today on foot by a stiff 300-metre climb up a narrow tarmac track, the ingenuity of its placement, adapted to the steep drops all around, would have demanded considerable construction skill, and required much knowledge of water management and terrace agriculture, in which Arab Muslims excelled. Other Arab features include the merlon crenellations of the bell tower, the *ajimez* mullioned windows, the blind arcades, the so-called Lombard bands and the vertical pilaster strips or lesenes. The four apses of the church chevet are likewise decorated externally with Lombard bands.

The site booklet rather coyly tells us that at the very end of the tenth century in Catalonia 'we see the emergence of a new art of building... as well as in Burgundy and northern Italy. It would have been the result', the booklet explains, 'of religious, cultural and political choices about which little is known.' The features of this new style, dubbed 'First Romanesque', are listed in the booklet as follows: the systematic use of vaults, the use of fieldstone, twin-mullioned windows, the use of vertical decorative bands called pilaster strips or lesenes, blind arcades, dog-tooth friezes and repeated features, especially on bell towers. All these features were brought into Europe from the Islamic world, as explained earlier.

Romanesque Capitals and their Interpretation

The Saint-Martin-du-Canigou booklet, like the material sold on-site at all the monasteries across Spain today, does its best to impart Christian meanings to the subject matter of the capitals in an attempt to make sense of them. 'We can only understand Romanesque art by means of a spiritual interpretation of the decoration', it states, whilst also acknowledging that this is 'a difficult task'. Sometimes these attempts verge on the ridiculous, as in the interpretation of the capital where the booklet sees 'winged rams which seem to be covering their mouths reflecting the rule of monastic silence. Unless they are chewing their wings to remind the monks of the importance of spiritual nourishment.' Far more likely, in my view, is that they are expressing awe, as the biting of fingers or nails in Arabic and Iranian paintings was a conventional way of depicting a psychological state of wonder.[6]

This whole question of interpretation needs to be understood within a wider context. When Bernard of Clairvaux denounced these 'ridiculous monstrosities' as distractions for the monks, taking their thoughts away from God (see Chapter 2), his condemnation tells us that such capitals and sculptures showing figures and monsters, real or imaginary plants and animals, were something new, an innovation that began in the eleventh century, seemingly from nowhere. But as we know, nothing in art or architecture appears magically in a completely new way unless it has been brought in from elsewhere. The Greeks with their Doric, Ionian and Corinthian capitals did not suddenly insert fantastical creatures or human heads and figures in their capitals. Indeed, they did not include any creatures at all in their capitals. The Romans were the same, following the Greek model.

8.3: This zoomorphic capital in the cloister of the Pyrenean monastery of Saint-Martin-du-Canigou shows rams appearing to 'chew their wings' or request 'monastic silence', typical misinterpretations by clergy seeking religious meaning in such sculpture.

Given that we know the construction world in the Iberian Peninsula at this time was dominated by Muslims and the skills they in turn had brought in from Syria and North Africa, this is the region where it is logical to look. The influences that craftsmen from Islamic Spain, and indeed from Sicily and southern Italy, would have been familiar with were Fatimid, where the inclusion of fantastical birds and beasts tangled within foliage and plant life was a common motif, and is seen on all surviving Fatimid ceramics, cloth, woodcarving and architecture, where birds, gazelles, lions, hares and serpents commonly inhabit the vegetation. The use of paired animals like lions or birds was a motif they had absorbed from earlier Iranian culture, Sassanian Iran, and the use of griffins, winged lions and other mythological beasts, especially dragon-like creatures such as the Babylonian *mushushu*, harked back to their Assyrian and Mesopotamian forebears and were the motifs commonly found on all ancient monumental sculpture, guarding entrances, warding off evil spirits and generally protecting the ruler and his elite entourage. Ancient Egyptian sphinx-like creatures, half man half beast, were likewise part of the inherited archetypal tradition deeply embedded in the psyche of those who lived in the eastern Mediterranean.

Here in these early Romanesque monasteries, were the masons shown pictures of what to carve on their capitals, either by people like Abbot Oliba or other clerics and monks? Did pictures of such scenes exist in illuminated manuscripts? The answer is no, they did not. So where did the ideas for these sculptures come from if not from the Christian clerics?

They can only have come from inside the heads of the master masons, from the inherited repertoire of subjects with which they had been familiar for generations, for centuries even, passed down within families. The use of the trepan, the drilling tool for making the small holes in the stone which appear on the capital sculptures to mark the edges, the frames of motifs, is another clue. The Canigou booklet says the holes were filled with lead which is no longer there and that they 'gave life to the sculpture', or that they 'could also have had a practical function, artists sometimes using them as markers for shaping the stone', remarks that once again illustrate the complete lack of understanding of the context. The writers of such booklets are not looking for meaning anywhere except through a narrow religious, Christian, Catholic lens.

Unlike the faces you see in Byzantine icons, no two faces in this distinctive early Romanesque sculpture are ever the same, which suggests these heads might well have been modelled on real people. A likeness to racial features from North Africa was pointed out to me by a very knowledgeable guide in Salisbury Cathedral, in the faces that look out over the nave from high above, and I noticed the same thing myself among the carved heads at Jumièges Abbey. The number of bearded men is also striking in many of these sculptures, and at Saint-Michel-de-Cuixà the winged and bearded angel found on a capital of the collapsed tribune is so notable that the on-site shop even features him in a special postcard in close-up, calling him simply *séraphin barbu*. In medieval Christian theology seraphim are in the highest choir of the angelic hierarchy as caretakers of God's throne, and always referred to in the plural. It is very unusual to find a single seraph, let alone a bearded one. In this cloister capital he appears by himself and seems to be modelled on an actual person. He has eyes that do not match, one pupil looking straight ahead, the other looking to the right, as if he has a lazy eye, a detail which must be deliberate given how well carved the remainder of the piece is.

In Islamic traditions the seraphim feature as Bearers of the Throne of God, often portrayed in zoomorphic forms, as in this illustration from Iranian manuscript 373 now in the Wellcome Collection, London, where one seraph is a human (like St Matthew), another a lion (like St Mark), another an eagle

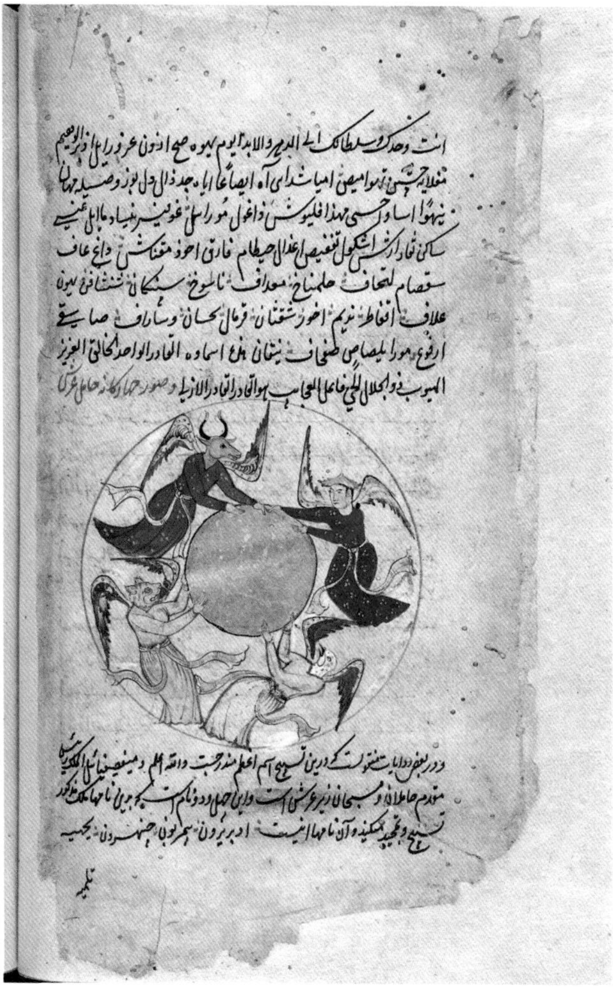

8.4: This Iranian manuscript known as 'Bearers of the Throne' shows the seraphim of the Islamic tradition carrying the Throne of God. They are represented in the same zoomorphic forms as in Christian art and architecture, where the Gospel writers Matthew, Mark, Luke and John are depicted as a man, a lion, an ox and an eagle.

(like St John) and the other a bull (like St Luke), not a coincidence, as the symbols derive from the ancient Babylonian signs of the zodiac, and were widely used in Assyrian, Egyptian and Greek art.

Muslim men were generally bearded, and it is hard not to see again in this sculpture an element of mischief and humour, given that in art of this period monks and saints are usually depicted without beards and angels are invariably clean-shaven. The monk and chronicler Orderic Vitalis (1075–1142) associated beards with debauchery, sexual activity, the devil and evil, writing: 'Now almost all our fellow countrymen are crazy and wear little beards, openly proclaiming by such a token that they revel in filthy lusts like stinking goats.'[7] Being clean-shaven on the other hand was associated with purity, humility and celibacy.

In 1096 the Archbishop of Rouen proclaimed that bearded men should be excluded from the Church, and by the 1100s the Latin Church had banned the wearing of beards among all monks and priests, especially among the Benedictines and the Cistercians. Depictions of Oliba always show him as beardless. Even Wilfred the Hairy was beardless. Charlemagne issued an edict at the end of the eighth century to root out beards among the clergy, though in art he is always shown with long hair, full beard and moustache. The pope was always clean shaven. It became a mark of the divide between East and West in Christianity, as the Eastern Orthodox wore beards and long hair following the tradition of the Desert Fathers of early Christianity, avoiding vanity and being more practical given the lack of water. The Greeks wore beards till Alexander the Great discouraged them among his soldiers, in case they could be grabbed by the enemy in hand-to-hand combat. The Romans wore their hair short and were always beardless, maintaining the view that only barbarians did not shave or cut their hair. In medieval times, ordinary lay Christians were allowed to grow beards and go unshaven, so when sculpted heads with beards appear on eleventh- and twelfth-century capitals, they must either represent lay Christians or Moors. As so often, the original iconography for seraphim can be traced back to ancient Egyptian icons—and they were clean-shaven.

In Anglo-Saxon England only the priests were fully clean-shaven, which is why King Harold's scouts, on first seeing the Normans camped outside Hastings, are said to have reported back, 'they have sent an army of priests!' In the Coptic frescoes and icons of Egypt and in the Fatimid ceiling of the Cappella Palatina in Palermo all the men are bearded.

Another important feature in the construction of Saint-Martin-du-Canigou is on display in the crypt. As the monastery's own booklet on the crypt points out, the fact that two vaulted spaces occur one directly on top of the other, both of similar size—namely the crypt below and the abbey church above—is rare and highly ambitious for the year 1000. In the crypt there are groined vaults resting on six monolithic columns, and barrel vaults reinforced by transverse supporting arches resting on cruciform pillars which divide the roof space into bays. There are no surviving documents which talk about the construction, but it was clearly highly sophisticated for its time. The nave of the abbey church above the crypt was also barrel vaulted, a technique that was not typical for the year 1000 and was only known on European soil in Muslim Spain.

Santa Maria de Ripoll

Many Benedictine abbeys like Ripoll were founded in northern Spain between the ninth and the twelfth centuries, as the region began to be repopulated by Christians after it had been under Muslim control. They were well funded thanks to grants of land and territorial legacies made by counts, nobles and other benefactors, as well as taxes raised on the subject Muslim population.

Today it is the portico at Ripoll, built in 1150, considered a masterpiece and one of the most notable works of Romanesque sculpture in Europe, that has come through the centuries intact, along with the twelfth-century cloisters. There are scenes in the portico with human figures, depicting the Old Testament stories with David, Jonah, Solomon and Cain and Abel, together with a handful of New Testament scenes from the lives of Peter and Paul. These are the features generally focused on by art historians, but the clues, in my view, are to be found in the other framing elements, like the zigzag border that runs across the top and round the head of the Christ in Majesty figure at the centre and round the innermost arch; the shell-like palmettes that frame the outer arch; the spiral pillars that frame the central doorway; the scroll of roundels running around the inner arch and horizontally across the bottom, containing animals or stylised plants or trees; the scenes of the mounted hunter killing a wild beast, directly above the roundels; and the row of arcades directly above them whose arches are decorated with the tell-tale beading. The Fatimid/Islamic features are clear in the way the whole composition is conceived, framed within its decorative elements, and in the typical subject matters of the Labours of the Months, scenes of everyday life, signs of the zodiac, intertwining arabesque foliage and imaginary animals. There is no symmetry in the framing of the arch; each pillar is decorated differently. Only the figures are vaguely symmetrical, which might well be because their inclusion was directed by Christian churchmen.

Poblet Monastery

Founded by Cistercian monks from France in 1153 with the help of royal patronage, Poblet Abbey is one of the largest monasteries in Spain. Inscribed as a UNESCO World Heritage Site in 1991 for its spiritual importance and its 'unique blend of architectural forms',[8] it bears many elements of Islamic influence. Perhaps the most dramatic is the ablutions fountain in the twelfth- and early-thirteenth-century cloister where the monks washed their hands and which still has running water today, just like the ablution fountain in a mosque courtyard.

8.5: The ablutions fountain at Poblet Abbey in Catalonia, set within the cloister as in a mosque courtyard, with constant running water where the monks washed their hands before meals.

The capitals of the cloister are a mix of intricate basketweave and complex floral designs with fantastic animals entangled. The thirteenth-century monks' dormitory has a magnificent series of pointed arches supporting the roof and resting on superb corbels in Moorish style. The Chapter House is the jewel of the monastery, with ribbed vaults branching elegantly upwards like the branches of a palm tree from the columns which resemble the tree trunks, just like the Chapter Houses at Wells and Salisbury. The keystones of its vaults are decorated with figures like the Virgin and Child, in the beaded framing typical of Islamic work, and the whole space is beautifully and harmoniously proportioned, with floral or geometric decoration on its capitals.

Lérida

The final focus in Catalonia is Lérida (Catalan Lleida) and the Lérida School of sculptors. *La Seu Vella* (the Old Cathedral) is the major landmark that dominates the city, built up on the central hill and visible from afar in all directions. Thought to have been built over the remains of the city's main mosque, the cathedral's construction began in the twelfth century. As a Muslim city, Lérida had had two main monuments: the mosque and what is still called *La Sudda*, an Arabic word meaning the seat or divan, that refers to the fortified enclosure on the highest part of the hill, built in 883, and which served as the seat of political and military power during Arab rule. Even after the Christian conquest in 1149 and to this day, the term *La Sudda* is still used to refer to the so-called 'Gothic' residential quarters that grew up around the castle. The mosque was built in 832. Both structures were heavily damaged when the Christians took the city, but then rebuilt in the same locations, almost certainly using local Arab masons who stayed and who continued to dominate the construction trade. It is they who are thought to be responsible for the exceptional late Romanesque carving, and who formed what has been called the Lérida School, which was influential in the surrounding areas, including Agramunt.[9]

The Taifa kingdom of Lérida was the refuge chosen by the last caliph of Córdoba, Hisham III, son of Abd al-Rahman III, when the caliphate fell apart in 1031. He requested political asylum and lived in Lérida till he died five years later in 1036. His choice of Lérida suggests that the city was at that time one of the most thriving and prosperous Muslim centres, and also illustrates how when a Muslim state fell, the ruler and his elite entourage left to seek protection elsewhere in other Muslim territories. The general population, however, which would have been predominantly Muslim, tended to stay put, accepting the terms of a peace agreement and continuing to work in their various specialisms, but under new masters. Had the new rulers simply expelled all the pre-existing population, not only would they have had no one to tax, but they would also have had no one to build their monuments, look after their irrigation systems, work their fields or make their clothes, shoes and household goods. For agriculture and trade to thrive, the skilled middle class needed to stay, on terms that were not so onerous as to drive them to leave.

The master of works at Lérida, according to the local guidebooks, was Pere de Coma, who was responsible for finding stonemasons, sculptors, labourers and other craftsmen. As so often, nothing is known of his background except that he was hired in 1203 to direct the construction, working for nearly twenty years on the site. Scholars suggest his origins might have been in Lombardy or in northern Catalonia, but they agree that the masons and sculptors responsible for the decorative carving were members of the so-called Lérida School and of Moorish origin, working to Pere de Coma's specifications for the structure and ground plan.

The cloister, one of Europe's largest, dates from the late thirteenth and early fourteenth centuries, boasting four massive galleries with huge, richly decorated windows. Unusually, its shape is slightly trapezoidal, as it was squeezed into the space in front of the original cathedral, because there was nowhere else for it on the rocky outcrop. Adapting a building to a tricky location is a technical skill known to have been a strength of Muslim architects; mosques like al-Aqmar (1125–6) in Cairo under the Fatimids were specially designed to fit the constraints of the pre-existing street layout. As a result of these adjustments, in Lérida you have to enter the church via the cloister in order to reach the Romanesque main church portal on the western facade. In this respect the cloister served the same purpose as that of a mosque courtyard in front of the prayer hall, a place where people gathered and chatted while children played games on the stones. The bases of some of the windows have carved qirkat boards in the stone, from the Arabic word *al-qariq*, meaning flat place. The boards were used to play games like noughts and crosses or draughts.

In the cloister, the finest of all the carved windows bears the six-pointed star, which in medieval times was used decoratively by both Muslims and Jews in mystical settings and was known as the Seal of Solomon (not the Star of David, which only became linked to a symbol for Jewish identity in the seventeenth century). The star frames a small Christ in Majesty in a multilobed frame, which shares similarities with the image of the seated caliph in the ivory at the tenth-century Umayyad palace of Madinat al-Zahra at Córdoba.

8.6: The cloister of the Old Cathedral of Lleida, where the carving by the Moorish 'Lérida School' on each arch is a different geometric pattern. This one bears the six-pointed Seal of Solomon framing a tiny Christ in Majesty sitting inside a polylobed frame.

It is the only cloister window with human figures, with the Virgin Mary and St John appearing as small standing figures at the bottom centre. Each of the carved windows also has its own rose window within the elaborate and delicate pattern, each with its own individual design. One is known as the 'palm trees'. Also striking in the cloister is the lack of symmetry in the arches on the side opposite the Star of David, where each of the three arches is a different size, in an apparently random way. Of the seventeen carved cloister windows, only two repeat the same pattern, while the other fifteen are all different. The capitals too are all different, depicting a whole world of fantastic animals and hybrid beings enmeshed in stylised plant and floral scrolls.

In the nave are the remains of a fresco, where even the church labelling mentions Islamic influence in the geometric interlacing decoration that forms the frame. The majestic vaulting of the nave uses pointed arches and ribs and has eight-spoke geometric-patterned rose wheel windows at each end of the transept, while the cupola at the crossing rests on squinches and more pointed arches, illustrative of the transition to Gothic innovations which the Muslim masons perfected.

Lérida's most precious relic, the Holy Swaddling Cloth, comically translated in the local guidebook as 'Jesus's first nappy', is kept in the main altar. It was secretly acquired in Tunisia from the sultan's treasures in his palace by a woman from Lérida who was married to the sultan's son, and who then donated it to the cathedral in 1297.

Castile and León

Santo Domingo de Silos

The remote Benedictine monastery of Santo Domingo (St Dominic) de Silos, set high in the hills southeast of Burgos at an altitude of over 1,000 metres, is famous for its two-storey eleventh- and twelfth-century cloisters. In addition to the exquisitely carved capitals, there are also sculpted panels of exceptional workmanship, sixteen in total, depicting biblical scenes like the Ascension. The capitals are thought to be the work of the same craftsmen who sculpted the beautiful capitals and entrance portal of Moissac Abbey in France.[10] Both sites were on the pilgrimage route to Santiago de Compostela, so it would have been entirely logical that the same craftsmen were used at several locations, being much in demand for the high level of their talents.

Cloisters always functioned as the centre of monastic community life, with all parts of the monastery connecting through them and moving out from them. Like the courtyard of a mosque, the cloister was the multipurpose central space where monks could meet, chat, walk and contemplate. They also served to preserve and proclaim the spiritual and memorial function of the monastery, and for that, they needed to be beautiful, magnificent even, fit for the aristocracy of the Church. At Silos, scholars have identified more than two hands at work, and the likelihood is that an entire workshop of masons and sculptors was involved both for the upper and the lower storeys—unless of course it was angels, as the on-site booklet, written and produced by the monks themselves, would have us believe:

> Your infrangible arcade and capitals,
> Who made them, poet or sculptor

> ... Or did angels come down from heaven
> With plans drawn out by Our Lord?[11]

In all the carvings there are the usual fantastical beasts like griffins and harpies, both confronted and addorsed, and birds and monsters, often entwined in foliage, while sometimes the capitals are simply covered in complex plant motifs. Vegetation emerges from the mouth of one feline creature, whose cat- or lion-like head is guarding the top of the foliage, just like the later Green Man so popular in Britain's Norman and Gothic cathedrals.

Arabs had occupied the area since the eighth century, but the monastery, founded during the Visigothic period, continued to exist, like many others in northern Spain.[12] The courtyard shape is irregular, with sixteen arches in the north and south, and fourteen in the east and west. All the lines are crooked, not straight, without symmetry; each capital is different, not just in its design but even in its shape, with no sequence or pattern, except that its underlying conception is geometric, in typical Islamic fashion.

American art historian Meyer Schapiro was the first to observe the Islamic characteristics in the early carvings of the cloister. Writing in 1939, he wondered if the sculptors were Mozarabs. Mozarabic art, he notes, 'shares in its symbolism and schematized imagery the broad medieval characteristics of Romanesque'.[13] He sees Mozarab stylistic characteristics in the carved figures, in their passive, constrained, tense and static form, as if they have no will of their own. He notes how their complex silhouettes are composed of short geometrical lines, how their bodies have an organic character. He sees a geometrised abstract environment that is quite unlike classical styles, which gives the whole composition a heightened sense of spirituality, like an unearthly cosmos, contrasting with intensely bright colours. He even detects that the musicians and dancers are not performing for God but for an earthly court, and notes how there are women musicians in the sculpture, a profession often denounced by the Church for females. Schapiro would not have known that female musicians are depicted in Islamic art from the eighth century onwards for the caliph's court, starting with the Umayyad frescoes of the Qusayr Amra bathhouse in today's Jordanian desert.

The ceiling of the lower cloister is decorated with a Mudéjar wooden painted ceiling made from carefully worked pine beams, probably dating from *c.*1390. It features scenes not of religious, but of secular life, in no logical or narrative sequence, but as isolated pictures of individuals and animals, in typical Islamic style, again reminiscent of the framed frescoes of the Syrian Umayyad craftsmen at Qusayr Amra.

8.7: One of the many framed wall frescoes in the Umayyad bathhouse of Qusayr Amra in today's Jordan, depicting scenes of everyday life, here showing carpenters at work.

Another unique feature in the cloister is the famous grouping of three columns twisted round each other, remarkably difficult to execute and requiring an extremely high level of skill to perfect. Again, it seems to have a playful quality, almost as if done solely to display virtuosity. No other such column has yet been found in either Islamic or Romanesque architecture.

One ornately carved Romanesque portal remains from the original church, known as the Portal of the Virgin, leading upstairs into the church from the cloister, framed by a Mozarab-style horseshoe arch. Its capitals depict scenes of men struggling with animals, another favourite Islamic theme.

The monks had a pharmacy that is still on display, along with a garden of medicinal herbs in the cloister courtyard. This was knowledge they vaunted as their own but which they had in practice learnt from the translations of Arabic

8.8: The unique twisted column in the cloister of the Benedictine monastery of Santo Domingo de Silos, in the hills above Burgos, northern Spain, one of many indicators of the exceptional carving virtuosity of the masons. They are recorded as being Muslims from Andalusia, displaced as the Córdoba Caliphate collapsed in the eleventh century and the Catholic Reconquista gained ground.

scientific manuscripts from the caliphal court of Andalusia in Córdoba. They also had a scriptorium where these manuscripts were copied between the tenth and fifteenth centuries. The monks' on-site guidebook tells us how 'monks have contributed to scientific studies throughout the centuries, to a very important degree'. No mention is made of where that knowledge came from.

The panel of Doubting Thomas was one of the last to be completed, and is suggestive of Mozarabic art in the way that there is no ground line, with the figures appearing to be suspended in a void. The central person is Paul, a figure much revered in the Eastern Orthodox Church adhered to by the Mozarabs, while Christ and Thomas are to the extreme left, even though Christ is larger than life; in other words, there is a complete absence of symmetry. Pearl-beaded borders decorate many of the hems of the robes, sirens sit astride seated lions and decorative geometry can be seen in the arabesques and interlace created by paws, tails and claws. The fantastic animals sometimes have fur carved as fine parallel lines ending in a tight spiral to suggest a curl. Sirens and birds have feathered plumage carved in finely striated lines as if to evoke embroidery or a finely woven textile. Most of the animals have almond-shaped eyes outlined by a double-incised line. Some of the intricate patterns on the capitals are like finely worked filigree. The capitals with fruits and pine cones seem to be arranged spatially as squares balanced on inverted cones. Experts have dated these extremely high-quality carvings, using comparisons with dated manuscript inscriptions at Silos, to the period after the Mozarabic rite was replaced in 1080–90 by the Roman Catholic rite, but before the Visigothic script disappeared *c.*1110, 'the very epoch in which monumental sculpture was being reinvented'.[14]

The term 'monumental sculpture', a reference to sculpture that was used architecturally to enhance a building's grandeur rather than its size, is usually described by art historians as 'Romanesque', and the period in which it appeared and was developed is agreed, by consensus, to be the late eleventh and early twelfth centuries, precisely the period when Muslim–Christian interaction—through displacement, wars and economic necessity—was at its height. In the inscriptions on the capitals, a Mozarabic script with decorative serifs and foliate terminals has been likened to the foliated Kufic script favoured in decorative calligraphy carved on stone facades in the Arab world since the ninth century. Kufic may even have been the original model from which such embellishments were copied when transposed into Latin script. The 'Silos epigrapher mixed forms freely, without concern for consistency'[15]—another Islamic characteristic. Many of the styles found at Silos are also found in the carvings at Saint-Sernin de Toulouse and in the cloister at Moissac, both dated by inscriptions to *c.*1100. After studying such links extensively, experts have often commented on the similarities: 'The geometric composition of the capital makes Moissac the only extant cloister comparable in spirit to the cloister of Silos.'[16]

None of these connections are surprising when the history of Silos is considered. It had acquired several Moorish villages during the eleventh-century warfare of the Reconquista. Santo Domingo's biographer tells of a Moorish convert to Christianity who lived at the abbey, and also its Muslim slaves. The earliest surviving Latin manuscript on paper is a mid-eleventh-century Mozarabic breviary in the library of Silos. The Silos treasury had a magnificent Moorish ivory casket, now in Burgos, dated to 1026, its Arabic inscription carved in the florid Kufic foliated style, and in the abbey itself a late-twelfth-century altar frontal is also decorated with a bold Kufic inscription. Another ivory found at the nearby San Millán de la Cogolla, also attributed to 'Islamic artists' working for Christians in the late tenth century,[17] is a processional cross with eagles, griffins, lions and deer entangled in decorative foliage, similar in style to the Silos cloister capitals. Like the cloister arcade mouldings, the cross arms show the interlace growing out of the mouth of a monster mask reminiscent of the 'Green Man'.

The whole artistic ambiance of the Silos cloister, with its sumptuous exotic capitals entwining flora and fauna in continuous arabesques, is unmistakeably Islamic in feel and spirit, redolent of the luxury arts associated with Andalusia. The monastic treasury had several Islamic ivories including a game board, a pyxis and the reliquary casket already mentioned, signed and dated 'Muhammad Ibn Zayyan, 1026 in Cuenca'. It has confronted beasts either side of a tree of life, with rows of small animals, just like those found on the Silos capitals. The silks that lined the ivory reliquaries were generally decorated with animals associated with death and resurrection like lions, eagles, griffins and birds, so prevalent in Islamic ornamentation and in the Silos capitals. Saints 'were posthumously honoured with Islamic textiles', and rulers, clergy and the wealthy also wore them, 'even to their graves'.[18]

All this evidence points to one thing—that the sculptors at the cloister of Silos were schooled in the tradition of Hispano-Muslim stone ornamentation, working for Christian masters, as was common. Despite the wars and political turmoil of the times, Muslims and Christians continued to live and work alongside and trade with each other, and even occasionally to marry each other. Alfonso VI of Castile's favourite mistress, later wife, was Zaida of Seville, a refugee Muslim princess. The Arab vizier of Badis Ibn Habus (Berber King of Granada, 1038–73) was assassinated by a Mozarab called Abu al-Rabbi, who then managed to get the king to nominate his grandson as the next king, instead of the king's own son, who was at that time a refugee in Toledo. The popular Spanish folk hero El Cid (*c.*1043–1099) also famously fought in both Christian and Muslim armies, at a time when loyalties were complex and fluctuated regularly.

Islamic styles and motifs are evident on many early Romanesque capitals across northern Spain and up into France in the Languedoc, Burgundy and

Aquitaine regions, especially in those monasteries that fell under the Benedictines; and whilst it is true that many of these motifs ultimately derived from earlier Sassanian, Byzantine and Coptic sculptural traditions, the fact is that they were brought to the European mainland, at this time, by Muslim artists and craftsmen who produced the luxuriant 'Romanesque' style of sculpture that was so much admired in Europe.

San Miguel de Escalada (Mozarab)

Located in a remote valley some 30 kilometres from León, on the road to Compostela, the monastery of San Miguel de Escalada was founded in 912 and constructed in just one year for a group of monks who had emigrated from what was then the Emirate of Córdoba. As Arabised Christians living under Muslim rule from 711, they had absorbed many cultural and architectural influences, as is evident in the refinement and quality of the stonework. Their craftsmen are thought to have formed a Mozarabic school of stonemasons who were active all over León.[19]

The on-site booklet explains that, though little of it remains today, painting was used extensively in Mozarabic art, with the interiors of buildings lavishly decorated in bright colours. The guide also highlights the Islamic origin of the use of ribbed vaults, a construction method it says reached its height in the tenth century, though many of the monasteries built in that style have now been lost and their ruins razed to the ground, leaving no trace.[20]

Among other Islamic features it lists the high *ajimez* double window in the tower, designed with a slender central column separating a pair of small horseshoe arches and set within an *alfiz*, or frame, and a narrow masonry frieze, made up of pointed stones set between two rows of bricks, which runs below the eaves all round the church. Typical of Mozarabic art are the scroll modillions decorated with circular swirls under the roof eaves. Like Muslim corbelling, they are both structural and decorative.

Inside San Miguel de Escalada the stone iconostasis (the screen separating the sanctuary from the nave) with its central black column is said to have come originally from North Africa. The interior sculpted and carved ornamentation of the screens marking off the transept (the side aisles that serve to separate the apse and that also form the short arms of the cross) is also very Islamic in style, focusing on continuous plant motifs with palm trees and stylised leaves together with geometric patterns, interlacing and braiding, and some zoomorphic representations like birds pecking at vine clusters. All the interior capitals are different, and the most famous is known as the triple capital because it depicts the ibis, the palm and the pelican. Another has the lion, the scallop of the Road to Santiago and the fleur-de-lys. The same motifs are repeated on the stone grilles that demarcate the nave from the sacred area for priests, sometimes in roundel-like circular frames.

In the Mozarabic rite, which was modelled on the Byzantine Eastern Orthodox and Coptic rite, a curtain was erected to screen the priest from the congregation during the blessing. In this they followed their Visigothic predecessors, who were followers of the Arian heresy from 507, that is, a position that was actually closer to Islam in that it denied the Trinity and Christ's divinity, believing that Jesus was subordinate to God. After the Reconquista the Catholic monarchs discarded the Mozarab rite and replaced it with the Roman Catholic rite, and Cluniac monks were often installed in the monasteries instead. In Santo Domingo de Silos, for example, the Roman Catholic rite was imposed by Alfonso VI and Pope Gregory VII in 1080 after they accused the Mozarabic liturgy of being tainted by Arian heresies. Despite this switch made by the top echelons, many Mozarabic architectural elements

8.9: The tenth-century Mozarabic monastery of San Miguel de Escalada near León, northern Spain, built by Christians from Córdoba, with its arcaded gallery of stilted horseshoe arches in the 'Cordovan Emiral style', also adopted many other Islamic architectural features both inside and out.

persisted, especially in the arches and the sculpture. All the arches at San Miguel de Escalada are Islamic horseshoe in type, sometimes also called 'stilted arches', in what was known as 'the Cordovan Emiral style',[21] particularly striking in the arcaded gallery of the porch.

Zamora Cathedral of San Salvador

Set on a distinctive rocky outcrop overlooking the Duero river, the medieval walled town of Zamora is sometimes called a museum of Romanesque architecture because it boasts no less than twenty-four churches from the twelfth and thirteenth centuries. No other city in Europe has as many. Mozarab builders arrived in the city in the tenth century from Toledo, and the city became one of the most thriving centres in Iberia, even surpassing León. After nearly a hundred years of Muslim raids and incursions, it developed into a bastion of Christianity. Of all Zamora's monuments the most memorable is the cathedral of San Salvador (1151–74), with its spectacular and exotic dome, conceived by a Cluniac monk named Bernardus under the auspices of King Alfonso VII, as a blend of Mozarabic and Andalusian Islamic influences. It inspired a construction fever so intense that the city was, in the words of its own publicity leaflet, 'choked with its enormous concentration of churches… where the arches began to rise upwards in the middle announcing the beginnings of the Gothic era which was to come'. It is described as an 'exquisite frontier architecture… with exotic Moorish notes.' The cathedral nave has pointed arches, but the most remarkable interior feature is the dome, 'embroidered stone' as the local leaflet calls it, with a continuous arcade of sixteen windows running round the base, and eight rib arches springing from the columns between the windows, that then criss-cross in the centre to make a star pattern.

The most beautiful church in the city is La Magdalena, thanks to the elegant decorative motif of its finely carved stone doorway, with its Islamic nine-cusped inner arch and delicately interlacing flower and plant patterns. It belonged to the Knights Templar and its stylised-flower rose window surrounded by zigzags, dating from the late twelfth century, resembles that of the Temple Church in London.

The fine thirteenth-century stone bridge across the Duero, with its sixteen pointed arches, is also a typical piece of Muslim engineering, with its clever circular holes to let the flood waters pass through at times of high water after the spring thaw.

Soria

Set on a high plain, the town of Soria in northeast Castile boasts two exceptional Romanesque buildings from the late twelfth century, both showing

8.10: The cloister courtyard of the monastery of San Juan de Duero in Soria, near Zaragoza, northern Spain, has an unusual combination of Islamic arches – pointed, interlocking and horseshoe, with different styles being used on each of the four sides, without symmetry.

unmistakeable Islamic influence. The first, in the town centre, is the church facade of Santo Domingo, with its double row of carved blind arches, topped by an eight-spoked wheel window, directly above the elaborately carved entrance portal, complete with tympanum. Sitting in the centre of the tympanum, holding Jesus Christ on his lap, is a regal God the Father, framed in a beaded mandorla. The style is very similar to churches found in the Poitou region of western France.

Outside town in a secluded wood on the banks of the Duero is the monastery of San Juan de Duero, with the most startlingly original and obviously Islamic-style cloister anywhere in Europe. Rather than doing anything as dull and conventional as having each of the four sides the same, each side is different, and not only that, but the style changes in the middle, not at the corners, as if to demonstrate, or maybe celebrate, the full gamut of arches that the stonemasons could construct—horseshoe arches, interlocking arches, round arches and pointed arches. The craftsmen enjoyed themselves and evidently had free rein. Inside the adjacent church there is also a variety of arches—pointed, rounded and horseshoe. There can be no doubt that it was the work of outsiders schooled in the Islamic tradition, since it is clearly on a level way beyond what any local masons could have managed.

The capitals of the cloister also show marked Islamic influence, each one different, with palm leaves, elaborate basketweave and geometric floral designs, together with highly stylised paired fantastical creatures. The vegetal interlace pattern runs continuously, without end, in typical Muslim style. Some are highly reminiscent of Madinat al-Zahra, the sumptuous exotic tenth-century caliphal palace built on hillside terraces just outside Córdoba, which represents the peak of Umayyad architecture.

Asturias

Santa Maria del Naranco

The sight of this remarkable structure, looking as if it has been lifted from the Dead Cities of the limestone massifs of northwest Syria and transplanted onto the hills of Asturias, is one of the most memorable images in northern Spain. Along with the church of San Miguel de Lillo, just 100 metres away, Santa Maria del Naranco (848 CE) was recognised as a UNESCO World Heritage Site in 1985. Together, they form an astonishing pair of buildings that give real insights into how architectural influences travel. Both are the only remaining relics of a palatial complex built in 848 by Ramiro I, King of Asturias, and are unlike anything else to survive from early medieval Spain.

8.11: The church of Santa Maria del Naranco in Asturias, northern Spain, with its sophisticated vaulting and decorative stonework, was originally the palace of a local king who was a contemporary of Abd al-Rahman II in Córdoba (r.822–52), from whose realm such techniques and styles were adopted.

Nothing is recorded about the builders, but both the context and the buildings speak for themselves. Ramiro I was a direct contemporary of Abd al-Rahman II, at a time when the Umayyad Emirate of Córdoba was at its peak and when the Córdoba Mezquita was expanded using new building techniques that were unknown in Christian Europe. The UNESCO entry describes these Asturian monuments as a pre-Romanesque 'unique artistic achievement which is neither a metamorphosis of Paleo-Christian art nor a feature of Carolingian art... These churches... entirely vaulted... have very rich decors inspired from Arab elements as well as shapes which associate them with the great sanctuaries of Asia Minor.'[22]

But it is inconceivable that a small kingdom like Asturias, during an extremely turbulent time in its history, with much internal strife and regular Viking raids, could have developed the skills necessary to build such advanced structures using ribbed barrel vaulting. The sophistication of the stonework and the decorative patterns used are clearly part of the repertoire of the Syrian Umayyads. When they made their capital in Damascus from 661 to 750, the Arab Umayyads absorbed the pre-existing early Byzantine architectural styles they found in Syria, learnt from them and developed them further, before bringing them into the Iberian Peninsula under their leader Abd al-Rahman I, builder of the Córdoba Mezquita in 785.

Running continuously round all the exterior vertical columns and arches of Santa Maria del Naranco is a band in a distinctive spiral pattern which locals call a rope design, but which looks more like palm fronds twisting on either side of a central branch; on the two spacious first-floor terraces, the columns are decorated with zigzags, spirals, palm frond capitals and pairs of winged creatures and fantastical beasts, which show both Syrian and Iranian influences; the upper throne room has blind arches and stone-carved arabesque roundel/medallions. The beaded frames on the zigzags recall the same beaded frame design that can still be seen on the original wooden

8.12: A section of the restored wooden ceiling of the Córdoba Mezquita showing the same beaded interlace framing as also appears on the zigzag column decoration of Santa Maria del Naranco, together with other ornamentation styles which had been taken over from the Syrian Umayyads, the eighth-century conquerors of Andalusia who were also highly skilled stonemasons.

ceiling of the Córdoba Mezquita, fragments of which have survived and now been recreated.

Two thirds of the church of San Miguel de Lillo (completed in 842) collapsed in the thirteenth century, but what remains also shows unmistakeable Islamic influence in its lattice windows of geometric patterns, all carved from one piece of stone and with a central eight-pointed star, its roundels with palms and its frames with arabesques, and its courtly scenes depicting a lion, symbol of royalty, and a ruler sitting on a throne while a musician plays a lute and an acrobat

8.13: A lattice window carved from a single piece of stone at the small Asturian church of San Miguel de Lillo, just 200 metres from Santa Maria del Naranco, with more features taken over from Islamic Spain, such as *ajimez* windows, arcading and geometric patterns.

performs. There is a geometric chequered pattern in red. Even the bases of the columns are carved, with tiny human figures inside a blind arcade.

Galicia

Cathedral of Santiago de Compostela

Santiago de Compostela (1075–1211) is Europe's most significant pilgrimage destination, its cathedral built over the reputed tomb of the Apostle James. Somewhat smothered today by Baroque and Gothic embellishments, the cathedral's underlying Romanesque structure nevertheless remains dominated by unmistakeably Islamic designs of interlocking and interlacing foliage, eight-pointed stars and lobed quatrefoils.

Like Santa Maria del Naranco and San Miguel de Lillo, UNESCO designated Santiago a World Heritage Site in 1985. The cult of St James the Moorslayer (Spanish *Matamoros*) grew in the ninth century and the shrine became a major Catholic pilgrimage site, aided by a legend in which King Ramiro of Asturias defeats the Moors in battle thanks to the saint appearing on a white horse and helping his troops win victory. Neither Asturian nor Arab chronicles of the period make any mention of such a battle, and its date in Latin sources was later altered by ten years to make it fit within Ramiro's reign. The legend was subsequently found to be based on a twelfth-century charter forged in Compostela, according to which Ramiro was said to have instituted another grant (also a twelfth-century forgery), the Voto de Santiago, a tax for the benefit of the church, only repealed in 1812.

According to medieval legend, the Apostle St James, son of Zebedee, brought Christianity to the Iberian Peninsula, but his tomb was not 'discovered' till 814 when a hermit named Pelagius saw strange lights in the night sky above a Roman tomb in the forest where he lived. He promptly alerted the local bishop. The bishop decided it must be a miracle indicating the location of the long-lost tomb of St James, and informed the king, Alfonso II, who ordered a shrine be built on the spot and reputedly then visited the shrine as its first pilgrim, thereby establishing its reputation. This shrine was followed by the first church in 829, and a second church in 899, which was then plundered and heavily damaged by al-Mansur (Almanzor), the army commander of the Córdoba caliph, in 997. A great deal of church treasure was carried off, but the tomb and relics were left untouched. Al-Mansur famously forced Christian captives from the raid to carry the cathedral doors and bells as booty to Córdoba where they were displayed in the mosque, but when Ferdinand III of Castile captured Córdoba over two centuries later in 1236, he repaid the ignominy by forcing his Muslim captives to carry them to Toledo, where they were then added to the cathedral of Santa Maria.

Thanks to al-Mansur sparing the tomb and relics, construction began again of the present cathedral, mostly built of granite, in 1075. From this time on, during the eleventh century, pilgrimages to Santiago increased, with considerable support from the Church and the monarchy. Without question, the huge cathedral built over the tomb and the phenomenal cult of the Way of St James, the Camino de Santiago, heavily promoted by the Catholic Church, has, in the words of the on-site guidebook, 'played a key role in the construction of the European identity'.[23] The powerful Benedictine Order, which has controlled the pilgrimage route across the centuries, funded and supervised the building of a series of cathedrals and churches along the Camino between 1000 and 1250, literally hundreds of monuments, using the top craftsmen wherever possible. As a result, the buildings themselves began to display superior vaulting techniques and elaborate decoration which had not been seen in Europe before. In other words, I would argue, the Camino de Santiago itself, despite its largely fanciful past based on medieval legend, brought real change into European architecture, though not in ways that have been generally acknowledged. The UNESCO listing calls it 'a symbol in the Spanish Christians' struggle against Islam',[24] which makes it especially ironic that so many Islamic techniques and decorative elements have found their way into the cathedral.

Later additions and amendments to the building have to some extent obscured the original Romanesque features, but it is among these—the crypt, the nave and its two aisles, the transept, the tribune and rose window and the exterior south facade—that the Islamic influences can still be clearly seen. Approached up a large flight of steps, the tower on the right of this southern facade has tall narrow blind arches and decorative vertical bands, while the double portals of the entrance are recessed with multiple decorative arches, divided by slender columns. Known as Las Platerias (meaning 'the Silversmiths' who used to sell their trinkets here), it is the sole remaining Romanesque facade and entrance, and the portals are mirrored by another pair of recessed arches, also framed by cinquefoil or five-cusped arches like those found in the Córdoba Mezquita. Dividing the upper and lower storeys is an overhanging cornice/lintel supported by corbels made up of a series of heads, mainly of animals.

Nothing is known about the men who built this facade beyond their names, listed in the Codex Calixtinus as 'Bernardus the elder, a wonderful master', and his assistants Robertus Galperinus, Esteban, master of the cathedral works

8.14: The oldest facade of the cathedral of Santiago de Compostela, known as Las Platerias, dates from the late eleventh century and has a double *ajimez*-style entrance, corbels decorated with animal heads, and a pair of Andalusian cinquefoil or five-cusped arches above the doors, like those found in the Córdoba Mezquita.

and, in the final stage, Bernardus the younger, who also built a monumental fountain in front of the north portal in 1122. Bernardus the elder and Robertus are recorded as working with about fifty masons to build the cathedral fabric.[25]

We can assume nothing from the names Robertus, Bernardus and Esteban, since it was normal at this time for Muslims to adopt Christian names to fit into their new environment, or, just as likely, to be given Christian names by their Christian co-workers which were then easier to pronounce. It is also possible that they were either Mozarabs, Arabised Christians who had emigrated from the Emirate of Córdoba, or Mudéjar Muslims who had elected to stay after their towns were conquered by Christians. But whatever their religion or ethnicity, their skills were in high demand in all things, not just for construction but also other areas of craftsmanship like carpentry, luxury textiles, carved ivory, glassware and ceramics, as well as in other cultural fields like literature, music, song, dance and fashion. The reason for this was simple. Arab-Islamic culture in the eleventh century was seen by Latin Europe as far more sophisticated and advanced than their own, and had become synonymous in the Latin imagination with 'chic and refinement'.[26]

On entering through the gate of Las Platerias, today's entrance for pilgrims, you are immediately struck by the tall, thin verticality of the long Romanesque nave, with its original barrel vaults, their transverse arches running right down to the ground into engaged columns which form part of slender composite columns, all designed to emphasise the sense of height. With its wide transept, lateral aisles, groin vaulting and choir with radiating chapels to display the relics, it is the largest Romanesque church in Spain and one of the largest in Europe. According to the 1936 Oxford PhD thesis of British architect Thomas Denny, both the nave and the triforium were the work of Muslim masons.[27] The central chapel in the ambulatory is one of the earliest parts of the cathedral, still in its original state. With arched windows on either side, it has stylish barrel vaulting. Its capitals sport stylised birds and animals in formal poses, such as two-tailed mermaid sirens. Santiago was one of five churches built around the same time with the same design, where pilgrims could walk up the length of the side aisles, round the transept and see the relics in the ambulatory chapels without interrupting services in the main nave. Those at Tours and Limoges have now been demolished, but those at Saint-Sernin de Toulouse and Sainte-Foy in Conques are still extant, and both also show clear Islamic influence with eight-pointed stars and sophisticated vaulting.

Study of the masons' marks (see Chapter 4) proved conclusively that the crypt was the work of the early masters, a construction that was unheard of in Galicia at this point. It is, as the official guidebook explains, 'unique both in shape and in function'. Its inner space is 'of a great architectural complexity, and is organized by a huge pillar comprising eight adjoining columns from which the arches support the vault stem. Moreover, that pillar is the root of the column in the mullion of the Pórtico de la Gloria, located just above.' Again, the sophisticated nature of the vaulting here, at this time, could only have been the work of Muslim engineers who understood this advanced level of geometry and stress loads. The crypt is sometimes called 'the old cathedral' because it is like a self-contained church in its own right, with rib vaulting and very high-quality carving on its capitals, embellished with floral patterns, animals and birds. Where the ribs cross in the ceiling are figures representing the sun and the moon.

Now on display as the highlight and centrepiece in the exhibition space of the Palace of Gelmírez, the famous rose window made of granite *c.*1200 is part of the lost west facade designed by the named architect Master Mateo. It has a striking Islamic design based on eight-pointed stars, repeated as the principal motif eight times round the circle, and intertwined with a continuous ribbon of tell-tale beaded interlacing. It has been adopted as the symbol of Compostela and is known as 'the mirror' or 'the great mirror', installed above the central western doorway to flood the nave with light, both literally and symbolically. Its complex tracery of circles, stars and interlaced ribbons was reconstructed in 1961 from fragments of the missing facade, a piece of jigsaw detective work reminiscent of the reconstruction of the very first rose window in the eighth-century Umayyad palace of Khirbat al-Mafjar, sometimes called Hisham's Palace, near Jericho in Palestine. The souvenir shops

8.15: Copy of the reconstructed rose window from the now lost west facade of the cathedral of Santiago de Compostela, known as 'the Great Mirror', built *c.*1200, used today as a symbol of the city, and based on eight-pointed stars repeated eight times in a circle, intertwined with a ribbon of continuous beaded interlacing. It is thought to be the work of the sculptor known as Master Mateo, who must have been schooled in the Islamic tradition.

are full of imitations of the pattern, in the form of coasters, mouse-mats, mirrors, notebooks and such like. From its design, it can only have been the work of a Muslim stonemason, leading us to conclude that there must have been Muslims amongst Master Mateo's workshop. Indeed, it is not impossible that Mateo could have been a Muslim himself, but adopted the name Mateo, even identifying himself with the St Matthew who is depicted in the portico, bearded, seated, concentrating on a scroll he is writing.

Of all Mateo's work, the most lauded for the sheer audacity of its conception was the Pórtico de la Gloria, the west facade he constructed in 1168–88 above the crypt. Its purpose and the reason for its magnificence was as the landmark to greet weary pilgrims on their final arrival at the shrine of St James, especially as it would originally have been painted in bright colours, hints of which have been recovered by recent restorers. The portico today has had its original function smothered by the eighteenth-century Baroque facade constructed in front of it, in line with the tastes of the time and no doubt considered far more magnificent.

The ensemble consists of over 200 sculptures, based on the Book of Revelation, the final book of the New Testament, with scenes depicting the Apocalypse and the Last Judgement. Recognised worldwide as an astonishing feat of human ingenuity, the portico is considered one of the most important works of Spanish Romanesque. The mullion pillar in the centre depicts the seated figure of St James holding a pilgrim staff. The twenty-four elders of the Apocalypse are shown framing the central arch, all sitting on a low divan and talking in pairs, each tuning a carefully carved instrument. Their instruments bear a close resemblance to those of the courtly musicians in the Fatimid ceiling of the Cappella Palatina, with a variety of stringed lute-like instruments being plucked, one closely resembling an early guitar, harps, various types of percussion like tambourines and castanets and an organistrum (a stringed figure-of-eight instrument played by two people, the earliest hurdy-gurdy or wheel fiddle, derived from the Middle Eastern *rebab*) in pride of place in the keystone. Islamic Iberia by the eleventh century had become a centre for the manufacture of musical instruments, promoted by the court of Córdoba from the ninth century, and the common Romanesque scene of Christ in Majesty surrounded by musicians may derive from courtly images of Islamic rulers being entertained.

Both the Old and the New Testament prophets are shown, and it is widely agreed that the sculptor behind it, Master Mateo, inserted himself as the small kneeling figure of St Matthew at the foot of St James, facing back into the nave. An inscription on the lintel reads that Mateo directed the work 'from

8.16: The sculptor Master Mateo is also credited with the spectacular Pórtico de la Gloria, part of the western facade of Santiago de Compostela cathedral, built in 1166–88 directly above the vaulted crypt. The twenty-four elders of the Apocalypse that form the centrepiece are tuning instruments resembling those of the courtly musicians seen in the Fatimid Cappella Palatina ceiling in Palermo, Sicily.

the foundations'. It is not known who appointed him to work on the cathedral, but there is no doubt that whoever that commissioning supervisor was would have gone to some lengths to find the best mason and sculptor money could buy, and such a mason, with skills at this level and a deep understanding of geometry and vaulting, is most likely to have been found living under the nearby culture of Andalusia, the most sophisticated civilisation in Europe at the time.

Such is the importance of the Pórtico de la Gloria that a full-size copy was commissioned in 1866 and made in situ for London's Victoria and Albert Museum, then shipped from Spain to the V&A with great difficulty after complex negotiations with the local authorities. Its enormous size dictated the width of the V&A's massive Cast Court, especially built for its display in 1873.

The tradition of swinging incense over the body of the church—using the famous *Botafumeiro* attached to the ceiling with a complex series of ropes and pulleys—began in the twelfth century, contemporary with Master Mateo, and was possibly reintroduced to Western Europe by Frankish Crusaders. Incense-burning has a long history in the Middle East, going right back to the ancient Egyptians and the Babylonians, who used incense in mummification rituals and to appease the gods at temples and oracles. The Copts still use it liberally during church services to this day, its properties originally thought to cleanse the building of bad or evil energy. The Fatimids continued the tradition, with the tops of their minarets even capped with what are called incense burners (*mabkhara*) in Arabic, more usually 'pepper pots' in European descriptions. The luxury commodity originated from frankincense trees growing on the mountains of southern Arabia in what is today Oman and Yemen. In one spectacular accident, when Princess Catherine of Aragon was visiting Santiago in 1499 on her way to marry Arthur, Prince of Wales, the eldest son of Henry VII, the *Botafumeiro* broke free from its ropes and flew out through the high window of Las Platerias—an omen maybe.

Aragon

Zaragoza

Al-Jaferia Palace in Zaragoza represents the apogee of Mudéjar art, an Islamic palace first built in 714 on the northern frontier of Andalusia. The style was brought to Spain by the Umayyad princes of Damascus, following models like al-Rusafa in Syria, as well as fine palaces like Raqqada in Tunisia, all of which had their own mosques. At al-Jaferia Mosque the horseshoe arch in the mihrab is flanked by a pair of concave rosettes/fleurons reminiscent of the Fatimid facade of al-Aqmar (1125–6) in Cairo, demonstrating how North African styles and traditions spread and were known to craftsmen in Muslim Spain. The same concave fleuron is then seen in Romanesque churches and cathedrals, most notably at Santiago.

Al-Jaferia's most beautiful rooms date from 1046–82, when it served as the palace of the king, Abu Ja'far Ahmad al-Muqtadir, from whom its current name al-Jaferia comes, though it was known by Abu Ja'far himself simply as 'the Palace of Joy'. As well as pleasure, the palace had a reputation for learning, attracting the finest artists, scientists and intellectuals of the day—be they Arabs or Jews. Abu Ja'far was himself a philosopher king, mathematician, astronomer and poet, composing a love poem to his palace which ended with the words: 'And though my kingdom were bereft of all else, You would be the only thing I would yearn for.'

The local booklet written by the Cortes de Aragón clearly grasps the essentials of Islamic architecture, saying:

> [H]ere we have an architectural style which is very much to the Moslem taste, based on the idea of creating spaces separated by series of archways which multiply in harmony and act as visual screens, creating an optical illusion and presenting the spectator with contrasting effects of light and shade.[28]

It comments on 'the profound tendency to project towards outside spaces', in this case towards the hub of the whole palace, the large central courtyard, and thereby to create 'a work of art that is sensual, if not imbued with a certain theatricality'. Arab texts describe it as a dream palace, its fragrant garden in the centre of the courtyard having a stream 'like a slithering snake', a pool with flowing water, and a pavilion whose ceiling and walls are decorated with gold and lapis lazuli. The whole complex was a much-copied model by the subsequent Almoravid, Almohad and Nasrid dynasties in Muslim Spain and is seen today as 'an indispensable basis for understanding how Andalusi architecture as a whole subsequently evolved'.[29]

Declared a UNESCO World Heritage site in 2001 as part of the category 'Mudéjar Art in Aragon', al-Jaferia Palace has been recently restored and now serves as the Aragonese seat of parliament, a project which has rescued it from ruin and neglect. It has seen many iterations and in the fifteenth century was even used by the Spanish Inquisition as a prison.

UNESCO's listing says that many elements of construction characteristic of Islamic art can be identified in these Aragonese monuments, such as *alfiz* panels, decorated eaves and lattice work. It then comments on how the mate-

8.17: The Patio de Santa Isabel is the largest courtyard of the Zaragoza emiral palace, al-Jaferia, its delicately carved arcaded portico enclosing a fragrant garden and flowing water.

rials used—brick, ceramics, plaster and wood—were chosen in order 'to follow the Islamic philosophy that everything is transitory and impermanent but for Allah, the only being that exists eternally',[30] a statement that is breath-taking in its ignorance, since Mudéjar art also used stone and marble, hardly ephemeral. In another side-stepping of historical reality, the UNESCO entry explains the decline in the Mudéjar tradition thus: 'historical and social factors in the 17th century led to a decline of the Mudéjar tradition and its replacement by other artistic movements such as the Renaissance and Baroque'. This conveniently omits the fact that Islam was outlawed in 1502 by the Crown of Aragon, and that even those who were forcibly converted to Christianity—the Moriscos, a pejorative Spanish word meaning 'Little Moors'—were suspected of being crypto-Muslims and expelled in 1609–14. Ironically, the Mudéjar style became popular again in the nineteenth century, when it was renamed Neo-Mudéjar.

A particular feature of Mudéjar art was its exotic painted wooden ceilings, many of which can be seen in al-Jaferia, decorated with heraldic signs, geometric patterns, plants, animals and people engaged in everyday activities,

Christian religious scenes and the fantastical beasts from the medieval bestiary. The thirteenth-century roof of the cathedral of Santa Maria de Mediavilla in Teruel is another well-known example, where there are scenes of the carpenters themselves busily making the ceiling, as well as biblical scenes. The style and composition of both the Teruel main ceiling and al-Jaferia's Throne Room, with their central decorative motif of eight-petalled flowers framed within eight-pointed stars, clearly demonstrate the continuous tradition that can first be seen on European soil in the painted wooden ceiling of Palermo's Cappella Palatina, dated to *c.*1140.

Al-Jaferia remained in Muslim hands till 1118 when it was captured by Afonso I, King of Portugal, for the Christians. Afonso turned it into the palace of the kings of Aragon and the political centre of Zaragoza, all the while still using local Mudéjar craftsmen. In 1301 the title of 'Master Builder of the Palace Works' was conferred on Mahomat Bellito, son of Jucef Bellito, who had held the title before him, illustrating how the skills were still passed down through Muslim families as late as the fourteenth century. When the Catholic monarchs Ferdinand and Isabella in turn took it over as their palace *c.*1492, they too appointed a Mudéjar chief master builder, Faraig de Galí, for life, whose son Mahoma de Galí then took over the position, not only for al-Jaferia but for all royal buildings in Aragon, a fact which seems to prove that no Christian master builder, even two centuries later, could rival such Muslim skill and building expertise.

9

GERMANIC ISLAMESQUE

The final three chapters, on Germany, France and Britain respectively, move from southern Europe, where Islamic rule had been endemic in large areas for centuries, across the Alps and the Pyrenees into northern Europe.

It has tended to be the usual reaction among European art historians, when confronted with a building in a style they did not recognise, and built in a way they struggled to explain, to attribute it to Byzantium or sometimes 'the East' and to leave it at that. But if progress such as complex vaulting based on the pointed arch was attributable to Byzantium, why had it not already happened sooner, closer to Byzantium or within Byzantium itself? The reality is that in Byzantium the arch had remained essentially the same, unchanged for centuries from what it had been under the Roman Empire, a rounded structure held together by mortar.

Likewise overlooked in this debate about the origins of Romanesque architecture is that, in addition to the import of top masons from the Islamic world by rulers for their prestige projects, there were also communities of Muslims living not only in France and Spain, but also in parts of the Rhineland in Germany and in Switzerland from as early as the ninth century, and that individual itinerant Muslims would have been present in these regions even earlier, since large communities already existed in the Iberian Peninsula, Sicily and southern Italy from the mid-700s.

Crossing the Mountains

By 930, 'the Saracens', as the Christian chroniclers called them (there is not a single contemporary account from the Muslim side that has yet been found), were well established in some northern Italian towns like Vercelli in the foothills of the Alps, from where they also controlled several north–south passes through the Alps, including the Great St Bernard. They pushed north of the Alps, and the Bishopric of Chur in the upper reaches of the Rhine Valley was sacked at least once, as was the great Abbey of St Gall near Lake Constance in 954, the same year that Grenoble to the west in France also fell to the Saracens. This seems to have been the high point of Saracen power in the Western European heartlands. The major reason for the ease of the Saracen conquest, so chroniclers tell us, was the disunity among the large number of Catholic petty princes, dukes and other nobility in these areas, some of whom even allied with the Muslims in order to gain the upper hand over their rivals. Hugh of Italy (r.926–47), for example, originally count of Arles in the Kingdom of Provence, entered into an alliance with the Saracens, giving them control over all the Alpine passes from the west to the east.

The German historian Manfred Wenner puts forward a plausible theory that the Saracens, rather than being defeated and driven out by the Christians, withdrew voluntarily from this area round the Alps after a change in policy by the Caliphate of Córdoba following the death of the caliph Abd al-Rahman III in 961, and the ascension of his son al-Hakam II, who by all accounts was a lot more peaceful and tolerant than his father. He may have refused to support the continued harassment of Christian Europe, which could explain why the Saracen presence appeared to melt away soon after 961. For the hundred years before that, however, when the Saracens were present, they did leave behind some traces at a time when, as Wenner points out, 'one of the most important geographical regions of Europe was only infrequently under the control of the indigenous Christian population'.[1]

Switzerland

Very little research into the Saracen legacy in Switzerland has been undertaken, but there are signs of Saracen occupation in concentrations of Arabic-derived place names in areas where they are known to have lived and the extraordinarily large number of place names beginning with al-, the Arabic definite article 'the', like Almagell, Albula, Albana and Albris. Other place names contain variations of the word 'Moor', like the Monte Moro on the Swiss–Italian border.

There is a local legend in one of the Rhône valleys that a particular variety of local grape was introduced by the Saracens when they settled there. Its local name is still *Heidenwein*, German for 'heathen wine'. During his field research of the 1970s,[2] Wenner was struck by the unusual characteristics of the population in the Saas Valley, an isolated valley which runs southward from the Rhône at the town of Visp and ends at Saas-Almagell in a relatively little-used pass, which leads to the similarly isolated Anza Valley in Italy (at the town of Macugnaga, known today as a ski resort). In the Saas Valley he found a remarkably high percentage of names which had a Middle Eastern or North African flavour to them; that the local people still refused to keep or raise pigs, despite the fact that pork was an almost traditional meat source for the population of the other Rhône valleys; and that they practised a particular method of sheep slaughtering for meat consumption. The Saas Valley has a noticeable lack of trees, which would conform with Saracen methods of clearing land for agricultural cultivation. Many writers have found evidence that a substantial amount of settlement and intermarriage with the local population took place—both in France and in Switzerland—during the period of hundred-year Saracen dominance of the area.[3]

Place names like Pontresina (from Pons Saracenorum), an important town on the Bernina Pass road, are not disputed by scholars, all of whom agree that the name comes from the Latin descriptive name, 'Bridge of the Saracens', a bridge which is recorded as having been erected there by the Saracens in the tenth century. A common family name in the area—Sarraz—is associated with a coat of arms containing a clear depiction of a bridge. There are also plenty of other place names—Château Sarrasin, Pont des Sarrasins—as well as the names of some small villages in western Switzerland as far north as the Berner Jura (La Sarraz), which could be assumed to have their origins in the Saracen invasions, especially as these names only appear locally from the tenth century.[4]

Most medieval European sources depict the Saracens as brutal or inhuman, but one contemporary account, by a traveller in the northern Italian hilltown of Vercelli, describes the Saracens as living within and among the local population in a manner which led him to assume they were well established: 'The Saracens neither carried arms nor were they molested by the local populace; indeed, they were apparently administering the town and the surrounding countryside with a "light hand".'[5] Ludovic Slimak, an archaeologist with the University of Toulouse and France's National Centre for Scientific Research, having studied patterns of settlement across Europe, said that 'All populations when they establish a "colony", create social networks and alliances with the locals, which is usually accomplished by exchanging women.' He concluded: 'Our old assumption must be completely reviewed and we have to rewrite the story of the colonization of Europe and the relationship between Europe and the Near East.'[6]

Despite the rather negative image of Arabs which is currently prevalent in Switzerland, one well-respected nineteenth-century local Swiss historian not only specifically acknowledged some Saracenic antecedents for the population, but also that they contributed substantially to making the entire Saas Valley cultivable.[7] He contended that the renowned Camargue horses were bred by the Arabs from Spain, and that it was even possible they had their origins in runaways from earlier Saracen campaigns into southern France in the early eighth century.

Carolingian Prototypes

Before focusing on a few specific examples of German Romanesque, it is worth taking a brief look at the earlier Carolingian architecture, often cited as a prototype for Romanesque. The Carolingian Empire (800–87), named after Charlemagne, King of the Franks from 768, King of the Lombards from 774 and Holy Roman Emperor from 800, had its heartland in what is roughly today's France, then known as Francia, and reached east across to the Rhine and south into Italy, while bordering the Emirate of Córdoba in the south.

Charlemagne was the first leader to unite central and western Europe in over 300 years and is on record as being a great builder. His secretary and biographer, Eginhard, tells us that the great emperor repaired the churches throughout his dominions, many of which had fallen into disrepair, but he only mentions two specific buildings: the Palatine Chapel at Charlemagne's capital, Aachen, 'constructed with wondrous workmanship',[8] and a bridge over the Rhine at Moguntiacum (Mainz), which has not survived since it was made of wood.

Searching for an architectural statement to cement his political and religious power, a building unlike anything that Europe had seen before, he commissioned his palace and chapel at Aachen, sparing no expense. He is on record as sending for the top craftsmen and the top materials, and Thomas Graham Jackson, writing in 1913, comments on its 'exotic' appearance, a work clearly of 'foreign origin'.[9] The architectural inspiration is known to have come from Ravenna, specifically the sixth-century octagonal domed church of San Vitale, visited three times by Charlemagne, a city with long-standing religious and commercial links to Antioch in Syria, where most bishops of Ravenna, including their patron saint Apollinaris, had come from.[10]

Syria and Palestine had a long tradition of dome architecture, and the likelihood is that given these strong connections between Antioch and Ravenna, stonemasons would have been brought to Ravenna from Syria, where such stonework was used in contemporary buildings.[11] Ravenna later served as a convenient quarry, the reason why its Palace of Theodoric stands today as a ruin without ornamentation. Theodoric's tomb in Ravenna also stands as a testament to Syrian stonemasonry, even sporting a joggled voussoir over its lintel, better to carry the massive weight.

As to the identity of Charlemagne's Aachen craftsmen, the clues, as ever, are embedded in the building. The only name recorded is 'Odo of Metz', mentioned in some sources as the master mason or architect. Metz was the first Carolingian capital before Aachen, so the name Odo of Metz probably just meant that Metz was where Odo was first based, not that he was a native of Metz. He is sometimes said to be of Armenian origin, because of a Latin inscription said to have been found in the Aachen dome stating that he came from 'the Land of Noah's Ark'.[12] Since the much closer and more familiar sacred Canigou mountain in the eastern Pyrennees was believed by local Catalan tradition to be not only the starting place but also the resting place of the Ark,[13] rather than the biblical Mount Ararat which stands on today's Turkish/Iranian/Armenian border, it is perfectly possible that Odo came from Catalonia, at that time under Muslim rule. Another reason for the supposed Armenian origin stems from the fact that some art historians have seen at the Aachen Chapel similarities with Armenian church architecture. However, as respected Islamic art historian Oleg Grabar explains, Armenian and Islamic architecture were heavily influenced by each other from early on,[14] as were Byzantine and Islamic architecture throughout the Abbasid period. Barrel vaults and domes on squinches, for example, became standard in Byzantine architecture only after being adopted from Islamic models, and the chapel in Aachen is the first vaulted structure north of the Alps since antiquity, according to the UNESCO website.[15]

There was also a thriving Carolingian–Abbasid alliance during the eighth and ninth centuries, based on shared interests and mutual enemies. Charlemagne nurtured the relationship, seeking close links with the Abbasid caliph Haroun al-Rashid (r.786–809) in Baghdad, whom he saw as a natural ally against his Christian rival, the Byzantine emperor in Constantinople, while the Abbasid caliph in turn saw Charlemagne as a natural ally against his own Muslim rivals, the Umayyads in Córdoba.

The two men, despite being theoretical enemies, courted each other with luxury gifts, the most famous of which was an elephant, to which Charlemagne was reportedly devoted, naming it Abu al-Abbas after the caliph. Historian Philip Hitti tells us that Haroun al-Rashid was undoubtedly more powerful than Charlemagne, and represented the higher culture. Immortalised through the fabulous stories of 'The Thousand and One Nights', he was a lavish patron of the arts and sciences during the Islamic Golden Age. Highly educated him-

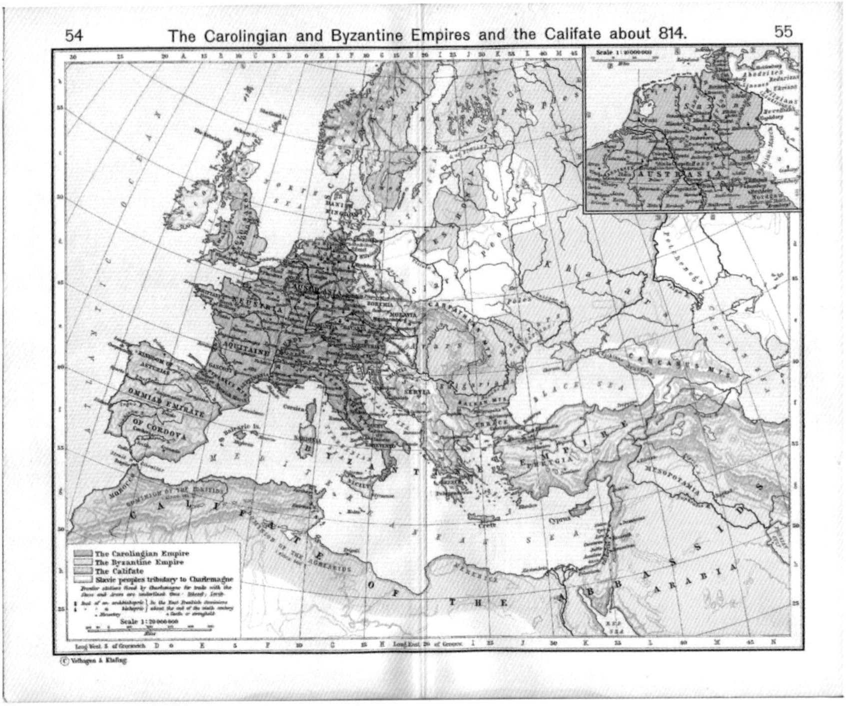

9.1: Map showing the extent of the contemporary Carolingian, Byzantine and Abbasid empires *c*.814. Charlemagne and the caliph Haroun al-Rashid had an alliance against their mutual enemies, the Byzantines and the Spanish Umayyads.

self, he encouraged learning through the translation of Greek and Persian texts into Arabic, at a time when Charlemagne and his lords, along with the rest of the European aristocracy, were largely illiterate, 'reportedly dabbling in the art of writing their names'.[16]

The fact that Islamic artistic influences start to appear in Christian religious architecture around the year 800, such as the contrasting black-and-white two-tone *ablaq* patterning of the Aachen Chapel arches, is unlikely to be mere coincidence. The exchange of embassies and gifts is documented in contemporary Western sources as taking place between 796 and 806, exactly the time when the Aachen Chapel was being built. The most plausible explanation therefore for the sudden appearance of Islamic features in the Aachen Chapel is that the caliph, as well as sending the elephant and other exotica, also sent Charlemagne a team of his top masons, who brought in their own styles, not seen before by European eyes. Charlemagne's relations with Byzantium were hostile throughout this period, with no such exchange of gifts or offer of Byzantine craftsmen. The evidence, as ever, is on view in the building itself.

Several years before the Aachen Palatine Chapel (792–805), the Córdoba Mezquita (785) had been built in Andalusia by Abd al-Rahman to mark his own conquests, employing the top Muslim craftsmen, many of them from Umayyad Syria, where skill in stonemasonry was literally as old as the limestone hills which formed the country's main building material. Charlemagne had crossed the Pyrenees in 778 when he was invited by a dissident Muslim faction to help fight against Abd al-Rahman, the Córdoba ruler, but after failing to take Zaragoza, his retreating army was defeated by Basque forces. It was the only significant defeat Charlemagne ever suffered in his military career.

The battle itself was romanticised by Christian oral tradition into a major conflict between Christians and Muslims, never mind the fact that the Basques of the period were mainly pagans and Charlemagne had been allied to some of the Muslims. In the tradition, the Basques were replaced by a force of 400,000 Saracens, and even though the Frankish military leader Roland died in the battle, he was popularised as a medieval chivalric hero of honour. *The Song of Roland*, written centuries later by an unknown poet between 1100 and 1120 to commemorate the battle from the Christian viewpoint, is the earliest surviving *chanson de geste*, or epic poem, of the troubadour culture of medieval France, a culture that had its roots in the Hispano-Arabic traditions of Andalusia through *The Ring of the Dove*, the influential book on courtly love written by Ibn Hazm (994–1064), a polymath and poet at the Córdoba court.[17] The French and German minstrels, like the *Minnesänger*, strummed their tunes on lutes descended from the Arab *'oud*. Kenneth Clark, too, while examining the enigmatic tapestries of the ever-popular 'Lady and the Unicorn' series at the Cluny Museum in Paris, wonders about the concepts of courtly love and chivalry that appeared in Europe towards the end of the Romanesque period. 'How did it begin?' he asks, before answering: 'The truth is that no one knows. But most people think that, like the pointed arch, it came from the East, and that pilgrims and Crusaders found in the Muslim world a tradition of Persian literature in which women were the subject of extravagant compliments and devotion.'[18] He links this phenomenon with the rise of the cult of the Virgin Mary in Gothic architecture, which at this point takes over from the Christ in Majesty theme that had dominated the portals of Romanesque cathedrals.

Together with the Knights of the Round Table in Britain, Roland and the Paladins (the twelve legendary knights of Charlemagne's court) have become archetypal icons of chivalry in Europe, their stories greatly influencing knightly culture and inspiring many Christian warriors that came after. During the Battle of Hastings in 1066, knights and soldiers under William the Conqueror chanted the poem to inspire themselves in their fight against the Anglo-Saxons.

Had Charlemagne ever entered Zaragoza, he would have seen with his own eyes the Moorish king's palace, al-Jaferia, with its own exquisitely decorated octagonal mosque, complete with an arcaded gallery of arches beneath the dome. The architecture of the earlier octagonal mosque is so similar in conception to that at Aachen, and indeed to the contemporary Carolingian Oratory of Germigny-des-Prés in central France, where many Muslim features have been noted, including in the mosaic decoration with its frieze of eight-pointed stars,[19] that it is impossible not to make the connection. Germigny-des-Prés was likewise associated with Odo of Metz, more evidence that the said Odo was likely to have originally been from Andalusia, or at the very least that he employed craftsmen from Muslim Spain, especially since Bishop Theodulf (750–821), the commissioner of Germigny-des-Prés, his own private chapel, was originally from Muslim Zaragoza. Andalusian horseshoe arches are used throughout the chapel.

9.2: The Carolingian Oratory of Germigny-des-Prés in what is today central France has Islamic features like a frieze of eight-pointed stars in its dome, in turn supported on an arcade of horseshoe arches.

A little earlier than Charlemagne's Palatine Chapel at Aachen, the equally curious and atypical gatehouse at Lorsch near Worms, thought to have been part of the famous Benedictine Lorsch Abbey, a monastery dedicated in the presence of Charlemagne in 774, stands as another testament to Islamic influence. Originally a two-storey hall, its facades are decorated in Islamic-style polychromy, chequerboard patterns of red and white lozenges and squares, topped with blank zigzag arcades, using the local red sandstone. Jackson observes that this 'extremely curious little building' shows 'in the execution of the carving a skill and knowledge superior to the local talent of the Germany of these days and betraying a Byzantine, or Italo-Byzantine hand', yet whose 'strange design of the upper storey shows no affinity with the art of the Exarchate or the East'.[20] In 1053 it was consecrated as a chapel, and its Norman-style zigzags and Romanesque capitals must date from that time.

9.3: The Carolingian gatehouse of the Benedictine Lorsch Abbey, southern Germany, shows striking Islamic influence in its geometric chequerboard pattern of lozenges and squares in the local red sandstone, topped with a zigzag blind arcade.

German Romanesque

The predominant influences on German, Swiss and Swedish Romanesque all entered from the south, travelling across the Alps, inspired by the north Italian examples, then up into the important trading communities on the great waterways of the Rhine, from where the style spread widely further north, often via other navigable rivers. The most brilliant examples appeared in the great Rhineland churches of Cologne, Worms, Mainz and Speyer, all of which were in close commercial contact with the Lombard cities, and so we find the same arcaded galleries, tall towers and blind arches seen earlier in Milan, Pavia, Como, Lucca and Pisa.

The Rhineland produced some of the most adventurous and sophisticated architecture of the Romanesque era, from great urban cathedrals to remote monasteries. Wealthy abbeys, burgeoning cities and ambitious princes and emperors instigated buildings of unprecedented size and magnificence. The same Islamic influences can be seen in these massive monuments as have been described earlier in the chapters on Sicily (Chapter 6) and Italy (Chapter 7), influences that had already crept up the boot of Italy from Sicily and Calabria in the south, into Lombardy and northern Italy, and which now crossed the Alps. The huge constructions and noble simplicity of form often masked a high degree of structural adventurousness and very considerable sophistication of design, symbolism and iconography. Many German churches suddenly boasted high towers and spires, complex ground plans and evidence of bold experiments in engineering. Inside Worms Cathedral, the vaulting is noteworthy, especially in the dome, which starts with a spherical pendentive that suddenly changes into a squinch arch to support the octagonal dome. The twelfth-century Strasbourg synagogue is modelled on Worms Cathedral, following the Moorish styles from Spain.

The tower of Cologne's St Columba has the familiar *ajimez* windows increasing towards the top and the same Venetian dentil decorating the different storeys at ceiling height; while the huge Abbey of Maria Laach in the Eifel region, built from the local lava, has cloister capitals decorated with interlacing foliage studded with the tell-tale beading, as does the carving on the west door at Boppard's church of St Severus. Despite the sheer scale and height of these churches and their tall towers, none of them used flying buttresses, suggesting that the vaulting must have been very advanced.

Speyer Cathedral

Speyer Cathedral (1030–61), built on a plateau directly overlooking the Rhine, is historically, artistically and architecturally one of the most signifi-

9.4: Strasbourg's twelfth-century synagogue is modelled on Worms Cathedral, with its tall round towers, arcaded galleries, Venetian dentil and high *ajimez* windows.

cant examples of Romanesque architecture in Europe, and the largest till it was superseded by the third and final abbey church of Cluny (Cluny III), built 1088–1130. UNESCO inscribed Speyer on their World Heritage Site list in 1981. After Cluny III was demolished during the French Revolution, Speyer Cathedral became once more the largest Romanesque church in the world. Even today only the Gothic cathedral of Cologne, built between 1248 and 1880, is larger. When construction on Speyer began in 1030, Christendom was still united, but the churches of East and West, the Orthodox and the Catholic, were split by the Great Schism in 1054. Then, 500 years later, the Christian West split once more during the Reformation. Pope John Paul II gave a sermon outside the cathedral in 1987, and spoke of the way it is interwoven with the history of Europe like no other building on the continent, and has witnessed the splendours of a common European culture in the realms of faith, science and art.

As well as its sheer size, it is also a forerunner, due to the modifications made to the ceiling vaulting between 1080 and 1106, in what came to be

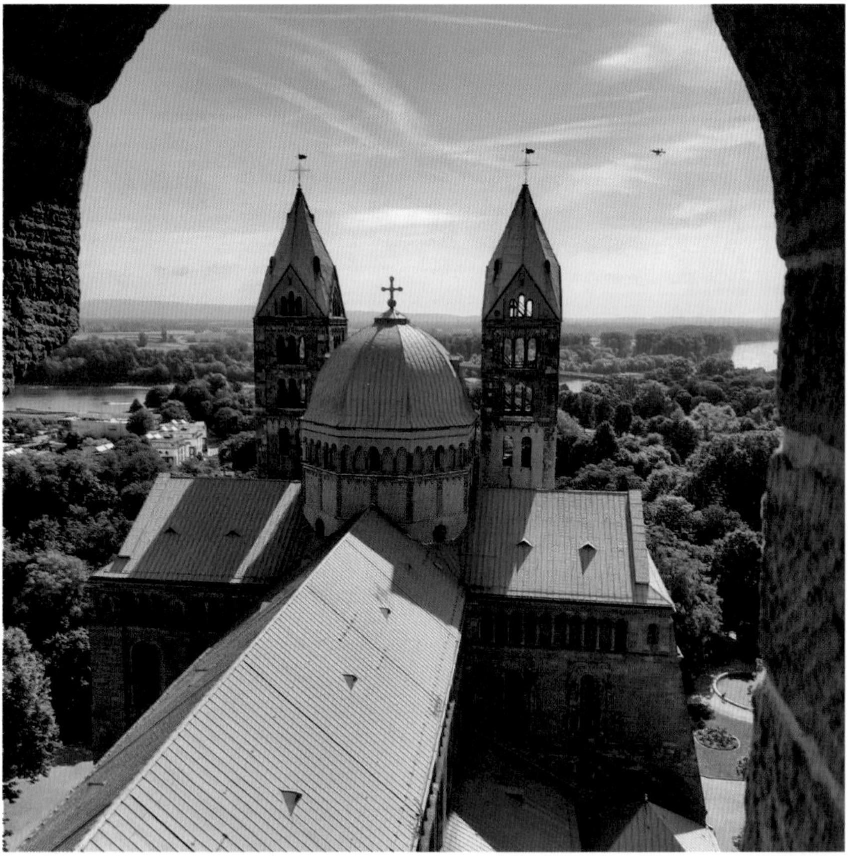

9.5: The vast eleventh-century cathedral of Speyer towers above the Rhine in southern Germany, still today one of the largest cathedrals in the world, with many decorative features derived from earlier Islamic models, such as arcaded dwarf galleries, two-tone stonework, tall blind arches, Venetian dentil, zigzags and *ajimez* windows.

known as Speyer II, the first to use the 'integrated system' whereby one vault of the central nave connected to the two side aisles. The other innovation was the arcaded dwarf gallery which runs under the roof around the whole cathedral, and which was subsequently copied by later Romanesque buildings including the Tower of Pisa.

But while all people, famous churchmen and politicians alike, talk of Speyer Cathedral in terms of a great European achievement, a monument to Europe's greatness, and one of the most important symbols for a united Europe available to us today, not once is there any acknowledgement of what lies behind this architectural achievement.

The place to begin is to examine the reason for these sudden, dramatic and massive innovations, less than twenty years after the first building, Speyer I, had been consecrated. The improvement works were carried out at the command of the future Holy Roman Emperor, Henry IV. Roughly a third of the cathedral was rebuilt, after first reducing the apse and whole main area of the church to ground level. The wooden ceiling of the central nave was replaced by stone arched vaulting. Henry's motivations are thought to have been political. Sharing his predecessors' imperial self-image as the protector of the church, Henry refused to accept the Pope's decree drawing a distinction between secular and spiritual power, and therefore resolved to use all means available to him to revitalise this building which most symbolised imperial responsibility for the Church.

The technical developments in construction and architecture between Konrad II's Speyer I (1030–61) and Henry IV's Speyer II modifications (1080–1106) are clearly visible in the two walls of the crossing, where the southeastern wall of Speyer I is the same thickness throughout, made up of irregularly hewn small ashlars and covered with a mud plaster, with the windows simply openings in the wall. The northern wall of Speyer II, on the other hand, is built quite differently: ornately structured, with three horizontal colour tones, two rows of windows and two openings for chapels at ground level. These chapels were created solely by hollowing out the wall and are not visible as individual rooms from the outside. In the corners and middle of the wall, a vertical pilaster runs from floor to ceiling and the stones are smooth and regularly hewn, so did not require plastering to disguise the poor construction technique of the earlier Speyer I. The whole structure—the transept, the square choir, the apse, the central tower and the flanking towers—was brought together into one harmonious building in an entirely new way. In that unity of vision, it resembles the same overall conception as a mosque, and was evidently the creation of one mastermind. As such, it became the model that would be copied at Mainz and at Worms.

Henry IV knew that there were no local architects or masons capable of constructing such a revolutionary new structure, but he must have heard of the new techniques, or maybe even seen them used in buildings elsewhere. He delegated the task to bishops Benno of Osnabrück and Otto of Bamberg, who in turn recruited stonemasons from Lombardy, the top craftsmen of their age. During the period of high architectural activity, a Jewish community settled in Speyer.[21] They were granted significant privileges by Bishop Rüdiger Huzmann and Emperor Henry IV and were protected by Bishop Johannes I from the anti-Jewish pogrom of the First Crusade in 1096. Towards the end of the construction phase in 1110, the Lombardic stonemasons were also involved in building the synagogue and the Jewish baths.

It is also significant that at the same time as the Speyer II construction, from 1088 onwards, the huge new monastic church at Cluny III was being built, designed to be just a few feet longer than Speyer Cathedral. From 1106 onwards, the new emperor Henry V continued the modifications begun by his father twenty-six years earlier by completing the towers. At the time of his death in 1125, the construction was complete. Along with Santiago de Compostela (begun 1075), Cluny III (begun 1088) and Durham Cathedral (begun 1093), it was the most ambitious project of its day. The red sandstone for the building came from the nearby mountains of the Palatine Forest and is thought to have been shipped down the local stream to the Rhine directly to Speyer itself. The closeness of the stream may well have influenced the choice of location, on the hill overlooking the Rhine, well above the high-water mark.

Speyer I had taken thirty-one years to complete, while the infinitely more complex structures of Speyer II only took twenty-six years, which again tells us something about the high level of skill, competence and experience of the masons and craftsmen employed on its construction. Their grasp of vaulting, stresses and geometry was the most advanced of the time, and they understood that walls only needed to be thick in places where weight was carried, and that lighter walls made the foundations more stable. This realisation enabled the ornate arcaded dwarf gallery to be built directly below the roof, an innovation that in turn led ultimately to all the subsequent innovations of so-called Gothic architecture, where the walls are reduced to pointed arches and filled with large stained-glass windows. The astonishing geometric harmony is apparent the moment you step inside the tall, slender nave, with its surprisingly delicate round engaged columns rising all the way to the top of the wall and then continuing seamlessly round into the twelve ribs of the groin-vaulted ceiling. The only other contemporary example of such a bay system is in the beautifully crafted stonework of the church of Sant Vicenç in Cardona, Spain, completed in 1040, using similar rounded arches running down the piers as pilasters and covered in stone groin vaults, which again gives clues as to where this vaulting expertise came from.

Speyer's double-bay vaulting system was copied in many monuments along the Rhine. The addition of groin vaults made the incorporation of clerestory windows possible without weakening the structure.

Apart from the overall unified harmony of the building, there are several striking features which are recognisable from earlier Islamic architecture, starting with the use of two-tone alternating stonework, both inside and out.

9.6: The vaulting of Speyer Cathedral was extremely advanced for its time, with a new integrated system whereby one vault connected the central nave to the side aisles. Its dome is supported on Islamic-style squinches and ringed with blind arcades.

It appears in the arches of the crypt and the nave, in this case red and yellow from the local sandstone. The central dome rests on squinches. Then, on the exterior, there are the *ajimez* windows in the towers, the tall blind arches, the blind arcades and the so-called Venetian dentil. The carving high up on the bands beneath the roof, especially running round the transepts, in style is all vegetal and geometric, with a framed frieze of palmettes below the cornices. The high exterior windows on the south and east walls of the south transept are flanked by elegant slender colonettes, and elaborately carved in decorative continuous bands of vine leaves and grapes, in which birds and a rabbit are entangled, with a pair of animals fighting each other. Framing the foliage bands are a continuous pearled/beaded border (German *Perlstab*) and a continuous spiral border.

The massive 7-metre-high vaulted crypt, like the cathedral itself, is the biggest Romanesque crypt in the world, begun in 1030 and consecrated in 1041. Even the guidebooks talk of 'the splendid rhythm of the pillars, hewn of red and white sandstone' and the atmosphere of 'awed silence' and harmony. The construction is like a hall divided into four rooms, centred round a square room beneath the crossing, divided into nine three-by-three bays, a construction emphasised by the ceiling vaults supported on their enormous round pillars.

Evolution of Capitals

The crypt has simple cushion capitals, a feature not found in England till *c.*1080, when they appear in the ambulatory of St John's Chapel in William the Conqueror's Tower of London. It also has scallop capitals, a slightly more complex development. Trefoil scallop capitals, a further advance which first appear at Henry I's Reading Abbey (founded 1121), very elegant and striking, seem to grow organically from the octagonal shafts supporting them. The next evolution in capitals was the waterleaf and flat leaf designs, commonly found in French Cistercian abbeys like Pontigny (1114) before spreading to Cistercian monasteries in England like Fountains Abbey in North Yorkshire (1132). From there the waterleaf capital design spread to every county in England, before dying out around 1200 and being replaced with stiff-leaf forms of capital. Naturalistic as opposed to highly stylised foliage did not begin to appear on church capitals in Europe until well into the thirteenth century, at places like Reims and Naumburg, and what is clear, looking at these waterleaf and stiff-leaf capitals, is that they are all derived from the highly stylised lotus capitals, some in bud, some in leaf, of ancient Egyptian temples, as seen in Karnak and Philae, and then taken over into Coptic then Fatimid motifs. Capitals with highly stylised waterleaf designs, representing nature and rebirth like the lotus, are clearly seen in the mosques of North Africa like Kairouan, and then again in the original Fatimid architecture that survives on Sicily, as at the Baths of Cefalà Diana in the mountains southwest of Palermo.

The Speyer nave capitals and the capitals in St Emmeram's Chapel (today's baptismal chapel), both dating to c.1100, have evolved into much more elaborately carved foliage, each carrying four bands, each different, and each separated by its own frame. Some are in leaf shapes, some in eight-pointed flowers or stars, or in endlessly scrolling arabesques of interwoven foliage.

The Sacred *Waldrapp*

During the 1999 restoration, the cathedral's construction team decided to take the opportunity to make a copy of a bird sculpture found high up on the uppermost capitals of the nave. About the size of a goose, in German it is called *Waldrapp Geronticus*. Perched in the foliage with its clawed feet holding tight to the stem below, the bird is turning its head backwards and plucking at its raised wing with its long thin beak. Its body and tail are covered with scaly feathers.

The original pair of *Waldrapps* sit so high up in the nave that it is hard to make them out at all from ground level, but their placement there was not random. There was always a meaning in these choices, especially here, where there are no other creatures in the carving, only vegetal forms.

German researchers looked into the origins of this strange bird and concluded that it was a bald ibis, native to Europe till the sixteenth century. Nine hundred years ago when it was sculpted into the Speyer sandstone they were still abundant, but they were later hunted to extinction for their tasty meat, especially the young who were served as delicacies at the banquets of European nobles.

In ancient Egypt they were seen as holy birds, like the sacred ibis, carriers of the souls of the dead, their distinctive shape serving as a hieroglyphic sign for 'blessed ancestor spirits'. Given their location so high up and on either side of the nave, they may well have had similar associations in medieval Germany, carefully positioned there to carry the soul upwards into heaven.

Today there are reintroduction programmes for the *Waldrapp* in Germany, Austria and Spain, and there are also plans to reintroduce the species in Morocco, where they used to nest high up in cliffs in the Atlas Mountains. In

June 2023 one pair was sighted nesting near Zurich Airport with two young, the first recorded breeding pair in Switzerland for over 400 years. They were tracked from the German reintroduction project at Überlingen.[22]

The *Waldrapps* are reminiscent of the pair of similar birds in a similar location on either side of the nave capitals at the ruined Abbey of Jumièges, where they are carved in limestone and still bear some of their original painted colours, mainly reds and yellows.

The sculpture at Speyer, the sharpness of the edges, is among the highest quality in Germany for the time. As well as birds, leaves, foliage and vines, there are fantastical beasts like dragons.

Cistercian Abbey of Eusserthal

Bernard of Clairvaux, founder of the Cistercian Order, favoured remote locations for his monasteries, away from the distractions of the cities, and not far from Speyer, tucked at the end of an enclosed valley and surrounded by the pine forests of the Rhineland-Palatinate, is all that remains of the once extensive Cistercian Abbey of Eusserthal (1148). It still serves as the Catholic church for the village. The monks worked as chaplains at the nearby Trifels Castle (where Richard the Lionheart was briefly imprisoned) and guarded the imperial jewels which were stored there. Built from the same local red sandstone as Speyer, St Bernard would have approved of its magnificent, austere vaulting, simple zigzag arches and lack of decorative sculpture—except that even here, an endearing dragon-like monster lurks in the northern side chapel. The prize possession of the church is a tiny relic of St Bernard himself, part of his jawbone, displayed behind a grille set into the wall beside the altar.

Hildesheim

Of all Germany's Romanesque churches in the north of the country, special mention must be made of St Michael's Church at Hildesheim, not far from Hanover, and its Islamesque features. The round towers of this ancient Benedictine abbey church have *ajimez* twin windows and the interior has a simple barrel vault with red and white alternating stonework on its main nave arches and the arches of its side aisles. The undersides of the side aisle arches are decorated with arabesque foliage designs, each one different, no symmetry, and the capitals are likewise decorated with a range of floral patterns.

The painted wooden ceiling is thought to depict the Tree of Jesse, the ancestral line of Jesus, and is dated between 1220 and 1240. The clues to Islamic workmanship, as ever, can be seen in the frame, which has a continuous frieze of lozenge shapes, inside which is a further frame of roundels, each with a figure

9.7: The village church is all that remains of the Cisterican Abbey of Eusserthal in the Rheinland-Palatinate, displaying zigzag-framed blind arches and austere but geometrically perfect vaulting. It boasts a tiny relic from the jawbone of Bernard of Clairvaux, co-founder of the Cistercian Order.

inside, while the central area has a series of different shaped framed figures, including circles, diamonds and quatrefoils, each containing a different king.

The same characteristics are shared by the other rare surviving Romanesque painted wooden ceiling that can be seen at St Martin's Church in Zillis, Switzerland. Dated to 1110, it consists of 153 painted wooden squares with mythical images, biblical scenes and episodes from the life of St Martin of Tours. The ceiling has been restored but was never overpainted, so the

9.8: One of only four medieval painted wooden ceilings to have survived in Europe, the ceiling at St Michael's Church in Hildesheim, northern Germany, shows the characteristic Islamic use of frames in various shapes—lozenges, quatrefoils and round medallions—together with an outer frame of continuous running lozenges.

frames of each square are as originally devised, enclosed within friezes of arabesque foliage, merlons, interlacing bands and eight-pointed stars. Each frieze is different and random, with no discernible pattern or symmetry.

Still at Hildesheim, the cathedral, built between 1010 and 1020, has *ajimez* twin windows high up in its towers along with arched arcades, tall narrow arches in its transept and high zigzag arches in its aisles, recessed arches in the main portal and a rose window. Its cloister, built from 1060 to 1070, has an upper storey of delicate triple-arched windows with slender columns. The cathedral's treasures include two of the four notable Romanesque wheel chandeliers, the Hezilo and the Azelin, richly decorated with openwork foliage and merlons and designed to hold seventy-two candles. The others are in Aachen Cathedral, attributed to Frederick Barbarossa (1122–1190), and Hartwig's chandelier in the Abbey of Comburg, also from the twelfth century. The design and concept of the wheel chandelier are derived from the Fatimids of Egypt. When the Fatimid palace was looted in Cairo in 1068–9, 50,000 dinars' worth of chandeliers, censers and ornamental objects were found, since the palace combined the roles of royal treasure house and royal necropolis, with tombs of the first Fatimid caliphs.[23] Today, a bronze Fatimid wheel chandelier can still be seen in Kairouan's Raqqada Museum of Islamic Art, dating to the tenth/eleventh century and belonging to a series of eight found in the Great Mosque of Kairouan, decorated with a stylised vine-leaf motif commonly used in North African art at that time. Similar chandeliers have been found in Egypt, Syria and especially in Spain, where the technique seems to have been taken up by Spanish Christians, as there is a similar chandelier from a Spanish church in London's British Museum.

Belgium

Tournai Cathedral in today's Belgium stands as a link between the Romanesque styles of northern France and Germany. Its nave was dedicated in 1066 and the nave pillars have half-columns on all four sides. The capitals are richly carved with interlacing foliage, grotesque animals, knots and twists of various kinds; much elaborated and highly finished, they are of a much more advanced style than one would expect at such an early date. There are similar capitals at the contemporary churches of William the Conqueror at Caen.[24]

Sweden

The work of the Lombard Comacene masons has been traced as far north as Lund Cathedral, one of the oldest stone buildings still in use in Sweden. Lund belonged to Denmark at the time of its construction in 1145, and the cathedral represents the most powerful example of Romanesque architecture in the Nordic countries.

Its architecture shows clear influences from contemporary north Italian architecture, conveyed via the Rhine Valley, and was richly decorated with stone sculpture on its capitals.

Their work has also been seen at Königslutter, some 70 kilometres east of Hildesheim, where the trefoil portal has one spiral column and one zigzag column resting on the backs of squatting lions and the capitals have heads spewing palmette-type foliage, all elements of Islamic styles we have come to recognise.

9.9: The portal at the Kaiserdom in Königslutter, Lower Saxony, Germany, shows several Islamic features, such as the recumbent sphinx-like lions supporting the asymmetrical columns, one zigzag, one spiral, the trefoil shape of the doorway and its recessed arches.

10

FRENCH ISLAMESQUE

The early Muslim presence in France is less well documented than in Spain, but the first arrival of Muslim forces on French soil took place in 719 with the Umayyad invasion of Gaul. It was a continuation of their conquest of Hispania to the south, and for a period of about forty years, till 759, they controlled the region known as Septimania, an area in southeast France that corresponds roughly to the modern region of Occitanie. Its main cities were Carcassonne, Nîmes, Beziers and Narbonne, the capital. At that time the Umayyad Caliphate, based in Damascus, was one of the world's foremost military powers. It had conquered and completely absorbed the Iranian Sassanian Empire, and much of the Byzantine Empire including Syria, Armenia and North Africa.

The northward Saracen advance was ended in 732 by Charles Martel (grandfather of Charlemagne), the de facto ruler of Francia and commander-in-chief of the foremost military power of Western Europe, at the Battle of Tours, also called the Battle of Poitiers and, by the Arabs, the Battle of the Highway of the Martyrs. It was widely regarded as the turning point in halting the Islamisation of Western Europe. In Christian sources the Muslims are referred to as 'Saracens' while their own forces are called the 'Franks'.

The Muslims then had a second period of presence in France that lasted close to a hundred years, from 890 till 973, mainly in the region of Provence in the hinterland of Saint-Tropez, from where they raided Aix-en-Provence and Marseilles, among other French cities. Medieval chroniclers referred to the area as Fraxinetum (today's La Garde-Freinet), with the nearby Mont des Maures (Mountain of the Moors) providing defence. The city of Castelsarrasin, whose name indicates that its castle was built in the Saracen era, is documented as being in existence from 961. Today it is a populous commune in central southern France, in the Tarn-et-Garonne department of Occitanie, with its own station on the Bordeaux–Toulouse line. In the local Occitan/Provençal language it is simply known as *Los Sarrasins*, the Saracens.

Systematic archaeological research into the Saracens in southeastern France and the Alpine regions has only been undertaken since the end of the Second World War. Various towers and fortifications are attributed to the Saracens, especially by local legend and occasional documentary evidence. The research revealed cemeteries, weapons, coins, wells, buildings, and, most significant of all, the discovery of mihrabs in the walls of some churches in southern France, notably in Narbonne. It is also possible that some other present-day churches and cathedrals in the department of Var (in the Provence-Alpes-Côte d'Azur region of southeast France) and the Rhône Valley may have originally been built as mosques and later converted.

The Arrival of Romanesque Architecture in France

Starting from the beginning of the eleventh century, the style known as 'French Romanesque' is said to have arrived from northern Italy and spread across southern France, especially in the provinces bordering Catalonia and Spain. Today's modern national borders are obviously very different to medieval boundaries, where entities like Normandy, Burgundy and Aquitaine were more or less autonomous, but I have attempted wherever possible to use current geographical regions for the reader's sake, even though, as has already become very clear, architectural styles were never constrained by such considerations.

More has been written about Romanesque architecture in France than in any other country. Maybe this is because the term 'Romanesque' was first invented in nineteenth-century France, and there are more Romanesque buildings in today's France than in any other European country. On my many road trips it often seemed to me that almost every French village had a Romanesque church, a reflection, perhaps, of the power of the Church in medieval times, and particularly the monastic orders like the Benedictines. This power was brought to an end by the French Revolution in 1789, when many churches and monasteries were sacked and heavily damaged, most famously Cluny itself, the Benedictine powerhouse. Five years later only a handful of France's 40,000 churches were still functioning. The vast majority were destroyed, sold, converted to other uses like prisons, schools, barns or cafes, or simply locked up. All this changed again in 1834, when the French government decided to restore its architectural heritage and appointed Prosper Mérimée as Inspector-General of Historical Monuments, on a high salary, all travel expenses paid, a job, Mérimée wrote, perfectly suited to 'his taste, his laziness and his ideas of travel'.[1] He held the post for twenty-seven years, appointing the young architect Eugène Viollet-le-Duc in 1840 to take charge of restoration projects. These two men can be largely credited with saving France's architectural heritage, starting with Vézelay Abbey in Burgundy before moving on to many other monuments, including Notre-Dame and Saint-Denis, over the next forty years.

Thomas Graham Jackson, at the end of his classic two-volume tome on Byzantine and Romanesque architecture, noted that the adoption of the pointed arch as the main element of design was the real game-changer in Romanesque, the technical innovation which led directly to Gothic. He summed it up:

> The Roman arch was a passive weight-bearing feature but the use of arcades and the pointed arch made the arches into active parts of the structure, opposing vault to vault, thrust to thrust, and thus beginning that method of construction by equilibrium of forces which was the motive principle of all succeeding architecture during the Middle Ages... Thenceforth the vault was the dominant factor in all the schools of Romanesque art and of the Gothic that followed, and from the exigencies of that form of construction arose all the later schools of western Europe.[2]

French architectural historian Jean Bony (1908–95) tracks the distribution into northern Europe of the earliest pointed arches from their sources in North Africa, Sicily and Spain, and does the same for the earliest ribbed vaulting from the same Islamic sources.[3] He shows that the earliest pointed arches are to be found in the palaces and mosques of North Africa, Sicily and Spain, from where they move northward through the west of France, from Moissac, Cahors and Périgueux, on to a cluster around Paris, from where they move across the English Channel and appear at Reading Abbey in England, built by Henry I, who is known to have benefited from the services of the Muslim master mason known as Lalys, as explained earlier. Bony tells us that the pointed arch was already in use 'in Islamic architecture of the Near East in the course of the eighth century and had propagated itself through Egypt and Tunisia to Sicily, then under Arab domination'.[4]

Even if the exact route of transmission into Europe is not known, the source in the Islamic world is not in doubt, just as Bony and others are not in doubt that the pointed arch then made its first proper appearance in Latin Christendom at Cluny in southern Burgundy, in the new church known as Cluny III, begun in 1088 under Abbot Hugh the Great. Cluny became the wealthiest and largest church in Europe and its abbots became leaders on the international stage. Monks had not always been so popular. When monasticism first arrived in the West in the fourth century, following the ways of the Egyptian Desert Fathers, it was regarded with great suspicion and disapproval. St Jerome tells us that in fourth-century Rome, at the funeral of a man who had died of excessive fasting, the people cried: 'When will they drive this detestable race of monks from the town? Why do they not stone them? Why do they not throw them into the river?'[5]

The massive expansion of the Benedictine monasteries over the eleventh and twelfth centuries under the leadership of Cluny was key to the further development of the style, as experiments began in the abbeys of Burgundy with different forms of vaulted ceiling. The Benedictines controlled and encouraged the vastly lucrative pilgrimage route to Santiago de Compostela and a total of seventy-one churches were built, specially designed to meet the needs of the pilgrims. The route was recognised by UNESCO in 1993 as having played an enormous role in religious and cultural exchange and in constituting 'outstanding witness to the power and influence of faith among people of all social classes and origins in medieval Europe and later'.[6] Abbot Hugh presided over 314 monasteries and reigned like a temporal prince, even striking money in his own mint like the king of France himself. At its peak there were 815 monasteries and over 10,000 monks under the Abbot of Cluny. The abbot sat at the head of a vast congregation whose spiritual and political influence was felt throughout Western Europe, especially in former Gaul, the Iberian Peninsula and Italy.

The wealth for all these building projects, Cluny III included, came in large part from the Muslim treasures and taxes that followed the rise of the Christians in the Spanish Reconquista, and the skill to build them came likewise from Muslim Spain. Though Cluny III is no more, destroyed in the wake of the French Revolution, the nearby Cluniac church of Paray-le-Monial serves as a small-scale replica, since both were completed within a few years of each other in an identical style. The new pointed arches and ribbed vaulting reduced the thrust, Bony tells us, by about 20 per cent, 'and this technical advantage explains its rapid diffusion in some areas of Romanesque Europe'.[7]

Ribbed vaulting, as Bony proves, entered Europe from the Islamic world and was, along with the pointed arch, the key long-lasting technical innovation of the Romanesque period, that then went on to provide the structural framework for all future buildings of the Gothic style, including Europe's best-known and most magnificent cathedrals, like the iconic Notre-Dame de Paris.

By the early 1120s, ribbed vaulting is evident at the northern Italian centres of Milan, Novara and Pavia. The link with Pavia, hometown of Lanfranc, William the Conqueror's first Archbishop of Canterbury, may be significant in terms of how and why William of Sens was chosen to bring the style into England, as Lanfranc would already have been familiar with the advances in Romanesque building techniques. By 1120–5, a system of diagonal ribs also developed in a cluster of buildings in Normandy, specifically in the abbeys of Evreux, Lessay and Jumièges, and a slightly different type of ribbed vaulting can be seen in the porch-tower of Moissac Abbey in central southern France, generally dated to Abbot Roger (1115–31). As Bony points out:

> it does not seem pure accident that, both in England and Italy, the first systematic experiments in rib-vaulting started within ten years of the capture of Toledo (1085), where could be seen—on a reduced scale but in a rich variety of types—some of the finest examples of Islamic rib-vaults.[8]

The two small mosques which are still extant in Toledo—Bab al-Mardum (now the church of El Cristo de la Luz) and Las Tornerías—are a little later than the ribbed vaulting at the Córdoba Mezquita, dating to the last years of the tenth century. Together with the Córdoba Mezqita, they therefore represent over a century of previous experimentation with the technique before it reached France.

Sculpture

Southern and western France are where the Islamic architectural styles and motifs are most similar to those in northern Spain. In the Languedoc, Burgundy and Aquitaine regions, the styles are especially pronounced in those monasteries that fell under the Benedictines, where the churches and cathedrals have the most similar Romanesque characteristics such as domes, elaborately carved facades and capitals and much detailed ornamentation like blind arcades and zigzags. All are on the pilgrimage route to Santiago, sponsored by the Benedictines, benefiting from the styles already introduced by Muslim craftsmen.

Only a handful of the many thousands of examples of Islamic-style Romanesque architecture in France can be covered here—a whole book could easily be written on those in France alone. The examples I have chosen follow the rough direction of travel of the style, from Spain northwards, starting with one of the least visited abbeys in Europe, due to its out-of-the-way location, far from the autoroute network.

Moissac Abbey

As at Silos, it is Moissac's magnificent cloister, one of the finest in France, if not in all Europe, that forms the unforgettable highpoint. Dated, like that at Silos, to 1100 by an in-situ inscription, the cloister's elegant double columns and capitals are well preserved despite the depredations wrought by the French Revolution. Its atmosphere of serenity is enhanced by an enormous cedar tree growing in the courtyard lawn, a serenity somewhat marred every time a train runs past the end of the abbey, out of sight but within close earshot, the result of a misguided planning decision in the mid-nineteenth century. The cloister was saved, and hurriedly added to Prosper Mérimée's 1840 'List of Historic Monuments', but the refectory was sacrificed to make way for the railway cutting. The abbey's early history, too, was not uneventful: sacked by the Moors of Andalusia twice in 732, looted by Norman pirates in the ninth century and by the Hungarians in the tenth.

Affiliated to Cluny, and an important stop on the pilgrim route to Santiago, Moissac was one of the most powerful Benedictine abbeys in France during its Golden Age in the eleventh and twelfth centuries, with buildings to match. It controlled lands and priories as far afield as Roussillon and Catalonia, known for their skilled stone workshops. Its splendour lies above all in the sculpture of its crenellated portal and cloister, features that have earned it UNESCO World Heritage Site status. Thomas Graham Jackson sees what he calls 'a Byzantine character' across the lintel of the portal, with its fine row of rosettes round a raised central flower. What he does not notice is that they are eight-petalled flowers in the style of eight-pointed stars. He also comments that the figure carving 'is the work of a very different school, which has little trace of either Roman or Byzantine influence, but in which, with all its imperfections, one seems to see the seeds of growth and of the future Gothic art'.[9] He sees the figures as 'drawn out beyond all proportion, forced and extravagant', exactly the kind of absence of realism that Islamic sculpture is known for. All the faces of the twenty-four elders of the Apocalypse in the portal tympanum are different; each one is dressed differently and sits in a different pose, as they look upwards to the figure of Christ in Majesty, so unlike the uniformity and symmetry that is the norm in Byzantine or classical art.

The whole effect of the twenty-four elders, to my eye, is imbued with a certain humour, almost mockery. Their gaze and postures are far from reverent. In the frames round the haloes of Christ and the upper figures, including the eagle and the pair of fantastical winged beasts, in the detailing of their

10.1: The sculpted capitals in the cloister of Moissac Abbey, one of the most powerful Benedictine monasteries in France in its eleventh- and twelfth-century heyday, rest on alternate slender single and double columns supporting pointed arches. The sculpture is thought to be by the same master as at Santo Domingo de Silos in northern Spain.

garments, and in the folds of the interlace banding that frames both sides of the semicircle, the tell-tale round pearl-like beading appears, the typical Islamic ornamental device seen so often before in Sicily, mainland Italy and Spain. Eight-pointed stars also appear in the decoration behind the Christ in Majesty, and eight-petalled flowers feature in his halo, more pointers towards Islamic craftsmen, for whom such backgrounds used as framing would have been second nature.

As to the subject matter, it is not necessary to be Christian in order to produce art of great beauty and spirituality. The Muslim craftsmen would have been following the subject matter requirements of their Christian employers, showing the typical biblical scenes specified by the abbot and his top clergy—such as Adam and Eve, the Temptation and the Expulsion, David and Goliath, and Daniel in the Lion's Den. Non-biblical scenes also feature, like the Labours of the Months, the Ascension of Alexander and various martyrdoms of saints like Stephen, Lawrence, Peter and Paul. Some cloister capitals are simply composed of arabesque-style intertwining foliage based on repeating palmettes, while others have fantastical versions of beasts, in pairs confronted or addorsed, like dragons, lions and birds, but clearly the work of the same artist.[10] These must have been the ones where the sculptors had free rein, not directed to create this or that biblical subject matter. The four sides of the historiated capitals (the ones that tell biblical stories) often follow a right-to-left sequence, the usual Arabic direction, the opposite of the Latin left-to-right sequence. In one capital a pair of goats stand either side of a palm tree, and the word '*cabra*' ('goat' in the Occitan language of the day) is incised behind each one; but on the right side it is written backwards with the letters reversed,[11] as if written by an Arab with the usual right-to-left flow of script. The fountain, now sadly destroyed, and *trumeau* (carved pillar dividing the doorspace of the portal, like an *ajimez*) were described by Moissac's fourteenth-century abbot as 'so wonderful that they were considered miraculous rather than human works'.[12] The craftsmen would be using their own repertoire of stylistic devices, supplying framing and background ornamentation from within their own imagination. Small wonder the style has caused such puzzlement among art historians, as they wrestled with these newly appeared and unfamiliar styles of sculpture.

American art historian Meyer Schapiro, whom we encountered at Silos in Spain, spent decades studying the sculpture at Moissac, starting as a student when his professor encouraged him to travel to France in order to make it the subject of his doctoral thesis. Schapiro dedicated the rest of his life to Romanesque sculpture. Looking at the Moissac sculpture style in the round, he observes a 'dominant restlessness' and 'ornamental abstraction or arithmetical grouping of repeated elements'. Each figure is different—some sandalled, some barefoot, some wearing shoes, some holding closed books, some holding open books or a cross. Even the pedestal for each is different, with some standing on steps or staircases. Schapiro is baffled by how 'the artist who did not observe the human eye correctly and misproportioned the arms and legs and head, was very careful to represent the stitching in the shoes of St Andrew and each separate hair of his beard'.[13] He sees some similarities to ancient Egyptian art[14] or sometimes, in the way a quadruped's legs move, Assyrian art, but struggles to place the style somewhere between what he calls the 'archaic' method of the northern early Middle Ages and 'the early baroque of Italy', noting its 'intricate rhythmical balance and coordinated asymmetries'.[15]

There is a gap of some thirty years between the cloister and the porch, with the earlier cloister sculptures being 'flatter and more uniform in their sur-

10.2: Each capital in the Moissac cloister is different, with no repetition or symmetry. The work is dated by an inscription to 1100, with many eight-pointed stars and eight-petalled flowers used in the frames and friezes both in the cloister and in the entrance portal.

faces', but Schapiro can see the stylistic similarities between the two, and how the later has developed out of the earlier, becoming 'more intricate and more intensely expressive... within a limited but greater space'. He also notes 'the earliest use of strong *chiaroscuro*... a schematic structure of illumination, a distinct division of light from shadow, in a primitive cosmogenic manner'.[16] All the capitals at Moissac share the same geometric composition as at the cloister of Silos, with zigzags and triangles embedded, often with legs of the figures going in diagonally opposite directions in dramatic postures. A poly-lobed Moorish archway appears as background in one capital, but normally the figures are set against no interior or exterior wall; even a ground is absent, giving an abstracted spacelessness. All these are characteristics now becoming familiar to us as signs of Islamic craftsmanship from the monasteries of Italy, Sicily and Spain already examined.

A few final details noticed by Schapiro might also point towards Arab sculptors, though he does not make the connection: first, in the relief of the Abbot Durand who commissioned the work and second, in the relief where the cloister inscription itself, giving the year 1100 in Latin words rather than numerals, is carved into a pillar. The Durand relief is carved on the broadest of the nine pillars, presumably at his own request, but he is shown in a posture that is

> extraordinarily strained... represented with a diagramatic precision, as if by compass and ruler... with a neat symmetry that suggests an almost mechanical indifference to expression, the forms are not in ideal repose or clarity... The artist who described with religious devotion the insignia of Durand's authority did not maintain in the smaller elements the ritual gravity inherent in the static architectural design of the whole.[17]

This would be consistent with a sculptor who was not best enamoured of his patron, and who was almost mocking him. Durand was not a popular abbot.

The second detail appears in the inscription which Schapiro notes is illogically spaced—sometimes crowded, sometimes with gaps—as if 'the artist could not accept two lines in clear unmodified parallelism'.[18] This immediately brings to mind the inscriptions in the Fatimid mihrab of the Ibn Tulun Mosque in Cairo, where the artist has got the spacing wrong, sometimes squashing letters into a cramped space, sometimes leaving gaps. The usual Arab approach in medieval times was not to plan out an inscription in advance, but to carve it spontaneously, which meant that mistakes were permanent and not correctable. Finally, in the capital depicting the Apostles fishing, their boat is meant to be a clinker-style vessel, but the planks are depicted overlapping the wrong way, from bottom to top, the same detail that occurs on the West Front at Wells Cathedral (see Chapter 5).

The elaborate carving of Moissac's cloister depicts exactly the kind of subject matter that provoked the wrath of Bernard of Clairvaux (1090–1153), founder of the breakaway Cistercian Order, and co-founder of the Knights Templar, who were then seen as the pinnacle of Christian nobility. Bernard's family was itself of the highest Burgundian pedigree, and he preached a faith based on the Virgin Mary as intercessor. This kind of sculpture was clearly new to the age, but the idea that such sculpture could have been crafted by

Muslims is so remote a possibility to the typical nineteenth-century art historian like Jackson, who assumes Islamic art was forbidden from sculpting humans or animals in any way, that he even compares Muslim art with Cistercian art:

> Just as the Moslem managed to build beautifully and romantically though his religion debarred him from the resources of sculpture, so the Cistercians, while obeying the severe restrictions of their rule in the matter of decoration, have managed to leave us some of the loveliest buildings of the Middle Ages.[19]

Pontigny Abbey

The biggest Cistercian church in the world, Pontigny Abbey was built in two stages, in 1137 and in 1150, during the transition to Gothic. It boasts the first ribbed vault in Burgundy. In the impressive nave and aisles it has quadripartite vaulting, which cleverly becomes five vault spaces between the ribs to handle the curve of the apse. At the apex of the apse itself, there are ten vault spaces between the ribs, terminating together at the centre in a foliated boss.

Throughout there are stylised papyrus/lily capitals of many varied types, and the purity of style lends a calmness to the space, which was enhanced on the day of my visit by an elderly man playing the harp. Jackson comments that some of the capitals of the nave 'are little more than geometrical blocks, as abstract as the Moslem capitals in the forecourts of mosques in Constantinople',[20] but he admires the beauty that comes from its delicate proportions, with its simply foliaged capitals, saying it should satisfy St Bernard himself. It is likely to have had the same team of masons who developed the early Gothic style at nearby Sens Cathedral, where it is generally assumed William of Sens first learned his craft, built between 1135 and 1140. The exterior has simple tall blind arches as decoration, in the Islamic style brought into France via North Africa, Sicily and Spain.

Domed Churches

The domed Romanesque churches of southwestern France solve the vault problem by having a sequence of domes, usually two or three, whose weight is borne entirely by massive pillars at the four corners, so that side aisles are not needed. Aquitaine has many examples and the province of Périgord once had about thirty, of which at least fifteen are still standing. Jackson sees it as 'Byzantine influence',[21] though he does wonder quite how the style found its way to Aquitaine unless it was through Venetian trading links. Jackson is not wrong to note Venetian links, as probably the best known of the domed churches, Saint-Front at Périgueux, rebuilt in 1120 after a terrible fire, is a five-domed cruciform building closely modelled on St Mark's, Venice, even in its dimensions, and one of the buildings singled out as 'of the Saracen style' by Christopher Wren. The great arches that carry Saint-Front's dome are slightly pointed, and as Jackson observes, 'there are certain variations in the construction of the domes and pendentives which seem to show that the architect of Saint-Front was not a Greek himself'.[22]

He also notes other unusual characteristics, as at the church of Saint-Hilaire le Grand in Poitiers, built in 1130, where the nave was vaulted by covering it with polygonal quasi-domes, irregular octagons, 'springing not from real pendentives but from "tromps" or squinch-arches thrown across the angles, like those we have seen in the churches of Syria'.[23] Notre-Dame in Poitiers also has an octagonal dome on squinches, as has Saint-Pierre in Chauvigny.

Both the squinch and the pendentive were ways of supporting a dome on a square base and both developed in the fifth century CE in the Iranian Empire and in Syria. The squinch is the simpler of the two, fixed in the corner of two walls, like a swallow's nest. The four squinches, one at each corner, have the effect of turning a square into an octagon, and so give enough support to hold a circular dome, either on a small arch or on a projecting stone or brick corbel. A pendentive is a more sophisticated concept, simpler to look at but more complex in its geometry, where the dome's weight is transferred to the ground via four supporting arches, thereby leaving the space beneath the dome open and light. Bony notes this effect at Poitiers Cathedral, begun in 1162, observing how 'the volume enclosed by those tall triple naves of half-churches became so continuous and disencumbered that the impression achieved was one of overwhelming spatial unity',[24] exactly the same sensation as when stepping inside a domed mosque.

The cathedral at Cahors, Saint-Etienne, consecrated in 1119, is a few years older than Saint-Front and has two domes, visible from outside, carried on pendentives with slightly pointed arches. The exterior facades are decorated with blind arches and inside its capitals are covered in ornamental sculpture, as we have come to expect. Sainte-Marie at Souillac, some 60 kilometres north of Cahors, has three domes in a row, visible from the outside but not the inside, again with no side aisles. Its remarkable feature on the inside is the astonishing twelfth-century carving, the so-called Pillar of Sin, where a semi-naked crowned aristocrat at the top is being bitten by the enormous beak of a bird, piled on top of multiple entwined fantastical beasts, all appearing to attack each other.

10.3: Inside the Sainte-Marie Abbey in Souillac, on the Dordogne in southwestern France, is this twelfth-century 'grotesque' sculpture, the so-called 'Pillar of Sin', where a half-dressed nobleman, still wearing his crown, is tormented by fantastical beasts. The three exterior domes that roof the nave are supported on Islamic-style squinches.

Sculpture in Aquitaine

The region known in medieval times as Saintonge, today's Charente-Maritime, with Saintes as its largest town and its own Benedictine Abbaye aux Dames, has a remarkable cluster of Romanesque churches with quite exceptional sculpture and ornamentation, all of it reminiscent of what we have seen in northern Spain and Italy. There must have been a group, if not several groups, of masons schooled under Islamic rule working in the area during this period.

All the churches have striking west facades of great beauty composed of blind arches, with ornamental detailing round the arches based on arabesque repeating foliage designs, zigzags or other geometric patterns, fantastical beasts and figural statues. Eight-petalled flowers and eight-pointed stars are commonly used in the decorative repertoire. Angoulême Cathedral, Fontevraud Abbey, Notre-Dame in Poitiers and Saint-Nicolas in Civray probably boast the most elaborate facades, with zigzags, lozenges and confronted pairs of fantastical animals. Angoulême (1101–36) and Fontevraud Abbey (1110) were both built within a few years of each other and are so close in design and dimension, as aisleless crucifom churches covered by a series of domes on pendentives resting on slightly pointed arches, that they must have been conceived by the same master craftsman and likely executed according to his techniques, all of which show Islamic influence. Both churches also have tall blind arches at ground level and blind decorative arcades higher up, together with Venetian dentil decorative friezes below the roofs of the tower and the apse. At Fontevraud the domes have been destroyed but the pendentives remain.

The highly carved triple facade at Civray, with its beaded foliage, palmettes and eight-petalled flowers, overlooks the main square, while its interior is very colourfully painted in the colours of the period, recreating the atmosphere that would have pervaded the church in its heyday. Civray also has slender recessed columns supporting the arches and Venetian dentil framing each storey, with the base of each arch carrying an individual head of either an animal or a person. Some of the animals, often in pairs, are recognisable, such as the bulls, but others are grotesques of some sort, presumably to ward off evil spirits.

Each person's face is different and appears to be based on some real likeness, another feature which is common to the churches of Saintonge. The higher levels especially seem to carry more faces, and it seems logical to assume that these were the faces of the masons, or their friends and families, immortalising themselves on the church facades. Though they are anonymous to us, the masons knew who they were, and this was one way of ensuring their work had a kind of signature.

Saintonge also has a collection of quite extraordinarily decorated smaller churches, in villages like Chadenac, Aulnay, Varaize and Blasimon, where the same master sculptor is thought to have worked on their twelfth-century facades and capitals, rich with winged monsters, lions and dragons in scenes of combat.

Some of these smaller churches also have the bird-headed design round their portals known in Norman Romanesque language as 'beakheads', which after first appearing in northern Spain found their way through

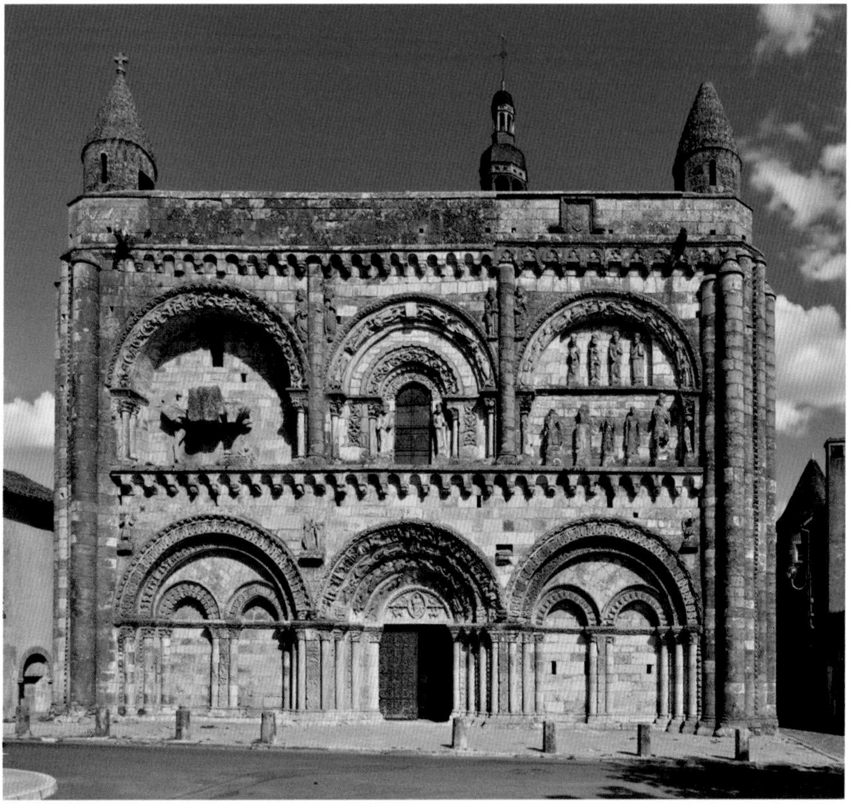

10.4: The twelfth-century west facade of Saint-Nicolas in Civray, Nouvelle-Aquitaine, western France, is decorated with richly carved fantastical beasts framing the recessed arches, slender columns, beaded foliage, palmettes, eight-petalled flowers and Venetian dentil friezes.

France to England, where they become a characteristic Norman feature (see Chapters 2 and 11).

At the twelfth-century village church of Saint-Pierre in Arces, the sculpted capitals of the interior have been painted, showing dramatic zigzags on the pillars, eight-petalled flowers and people wrestling with snake-like dragons whose bodies are framed by beaded interlace.

At the church of Saint-Pierre in the village of Aulnay, dated 1120–40, there are many acknowledged 'oriental' influences, from the tall blind arches of the exterior to the obviously oriental portal with its fantastical animals in roundels, and the exotic carvings of the nave capitals, including one with an elephant, topped with a zigzag frieze.

10.5 The capitals and interior arches at the church of Saint-Pierre in Arces, Aquitaine, are painted with what are thought to have been the original styles, showing highly coloured zigzags on the columns, beading on the dragons' bodies, felines spewing interlace foliage and friezes of eight-petalled flowers.

10.6: At the church of Saint-Pierre in Aulnay-de-Saintonge, western France, the capitals are carved with many exotic beasts, including elephants, framed with zigzag friezes.

Saint-Savin-sur-Gartempe

Sometimes described as the 'Romanesque Sistine Chapel', the abbey church of Saint-Savin-sur-Gartempe dates from the late eleventh and early twelfth centuries, and possesses, according to UNESCO, 'the largest area of Roman murals ($420m^2$) resulting from a single and same [*sic*] campaign, a unique artistic realization in a remarkable state of conservation'.[25]

Old myths about monks imbued with religious fervour painting the frescoes of their monasteries themselves have been well and truly discredited in recent years. When I visited Saint-Savin, the lady at the ticket office confirmed that it is now known, because it is stated in the church's own archives, that professionals were brought in for the job, though no one knows from where or who they were, since nothing was recorded about them. Why might that be? It seems extraordinary, given the extent of the work, all over the interior walls

10.7: The murals at the monastery church of Saint-Savin-sur-Gartempe were painted by a team of professional artists, possibly Mozarabs, and show many Arab traditions like the use of individualised faces, expressive hand gestures and brightly coloured sinuous robes, with palm trees and background architecture. There is also pearl-beaded framing, with trefoils, arabesques, lozenges and diaper motifs.

of the abbey church, that no mention has ever been made of who these artists were or where they came from. The subject matter is an immense biblical narrative, Old and New Testament, thematically organised, which would presumably have been commissioned by the abbot and senior clergy.

Based on examining the frescoes themselves, my own theory is that the painters are likely to have been a highly skilled team of Mozarabs from Muslim Spain. Just as their Muslim contemporaries in Spain enjoyed painting their mosques in bright colours, so too the Mozarabs were known to paint the interiors of their churches with highly coloured scenes. Islamic culture under the Abbasids, the Fatimids and the Andalusian Umayyads used pictorial and figural representation in many settings, and even surviving medieval Syriac manuscripts show how Christian styles were influenced by the Arab tradition of individualised faces, with strong movement, expressive hand gestures, brightly coloured sinuous robes, palm trees and the use of architecture in the background, with trefoils, arabesques, lozenges and diaper motifs.[26] Of course they could also have been Arab Muslims, given the tell-tale white beading that frames the frescoes.

Auvergne and the Massif Central

The ever-perceptive Jackson comments how during the Romanesque period the Auvergne region developed a distinct architectural style of its own, 'so original and so satisfactory that one regrets the wave of Gothic architecture that came to sweep it away. In such able hands one might have imagined it would have led to some further development of surpassing interest.'[27]

It is thus no accident that it is here in the Auvergne, more than anywhere else in France, that Islamic influence is most apparent, both in the architectural styles and techniques and in the decoration, both internal and external. The key buildings are all around the same date and seem to be designed on roughly one model. Jackson notes that the style 'is so complete in all its parts that one does not see an opening for anything to proceed from it'.[28]

Statues are seen only very rarely, and such sculpture as does occur is mainly confined to the capitals. The painting of interiors in bright colours seems to have been common, to judge from the traces that still remain in places, and as a result some churches like Issoire have been repainted to recreate that effect inside.

Polychrome effects in the stonework are a distinctive Islamic feature in the churches of the Auvergne, using masonry with the black volcanic basalt of the Massif Central in contrast with yellowy white limestone, exactly as is found all over Syria with its own widespread volcanic black basalt and white limestone. One of the most famous French examples is Notre-Dame du Port at Clermont-Ferrand, which not only has black-and-white arches on the semicircular chevet at its eastern end, but also black-and-white patterned mosaic *intarsia* stonework with eight-petalled flowers in a continuous series of roundels, calling to mind the churches on Sicily, especially at Messina.

Le Puy Cathedral

Le Puy is the most famous example in all the Auvergne, the cathedral in which even the French admit there is Islamic influence, above all in the charming *ablaq* arches of the cloister and in the internal dome construction. It is the starting point of one of the four symbolic pilgrim routes to Santiago de Compostela, the others being Paris, Vézelay and Arles, and therefore forms part of that UNESCO grouping of churches.[29]

10.8: In the Auvergne, central France, many churches like Notre-Dame du Port at Clermont-Ferrand are decorated with local volcanic black lava *intarsia* inlay in roundels of eight-pointed stars, together with black-and-white *ablaq* arches, reminiscent of those found all over the Islamic world.

10.9: Le Puy Cathedral in the Auvergne is so heavily influenced by Islamic architecture that even the French acknowledge it. The arches and facades are all decorated in two-tone black-and-white *ablaq* using the local black lava. The tall ground-level arches are echoed in the upper-level blind arcades on this western facade.

There was a strong connection between Aquitaine and the Auvergne, and the cathedral at Le Puy-en-Velay shows considerable Islamic influence in the dome and its vaulting. Set high on a hill, the unusual entrance was below the church ground level, via a flight of steps, into the centre of the nave, and the on-site guide quotes an old monkish chronicler saying 'one entered the church by the nostril, and left it by the ears', meaning by the side doors of the transepts. The original facade has porphyry columns, pilfered from somewhere in the Eastern Mediterranean, and the original Levantine cedarwood doors still remain, complete with Arabic inscription in Kufic script, the endlessly repeating phrase '*al-mulk lillah*' (meaning 'Sovereignty belongs to God'), a phrase often found on Islamic objects and sufficiently ambiguous to be used in Christian contexts. The doors of the tenth-century Madinat al-Zahra have fleurons which are very similar to the vegetal fleurons of Le Puy Cathedral, and similar ones also appear in the ninth-century Kairouan Mosque and in Egypt and in Sicily. They have a very Fatimid character, like palmettes with three lobes or with five lobes.

The vaulting of the nave is achieved through a succession of octagonal quasi-domes on squinch arches, as at Saint-Hilaire in Poitiers, which are coloured in *ablaq* stonework supported on pairs of slender columns with a pronounced Islamic influence.

The treasury has a piece of cloth claimed to be a piece of the Virgin's Belt, which is clearly Islamic silk.[30] Georges Marçais also saw in the polychrome cathedrals of the Auvergne architectural styles similar to those used in the Italian churches of Abruzzo, like Santa Maria di Collemaggio, moving north from Sicily, having first entered from Egypt via North Africa.[31]

The basalt tower of Le Puy also has windows with the characteristic horseshoe trefoil arches found in most of the Auvergne churches, as seen above the mihrab in the tenth-century extension of the Córdoba Mezquita. The horseshoe arch was the earliest Muslim arch adaptation, used in the Umayyad Great Mosque of Damascus, built between 706 and 715, and brought by the Umayyads into Spain. In Islam the horseshoe is a symbol of sainthood and holiness, not luck as in Western cultures. From Córdoba the arch travelled north with the Mozarabs thanks to the movement of artists, scholars, builders and architects between the Muslim southern and northern Christian parts of Spain. An example of this movement can be found in some of the architectural drawings seen in tenth-century Mozarabic illustrated manuscripts such as the Beatus of Facundus or the Beatus of San Miguel de Escalada Codex, or *Morgan Beatus* (after its present repository at the Morgan Library in New York), commissioned for Abbot Victor of the San Miguel de Escalada Abbey.

At the church of Saint-Michel d'Aiguilhe, set on its pinnacle in a suburb of Le Puy, the large horseshoe trefoil is particularly striking directly above the entrance doorway. This, combined with its polychrome decorative stone and brickwork in red, black and white, gives it a very Islamic flavour.

10.10: The interior vaulting at Le Puy Cathedral makes use of Islamic-style squinches supporting the octagonal quasi-domes that cover the nave, their arches framed by black-and-white *ablaq* patterning.

Toulouse, Saint-Sernin

Romanesque remains in the County of Toulouse are not abundant because of the devastation to which the area was subjected during the Albigensian Crusade (1209–29) against the Cathars, a war which the Catholic northern French prosecuted 'with every atrocious barbarity which superstition the mother of crimes could inspire'.[32] The Cathars were a Christian sect that emerged in southwest France in the eleventh century, whose dualist beliefs are thought to have originated in Iran or the Byzantine Empire.[33] The Catholics referred to their beliefs as 'The Great Heresy'.

The vast church of Saint-Sernin is the most important to have survived. Built between 1080 and 1120 in a mix of red brick and stone, often in alternating colours, especially inside the arches, it is the largest remaining Romanesque building in Europe. Brick was commonly used decoratively by Mudéjar craftsmen as their main material.

The nave is unusually slender for such a large building, leading Viollet-le-Duc to study the proportions of the church. He found that the whole structure had been laid out on angles of 60 degrees and 45 degrees, in isosceles triangles and equilateral triangles.[34] The plan bears such a close resemblance to the basilica at Santiago de Compostela that the architect of the original Romanesque building is thought to be the same. The remarkable tower rises in five ever-diminishing octagonal stages, with a pair of blind arches on each of the eight sides.

Conques Abbey

Nestled in a wooded valley surrounded by medieval timbered houses, the abbey church of Sainte-Foy in Conques feels like a cross between a fairy tale and a Hollywood stage set. Another important stop for pilgrims on their way to Santiago de Compostela, its early-twelfth-century construction was inspired by the churches of Saint-Sernin and Santiago. Its west facade is decorated with eight-pointed stars and its twin towers are pierced with double *ajimez* windows, while its walls carry large vertical lesenes and tall blind arches. The interior vaulting at the crossing has a delicate octagon resting on squinches, in which angels with expressive faces and eyes are positioned, each different. There are over 200 columns, carved with palm leaves, fantastical monsters in pairs, confronted or addorsed, and biblical stories. Some still have traces of the original colour painting. The sculpted tympanum over the doorway is full of humour, with grotesques being eaten by outsize monsters, a grinning devil and someone identified as a local bishop caught in one of the nets of hell. The sculptor appears to have enjoyed himself, depicting the miserable naked sinners being taken to hell while an impassive Christ in Majesty sits above. Some poachers are shown being roasted by the very rabbit they had poached from the monastery, a comic scene reminiscent of the zoomorphic humour found in Egyptian Fatimid artworks, poking fun at authority figures.

Burgundy

Vézelay

The abbey church of Sainte-Marie-Madeleine at Vézelay, on a hilltop dominating the surrounding landscape, was begun in 1089, at much the same time as Cluny III, but a major innovation was introduced in the ribbed vaulting of its nave *c.*1120–40. This had the great advantage of allowing the nave height to be raised so that a clerestory could be added to let in more light. In barrel vaults the light can only enter the nave from either end, leaving the space very dark. These Vézelay ribbed tunnel vaults closely resemble those at the Ribat of Sousse, Tunisia, built nearly two centuries earlier in 821–2.

The alternate use of white and dark brown stone in the round arches of the nave ribs is one of the few instances of polychrome masonry in France outside the Auvergne. The style is sombre, almost like a mosque, with the only decoration being small rosettes running in continuous repetitive bands round the tops of each of the rib vaults, similar to those found running in frames round the wooden ceiling of the Córdoba Mezquita. Across the nave side arches a different pattern runs endlessly, like a wavy, continuously looping line, which serves as a kind of frame, similar to one of the multiple frames used for the lozenges in Peterborough Cathedral's painted ceiling. All these features combined in one place suggest an Islamic identity for the masons involved at Vézelay, lending their styles and high-level skills to new masters.

The narthex (the spacious separate porch area), from where you enter the church proper, was added onto the western end of the nave by 1132, as at Cluny—another way of propping up the Romanesque nave, this time with the benefit and strengthening properties of the pointed arch. With its own central nave and side aisles it is almost like a separate church by itself. The Great Mosque at Kairouan built by the Aghlabids in the ninth century also has a separate porched entrance portal, topped with a ribbed dome, through which to enter the main prayer hall, as does the eleventh-century northern portico of the Fatimid Great Mosque of Mahdia in today's Tunisia, and the Fatimid al-Hakim Mosque in Cairo, completed in 1013.

Vézelay's most famous feature, however, is its great west doorway that leads from this narthex into the nave, boasting a tympanum which Jackson calls 'perhaps the finest product of Burgundian Romanesque',[35] depicting the usual Christ in Majesty framed within a mandorla. As for the smaller figures in the compartments of the arch and in the lintel, Jackson tells us they have defied interpretation. 'It is difficult to see the meaning', he writes, 'of the men and women with dog's heads or pig's snouts, or of the dwarf about to mount on horseback with the aid of a ladder.'[36] In the larger figures like Christ himself with their 'convoluted draperies', he sees the influence of Byzantine art:

> All trace of classic grace is gone, and the design is rather barbarous. The figures are attenuated, and disproportionate, and thrown into attitudes that are forced

> and extravagant. And yet in spite of its barbarism, the work has not only an undeniable life and spirit but also a kind of primitive refinement. A certain delicacy is given by its peculiar method of execution. The figures are carved as it were in low relief on a flat surface which is then sunk all round them to some depth. This same treatment may be observed in the beautifully Byzantinesque scrolls on the lintels of the north and south doorways at Bourges (mid-twelfth century) where the leaves and flowers are carved with a very flat treatment, and much undercut, which gives them a very precious and delicate effect and apparently almost the frailty of paper.[37]

As a technique, this is a style associated with Fatimid carving, as seen in the wood and stone fragments on display today in Cairo's Islamic Art Museum, and Jackson, without realising it, is giving a remarkably accurate description of all the characteristics of Islamic art. The haloes also have tell-tale beaded frames.

Autun Cathedral

The cathedral at Autun (1120–32) is later than Vézelay but the nave retains the early construction style of a barrel roof, resting now on pointed arches instead of round. Even so, because they spring from so low down, there is only capacity for very small clerestory windows, making the church very dark. Its dome rests on Islamic-style squinches.

The famous Christ in Majesty tympanum, which is what brings most people to Autun, can be found outside the church in a porch overlooking the street below. With the typical medieval warnings of doom at the Last Judgement, it carries a Latin inscription which translates as: 'May this terror terrify those whom earthly error binds, for the horror of the images here in this manner truly depict what will be.'

The phrase '*Gislebertus hoc fecit*' is written right in the middle, and though some have seen in this the name of the sculptor himself, it seems extremely unlikely, since the names of sculptors did not appear on their work at this period. Only the patron or official, often a bishop or abbot, who commissioned the work, would ensure his name was immortalised in this way. Maybe it was the bishop, supported by two angels, who is represented in the central column supporting the lintel of the tympanum. The long, thin style of the human figures is strongly reminiscent of the stucco figures at Cividale del Friuli in Italy. One exterior column is decorated with a striking motif of hanging pine cones, while another is covered in a pattern of interwoven beading so delicately carved that it makes the stone appear to be draped in a luxurious cloth. The south entrance is framed by columns with deeply incised zigzags and lozenge shapes strongly reminiscent of the columns in the nave of Durham Cathedral.

10.11: The sculpted tympanum of Christ in Majesty at Autun Cathedral in central-eastern France shows the long, thin, almost abstract figures that recall those at Cividale in Italy. There is also extensive use of pearl-beaded interlace framing the arched borders, Christ's halo and the capitals, together with a complete absence of symmetry in the entire decorative carving of the portal.

There are several indicators that the highly skilled sculptors at work in Autun were schooled in the Islamic tradition in clues like the extensive use of beaded interlace in the scrolling frames of the tympanum and in the outermost arch border, on God's halo and on capitals like the three-headed bird.

There are also clues in the series of roundels containing seasonal and astrological symbols in the arch that frames the tympanum; the repeating arabesques of foliage, fruit and leaves; the over-large hands of the Christ figure; the use of winged grotesque hybrid beings; and the humour in some of the scenes depicted, like Adam and Eve lolling naked on the ground, the comic-strip Hanging of Judas with winged grotesques and the naked 'pygmy' mounted on the back of a crane, trying to stab it with his sword. The way the crane's feathers are carved shows similarities with Assyrian sculptural styles, making the feathers look more like scales.

There is also an astronomical clock at the cathedral, something which often indicates the presence of Islamic craftsmen, since they were the only ones capable at this early time of constructing such complex devices. Timekeeping was vital in a religion that prescribed five prayers a day at specific times, so that mosques would know exactly when to proclaim the call to prayer.

Iguerande

There can be few places more atmospheric than the lovely church of Saint-Marcel at Iguerande, beautifully situated on a hilltop overlooking the Loire, the sole remaining vestige of a Benedictine monastery dating to *c.*1088–1110. It has many Islamic-influenced features, from the *ajimez* windows of its bell tower with their fine recessed arches to its wall buttressing like that at the Kairouan Mosque; external corbels with human and animal heads and the mysterious carvings of the nave, both the bases and the capitals; a mix of plant motifs and fantastical creatures, often paired; beakheads and even a musical Cyclops-like monster playing the pan pipes, framed by the tell-tale beaded decoration, which is widely used throughout the foliage ornamentation. The whole interior has a wonderfully tranquil feel, the effect of its harmonious proportions, simple lines and perfectly balanced lighting. Its fine octagonal dome at the transept crossing rests on squinches. The main entrance on the western facade is flanked by columns sculpted with pomegranates, symbol of immortality, on their capitals and bases. Many elements of the sculpture have similarities with the motifs as Kilpeck church of St Mary and St David in Herefordshire, built a few decades later, in the iconography of pomegranates, the ornamental beading interlace and even the style of the carving, deeply incised in the Fatimid way.

Normandy

The Normans were the last of the Norse tribes who conquered and founded settlements in Western Europe. Their Viking longships swept up the Seine with regularity during the ninth century, even reaching as far as Paris, pillaging and looting churches and monasteries along the way. They carried off the Abbot of Saint-Denis and ransomed him for 685 pounds of gold, but later returned to rebuild the same monasteries they had earlier destroyed.[38]

Under their leader Rollo, the Vikings invited William of Volpiano, a great Italian builder from Lombardy, to build first the abbey at Fécamp and then the famous monastery at Mont Saint-Michel, which had burnt down in 1001. They thereby introduced the influence of the Lombard school into northern France, Lombard traditions which were already rooted in Arab styles and techniques, especially those from Syria, with which Ravenna had very strong connections. The Romanesque tower at Fécamp bears the characteristic tall blind arches of Lombardy and Venetian dentil round the roofline of the apse.

Jumièges Abbey

As one of the earliest and most important monasteries to be founded in the Seine Valley, Jumièges (1040–65) epitomises the Norman phenomenon. It was repeatedly sacked by the Vikings during the 800s, only to be rebuilt by them in the eleventh century as part of their new-found religious fervour. It was here that the history of Normandy and the Normans began.

Consecrated in the presence of Duke William II (later the Conqueror), only the imposing west front of Jumièges and its nave, the tallest Romanesque nave in Normandy, remain from that period. It has eight bays, resting on massive chunky pillars with lotus-like capitals, and even in its heavily ruined state, it is still possible to feel the new rhythm and way of dividing the space that Jean Bony detects as a major consequence of the new rib vaulting, the repetitive all-over pattern that he notes first beginning in the Santiago Pilgrimage Road churches and initiated in Catalonia in the 1030s and 1040s.[39] On the first storey of the transept is a narrow circulation gallery fitted into the wall thickness, one of the oldest examples of gangways characteristic of Norman Romanesque churches, *c.*1050, which then evolved into the first arcaded triforium gallery at Caen's Abbaye aux Hommes (1067–79), where the loggia treatment of the clerestory was also initiated.

At Jumièges, still set into the top of the original Romanesque pillars at the head of the nave, are a pair of eleventh-century birds very reminiscent of the Speyer *Waldrapp*, in the same location and of a similar date. Like the Speyer *Waldrapp*, the birds sit within encircling foliage and have their heads turned backwards, looking towards their tails, with their wings raised in typical Eastern fashion. Traces of red paint can still be seen in the deeply carved recesses. From studying what evidence remains of the roof structure, experts think the nave would once have had a painted ceiling supported on rafters and tie beams, as at St Michael's, Hildesheim, in Germany and Peterborough Cathedral in England, a feature in which Muslim craftsmen excelled.

Excavations are ongoing into the earlier Carolingian nave, but even above ground, the striking Islamic influence is apparent in the *ajimez* windows and the circular blind oculi which would have been filled with inlay, probably coloured mosaics, very typical of Islamic ornamentation.

The ruins of the late-eleventh-/early-twelfth-century Romanesque chapter house show that it was once covered with an intersecting ribbed vault which is, together with that at Lessay Abbey, one of the oldest examples of this type of Norman roofing.

To the right of the nave as you enter the site is the early-twelfth-century hostelry, a grand vaulted hall to receive distinguished guests. Its west facade is decorated with blind arches framed by zigzag friezes, trefoil arches and a row of heads, who seem to be real people, just below roof height. Probably representing the masons themselves, this would have been their only way of documenting themselves and their involvement in the building project. Some are bearded, some have thicker lips more like North African features, as at Salisbury Cathedral.

Lillers

Inland from Calais, the Saint-Omer Collegiate Church stands in its own square near the centre of Lillers. Built between 1125 and 1135, it has early pointed arches and is the largest Romanesque building in this part of northern France, with an imposing west facade topped by a row of blind arcades and many zigzag teeth round the arches. The nave inside has 120 capitals, with some rare examples from the medieval bestiary. One, carved on a bracket in the north angle of the nave western wall, shows a hybrid bearded man-siren with a mermaid's tail, looking startled. In the choir arcade there are twelve unusual capitals mostly carved with 'water leaves', called 'Lys Romanesque' (French *lys* means 'lily'), apart from two which are in the rare pattern of running foliage decoration. The leaves themselves are usually keel-shaped, a characteristic Fatimid shape used in arches and decorative sculpture, as at al-Aqmar Mosque in Cairo. From Normandy this 'waterleaf' style then appears in the column bases of William of Sens's work in Canterbury Cathedral after the fire of 1174, before spreading widely across England.

Caen

In Normandy the two Romanesque buildings most notable for their vaulting are in Caen, namely, the Abbaye aux Hommes (Men's Abbey) and the Abbaye aux Dames (Women's Abbey). Both were built from the local high-quality Caen limestone under the direction of Lanfranc, who once again brought in architectural influences from his native Lombardy. The abbeys were commissioned by William the Conqueror and his queen, Matilda, to reconcile the Pope to their marriage, in the same year that he crossed the Channel to conquer England in 1066. The pair were third cousins once removed, and under the very strict rules on consanguinity imposed by the Church at the time, the Pope had decreed their marriage of *c.*1050 to be against canon law.

When the 8-metre-high ceiling in the choir of the Abbaye aux Dames became structurally unsound, it was replaced in 1120 with a sexpartite rib

10.12: The stone roof of the nave at the Abbaye aux Hommes in Caen, Normandy, commissioned by William the Conqueror in 1066 just before his conquest of England, shows very early sexpartite vaulting, where three transverse ribs are crossed by a pair of diagonal ribs to divide the space into six parts. Such advanced ribbed vaulting was first seen on European soil in the tenth-century extension to the Córdoba Mezquita, Andalusia.

vault using rounded ribs, one of the earliest examples in France, progressing to quadripartite vaults with pointed ribs in the sanctuary. Both abbeys are considered important forerunners of Gothic in their advanced vaulting.

A sexpartite vault is a type of rib vault divided into six bays by two diagonal ribs and three transverse ribs. Other notable early examples of this type of rib vault, now seen as transitional, are at Notre-Dame de Paris and the cathedrals of Laon, Senlis and Sens. William of Sens brought the sexpartite vault to Canterbury Cathedral from Sens, and it was later seen also at Lincoln Cathedral and in St Faith's Chapel in Westminster Abbey. Quadripartite vaults, the next stage in development using pointed ribs, had the structural advantage of shifting the weight to the corners, where it could be supported by piers, columns or walls, enabling higher walls and larger windows.

The timing of these innovations is important since it also follows the First Crusade of 1096–9, a period during which Norman knights were known to have brought back Muslim prisoners with non-local skills. This would also explain why slightly different types of ribbed vaults suddenly appeared within a decade or two, as the newly imported masons and engineers began the process of putting their skills to use in different building projects under the direction of new Christian masters.

At the Abbaye aux Hommes, the other Islamic features beyond the vaulting are rows of blind arcades, some beakhead carvings inside the nave and on the exterior, corbels with heads of people and animals, and eight-petalled-flower rose windows in the apse. Consecrated in 1077, Lanfranc was its first abbot. The interior is unusual in France in that the two storeys in the nave are of almost equal proportions, a characteristic that is found in Norman cathedrals in England at Ely, Peterborough, Norwich, Southwell and Winchester and, significantly, in Lombardy at Sant'Ambrogio in Milan, which was completed during Lanfranc's lifetime.

At the Abbaye aux Dames the triple doorway has been likened to al-Hakim Mosque in Cairo, while inside there are many heads of men, presumably the masons themselves, looking down on the women, and on the right-hand side of the transept are two heads of women, one large fat abbess and one young woman, both added later as an afterthought. The capitals carry many fantastical creatures.

Bayeux and its Environs

In the area around Bayeux, a group of sculptors schooled in the Islamic tradition of decorative patterns must have been at work in the early decades of the twelfth century, judging from the concentration of highly ornamented churches in close proximity to each other. Outside the town of Thaon, all by itself in an isolated valley beside a stream, the small church of Saint-Pierre, whose nave and chancel are dated *c.*1120–30, must be one of the most exquisitely decorated in all of France. It is kept locked these days and is clearly not in use, so its interior with capitals carved into fantastical animals, often in pairs confronted or addorsed, is hard to see, squinting through small holes; but the exterior is a perfect gem of stonework so delicate it looks like embroi-

10.13: The interior walls of the nave of Bayeux Cathedral are covered in rich ornamentation, including a frieze of sixty-two 'beakheads' framing one of the main arches, each head different, with no symmetry.

dery or tapestry. The earlier eleventh-century bell tower has *ajimez* double windows and the twelfth-century exterior walls have tall blind arches, blind arcades and continuous billet moulding, while the corbels are carved with heads of animals and people.

Bayeux Cathedral has similarities with Saint-Pierre de Thaon's exterior embroidery or tapestry-style decoration, except that here it is in the interior, covering all the flat surfaces between the arches of the nave, suggestive of weaving, basketry or stitchwork, with multiple geometric patterns such as lozenges. This part of the cathedral was rebuilt after the fire of 1105. One of the arches in the nave is decorated with a staggering sixty-two beakheads, none of them identical, with a mixture of people's faces: sometimes a man with a crown, sometimes bearded, sometimes animal faces, always clasping the rim of the arch.

Round some of the sculpted reliefs is a frame of pearled beadwork of exactly the same type as in the Cappella Palatina ceiling, a clear indication of Islamic craftmanship. Another distinctively Islamic feature is the use of holes drilled in stone using a trepan, over intense black backgrounds, to decorate some of the animals' bodies, the same as seen in the cloister capitals of Saint-Michel-de-Cuixà. The creatures depicted are evidently inspired by ancient Middle Eastern archetypes, and the fact that these same styles and skill levels were found at this time and in earlier centuries in exquisitely carved ivories and metalwork executed by Muslim craftsmen in Andalusia and in Fatimid Egypt once again points to the identity of the artists.[40]

Nothing is known about the origins of French sculpture, except that it goes back to the early twelfth century. Before the year 1000, buildings in France had very little or no sculpted decoration, just blind arches and pilasters dividing exterior walls into sections which projected a simple, geometric aesthetic. The very first known figural forms were those on the lintel at Saint-Génis-des-Fontaines, dated to 1019/20, discussed in detail in Chapter 4, closely followed in 1030 by historiated capitals in the tower of the great royal monastery of Fleury in Saint-Benoît-sur-Loire. These capitals are decorated with apocalyptic figures thought to be inspired by the Mozarabic Beatus, brightly coloured manuscripts illustrating the Book of the Apocalypse which were produced by Christians in newly Arabicised areas like Córdoba and León in the tenth century. These illustrations are the earliest examples of Mozarabic art and show how the Christian artists were influenced by the new Islamic culture around them. In one example, of *The Woman clothed with the sun escaping from the dragon*, the intertwined red and purple dragons, with their perturbing red tongues and bulging eyes, are directly adopted from Islamic art in its characteristic use of vibrant colours, patterned borders and abstract depictions of humans, animals and plants. There are also many eight-pointed stars.

The most likely explanation therefore for why French sculpture blossomed so quickly over the eleventh and twelfth centuries is that Mozarab artists, as the Córdoba Caliphate began to fall apart from the year 1000 onwards, moved north into France in search of new, more stable, work. It appears they were laymen, familiar with the Christian biblical stories and iconography, but bringing with them the influences of the Islamic environment and culture in which they had by that time been immersed for centuries. These influences included a great variety of facial expressions and postures, a sense of the abstract and unreal, and disproportionate people with dislocated limbs and impossible hand gestures. French Romanesque sculpture later evolved into the elaborately decorated facades of Gothic cathedrals, and it is thought that some Romanesque sculptors who had been working in central France were involved in carving some of the earliest parts of the first Gothic cathedrals, from Saint-Denis onwards. At Chartres Cathedral, for example, one of the portals has incredibly tall, thin figures with their mantles' folds falling vertically like column grooves in an abstract stylisation very typical of Islamic art.

Within a short radius of Bayeux are the early-twelfth-century village churches of Saint-Gabriel-Brécy Priory (1140), Saint-Martin-de-Creully and Saint-Martin-de-Ryes, all of which are fitting examples of this high level of decorative carving, with beakheads and human heads, both on the inside and the outside. Saint-Martin-de-Ryes is the most exceptional, with many stiff-leaf capitals based on stylised lotus or papyrus, zigzags galore, and many carved beakheads, one grasping the body of a lion. The capitals are carved

10.14: The jambs of the central doorway of the Royal Portal at Chartres Cathedral, widely seen as a transition to Gothic architecture, are decorated with highly stylised, impossibly tall, thin figures, an abstract style typical of Islamic art. They stand on columns of different geometric patterns, whose bases carry elongated beaded circles.

with many weird unidentifiable creatures, as well as one that is suggestive of a primitive Alexander being escorted to heaven by two griffins.

Lessay

Founded in 1056, but faithfully rebuilt after 1944, the Benedictine Abbaye de la Sainte-Trinité (Abbey of the Holy Trinity) in Lessay is one of the most important Norman Romanesque churches, which, along with Durham Cathedral, boasts one of the first examples of the rib vault, erected in 1098 to cover the choir. When you step inside, the superb workmanship of the stonework is immediately striking, with very harmonious proportions and a delicate, pleasing aesthetic. On the outside, the two arches to the left of the apse appear to have *ablaq* two-tone stonework, and faces hidden among the capitals seem like real men, often bearded. The exterior walls are decorated with vertical pilasters like the Lombardy lesenes, with blind arcades on the tower. There are engaged pillars, tall blind arches and rows of heads at both levels below the roof, and high up on the exterior wall there are three blind arches which are not symmetrical, one much smaller than the other two. Islamic architecture does not value symmetry; it is not important in the way that it is in Latin Christendom. Far more important are the continuous running patterns, with no beginning and no end.

Mont Saint-Michel

There is much embedded evidence of Islamic craftsmanship and technological know-how in the buildings of the island monastery of Mont Saint-Michel, a UNESCO World Heritage Site since 1979. Firstly, the building contractor chosen for the Romanesque expansion of the abbey church was the Italian Benedictine William of Volpiano, whose work we have already seen in Lombardy and in Fécamp, and who already had experience of using the top-level masons who would have been up to this very challenging job. He is generally described as the 'designer' of the daring decision to place the church transept right at the top of the mount. It is far more likely that the plan was proposed to him by a master mason who had full understanding of the complex geometrical and mathematical calculations required to design the necessary underground vaulting and construction of three crypts and chapels with enormous supporting granite pillars to take the weight. The only masons with this level of skill and expertise at this time would have been those who had been trained in the Islamic world, where such technology was already in use under the Fatimids, as in Cairo's Mosque of al-Lu'lu'a, built in 1015–16 in al-Qarafa cemetery from three superimposed vaulted rooms.[41] William of

Volpiano died in 1031, well before construction of the abbey church itself began in 1060.

Even from afar, as you approach the island from the causeway it is striking how the tall, thin blind arches, with their triple recessed slender columns framed by larger arches, decorate the exterior fortification walls, adding the elegance and impression of lightness familiar from Islamic architecture. Further round the walls, the pattern changes to wider blind arches framed within pointed arches, serving no defensive purpose, purely ornamental. There is Venetian dentil running beneath the pyramid slate roof, zigzags round the arches, and the heads of animals and humans carved on the corbels all round the lower line of the tower.

After finally reaching the main abbey church entrance, having climbed the endless stone steps zigzagging up the mount, you are greeted by a joggled voussoir lintel, a technique requiring a high level of skill, but in common use in Islamic architecture to add strength and elegance to a portal.

The nave, rebuilt in the twelfth century, has rounded as opposed to rectangular engaged columns, running all the way from top to bottom, adding elegance to the tall, thin proportions of the vaulting. The thirteenth-century cloister which adjoins the nave feels more like Islamic Spain, with slender twin columns, pointed arches and another joggled voussoir over the arch leading into the refectory.

The kitchen which lies beneath the refectory has more joggled voussoirs in the lintels of its giant pair of fireplaces, and then another one over the single hearth in the guest hall at the next level down. All these techniques are adding extra strength to parts of the construction like doorways and hearth openings where there is a need to carry extra load. Going down a further level, you can inspect the massive vaulting in the crypt, supported by hugely thick round columns, constructed from the local granite.

William of Volpiano was also put in charge of rebuilding the Abbey of Saint-Germain-des-Prés in Paris. A few telling Islamic features remain, such as the striking top-storey *ajimez* windows of the tower, with its unusual geometric window grilles in the lower storeys.

Swiss Normandy

In what is today known as Swiss Normandy because of its hilly terrain and rural character, there is a very interesting group of Romanesque buildings, all of which show clear Islamic influence.

The heavily ruined Savigny-le-Vieux, sister foundation of Neath Abbey in Wales, known to have been built by the Saracen mason Lalys, lies in a remote

10.15: The tenth-century bell tower at the abbey of Saint-Germain-des-Prés in Paris has some of the earliest *ajimez* windows in France in the top two sections, along with geometric patterned window grilles lower down, set in recessed arches.

valley, and was once a very large community with 300 monks. Its excellent workmanship still shows in the one remaining very attractive double portal, with its delicate zigzag decoration, rounded engaged columns, and superior stonework around the windows. The walls still stand tall enough to show the beginnings of the roof vaulting.

L'Abbaye Blanche was founded as a nunnery in 1112, located in its own heavily treed valley beside a rushing stream, below the hilltop town of Mortain. Today it is private property and fenced off, bought by an investor who plans to make it into a language training centre for diplomats. Its twelfth-century cloister has very beautiful carvings, still unrestored, an example of how the French state has not been able to afford the restoration costs of all its many Romanesque buildings.

Lonlay-l'Abbaye

The Benedictine abbey church of Lonlay is one of the most memorable in terms of the exceptional quality of its stonemasonry, crafted from the local sandstone with a level of skill that stands out as beyond anything local masons could possibly have achieved. Nestled in the long valley (hence 'Lonlay') at the heart of the town, it was founded in the early eleventh century and had an immense wealth of land and priories, including on the other side of the English Channel. War and fire damaged it on several occasions, but its magnificent Romanesque capitals are still intact from the late eleventh century, carved with fantastical beasts and intricately detailed foliage.

Domfront

Situated on the southern margins of the Duchy of Normandy, Domfront, where Richard the Lionheart employed his 'Saracens', boasts a dramatic if largely ruined castle on the cliff edge of the town. The Tourist Office sells a publication with a short article entitled 'Le Roi Richard et ses Sarassins'. One of the towers of the castle is known as Tower of the Moors, and the quality of the stonework and construction is unusually high. The keep and the chapel date from the time of Henry I Beauclerc, son of William the Conqueror, Lord of Domfront from 1092, then King of England from 1100 and Duke of Normandy from 1106, who went on to build Reading Abbey. The Great Hall was vaulted with three granite pillars. On the riverbank below, near an ancient ford and mill, is the church of Notre-Dame-sur-l'Eau, built *c.*1100, the original parish church and a priory of the nearby Lonlay Abbey, and reportedly visited by many Anglo-Norman kings like the Plantagenet Henry II, Eleanor of Aquitaine, Richard the Lionheart and Thomas à Becket, Archbishop of Canterbury. Its windows are decorated with billet mouldings and the tower has a row of blind arcades topped with twin windows, while its corbels are carved with heads of humans, probably representing the masons who worked on this and other local projects. The local historian Jean-Philippe Cormier confirmed that Saracens were present in Domfront even after Richard, well into the thirteenth century, and sent me copies of his various articles, where he hypothesises that they were prisoners captured during the Third Crusade, probably during the siege and conquest of Acre, and assigned by partition of booty in the normal way to the king. They seem to have been well treated, given clothing and a horse, as the accounts of the Norman Exchequer for May 1195 detail, so must have been useful to Richard in some way. Local names like La Table des Sarrasins and La Maison des Sarrasins make it clear that they stayed in the area, and the last mention in local records comes from 1292, in connection with Count Robert II of Artois, nephew of King Louis IX (the Saint), who is known to have gone on the 1270 Crusade and to have had long stays in Sicily or southern Italy. Louis himself is recorded as arriving at Cyprus in 1248, accompanied by his chamberlain Jean Pierre Sarrasin (John the Saracen).[42]

In 1288 Count Robert began work on a great park at Hesdin, between Calais and Amiens, in which 'Saracens' may well have contributed their expertise, since as well as mechanical statues of waving monkeys draped in skins (such robotic automation was well developed in the Islamic world), the magnificent park boasted a menagerie, aviaries, fishponds, orchards, enclosed gardens and facilities for tournaments, all of which Robert would have first seen in the Holy Land on Crusade, when crusading knights copied the Saracen horsemen who held jousting tournaments on the plains of Syria.[43] The elites of medieval Europe revelled in such elaborate entertainment to showcase their wealth and power; banquets featured wine pouring from fountains and Islamic delicacies like sugared almonds and rosewater showering their guests' heads like hail.[44]

Gardens were another feature introduced into monasteries and abbeys at this time, as knowledge of the medicinal properties of herbs and flowers passed over from the Islamic world. The Abbey of Saint-Georges-de-Boscherville near Rouen has one of the finest and most extensive, with special areas for medicinal and other aromatic plants.

The cloister courtyard of Mont Saint-Michel, with its spectacular view out to sea, has a geometrically laid out garden of medicinal herbs and even Damascus roses, the work of a Benedictine monk who in 1966 sought to recreate the medieval garden the monks would have enjoyed. The concept of a garden for beauty, contemplation, meditation and health, as opposed to a more utilitarian allotment-like garden for food, was introduced to Europe via the Islamic world and embraced by the monks.

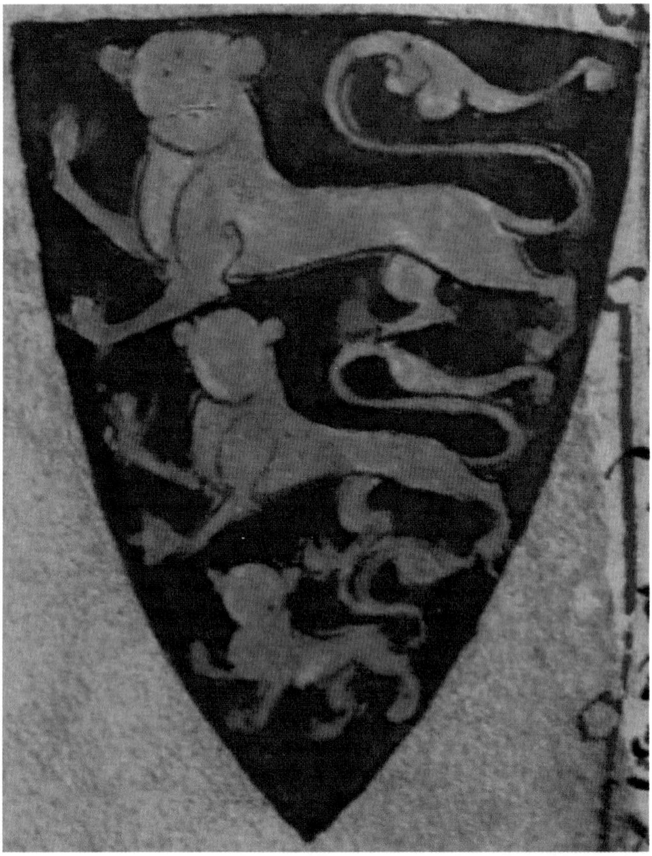

11.1: The Royal Coat of Arms of England—the familiar three gold lions on a red background—was first used by Richard the Lionheart on his seal in 1198. It was the same year he completed his beloved Chateau Gaillard overlooking the Seine, using many innovative 'Saracen' military styles first encountered on crusade in the Holy Land. On return to France in 1194 Richard employed 'Saracens', as recorded in the Norman Exchequer of 1195, and the timing suggests he also adopted the 'Saracen' symbol of the lion. In an identical stylised pose, moving from right to left, right paw raised, tail curled upwards, face turned towards the viewer, mouth open, tongue out, it was already in use on Fatimid banners of the period.

11

ISLAMESQUE IN THE BRITISH ISLES

Every Norman church and cathedral in the British Isles stands as a testament to the Islamic influence highlighted throughout this book; so much so that it has been very difficult to select just a few for this chapter. As with France, a whole book could very easily have been written on the Norman monuments in England alone. The terms 'Romanesque' and 'Norman' are interchangeable in the context of Britain, but it is worth looking briefly, to begin with, at the pre-Norman context.

Insular Art

The term Insular (Island) Art or Hiberno-Saxon Art is generally used by art historians to describe the style used across Great Britain and Ireland between the end of the Roman era and the beginning of the Romanesque or Norman period, broadly from the fifth to the eleventh centuries. Most Insular art originates from the Irish monastic movement of Celtic Christianity, itself heavily indebted to Coptic art and artefacts brought back from Egypt by the first Irish monks, as explained in Chapter 3.

One major distinctive feature of Insular Art is interlace decoration, as found on metalwork at Sutton Hoo in East Anglia, like the belt buckle (now in the British Museum) covered in zoomorphic complex animal interlace, a decorative style copied from the Mediterranean world and then applied to other media such as illuminated manuscripts, most notably the Book of Kells (dated to *c.*800).

Kenneth Clark confessed himself baffled by the origins of such decorative designs, remarking:

> The strange thing about these books is that the monks who decorated them seem to have had so little consciousness of any form of Classical or Christian culture.

> They are all Gospel books, but they are almost devoid of Christian symbols, except for the fierce oriental-looking beasts who symbolise the Four Evangelists.[1]

Much of the exceptionally high quality of the metalwork finds at Sutton Hoo shows its roots in the Byzantine Eastern Mediterranean, often from earlier Sassanian models.[2] This is unsurprising, since the Vikings had traded and raided as far as Iran and Baghdad by 800, via the Volga river and the Caspian Sea, exporting furs, wax, honey and slaves while importing silver, spices, textiles, fruits, wine and jewellery. They referred to it as 'Serkland' or 'the land of the Serkir', usually identified as Saracens. From the tenth to the fourteenth centuries, the Norsemen even served as mercenaries in an elite unit of the Byzantine army known as the Varangian Guard, personal bodyguards to the Byzantine emperors. Scandinavian museums boast the highest number in the world of silver coins from the medieval Islamic world, almost 500,000 dirhams. Some of the coins also found their way to Britain, where they were often turned into jewellery.[3]

These interweaving zoomorphic braid patterns were thought to have been transmitted directly to Irish monasteries through the travels of the Irish monks to the Coptic monasteries of Egypt, or possibly to have come via Lombardy in Italy, where Irish monasteries had schools. Pairs of elongated beasts intertwined with foliage and whole pages in manuscripts were covered in decorative, highly coloured abstract and geometric interlacing patterns, known as 'carpet pages' because they often had border frames like Middle Eastern carpets. Interlace and knotwork were not especially prominent in Byzantine art, but Islamic art adopted geometric interlacing patterns with great gusto, building on the earlier Roman and Coptic patterns. It was used especially in Islamic architecture from the eighth century onwards in floor mosaics, window grilles and carved stucco wall decoration, as well as on metalwork. In a stone relief from the Umayyad Mosque in Damascus (completed 715) the typical pearled beading also appears decoratively on some of the leaves, to emphasise the stems.

Many commentators have noted that Irish sculpture from around 900 CE, in the form of its elaborately carved crosses from early Irish monasteries, appears to anticipate the emergence of Romanesque art in Europe a century or so later. Sometimes Irish sculpture is even described as proto-Romanesque, with clear parallels in iconography and technique. The artists were anonymous, only the patron being named—as with the Abbot Muiredach after whom the Muiredach Cross at Monasterboice monastery is named. The mystery craftsman himself is simply referred to as the 'Muiredach Master'.

The iconography of these Celtic crosses shows clear parallels with far earlier Coptic designs,[4] as covered in Chapter 3, so it is not unreasonable to presume that, as with Romanesque sculpture, foreign craftsmen were at work. The way in which the scenes on the crosses are set in frames is reminiscent of earlier Coptic and Islamic work, as is the use of interlace separated by bosses and the use of the pump drill to make the patterns of beaded interlace. The sculpture of the two men pulling each other's beards, also found on Romanesque capitals in France, has been thought by Zehava Jacoby to be taken from Islamic art,[5] a scene of humour rather than aggression, judging by their faces. Descriptions of beard-pulling exist in early Arabic literature and the motif also occurs on Fatimid plates in Egypt, with mock battles and tests of strength thought to represent courtly entertainment for the caliph, in the same way as wrestling, music and dancing.

As well as the Celtic High Crosses, the other intriguing buildings which appear in Ireland *c.*900, as if out of nowhere, are the Irish round towers, thought to be monastery bell towers, some seventy of which are found across the island. Irish architectural artist Hector McDonnell, marvelling at the phenomenon, wrote: 'The actual erection of the towers required a level of constructional knowledge that was new in Ireland.'[6] All have extraordinarily shallow foundations, yet many still stand to over 30 metres, tapering to the top in registers, usually with four windows on the top register, thereby lightening the load as the tower gets higher. Early Islamic architecture is known to have unusually shallow foundations, often less than a metre deep, as long as the construction is built on firm rock. Examples of these traditional early Arab construction techniques can still be seen in parts of Rijal Almaa, a village in Saudi Arabia on the pilgrimage route to Mecca. Its tall houses, sometimes rising to eight storeys, were built from the inside out by local master builders, carefully laying each stone to fit perfectly with its fellows. Tall round stone watchtowers also still stand as isolated structures in the hills to defend the villages, built in the same way.[7] Scaffolding was not used, as the master builders relied on the accuracy of their techniques, notably the running bond, where one brick or stone was overlapped by the two above.

The only places where round towers were to be found in continental Europe were in Italy's Ravenna, the Byzantine capital in the West till it was captured by the Lombards in the eighth century. Ravenna is known to have had Irish monastic connections as well as close links with Antioch, where all its early bishops came from, including Ravenna's patron saint Apollinaris. Ravenna also had strong trading links in the eighth and ninth centuries to Egypt and North Africa, where the earliest minarets were often round towers placed on top of existing buildings, like the seventh-century mosque built on the upper platform of the round Pharos lighthouse after the Muslim capture of Alexandria. The word minaret is thought to derive from the Arabic *minara*, meaning lighthouse.

The use of lime mortar seen between the carefully curved stones of the Irish towers is another unusual feature, having largely fallen out of use when prestige building commissions dried up across Europe following the fall of Rome. All over the Middle East, however, it remained in common use, much in demand in the continuous high-level building projects. To this day all restoration work to old buildings in the Middle East uses lime mortar, as it was during the restoration of my own Damascus house, where the lime (Arabic *kilis*) was slaked for at least four months. In Ireland, around the date of the round towers, only a king would have been able to afford such costly mortar, let alone the high-quality stone and skilled craftsmen to go with it.

Anglo-Saxon Pre-Norman Architecture

The earliest Saxon buildings were built of wood, but the first step towards a Saxon Romanesque style was taken in 674 when Benedict Biscop (*c*.628–690), an Anglo-Saxon nobleman who had already travelled to Rome three times from his native Northumbria, was charged by King Ecgfrith to build a monastery at the mouth of the River Wear. After spending nearly a year laying the foundations, despairing of finding masons in England, Biscop crossed to Gaul, found some masons and brought them back with him. Within a year the church was built.[8] He then sent for glass-makers to glaze the windows, 'the art of glass-making being unknown in Britain at that time',[9] who subsequently taught the English how to do it for themselves.

Rome at this time was under Byzantine rule, so many Byzantine influences passed into English church styles and practices via men like Biscop, who was made a saint on his death. The architectural styles found in churches of this Anglo-Saxon period, like Monkwearmouth, Earls Barton, Barton-upon-Humber, Barnack, Bradford-on-Avon, Carhampton, Dover Castle, Repton and St Bene't's, Cambridge, are sometimes described as a unique Anglo-Saxon pre-Romanesque style of architecture, but when examined carefully, all the characteristics they exhibit can be traced to foreign craftsmen who had been brought in, since such styles had no forerunners in England. Jackson tells us that he has never seen such styles in Italian architecture of the same period either, and believes them to have been 'inspired by the art of eastern rather than that of western Rome'.[10] He cites the examples of the western doorway porch of St Peter's Church, Monkwearmouth, with its two curious serpentine creatures intertwined and with beaked heads, together with a frieze finely sculpted with animals and the cross of Acca, Bishop of Hexham (d.740), in the cathedral library at Durham, 'enriched with an arabesque pattern of singular delicacy and beauty, instead of the usual knot-work'.[11] All Saints' Church at Earls Barton has a tower covered in decorative lesenes.

He notes that the triangular twin windows in the nave of St Mary's Priory, Deerhurst on the Severn, resemble the arcading at Lorsch, as does the fluted pilaster dividing the twin windows. The Islamic antecedents, on the other

11.2: The exterior of the tenth-century crenellated tower at All Saints' Church in Earls Barton, Northamptonshire, England, is decorated in a variety of Islamic styles including the row of five *ajimez* windows at the highest level, and tall slender lesenes that form lozenge patterns and a frieze of semi-circles.

hand, of the lesenes decorating the tall rectangular tower at Earls Barton, of the *ajimez* windows in the towers at Monkwearmouth and Barnack and of the blind arcading and slightly stilted horseshoe chancel arch of St Laurence's at Bradford-on-Avon go unremarked.

Norman Islamesque

Most Norman churches and cathedrals across England were built within the first eighty or ninety years after the conquest in 1066. Saxon architecture had already suffered waves of destruction at the hands of the Danes and the Norsemen, and in the 469 years between the coming of Augustine and the coming of the Normans, local architecture had sunk into what Thomas Graham Jackson calls 'a sort of Byzantine immobility',[12] with little or no change. All the more phenomenal, therefore, is the amount of construction undertaken by the Normans across Britain and Ireland. Never was there a time when 'so great a burst of architecture took place',[13] leaving its mark on most churches and cathedrals. Even village churches usually have at least a Norman doorway or chancel arch. The chronicler William of Malmesbury summed it up: 'Nearly all try to rival one another in sumptuous buildings of the style which Edward the Confessor had first introduced into this country. Everywhere you may see in villages churches, in towns monasteries rising in the new style of building.'[14]

So determined were the Normans to mark their new territory with their own style, and so unconvinced by the local ability to contribute anything beyond the most basic labour, that they imported both the top craftsmen and the top stone from Caen across the English Channel, starting with the magisterial White Tower, the keep or *donjon* of the Tower of London, built by William the Conqueror in 1078, with its part-decorative, part-structural lesenes (vertical pilasters) on the exterior walls and corners, together with its elegant *ajimez* windows set in decorative blind arches.

The particular features associated with the Norman style across Britain and Ireland, from the advanced vaulting to the distinctive styles of ornamentation, all derive without exception from the Islamic world, brought in by the Normans influenced by the Arabic style they had learnt in Sicily, in the Italian mainland and in Muslim Spain. These features include quadripartite and sexpartite vaulting based on the pointed arch, decorative blind arcades (Lombard bands), tall blind arches, intersecting arches and arcades, Venetian dentil, lesenes, *ajimez* windows, polychrome masonry effects, corbels, continuous bands of arabesque and geometric patterns including zigzags (chevrons) and

11.3: The White Tower or keep of the Tower of London, built under William the Conqueror in 1078, shows Islamic influence in its elegant *ajimez* windows set in recessed blind arches and the part-decorative, part-structural lesenes on its exterior walls.

lozenges running round doorways and arches, beakheads, and continuous bands of dog-tooth, a motif of four flower petals in the form of pointed teeth like canines. This last was brought back by the Norman Crusaders in the early twelfth century from the Holy Land, where the very first example was seen running round the arch moulding of the blind arcades in the great hall of Rabbath Ammon in Moab, Jordan, built by the Sassanians in 614 CE. On top of all these features, there are also the carved capitals, progressing from simple 'stiff leaf' to highly animated zoomorphic scenes of fantastical beasts, all of which will be discussed, as in earlier chapters, and have their Islamic antecedents explained.

Westminster Abbey

The earliest building identified as Romanesque in Britain in fact predates the Norman conquest of 1066, and was built by Edward the Confessor, whose mother, Emma, was a Norman. He lived in exile in Normandy till he became King of England in 1042, and was more a Norman than an Englishman. He died in 1066 and is buried in Westminster Abbey, erected in the Norman style with which he was familiar, and which went on, after the Norman conquest, to revolutionise the art and architecture of England. He is known to have brought in masons from France to carry out the work, who, given the timing, can only have been schooled in the Islamic tradition.

Just a few parts of the Romanesque building remain, notably the eleventh-century Pyx Chamber, whose capitals were enriched in the twelfth century; but we know what the original abbey looked like because it features in the Bayeux Tapestry as the destination of a procession carrying Edward's body for burial. It is shown with a blind arcade along its nave facade, but also, most remarkably, with a large central tower topped by a bulbous pepper-pot, Fatimid-style dome like the Arab-Norman churches of Palermo, and flanked by a pair of pointed minaret-style slender square towers topped with ribbed cones. Given the tapestry is thought by scholars to have been made in Canterbury soon after the Battle of Hastings, the likeness must be realistic, since everything else in the tapestry is faithfully depicted and details of this sort are most unlikely to have been pure fantasy.

The Islamic influences continue into the later additions, such as the octagonal Chapter House (1245–53), surrounded with blind arcading, perched directly above the octagonal eleventh-century crypt, with its pier of eight shafts carrying the vaulted ceiling. The style is today referred to as Geometric Gothic, and the geometry underlying the design is also visible in the Cosmati pavement (see Chapter 6) in front of the altar, where coronations take place—most recently that of King Charles III in 2023.

The abbot Richard of Ware arranged for the transportation of the craftsmen and the stones from Rome in 1258, by which time these Islamic geometric techniques are likely to have passed over to Christian artists. The porphyry, pilfered from Roman villas, would originally have been quarried in Egypt's Mons Porphyrites in Roman times; it was much favoured by the wealthy for its colour and rarity in their monumental sarcophagi, some of which are still on view in Rome's Vatican Museum and in Palermo Cathedral.

The geometric designs themselves, according to art historian Richard Foster, 'were thought to help the abbeys' monks in their contemplation, and conveyed medieval Christian ideas on the nature of the universe that could not easily be put into words'.[15] These are precisely the same theories behind the use of geometric patterns in Islamic art, predating the Cosmati pavements by centuries. The patterned floor at Westminster Abbey was the first of this type in England and went on to influence those at Canterbury Cathedral and St George's Chapel Windsor; an example even appears in Hans Holbein's 1533 painting *The Ambassadors*. The design is based on a Greek geometric principle known as the doubling of the square, a technique considered a trade secret among stonemasons, lost for centuries in Europe after the fall of Rome, but continuously developed without interruption across the Islamic world.

Geometric Gothic was also known as Decorated Gothic because of the amount of decoration and ornamentation. Westminster Abbey's north transept rose window is a geometric design built round an eight-petalled flower, expanding to a sixteen-petalled flower.

11.4: The geometric design of the Cosmati pavement in Westminster Abbey, where the coronation of kings takes place, most recently of Charles III, is one of many Islamic-influenced features found throughout the building. It was the first such pavement in England, laid down in 1268.

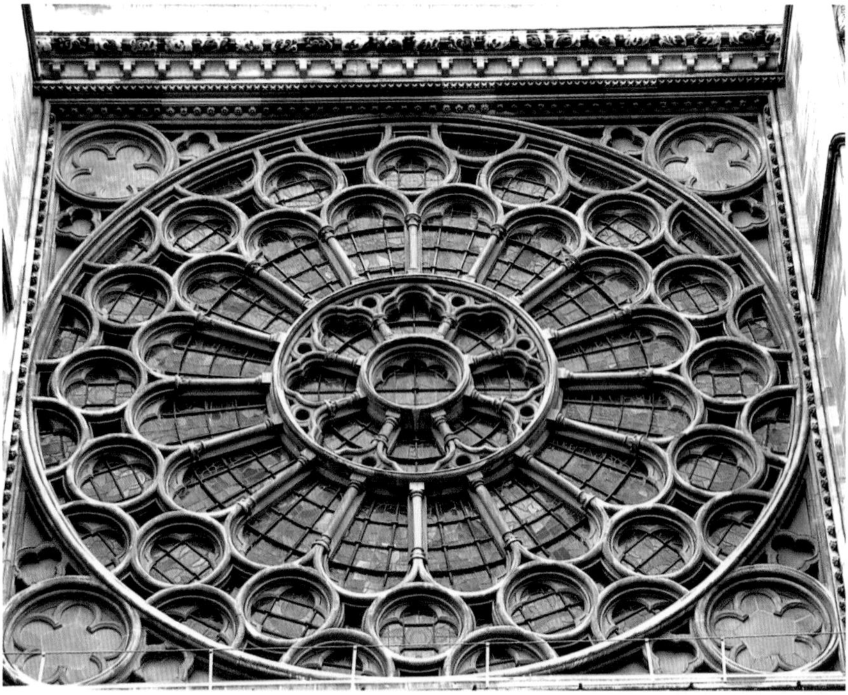

11.5: The eleventh-century north transept geometric rose window of Westminster Abbey is based on an Islamic design around a central eight-petalled flower, expanding to a sixteen-petalled flower.

Almost every facade and interior surface is decorated in the same way that Islamic architecture had been in its tenth-century heyday in Islamic Spain at Madinat al-Zahra, with cinquefoil cusped arches framing the multicoloured choir screen. High in the exhibition galleries of the triforium the original altarpiece is on display, the oldest in the country to survive, decorated with eight-pointed stars.

Canterbury Cathedral

While the Tower of London was the first secular Norman construction after the 1066 conquest, the first major religious one was at Canterbury Cathedral (consecrated in 1077) in a rebuilding project overseen by Lanfranc. Lanfranc himself, the Italian monk from Pavia in Lombardy, would have seen in his native city during his youth the fine Lombard Romanesque style, with its arcaded walls, rich in marble and sculpture. He would have been very familiar with prestige building projects and known where to source the best craftsmen, and would almost certainly have had several teams of top-class masons already on his payroll. His Canterbury Cathedral was completed in a remarkable time of just seven years, a testament to the skill of his builders. The plan was very similar to that of Westminster Abbey, and the dimensions corresponded very closely to those of the Abbaye aux Hommes in Caen (see Chapter 10), where Lanfranc had been the first abbot as well as the director of the building project. The nave had originally been fitted with a magnificent colourfully painted wooden ceiling, praised by the contemporary chronicler

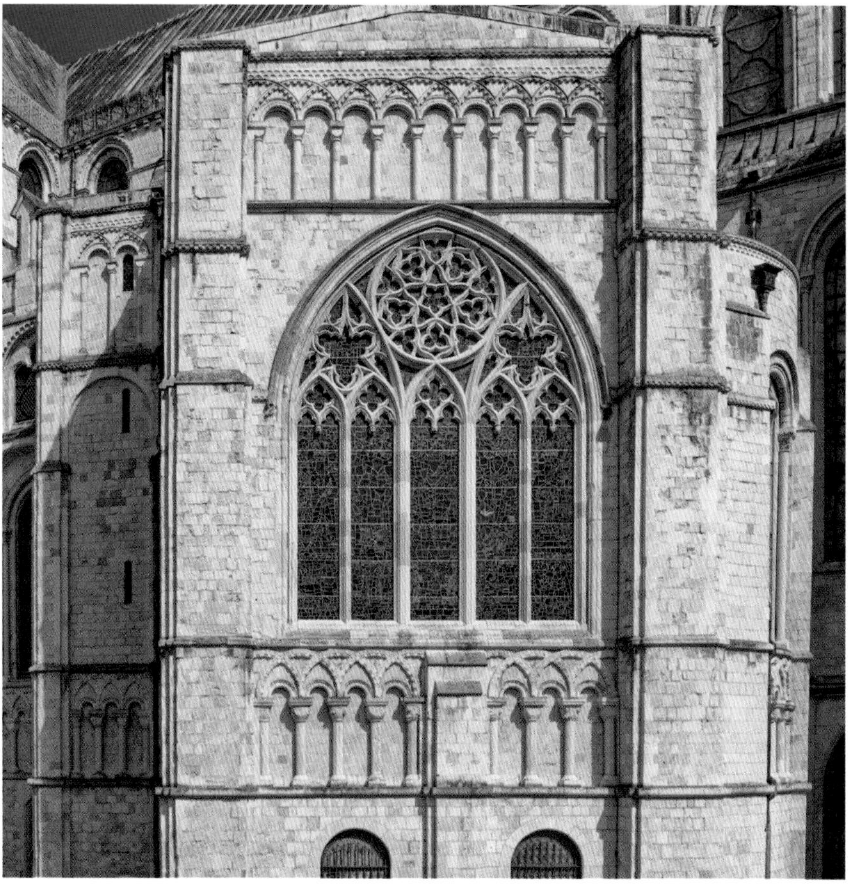

11.6: The early-twelfth-century parts of Canterbury Cathedral in Kent, England, at the southeastern end towards the apse and Corona, show the distinctive ornamental Andalusian-style interlocking arches of the stonework, blind arcades, tall blind arches, cusped tracery and quatrefoils. The slender columns are decorated with zigzags, lozenges and spirals, each different, with no symmetry.

William of Malmesbury: 'Nothing like it could be seen in England either for the light of its glass windows, the gleaming of its marble pavements, or the many-coloured paintings which led the eyes to the panelled ceiling above.'[16] As we know from both Sicily and Muslim Spain, only Muslim craftsmen had these kinds of skills at that time. When William of Sens introduced the Islamic sexpartite vault, he also brought the typical Islamic use of contrasting stones (*ablaq*) in the dark Purbeck marble and the pale Caen limestone.

The earliest parts of the Romanesque cathedral remaining today, after the ravages of the 1174 fire and Gothic rebuilding programmes, bear all the same hallmarks of Islamic decorative styles already seen in Lombardy. At the exterior eastern end, the walls are decorated with the characteristic rows of blind arches and arcades as already seen in Sicily, with highly ornamental zigzags, lozenges and spirals on slender columns and arch frames. The water tower on the northern side, with its alternate black and white banding, is also distinctive, covered with zigzags as you would expect from a feature whose function was to bring flowing water into the monastery from a nearby spring. Higher up on the exterior wall, on both the north and the south sides of the eastern end of the cathedral, are a pair of multilobed Andalusian-style blind arch frames.

Inside the cathedral, the oldest Romanesque work can be seen underground in the astonishing crypt, the largest in England and still containing the best and most enigmatic sculptures of the Romanesque period to be found anywhere in Britain or Ireland. Dated to *c.*1100, their subject matter, with fantastical beasts animatedly playing musical instruments, hybrid monsters spewing beaded interlace from their mouths, and bizarre two-headed beings riding stylised dragons, has puzzled art historians and clergymen for centuries—not least Bernard of Clairvaux. It has often simply been dismissed as 'pagan', with excuses like 'the meaning of many of these (capitals) was probably unclear even to those who carved them', a view that the author of the cathedral's own archaeology website has arrived at from studying a wide range of sources.[17] Writing in 1851, Charles Cockerell, Professor of Architecture at London's Royal Academy, likewise dismissed them: 'there are some barbaric sculptures in the capitals of the pillars, possibly erected by Lanfranc (1077): they appear to be without meaning'.[18]

There are models from the ancient Middle East for many of these images and archetypes, but the way in which they found their way to Canterbury needs to be properly understood. These ancient Middle Eastern models would have been assimilated first by the Egyptian Copts and then by the Muslims of Fatimid Egypt, with whom these sculptures are contemporary.

Even the Umayyads in Syria, the very first Islamic dynasty, had a fresco of a bear playing a harp in the palace bathhouse of Qusayr Amra, in today's Jordanian desert. There is no such tradition in Byzantine art, but there certainly is in Islamic art; a visit to Cairo's Museum of Islamic Art will show you fragments of wood and stone carving in precisely such styles from secular settings like the Fatimid caliph's palace in Cairo, depicting the caliph being entertained by dancers, musicians, wrestlers and sometimes wild beasts trained to perform antics.

In the Canterbury crypt capitals, as in the artworks of the Syrian Umayyads and the Egyptian Fatimids, there are precisely such scenes of entertainers, like the acrobats tumbling with a fish and bowl, where the fish is always vertical; a stylised dragon biting the wrist of the goat who is blowing into a wind instrument; a two-headed dog with fangs and breasts sitting astride a dragon with heads at each end; and a winged monster spearing a dog.

Close to Canterbury are a pair of twelfth-century village churches, which also display a remarkably high level of stone carving, at Barfrestone and Patrixbourne. The Barfrestone church is sometimes called 'the Kilpeck of the South', as it boasts a similar level of complex sculpture round its portals and on its corbels as its more famous counterpart in Herefordshire. So distinctive is its portal that the Victoria and Albert Museum's Cast Court even has a full-size replica of it for those who do not have time to make the pilgrimage to the remote village in the Kent Downs. Like Kilpeck, it is obviously way above the level of craftsmanship that local sculptors would have been capable of, and skilled artists from abroad must have carried out the commission.

Beyond all the decorative details, it is the whole ensemble, the entire conception of the doorway and its arches, that is unmistakeably Islamic. The individual elements within the roundels will change according to the context of what the patron might request or require, but the ornamental framework that the artist begins with, namely the arabesque scrolls, the panels and recessed engaged columns and blind arcades, are all elements that remain consistent and are therefore recognisable to the trained eye. Immediately above the roundels, the arch of the portal still bears clear fragments of its original pearl-beaded framing.

The churches at Barfrestone and Patrixbourne are so similar they are likely to have had the same master mason. Each boasts a rose window on its east facade, therefore accounting for two out of the only five rose wheel windows in the United Kingdom. Wheel windows differ from typical rose windows in their use of simple circular or semicircular mullions as spokes radiating from a central boss, and the term 'rose window' was in any event only introduced

11.7: The twelfth-century village church at Barfrestone may well have had its decorative sculpture carved by the same master mason as at the nearby Canterbury Cathedral, given its familiar repertoire of blind arcades, corbels with animal heads and the pearl-beaded framing of the elaborate entrance portal.

11.8: The twelfth-century village church of Patrixbourne near Canterbury is similarly familiar, with its eight-petalled 'wheel' window, its spokes being eaten by fantastical beasts, the whole ensemble framed with zigzags spewed by a central head.

in the seventeenth century. Each has eight spokes, modelled on the eight-pointed star and the eight-petalled flower as seen in the Santiago rose window of Master Mateo. At Patrixbourne, a Green Man appears at the top of the rose window, his moustache a continuation of the zigzags round the window rim decoration. In both churches the spokes of the wheel are being eaten away by monstrous creatures.

Reading Abbey

Though sadly now in ruins, this vast and powerful Benedictine abbey was hugely influential in its day as the most richly decorated building in the area. It was founded in 1121 by King Henry I (r.1100–35), fourth son of William the Conqueror, and endowed with generous gifts of land, privileges and money. The fourth longest church in England, it would have required a small army of builders and enormous quantities of materials. No expense was spared in its construction, and we are told that monks from the Benedictine headquarters of Cluny in Burgundy, to which Henry also gave large sums of money, came to supervise. Some of the stone was shipped over from Caen then transported up the Thames, and some was brought from Taynton in Oxfordshire, further upstream. There is no mention of who the master mason or architect was, but we do know that Lalys, the skilled mason from Palestine, brought back from Crusade by the Glamorgan knight Robert de Grenville (see Chapter 5), was working for Henry I as his architect. Neath Abbey, Lalys's construction for de Grenville, was complete by 1129, while Reading Abbey was not yet complete at the time of Henry's death in 1135, so it is possible that Lalys was involved in both projects.

The quality of Reading Abbey's craftsmanship can thankfully still be seen at the neo-Gothic Reading Museum which displays its salvaged sculpture, one of the richest collections of Romanesque or Anglo-Norman stonework in Britain. Many of the carvings on display today were tracked down from other buildings, but the remnants are extremely important as they give the clues relating to certain mysterious elements of Romanesque sculpture like the so-called beakheads, and they also offer the chance to examine the stonework in close-up. Most are from the cloister, and the influence of the Canterbury crypt capitals is clear in the subject matter, like the pair of winged fantastical beasts, and a head spewing vine scrolls in the form of pearl-beaded interlace which then becomes a continuous border of roundels, each of which contains an animal, a motif which is seen in Coptic fabrics and that continued into Islamic ornamentation.

As late as the nineteenth century it was fashionable to look for moral messages by identifying monstrous creatures with the animals described in medieval bestiaries, which had Christian ethical messages attached to them in the text. Gargoyle waterspouts, for example, were seen as devils conquered by the church, set to perform menial tasks. The on-site sculpture captions at Reading follow the same trend, telling how 'terrifying inventions like this, which deliberately contradicted the divinely ordered nature of the world, were there to remind the monks of the constant presence of the devil at their shoulder'. Another tells us that the carving of a man with a bishop's crozier surrounded by entangling vegetation means that 'a holy person must guard against being entangled in the temptations of the world and the devil'. One top-quality so-called 'trefoil capital' has been carved from a single stone, in a very high-risk strategy. One mistake would ruin the whole thing—such a technique would only be attempted by someone at the top of his game, highly skilled and experienced. The whole capital is framed by the typical Islamic pearled beading.

Beakhead Motif

Beakheads make their first known appearance on English soil at Reading Abbey, and one striking example has been salvaged and put on display in the museum. It is described as the 'head of a savage bird with almond-shaped eyes and a long beak gripping the decorative arch moulding'. The caption claims the design was created especially for Reading (even though earlier examples exist in France and in Spain; see Chapters 2, 8 and 10). The motif 'must have been popular with visitors', we are told, 'because it quickly spread to other monasteries and churches'. Within a 40-kilometre radius of Oxford a total of fourteen churches with well-preserved beakhead arches have been identified. The church of the Assumption of the Blessed Virgin in Twyford, Buckinghamshire, has a very fine south portal with beakheads, zigzags and eight-pointed stars. An interesting feature of the beakhead motif is that it produces alternations of light and shadow across the arches, which are effective in conveying a feeling of richness and solidity and echo similar effects produced by the corbels below the roof line, and indeed by zigzags. Bands of zigzags and beakheads often occur together in the archivolts of arches, and have exactly the same play on light and shade in exterior decoration that was, and is still, so important in Islamic architecture.

The ultimate example is the highly complex *muqarnas* vaulting system, as seen in ceilings like the Cappella Palatina, where its effect is to blur the distinction between the solid and the ephemeral, the transition zone between the earthly and the divine.

Within England the distribution of beakheads is extremely uneven. It is very scarce in Kent, Hertfordshire, Dorset, Lancashire, Bedfordshire, Northumberland, Shropshire, Leicestershire, Warwickshire, Somerset and even Herefordshire; but in Yorkshire there are more than fifty sites with beakheads, and a further forty in the area between the Chilterns and the Cotswolds, covering the counties of Berkshire, Oxfordshire, Gloucestershire and Buckinghamshire. This suggests that, just as in France where its appearance comes in clusters, only a few workshops of sculptors were responsible for its introduction into England, and the evidence strongly suggests a connection with royal works carried out under Henry I. The beakhead was short-lived, no longer found after 1160–70, when Geoffrey de Clinton, patron of St Mary the Virgin, Iffley, was the last to employ it, which again suggests that the masons who brought it in did not settle in England.

Old Sarum

At roughly the same time as Reading Abbey was being constructed, Old Sarum Cathedral in Wiltshire was being enlarged and elaborated by Roger, Bishop of Salisbury (d.1139), Henry I's chief justiciar for most of his reign (the justiciar was roughly equivalent to the prime minister today), also using beakheads, which suggests some of the same workforce was employed. Further examples can be seen at Sherborne Old Castle, and the castles at Devizes and Malmesbury, all associated with Roger.

As Lord Keeper of England and Lord Chancellor, Roger was the most powerful man in the kingdom, acting as Regent during Henry I's frequent sojourns abroad in Normandy. From his origins as an impoverished monk at Caen, his rise to power was nothing short of meteoric, and once he had control of the Exchequer he evidently spent freely on his building projects, using the best craftsmen money could buy. His taste was described as being in advance of his age, and he had a great love of extravagant ornament, not only in his buildings; he also wore exotically decorated and bejewelled garments and owned extravagantly engraved gold and silverware, none of which, sadly, has survived. Very little too survives of his great constructions, so we can only get a glimpse of their magnificence through medieval chroniclers and the splendid carved stone fragments that have been salvaged and which are now on display in the Salisbury and South Wiltshire Museum.

Many of these bear tell-tale signs of Islamic influence which we have now come to recognise, such as the carved lions with their beaded spines, manes sculpted as curly tufts, long claws, elegant tails curling over their bodies and large oval bulging eyes with drilled pupils. There are sections of interlaced arcading edged with pearl-beaded frames, palmettes, leaves with a central spine of beads, and criss-cross strapwork decorated with drilled beads. One stone has a mason's mark in the form of a five-pointed star. There are many examples of quatrefoils with more elaborate curved forms, nicknamed 'ravioli', decorated with small drill holes along their edge, resembling pinched and folded sheets of pasta. The fluidity of the form, compared with the simple geometric form of some stones, suggests it is the work of carvers with a higher skill level.

The exceptional quality of the architectural detailing in the twelfth-century fragments remaining from Old Sarum suggest that when the workshop disbanded, around 1139, its craftsmen would have been in great demand. Their work has been detected in churches that are often connected with Roger in some way, in Wiltshire, east Somerset and South Wales, and one of the most remarkable is at the little Somerset church of All Saints, Lullington, where beakheads, the distinctive 'ravioli', paired muscular lions with tufty manes and long curling tails, paired heads with drilled oval pupils and the tell-tale pearl-beaded roundels are all on view, in characteristic Islamic deeply incised style. The beakhead arch is framed with pearled beading and the font has an arcade of interlocking arches resting on twin pillars, another clue that points to Muslim Spain. Further north at Chirton and at Devizes in Wiltshire, also under the influence of Roger of Salisbury, similar sophisticated motifs appear, including the use of rib vaults, while Leonard Stanley's priory church in southern Gloucestershire also shares some similar Old Sarum characteristics, like the pair of lions with drilled oval eyes in the tympanum, with their muscular legs and beaded manes. Further afield, the same detailing is on view at Newark Castle, Kenilworth Priory and Lincoln Cathedral, where the presence of motifs from Old Sarum is probably due to Bishop Roger's nephew being the Bishop of Lincoln (1123–48).[19]

Roger's tomb memorial slab of *c.*1140–50 is made of Tournai black polished marble, and the decorative details bear the typical Islamic beading pattern among the foliage. At his feet a fantastical creature lies coiled. A plaster cast copy of the slab, made in 1882 for display at the Crystal Palace exhibition in Sydenham, survived the fire there and is now on display at the Cast Court in the Victoria and Albert Museum. The original is in Salisbury Cathedral.

Old Sarum also had links through southern Wales, where it owned some land, and its influence even spread into Ireland. Roger is known to have spent time in Llanthony Priory, one of Wales's great medieval buildings. Now a ruin, its former magnificence can still be seen in its richly decorated red stonework and superb arcade of pointed arches.

Rochester Cathedral

Rochester's Great West Door, with its stonework substantially unaltered, marks the highest level achieved by Norman architectural sculpture. It is 'the most ancient example', as Cockerell writes, 'of iconographic art, of ascertained date, in this country, having been begun by Bishop Gundulphus in 1103', the third year of Henry I's reign. The joggled voussoir (see Chapter 3) of its lintel, therefore, 'locked into its neighbour in the Saracenic fashion',[20] as Cockerell correctly observes, is all the more significant, unlike anything else seen before or since in England. Its purpose was to ensure there could be no slippage in the important sculpture directly above the West Door, originally the main entrance to the cathedral.

Rochester Cathedral's website gives the results of their survey of masons' marks found in the cathedral—all 3,912 of them. Analysis of the marks showed a clear distinction in mark types across both building campaigns, from the earlier west end construction of the 1140s to the 1160s, and the rebuilt east end after the fire of 1179. The only complex mark type to occur across both campaigns is the trefoil 3a282,[21] a curved sign already seen earlier, as at Santiago in Spain, which hints at a mason schooled in the Islamic tradition. Given the time span, the mark may have been passed down from father to son, which would also explain its appearance at multiple locations. In the nave, with its stiff-leaf capitals, there is elaborate embroidery-like patterning between the six Romanesque arch spaces on either side, each one different, with no symmetry.

The Norman monk Gundulf (*c.*1024–1108) is often credited with the buildings of Rochester, both castle and cathedral (*c.*1103–60), as well as the Tower of London, Colchester Castle and St Leonard's Tower in West Malling. He was a friend, pupil and chamberlain of Lanfranc, appointed by him to be Bishop of Rochester in 1077, and was described as 'competent and skilled at building in stone'.[22] Through Lanfranc's Lombard connections, he would have known where to source the best masons. Gundulf served under three kings of England, starting with William the Conqueror, and is often called the first 'King's Engineer' and regarded as the father of the Corps of Royal Engineers to this day. His statue stands on the west front at Rochester, holding a model of the White Tower, remarkably accurately depicted with its lesenes and *ajimez* windows, the hem of his robes framed with a bead and zigzag pattern and his feet standing on a beaded roundel.

Salisbury and Wells

Rochester is also the place where the figure of Elias of Dereham (1167–1245) first appears on the architectural stage, credited as the architect of Salisbury Cathedral, a commission he was given aged fifty-five at the height of his powers. Salisbury is widely seen as the first example of a fully Gothic cathedral on

English soil, and was completed very quickly by the standards of the day in the thirty-eight years from 1220 to 1258. A close scrutiny of Elias's earlier career reveals some interesting details which shed light on how Salisbury Cathedral was built so fast and with such homogeneity of style.

Elias was a high-level administrator and had worked for a string of influential bishops, always keen to introduce innovative techniques into the many prestige commissions he oversaw. Before Salisbury, his name was associated with Winchester's Great Hall, Clarendon Palace, and Wells, Durham, Lincoln and Laon cathedrals. During the so-called Interdict from 1208 to 1214, when King John was excommunicated by Pope Innocent III and when priests were banned from holding church services, all building work in England came to a halt. For those turbulent six years, Elias was forced into exile in France, along with several bishops including Richard Poore, Bishop of Salisbury, where he and his eminent companions lived as guests at Pontigny Abbey, the same Cistercian monastery Thomas à Becket had fled to before them.

As we learnt in Chapter 10, Pontigny is where the first rib vaults occur in Burgundy, the nave and the aisles have early quadripartite vaulting, the ribs of the apse meet at the centre in a floral ceiling boss for the first time (very like those at Wells and at Salisbury), there is a high rose window in an eight-petalled, multi-cusped flower shape, and the capitals are carved in elegant, stylised lotus and papyrus buds—the clear antecedents of those found at Salisbury Cathedral. During these years, Elias would have had ample time to absorb his new and elegant surroundings at Pontigny and to make enquiries about who the builders had been.

Not long after he and Richard Poore were allowed to return from exile in Pontigny, work began on Salisbury Cathedral and by April 1220 the foundations of the whole cathedral had been dug. The likelihod is that builders were brought over from France, and then worked without a break till its completion in 1258. This suggests Elias returned from Pontigny with a plan and a design, after discussing the new cathedral with Bishop Poore. Poore later moved to Durham and may well have used Elias again, this time to administer the addition of the eastern Chapel of Nine Altars at Durham Cathedral, which—and this can be no mere coincidence—is remarkably similar in style to Salisbury. At Salisbury, Elias would have had many assistants and clerks to help him, in addition to the cathedral workforce. None of these people are ever named, though the fabric fund (monies allocated for the cathedral building works) at Salisbury shows there were 300 men on the payroll, plus transporters and suppliers. It was a vast project, and while local men would have been recruited for the basic menial labour, it is not credible that the master mason and skilled sculptors would have been sitting waiting for work in Salisbury during that fallow period of the Interdict. A statue of Elias stands today inside the cathedral, the gift of the Freemasons of Salisbury in 1946, with a plaque describing him as 'Canon and Architect'.

Very significantly, the dates at Salisbury also fit with the West Front at Wells Cathedral, where Arabic numerals were found on the sculpture of the Resurrection Tier. In addition to all the earlier analysis provided on the use of Arabic numerals in Chapter 5, there is more evidence that the Wells masons were likely to have been Arabs. Apart from the Islamic decorative interlocking arches, there are the quatrefoils and the central ten-cusped niche designed for the central figure of Christ. But the clinching proof comes in Jerry Sampson's own forensic archaeological work, as recorded in his 1998 book. Compiled during the Wells restoration programme of 1974–86, it analyses the sculpture of the West Front, seeing it as 'a unique opportunity,' as he put it, 'to study the operation and technological property of a thirteenth-century English stone carvers' workshop'.[23]

He describes the stylistic unity of the 300 sculptures, the largest concentration preserved from the Middle Ages anywhere in England, as evidence that the work was produced in coherent fashion by one workshop over the course of twenty years or so (1220–43). Not only that, but he is certain that 'the forging of such unity of expression and style implies a considerable body of previous work'[24] not seen before, and certainly not produced by the local Wells workshop and indigenous masons, whose previous work in the nave is not to the same standard or on anything like the same scale that would now be required for such a large group of statuary: 'It seems unlikely that anything of this magnitude had been attempted in England before... Such an operation must have been well beyond the scope of the local workforce.'[25] He also provides proof, through the many photos in his book, of the sheer technical sophistication of the sculptures, quoting Bertrand Monnet of the French *Monuments Historiques*, who on seeing them up close for the first time during the restoration programme in 1976 commented: 'I have always admired Wells for the exceptional quantity of its statues. I now see for the first time the exceptional *quality* of its sculptures'[26] (original italics).

In the Madonna and Child group, which was the iconically most important group in the entire ensemble, and one of the first to be carved and placed, Sampson detects the work 'of the best and most innovative of the carvers' in a style that 'had already been perfected elsewhere'.[27] He describes the decoration of the throne as unique,

> the example of the mature workshop style... with extensive drill-work... and a fine diaper pattern... the drapery is varied and adventurous: the folds tend to be deep, often with a triangular section rather than the flatter ribbon-folds of the Madonna... The prolific use of the drill, both in the provision of decoration and in the mechanics of carving, is quite different from the normal usage, and it is so prevalent as to suggest for this carver an origin in a different school of training.[28]

He adds that this use of the drill indicates 'a differently technically orientated school of carving, rather than merely a different approach to a finer stone by the same carvers'.[29] Sampson sees similarities in the life-size heads, carved from the same white limestone, as those found in excavations at Glastonbury Abbey. The Glastonbury Lady Chapel north door shows the decorative use of interlocking arches above the portal and much delicate vegetal ornamentation typical of Islamic architecture. A beautifully carved double capital of Blue Lias limestone, now on display at the Salisbury and South Wiltshire Museum, with gracefully curling leaf forms, the stalks decorated with tell-tale Islamic pearl beading, zigzag interlace and decorated triple clasps, is thought to be a fragment from the cloister sculpture of Glastonbury Abbey.

At Wells, Sampson sees this uncommon use of the drill as 'experiments with undercutting' in some of the Old Testament quatrefoils, like The Forbidding of the Tree and The Fall, 'where the stone becomes a fretwork bridged together by the trunks and branches of the trees' as well as in the 'arms-akimbo postures of the seated kings' and 'the exaggerated position of the arms of some standing figures', as well as 'the tendency towards richness of the treatment of female drapery'.[30]

Sampson speculates that the sculptors might have come from Bristol, as a rich maritime city close by, but he is unaware that this use of the drill for precisely these kinds of effects in delicate detailing on drapery and decoration is characteristic of Islamic craftsmen, who were specialised and expert in the use of the drill, a fact which can be corroborated both by the work itself in the monasteries of Catalonia, like Saint-Michel-de-Cuixà in the cloister capitals, and by the painting by Il Sodoma on the cover of this book, showing what appears to be an Arab craftsman using the drill while working on a capital in an Italian monastery, as described in Chapter 8. The earliest use of the bow-drill was in ancient Egypt, as depicted on wall paintings in tombs, a skill then passed down to the Copts and the Fatimids of Egypt, used on both wood and stone.

Sampson concludes there must have been a drill workshop at Wells,[31] as there was at Glastonbury in the mid-1180s. The use of the drill in both the

Glastonbury and the Wells sculpture is very advanced, he notes, with remarkable portraiture, very different to the flat chisel work of Bristol. The sculptors must have been employed based on their reputations, since they could hardly go round showing sculpture samples—another factor that suggests they might have been brought from Pontigny where their reputation was well established and tested. There are no surviving workshop manuals on sculpture till the Italian Renaissance, so 'the history of medieval sculptural technique remains to be written', as Sampson rightly says.[32]

What he is certain of, however, is that the sculpture was carved in a workshop, not in situ from a scaffold, and that it was all the work of the same team of masons, because of the homogeneity of the style and the speed of execution without a break till 1243. Sampson concludes:

> there here can be no doubt that a single guiding intelligence was behind the production of the Wells figure sculpture, but how his ideas were first worked out, how his instructions were communicated and how his vision was recorded and preserved during the years it must have taken to carry it out, we cannot know.[33]

He says there must have been involvement from a clerical theologian to decide the details of the iconography, but that otherwise, 'one of the hallmarks of the Wells work is its complete lack of repetitiveness (except in some of the bishops)',[34] again a hallmark of Islamic art with its random element and disregard for a rigid plan or symmetrical layout, quite unlike classical work. In the Resurrection Tier where the Arabic numerals occur, every single sculpture is an individual with a different posture and face, some showing delight, some showing dejection at their fate, and the fact that they are naked but for their crowns (if they are kings) or their mitres (if they are bishops) is again full of humour.

No doubt the faces are those of people the masons knew and saw around them, and they may even have enjoyed deciding who went to hell or to heaven from among their masters and colleagues. There is certainly, to my eye, a playful element in the way they emerge from their coffins, pushing the lids away to discover their fate, a playfulness I also see in the Romanesque capitals of monastery cloisters in southern France and northern Spain where Muslim masons are known to have been at work, not to mention in the crypt of Canterbury Cathedral. The worlds of the sacred and the earthly overlap in the Resurrection Tier, representing the Second Coming, believed in equally by Muslims, who named the tallest minaret of the Damascus Great Umayyad Mosque the 'Jesus Minaret', believing it to be the spot from which Christ would descend on the Day of Judgement—a blending of Muslim and Christian traditions that is common in Syria to this day.

Though it generally receives far less attention than the West Front, the oldest and maybe even the the finest architecture of Wells Cathedral is the North Porch, dating to 1185 and housing in its attic room one of only two medieval tracing floors to be found in the country. Experts have detected in the drawn patterns the exact shapes of the arches used to build the cloisters, in what appear to be experimental templates. Writing in 1898, the Reverend Percy Dearmer is a particular fan of the refined sculpture of the North Porch, with its 'Norman zigzags' and its capitals 'very boldly undercut', commenting on the 'love of delicate ornament that is so characteristic of this architect... the more amazing when we consider that the architect and his masons had only just emerged from the large methods of Norman building'.[35]

One final curiosity that is hard to write off as coincidence is the mechanical clock at Wells Cathedral, a specialist skill of the Islamic world, a novelty in Europe, but certainly known to the Normans. A trilingual mechanical clock in Arabic, Latin and Greek is recorded as being installed in their palace in Palermo in 1142. Such mechanical clocks were often marked with the signs of the zodiac and sometimes operated by water, with exotic bronze clashing cymbals to mark the hours.

Bristol Cathedral

Second only to London in wealth at the time, Bristol boasts one of England's great medieval cathedrals, unusual for being founded by a wealthy Anglo-Saxon merchant. He was one of the very few Anglo-Saxons to integrate successfully within the Norman nobility, thanks to his position as financier to the future King Henry II (1133–1189). The cathedral (1140–8) is among the finest examples in the world of what is known as a medieval 'hall church', more commonly found in German Gothic architecture, where the vaulted ceilings of the nave, choir and aisles are all the same height, creating a light and airy space with a series of elegant arches.

On stepping inside it is the vaulting that is immediately striking, the columns like tree trunks, rising continuously up into the vaults like branches spreading gracefully upwards into the ceiling, where the ribs criss-cross in patterns of breathtaking beauty. The blind ogee arches in the side walls are decorated with inner multifoil arches. The hall church effect means that the vault is comparatively low, about half the height of that at Westminster Abbey, and thus more visible from the ground, similar to those in mosques, where height is not the effect being sought but rather a sense of space and openness spreading horizontally, not vertically. The north and south aisles employ a unique technique where the vaults rest on tie-beam-style bridges supported by pointed arches.

Bristol also boasts what is arguably the most beautiful Norman Chapter House in the country, with an astonishingly high level of intricate carving. Built *c.*1160, it is described by its own plaque as 'tapestry turned into stone', with some of the earliest use of pointed arches in England. This type of plaster embroidery is reminiscent of the stucco wall decoration used in the

11.9: The Chapter House at Bristol Cathedral, dated to 1160, in England's West Country, is described as 'tapestry turned into stone', so heavily decorated is it with delicate zigzags on its walls and even on the ribs of its vaults, together with beaded spirals, lozenges and blind arcades.

cathedrals of Lérida, Santiago and Toledo. Together with the Abbot's Gatehouse, outside the abbey a few metres to the south, these two structures are among the finest works of twelfth-century architecture in the country. The Islamic influences here are extremely striking, notably the way all the wall surfaces, from floor to ceiling, are covered in abstract ornamentation and interlocking arches, as at the Córdoba Mezquita, framed with the telltale pearled beading, in elaborate geometric patterns with zigzags and beaded spirals on the columns. The columns have papyrus capitals while the ceiling vaulting is supported by zigzag ribs which are both structural and ornamental. The vestibule of the Chapter House has some of the earliest experiments in vaulting, 'from which the Gothic style was born', says the guidebook, with beading also framing the ribs of the vaulting. There is no symmetry and all the capitals are random, with stylised floral motifs and palms in stiff-leaf form. At ground level there are blind niches where the monks would have sat, and of the four arched side walls, only one seems finished, with zigzags falling vertically like a cascade of water and the beading resembling drops of water. All four patterns are different, with no symmetry, but all have continuous carved patterns, with a complex interplay of zigzags, spirals, beading and lozenges, with no beginning and no end. The entrance is flanked by a pair of *ajimez* windows.

Outside was the monks' herb garden for their medicinal needs, and there is an unusually decorated small door, its arch ornamented with zigzags and eight-pointed stars.

All the evidence tells us that when something exceptionally rare and unusual appears, quite different to the normal local work, it can only be the result of outside craftsmen coming in, not just 'the Bristol Master' but an entire team of workmen, as he could not possibly have done it all on his own using local builders. The techniques and skills would not have been available locally until much later, assuming the workmen stayed, and even then only after generations had passed their skills on to others who were local, possibly through intermarriage.

The West Country and Herefordshire

The so-called 'Herefordshire School' was a term coined in the twentieth century by Romanesque art historian George Zarnecki to explain the phenomenon of a group of churches in the Herefordshire area, within a few years of each other in the twelfth century, that together suddenly exhibited a remarkably complex and advanced style of ornamental sculpture, both on the exterior and the interior. There is nothing similar in the region, so they stand out from the local craftsmanship. Zarnecki, who was always keen to argue for Celtic and Nordic influences, posited that a group of master masons formed a local workshop to carry out these sculptures, not just in Kilpeck, the most famous and distinctive example, but also in nearby Rowlestone, Eardisley, Shobdon, Castle Frome and Rock (in Worcestershire). Romanesque specialist Malcolm Thurlby has written a whole book on the phenomenon in Herefordshire. Other historians have speculated that master masons may have been recruited from abroad by a local lord who, on his return from pilgrimage to Santiago de Compostela, ordered a church to be built at Shobdon (now largely ruined) which so impressed his relation Hugh de Kilpeck that the latter employed the same builders for his own church in Kilpeck village.

Kilpeck

Built between 1140 and 1143, the distinctive Islamic characteristics of the sandstone and limestone carvings at the church of St Mary and St David at Kilpeck, and at the other group of Herefordshire churches, are striking. They share many similarities with the decorative carving at Henry I's slightly earlier Reading Abbey, especially in the prolific use of tell-tale beaded interlace in both foliage and frames, and in the overall style of carving, not to mention the fantastical monsters and beakheads. The whole church is in a remarkably good state of preservation, with all the sculpture intact and still in its original positions. This Herefordshire grouping of churches shares the common motif of the palmette with long attenuated leaves, often irregular in its design, no strict symmetry, with beaded interlace and a play on light and shade. They also have serpents with fleshy bodies interwoven with ornamental plant scrolling which winds itself round animals and human figures. The birds in profile have one wing raised and are often set within roundels of beaded interlace, similar to those at both Jumièges and Speyer, while the paws of the animals are long and pointed downwards, with the front leg closest to the background raised with the paw drooping heavily.

A total of eighty-five corbels run round the tiny Kilpeck church, each one different, no repetition, a mix of human, animal and fictional creatures. The elaborately carved main portal is possibly the most distinctive piece of Romanesque sculpture anywhere in the country, startlingly disproportionate in such a minor village church. Its whole composition is recognisably Islamic in style, in its blend of abstract patterns and fantastical creatures, each apparently separate and not part of any overarching narrative.

European art historians once again confess themselves confused by what the whole is meant to convey, desperately trying to see some form of Christian message among the beasts. But they will search in vain, for the message is not religious; it is secular, humorous and playful. The monsters all look harmless, as if laughing. The sculptors carrying out this commission were evidently given a free hand, with no bishop issuing directives or paying too much attention to what they were creating. The tell-tale beaded interlace decorates the bodies of the beasts and is used as foliage spewing from the mouths of monsters and as framing for roundels enclosing more monsters, like the Green Man, bursting with the energy and exuberance of Nature.

The semicircular tympanum above the main door shows a heavily stylised tree of life. Beaded interlace represents the branches and zigzags beneath it symbolise water. The deeply incised and bevelled foliage is typical of Fatimid carving, as is the way the leaves terminate and are tied, together

11.10: The village church at Kilpeck in Herefordshire, central-western England, is elaborately carved in the local red sandstone. Its tympanum shows a typical Islamic tree of life with pearl-beaded branches and deeply incised foliage, and a zigzag-patterned lintel, all framed by a complex mix of fantastical creatures, including beakheads.

11.11: Among the Islamic features of the delicate carvings on the portal at Kilpeck are serpents eating their tails and pearl-beaded roundels containing birds with one wing raised. The whole ensemble is more like a homage to Nature than an attempt to convey any religious message. It is devoid of any Christian theme or content.

with the use of the pomegranate growing on the tree, emblem of both fertility and eternity.

Inside, in the holiest space above the chancel and the altar, is one of the very few places where the zigzags seem to have been understood to represent flowing water, carved into the four supporting ribs of the dome, flowing down like the four rivers of Paradise from the central boss, from heaven to earth.

Some of the monsters, a kind of cross between serpents and dragons, are depicted swallowing their own tails, their bodies also decorated with the tell-tale beading.

Oxfordshire

The church of St Mary the Virgin, built on a hillock overlooking the Thames at Iffley, just outside Oxford, was built *c.*1160 by the de Clinton family for their private use. It is a remarkable gem of carving full of Islamic influences, the same as at Kilpeck. The family was one of the most important in the land, with Geoffrey de Clinton serving as Chamberlain to Henry I, and his son, also

Geoffrey, serving as Chamberlain to Henry II. This elite patronage and wealth are obvious in the lavishness of the construction, as the family clearly employed the top craftsmen. The external walls are decorated with a feast of zigzags round the recessed blind arches, corbels of sculpted heads and a cusped arch like those found in Aquitaine and Moorish Spain. The west portal has possibly the best display of beakheads in the country, a continuous double row all round the arch surmounted by fantastical beasts like griffins.

The zodiac signs of Aquarius, Pisces and Virgo feature in the decor, as well as the lion, ox and eagle of the Evangelists, often in lobed shapes with typical Islamic beaded frames. The smaller south door is flanked by two very distinctively decorated columns, one with lozenges, the other with zigzags, both framed with the usual Islamic beading. Many of the sculptures of beasts and birds are likewise decorated with beading, emphasising their curves and contours. Inside, as at Kilpeck, four rivers of zigzags run down the rib vaults from the central boss of the chancel vaulted ceiling, each gushing from a head, in a style far removed from the classical; each one is different, but each has the staring bulging eyes and drilled pupils characteristic of Mesopotamian sculpture, reminiscent of the statue of King Idrimi in the British Museum. Both the heads and the central boss itself, extremely complexly carved and deeply incised to represent a coiled winged serpent, are decorated with more beading used as frames, together with four Phoenician-style pine cones. The whole ensemble is conceived as a dramatic representation of fertility, with pine cones pointing downwards through the running water zigzags.

Norfolk

Another remarkable cluster of buildings with clear Islamic influence can be found in Norfolk. Norwich Castle, with its series of blind arcades on all four main facades and windows decorated with beakheads, is the most highly ornamented keep in England, made of Caen stone over a flint core. The striking highly decorated exterior is enhanced by its dominant position on a natural mound overlooking the city. It was founded by William the Conqueror, but probably substantially built by his son Henry I before he began work on Reading Abbey, so all the same craftsmen are likely to have been involved.

Norwich Cathedral has one of the most ambitious of all Norman towers to survive in England, decorated with geometric circles, lozenges and interlaced arcading.

11.12: Norwich Castle in Norfolk, East Anglia, faced with superb Caen stone, is the most highly ornamented keep in England, with its series of blind arcades on all four main facades and its windows decorated with beakheads. Founded by William the Conqueror, it was mainly built under his son Henry I, before he began work on Reading Abbey, so the same craftsmen are likely to have been involved.

Castle Rising

With its extensive pilaster buttresses and blind interlocking arcading, Castle Rising is one of the finest Norman keeps in England, built *c.*1138 by William d'Aubigny, 2nd Earl of Arundel, who is known to have gone on pilgrimage to Jerusalem from 1155 to 1158.[36]

Inspired by the decorated facades of the keep in Norwich, the greatest royal castle of its age, Castle Rising was never defensive, serving purely as a palatial residence-cum-hunting lodge. The immediate parallels that spring to mind are the grand hunting lodges of the Norman lords on Sicily, modelled on the earlier palaces of the Arab Fatimid rulers. The most famous of these are La Zisa and La Cuba on the outskirts of Palermo, the Norman capital, which not only took over the earlier Arab buildings, but also incorporated the extensive gardens that already existed and which served as hunting grounds for both cultures, first for the Arab, then for the Norman ruling class (see Chapter 6). The Arab tradition of pleasure palaces, away from the cares of the city and royal duties, where caliphal families could relax and hunt, dates right back to the eighth century and the earliest Islamic dynasty of the

Damascus Umayyads, some of whose desert palaces still stand in remote locations in today's Syria, Jordan and Palestine. Birds, rabbits and gazelles of various sorts formed the prey of the hunters at Castle Rising, who used hawks or falcons—another skill learnt from the Arab world. The twelfth-century seal of Isabel, daughter and heir to William de Warenne, 3rd Earl of Surrey, at nearby Castle Acre, shows her with a hawk perched on her wrist, a symbol of her high status. In the Bayeux Tapestry, Harold is likewise shown with a hawk on his wrist. At Castle Rising, researchers have tracked the boundaries of the extensive deer park that adjoined the castle. Not only the concept but also the decorative elements of this English pleasure palace can be traced back to Arab Sicily.

On crossing the moat and entering through the gatehouse of Castle Rising, you are confronted by a facade which, despite showing the wear of 900 years' worth of erosion, is described by the on-site booklet as 'the best surviving

11.13: Castle Rising (*c.*1138) in Norfolk, East Anglia, is modelled on Islamic pleasure palaces-cum-hunting lodges. It is surrounded by an extensive deer park, with high *ajimez* windows, decorative interlocking arches and buttress-like lesenes on its outer walls.

forebuilding of any twelfth century castle in the country... particularly noteworthy for its elaborate decoration on the outside, which makes a stunning impression'. Singled out for particular mention is the interlocking arcading, 'an incredibly expensive feature. It served no military purpose whatsoever and was only there to display the grandeur of the builder.'[37] As well as the stonework of interlocking arches, familiar from the tenth-century extension to the Córdoba Mezquita, there are rows of blind arcades, as seen in the ninth-century Fatimid mosques of North Africa.

The palatial ostentation continues through the main entrance and the wide staircase that leads up past elaborately carved capitals to make a grand approach to the first floor and the Great Hall, the most important room in the castle. Two of the exterior windows on the Great Hall level have ornate polylobed arches, another expensive feature of top-class workmanship, which again recalls the multifoil arches of the tenth-century Córdoba Mezquita extension. The exterior facade is ornamented with strong blind arcades defining the vertical space and the tall blind arches so typical of Islamic buildings in Spain, Sicily and North Africa.

Ely Cathedral

Ely Cathedral, rising above the Fens, has always been a magical sight, enhanced by the decorative features we now recognise as Islamic in origin. Every single part of the exterior surface is covered with exuberant and textured patterning of the stone, highly elaborate blind arcades and blind arches, both round and pointed, framed with beading, often recessed and flanked by slender colonettes, quatrefoils set in blank roundels, trefoil and multifoil tall blind arches, and trefoil friezes demarcating different tower sections and roof levels. The animal and human heads carved on the exterior corbels are very similar to those with animal heads on the door of Las Platerias, the Romanesque southern facade of Santiago de Compostela. These highly decorated and sculpted medieval cathedrals are often referred to by Christian commentators as representations of the Heavenly Jerusalem, without apparent awareness that the entire purpose of Islamic art and architecture too is to recreate visions of Paradise, and to create a transitional space in which it becomes possible to transcend earthly concerns and the material world in order to glimpse the spiritual reality of heaven.

The cathedral was begun in 1083 by Abbot Simeon, who was eighty-seven years old on his appointment to Ely in 1081. The distinctive octagon tower was built after the original Norman tower collapsed in 1321, and the Galilee Porch, Lady Chapel and choir were also rebuilt in Decorated Gothic style.

Every surface is highly ornamented with exotic and lavish detailing throughout. The north transept has distinctive 'pepper-pot' turrets, reminiscent of the shapes on the tops of Fatimid minarets in Cairo and in Palermo.

The interior sculpture at Ely Cathedral closely resembles the styles already seen in Lombardy, especially Pavia, with palmettes on the capitals of the triforium. The twelfth-century Prior's Door also shares with Pavian sculpture an intense and expressive *chiaroscuro*, as it does too with the sculpture of the churches already discussed in western France (see Chapter 10). A pearl-beaded frame runs all the way round the arch of the tympanum depicting Christ in Majesty in a mandorla, thought to date to 1135 and with much beaded interlace marking the hems of the garments. Roundels enclosing animals run up both sides of the door jambs. The arch is enriched with many devices of scrolls and interlacing ornaments, and on the corners of the capitals twin-headed birds face each other. The bases of the jamb shafts rest on what are now decayed projecting blocks of stone, but which seem to have been little lions, like those in the portals of Santa Maria Maggiore at Tuscania. Squatting on each of the lions' backs is a human figure, naked, embracing the colonette with his arms, his back towards the beholder.[38] It is a feature unique in England, but the motif of a pair of lions guarding the bottom of the portal is found throughout Italy, especially in the south, as it was before that in Fatimid Egypt, derived ultimately from the ancient Egyptian practice of placing lions at the entry to the temple to keep out impure people. The first gargoyles were those on Egyptian temples, charged with dissipating harmful influences which might attack the sacred edifice.[39]

The Monks' Door (South Door), dated to *c.*1100 and even better preserved than the Prior's Door, is widely considered one of the most outstanding and beautiful achievements of Romanesque art in England. Like the Prior's Door, it has clear Islamic influences in its lavish ornamentation, with each of the four bands of carving becoming ever more ornate as they move towards the innermost one, the arch of which is formed into a cusped trefoil with clear antecedents in Muslim Spain.

Lincoln Cathedral

As well as being the fourth largest cathedral in the country, Lincoln is also one of the most strikingly Islamic in its influences. Modelled on Rouen Cathedral, it was started in 1072 and its west front is nothing but rows of blind arcades, tall blind trefoil, pointed and round arches and zigzag friezes. Its main door has a row of nine trefoil arches above the portal, recessed with many arches, five engaged columns on each side, a rose window ornamented only with foliage patterns, and complex vaulting that is different in each section of the cathedral.

Above all, though, it is the exquisite craftsmanship of the decorative sculpture surrounding the three west front doorways where the Islamic influence is especially strong, in its rich use of pearl-beaded frames on roundels with pairs of confronted beasts and birds, and lozenges with flower motifs, as well as framing the entire arch. In its lavish style it has something in common with the exuberant twelfth-century sculpture carving at Kilpeck, though more delicate and with many more beakheads ringing the main west front arch, their eyes with drilled pupils. Here at Lincoln some of the beakheads even have pearl-beaded strands almost looking like beards dangling from their

11.14: The decorative sculpture on the eleventh-century West Front of Lincoln Cathedral is of an exceptionally high standard, with many Islamic ornamental details, like pairs of addorsed or confronted creatures set within roundels of pearl-beaded frames, scrolling foliage entangling animals and human figures, beakhead-like monsters spewing tongues or strands of foliage, all within zigzag frames. There is no overall symmetrical scheme.

chins. Each of the many beakheads is different, no symmetry, no pattern, just as the decorative carving flanking the pillars of the doors is equally random, without a consistent theme.

There are also a few interesting details in the stained-glass windows, where the right-hand grisaille window, beneath the Dean's Eye rose window, is known as the Masonic Window and has geometric stars created out of beaded frames. Much of the stained glass now in the cathedral is later nineteenth-century work, and in the quest to recreate the 'old' feel of the original windows, the pearl-beaded framing has been reintroduced, as if the British craftsmen understood that this was a feature found in the earliest designs, though they were unaware that it was a key signature of Islamic workmanship. The same thing can be seen in the nineteenth-century apse ceiling at Peterborough Cathedral, where the Christ figure sits within a pointed mandorla framed by a double pearl-beaded border.

Peterborough Cathedral

Rebuilt between 1118 and 1193 after a fire, Peterborough, Cathedral, along with Durham and Ely, is one of the most important Norman buildings in the country to have survived largely intact to this day. Its imposing west front has the characteristic tall blind arches of Islamic architecture, blind arcades and interlocking arches, together with the three huge recessed arches on the west front, and Venetian dentil running round the exterior roof line. The central wheel window is an eight-petalled flower.

The most astonishing survival at Peterborough, though, is the painted ceiling, completed between 1230 and 1250, the only one in Britain and one of only four to survive in the whole of Europe. Unlike the painted nave ceiling at Ely, which is entirely a Victorian creation, the Peterborough ceiling is known to have retained its original character and style, despite being over-painted in 1745 and 1834. Its lozenge design shows clear Islamic influence in the extensive use of frames, seven for each lozenge, three of them variations on a zigzag pattern, with a different and unrelated image inside each lozenge, sometimes floral, sometimes animal, sometimes human. Stalks end decoratively in trefoils, like foliated Kufic lettering.

Between 1998 and 2003, a major restoration took place that enabled modern conservation experts to examine the ceiling at close quarters from scaffolding for the first time. They were able to deduce, despite the invasive and lower-quality eighteenth- and nineteenth-century interventions, much information about the way the ceiling was originally constructed, and they recorded their findings in a detailed and well-illustrated book. In a few undisturbed sections of the original thirteenth-century carpentry they noted 'a sophistication of edge detail and surface grooving',[40] finely executed and with remarkably tightly fitting joints, features pointing to the high quality of its joinery. They also noted the way the motifs were slightly raised, carved to stand just proud of the background wood. An extremely difficult technique to master, this is exactly what was found in the original ceiling of the Córdoba Mezquita during restoration, where the six-petalled flowers demarcating the frames of the motifs and borders are slightly raised.

The craftsmen at Peterborough used an extremely rare clinker-style construction of overlapping boards, creating an upwards curve in the centre, like an upturned boat (the same shape as the Fatimid keel arch), such that the visual optics of the ceiling when seen from the floor of the nave gave a feeling of additional height. The only position marks found by the restorers were

11.15: Fragments of the original wooden ceiling of the Córdoba Mezquita on display in its courtyard still show how the six-petalled flowers were carved to be slightly raised, standing proud of the surface, an extremely difficult Islamic technique that was also used in the wooden ceiling of Peterborough Cathedral.

circles and crescents, and they also found that the original delicate frame decoration of the lozenges had been coarsened by the later overpainting.

Most remarkable of all was the exceptionally complex and skilful design, which had 'required extraordinarily intensive attention to detail'[41] in the way the lozenge pattern was conceived. It must have necessitated an astonishingly high grasp of geometry, yet all the evidence was that it was drawn freehand, with no templates involved. Such an advanced understanding of geometry and optics only existed in the medieval Islamic world.

The Bishop of Lincoln at that time, Robert Grosseteste, who was recognised as one of the greatest minds of the day (hence his nickname 'Great Head'), had previously been Chancellor of Oxford University and had written a scientific treatise on optics. He is known to have acquired this knowledge by reading the Latin version of the Arabic seven-volume *Book of Optics* (*Kitab al-Manazir*) written by Ibn al-Haytham between 1011 and 1021, which correctly explained for the first time how vision, light and colour theory worked.[42] Bishop Grosseteste would therefore also have known that the only carpenters and craftsmen capable of executing such a highly technical ceiling would have been 'the Moors', and he must therefore have sent for a special team to come over. It has been commented that there are many more pagan symbols on the ceiling than would have been normal for later centuries, but in the twelfth and early thirteenth centuries this subject matter, with its fantastical beasts,[43] some playing musical instruments, then here and there the occasional churchman and the Labours of the Months, and even personifications of liberal arts like geometry, mathematics, astronomy and music, was common fare in so-called Romanesque.

Durham Cathedral

To end with where we began, at the 'zigzag capital' of Britain, it has become abundantly clear that zigzags are indeed just the tip of the iceberg. Far from this being a solitary case of appropriation, Durham exhibits all the 'Islamesque' features we have been exploring.

The way its massive three-towered structure dominates the city as a Norman show of strength on the rocky promontory overlooking the River Wear led Sir Walter Scott to describe it as 'half church of God, half castle 'gainst the Scot'. Its two western towers were originally integrated into the castle wall and the width of its upper galleries indicate its dual purpose as church-fortress, just as in Norman Sicily at Palermo Cathedral (see Chapter 6), built by the local Arab workforce and derived from Moorish and Fatimid

11.16: The painted ceiling at Peterborough Cathedral, constructed between 1230 and 1250, is the only one to survive in Britain. It is based on an Islamic lozenge pattern where each lozenge has seven separate frames, three of which are variations on a zigzag pattern. The exceptionally complex design would have required a very advanced grasp of geometry and optics, curving upwards in a keel shape to give the illusion of height.

antecedents. The overall length, width and apsidal east directly copied the dimensions of Old St Peter's in Rome, no doubt as specified in the design outline by William de St-Calais, patron and paymaster for the cathedral. The innovative vaulting, on the other hand, together with the decorative repertoire of zigzags, spirals, lozenges, dog-tooth, corbelling and beading, is clearly the product of skilled masons schooled in the Islamic tradition. Over a thousand sculptures have been counted,[44] inside and out, a riot of foliage, faces and fantastical creatures. The delicate interlocking arcades of the Galilee Chapel and the eight-pointed star vaulting of the octagonal Great Kitchen are acknowledged by the Durham World Heritage Site's own website[45] as derived from far earlier tenth-century Andalusian models, like the Córdoba Mezquita and El Cristo de la Luz (Bab al-Mardum mosque) in Toledo, both of which are still extant and visitable.

In summary, it is apt that in his book *The Architecture of Norman England*, a standard work on the subject, respected Romanesque art historian Eric Fernie inadvertently argues my case, declaring:

> Decoration was a standard feature of Roman buildings, but from the sixth to the tenth, jambs and arches of buildings in western Europe were almost completely plain, as is the palace chapel at Aachen, or the churches at Brixworth in Anglo-Saxon England, Steinbach in Carolingian Germany, and Pomposa in early eleventh-century Italy. For whatever reason, but perhaps in association with an advance in stone-cutting techniques, this changed markedly in the course of the eleventh century, with increases in the number and complexity of the orders, mouldings, and all forms of carved decoration, especially on the capitals.[46]

Among the photos he provides to illustrate this new change is the chancel arch of St Mary's, Kempley in Gloucestershire, near the Herefordshire border, dated by dendrochronology of the roof beams to 1120. It exhibits all the usual Islamic patterns; first the frame of circular beading round the innermost arch surface, then a frame of zigzags, and on the soffit of the arch a red and white lozenge chequerboard pattern. All these ornamental motifs occur widely elsewhere in the church too, notably in the astonishing wall paintings in the chancel. The beaded frame is used to decorate the arcade of arches enclosing the haloed Apostles gazing up at the Christ in Majesty in his polylobed mandorla, in exactly the same way as it was used in the carved lintel at Saint-Génis-des-Fontaines a century before, the earliest known prototype for all such subsequent Christ in Majesty depictions.

Wall paintings of a similar date to those at Kempley can also be seen in a trio of West Sussex churches at the villages of Hardham, Coombes and Clayton, sharing the same use of red and white lozenge chequerboard patterns. These so-called 'Lewes School' paintings are linked by some commentators to Cluny, under whose patronage they fell via the nearby Lewes Priory, but no less an authority than Nikolaus Pevsner in his *Buildings of England (Sussex)* tells us the style is not Cluniac. The frescoes in all three churches also feature an identical style of arcaded architecture in the form of tall towers or enclosures. Those at Clayton depict the Book of Revelation's 'Heavenly Jerusalem' (or Paradise) as elegant arcades of stilted horseshoe arches, closely resembling those at the Spanish Mozarab monastery of San Miguel de Escalada and the magnificent garden city of Madinat al-Zahra built when the Córdoba Caliphate reached its civilisational peak in the tenth century.

Once again, the timing, the dates and the sudden appearance of these new but recognisable ornamental styles all point to the same thing; namely, that an influx of highly skilled Arab and Arabised artists, sculptors and master masons, be they Muslim or Christian, it does not matter which, entered the European workforce from the late tenth/early eleventh century onwards to work for new Christian masters, applying their talents in new ways in new environments. Some will have come as a result of the gradual collapse of the Córdoba Caliphate in Spain, seeking new commissions, while others will have been brought back to England as prisoners by Crusaders returning from the Holy Land or from Norman Sicily. They put their expertise to work on prestigious new building projects like cathedrals, monasteries, palaces and castles, embellishing medieval monuments all across Europe.

11.17: The twelfth-century frescoes at the Church of St John the Baptist at Clayton, a village in West Sussex, southern England, show the architecture of the Book of Revelation's 'Heavenly Jerusalem', depicted as a hexagonal enclosure ringed with elegant arcades of stilted horseshoe arches like those found at the tenth-century caliphal palace city of Madinat al-Zahra in Córdoba, or the portico of the Mozarab monastery of San Miguel de Escalada in northern Spain.

12

ISLAMESQUE BUILDINGS OF EUROPE

A Gallery of Images with Key Influences

The following gallery of images is arranged by country.

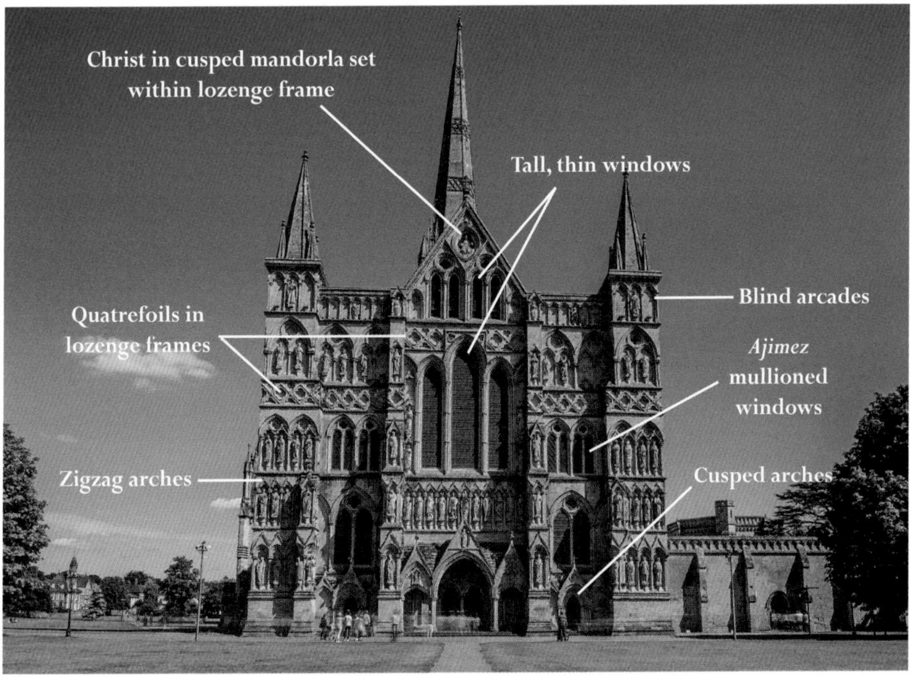

WEST FRONT OF SALISBURY CATHEDRAL

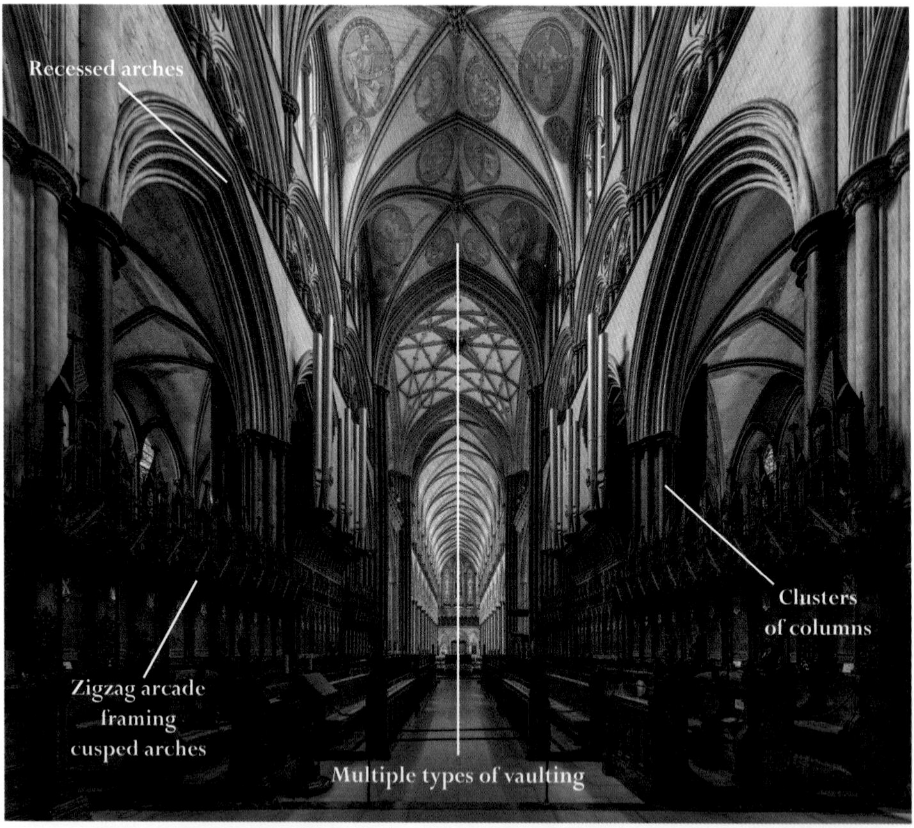

CHOIR AND NAVE VAULTING AT SALISBURY CATHEDRAL

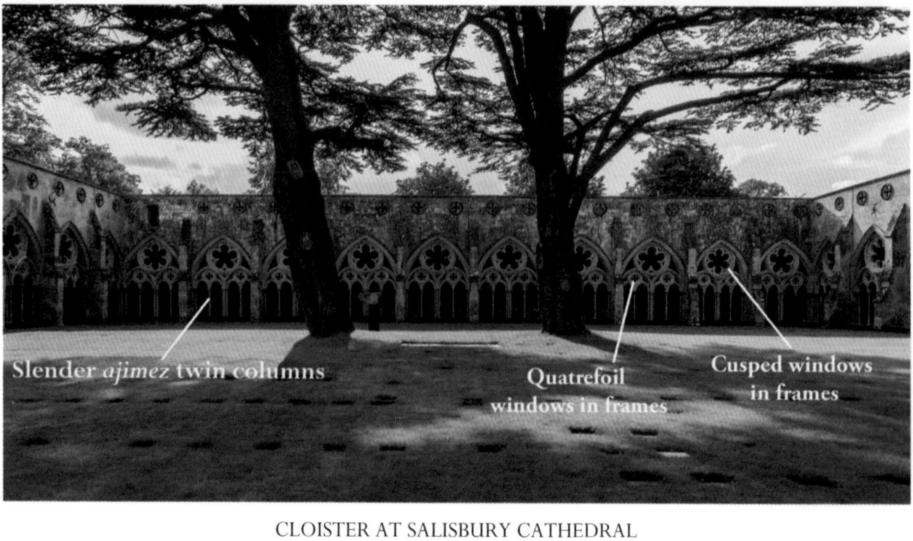

CLOISTER AT SALISBURY CATHEDRAL

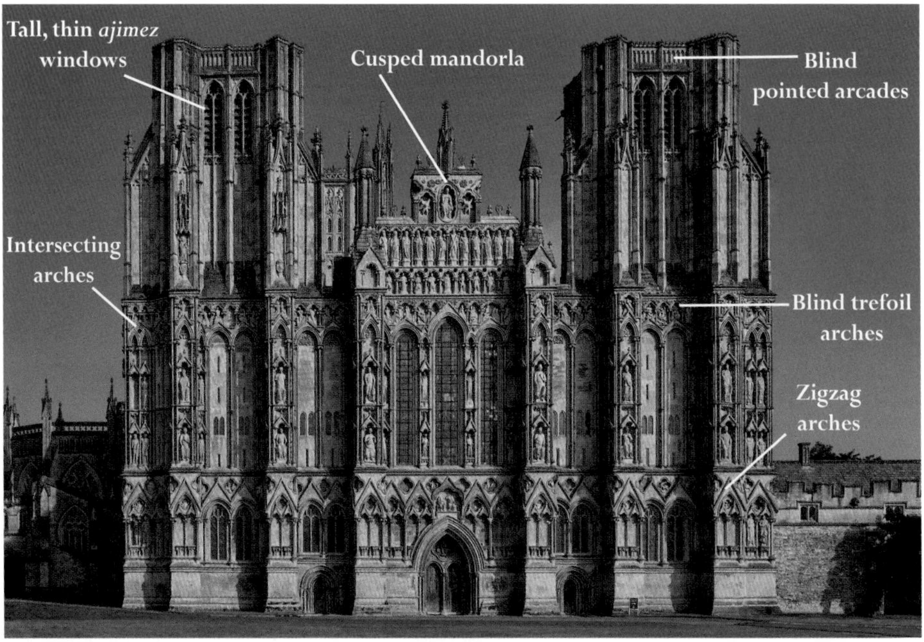

WEST FRONT OF WELLS CATHEDRAL, SOMERSET

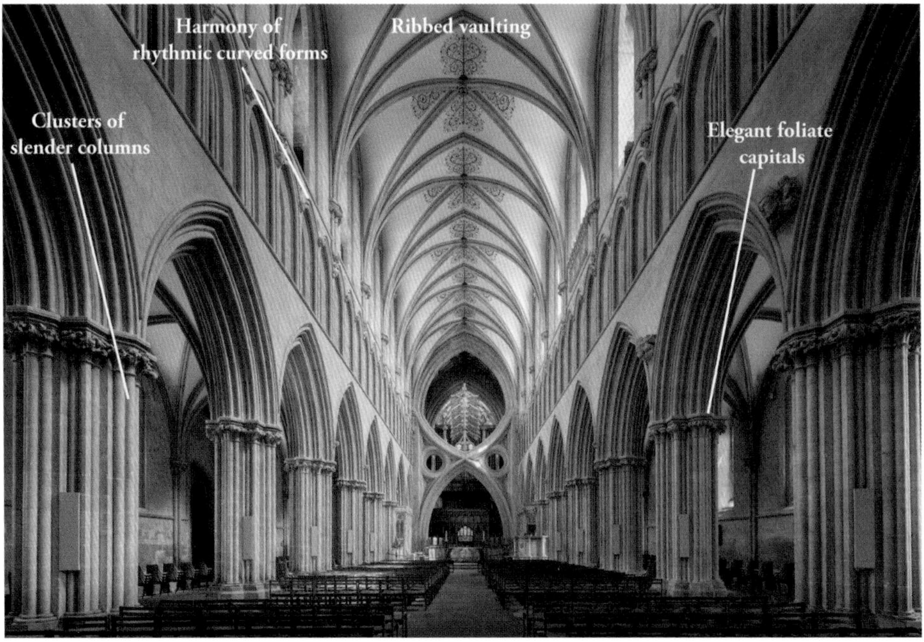

NAVE VAULTING AT WELLS CATHEDRAL

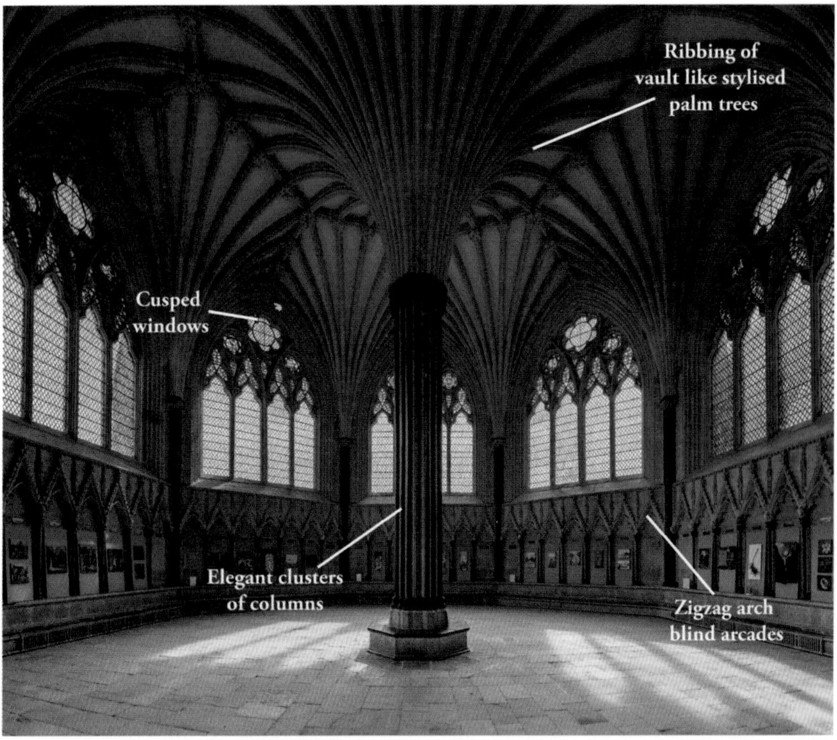

CHAPTER HOUSE AT WELLS CATHEDRAL

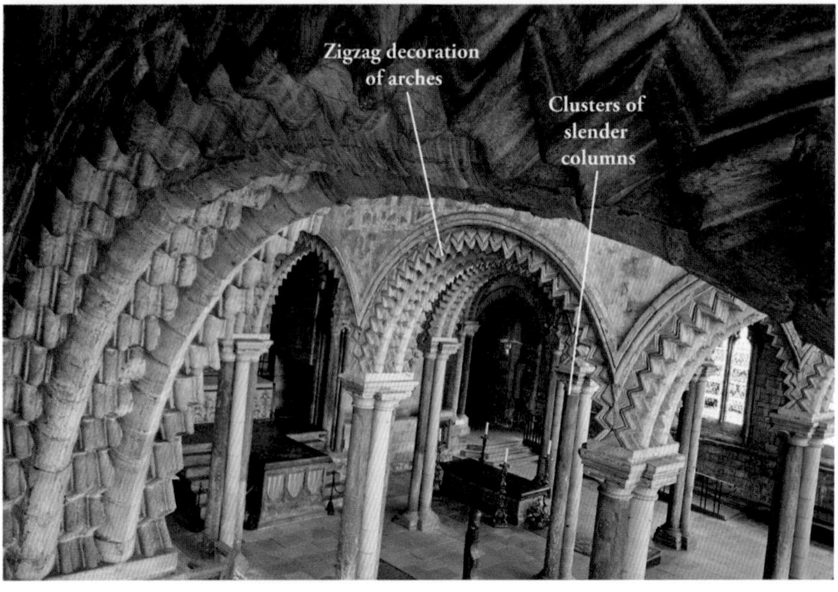

ZIGZAG ARCHES IN THE GALILEE CHAPEL, DURHAM CATHEDRAL

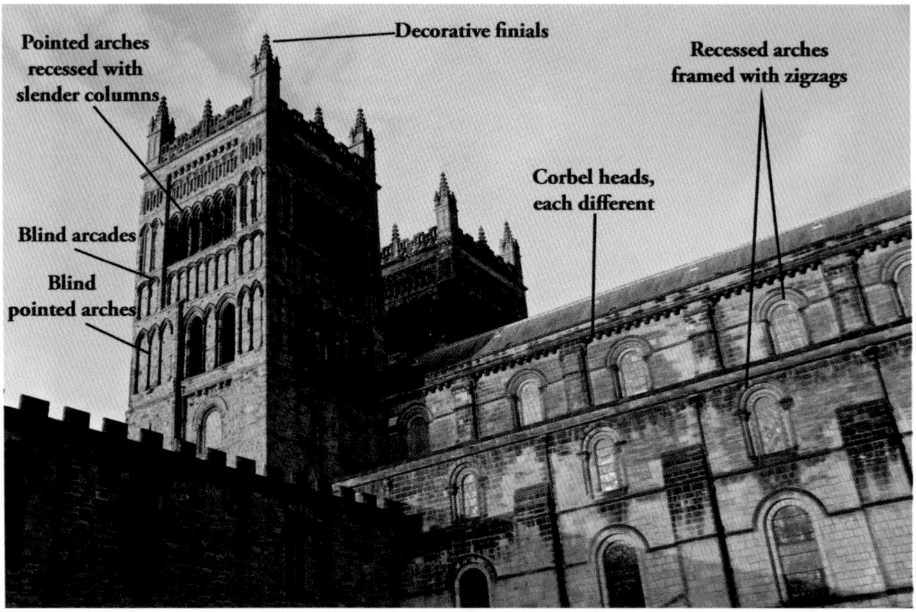

ROMANESQUE TOWERS AT DURHAM CATHEDRAL

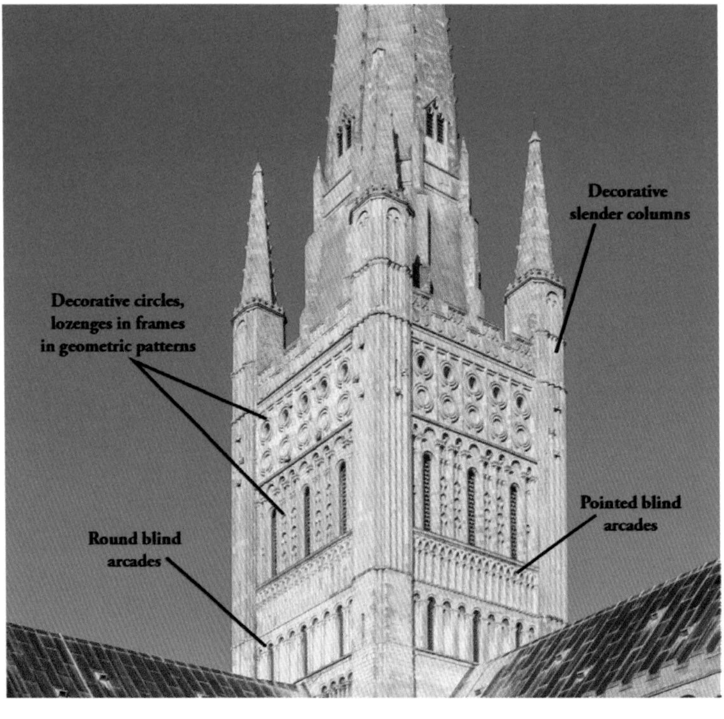

DETAIL OF TOWER AT NORWICH CATHEDRAL

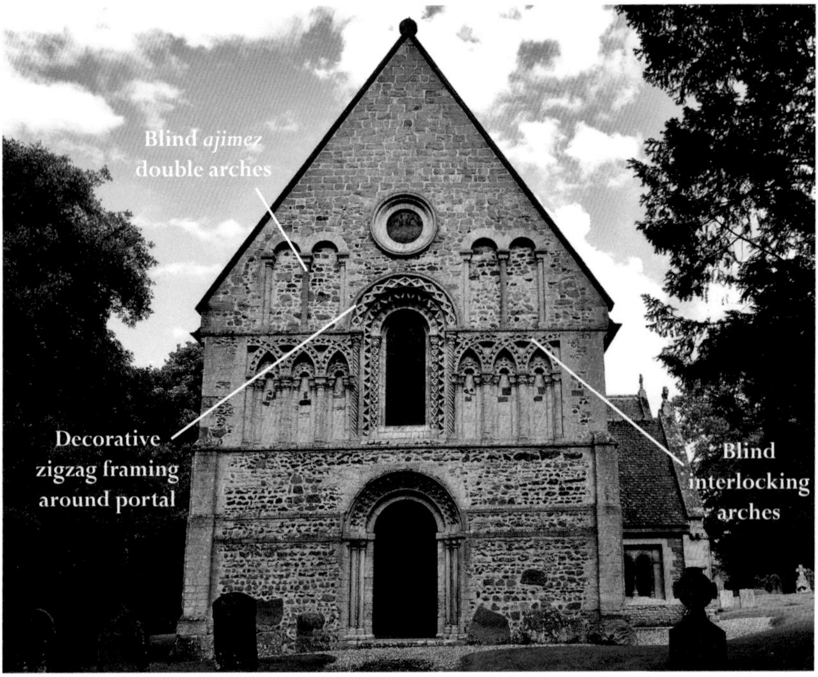

WEST FRONT OF ST LAWRENCE'S CHURCH, CASTLE RISING, NORFOLK

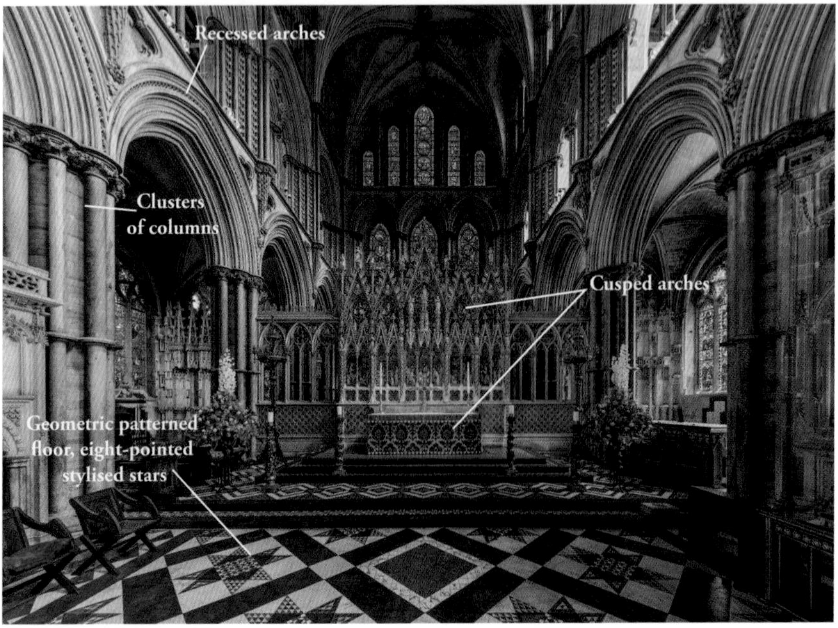

HIGH ALTAR AT ELY CATHEDRAL

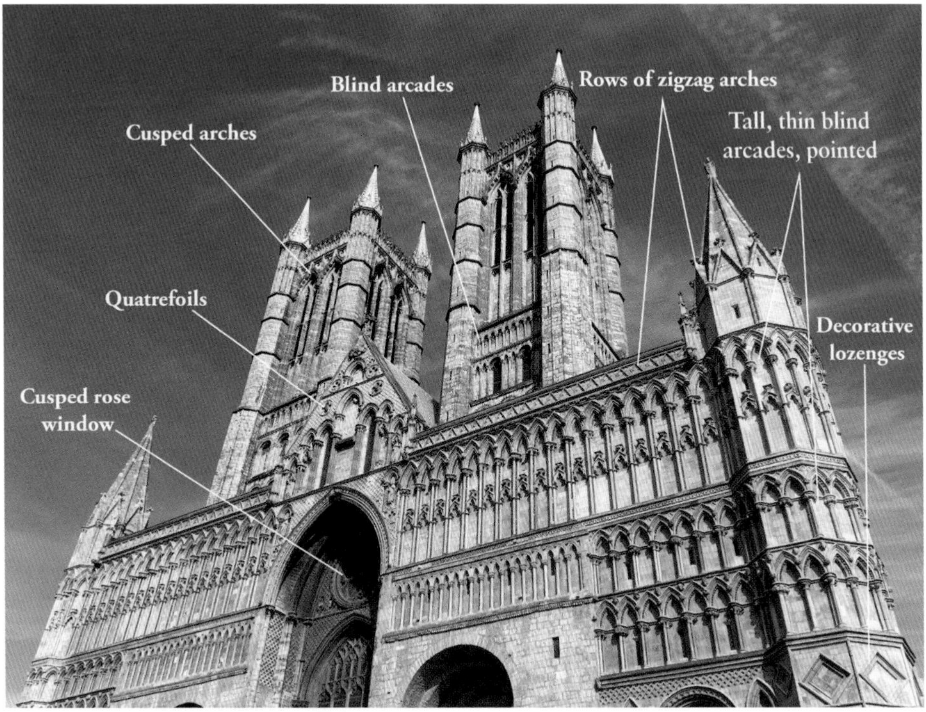

WEST FRONT OF LINCOLN CATHEDRAL

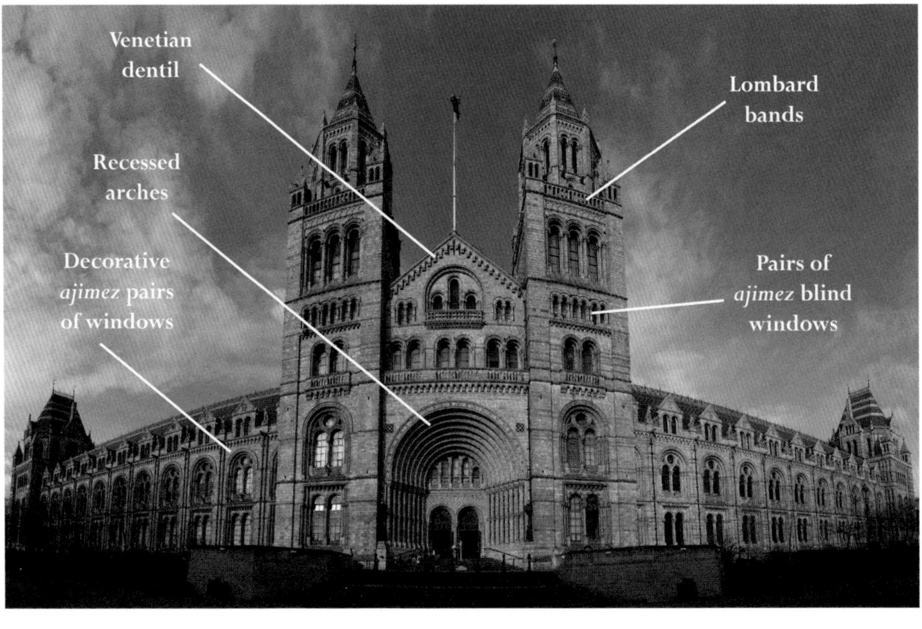

NEO-ROMANESQUE FACADE OF THE NATURAL HISTORY MUSEUM, LONDON

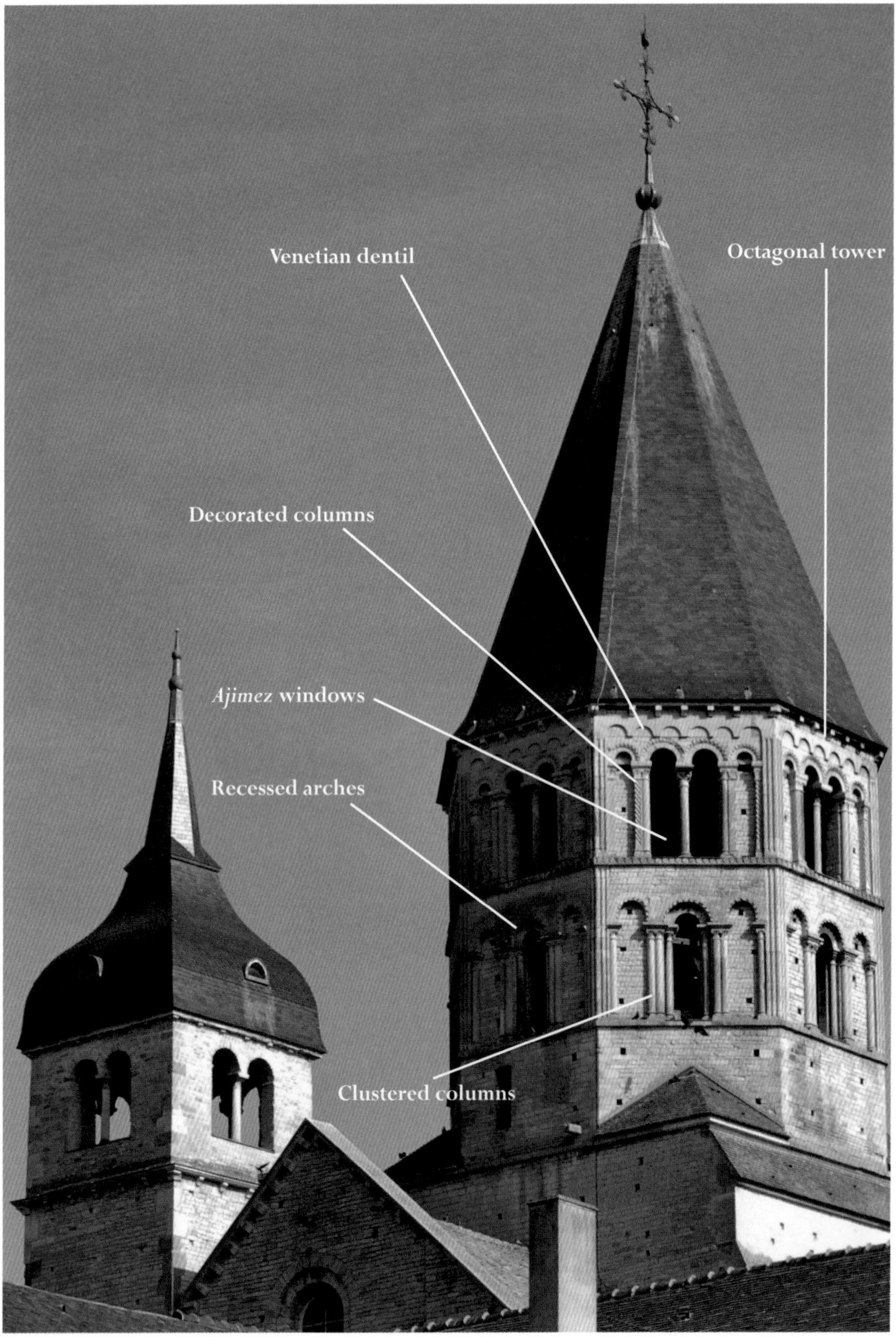

TOWER AT CLUNY ABBEY, FRANCE

MONT SAINT-MICHEL ABBEY, FRANCE

SAINT-SERNIN BASILICA, TOULOUSE, FRANCE

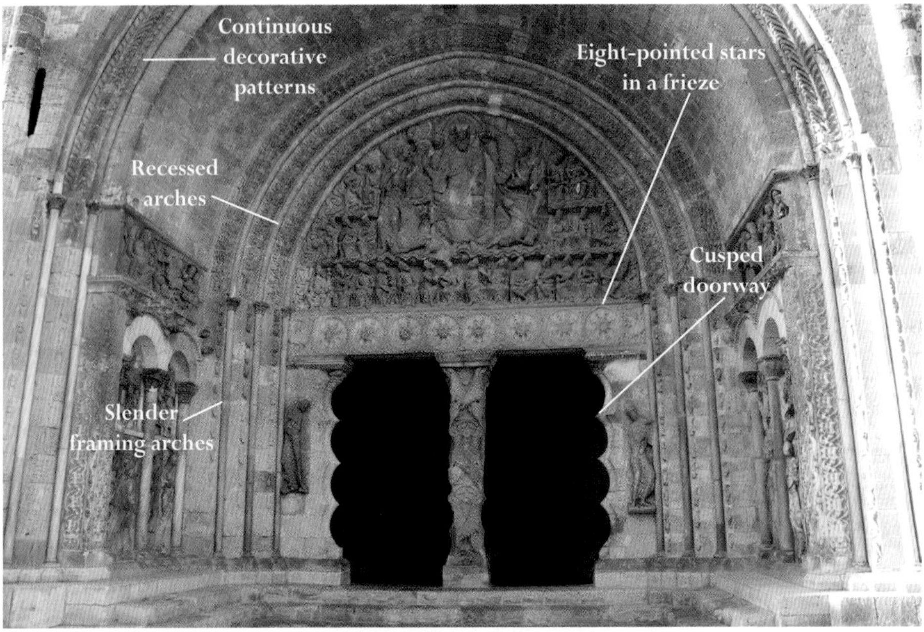

PORTAL AT MOISSAC ABBEY, FRANCE

CAHORS CATHEDRAL, FRANCE

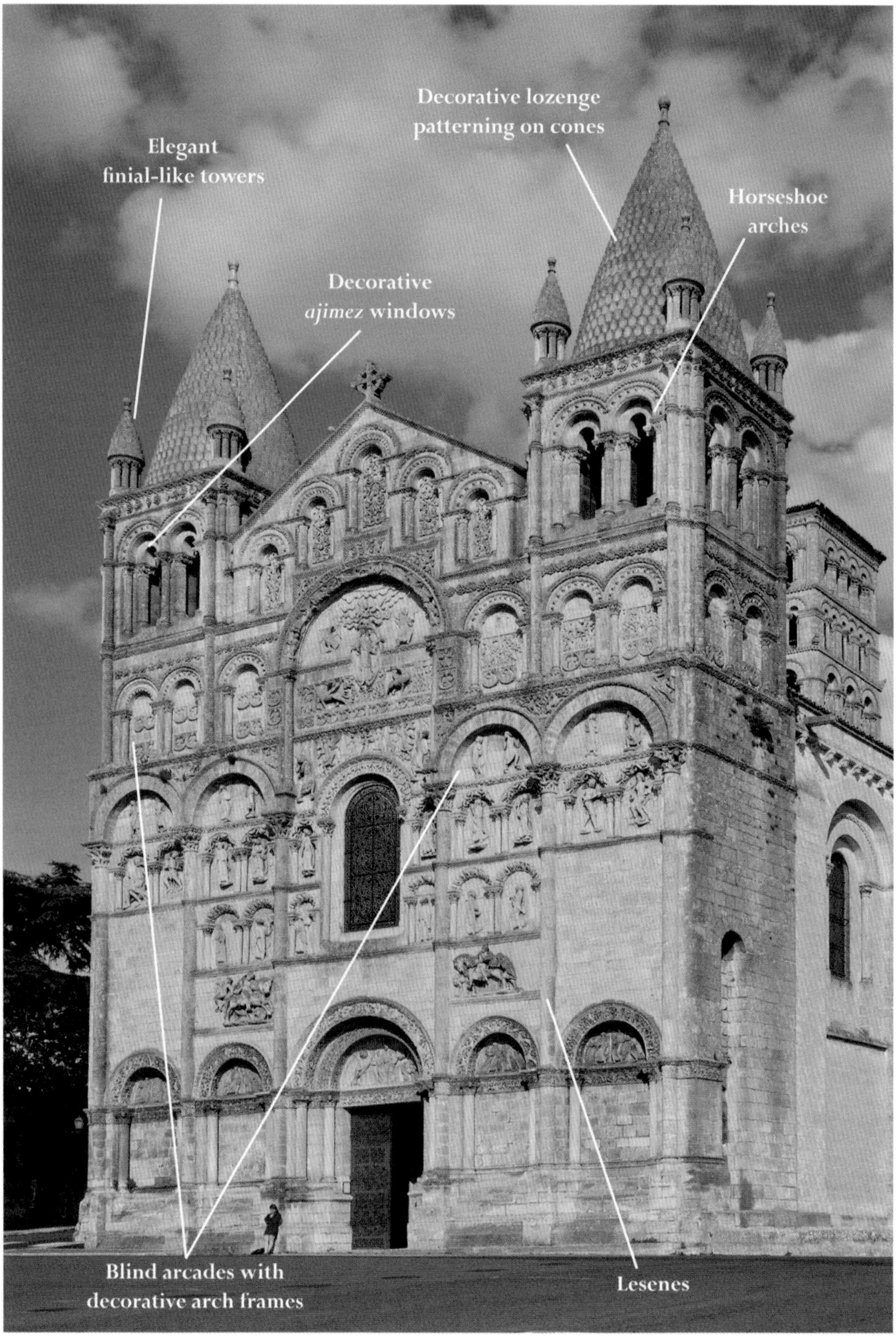

ANGOULÊME CATHEDRAL, FRANCE

CHAPEL OF SAINT-MICHEL D'AIGUILHE, FRANCE

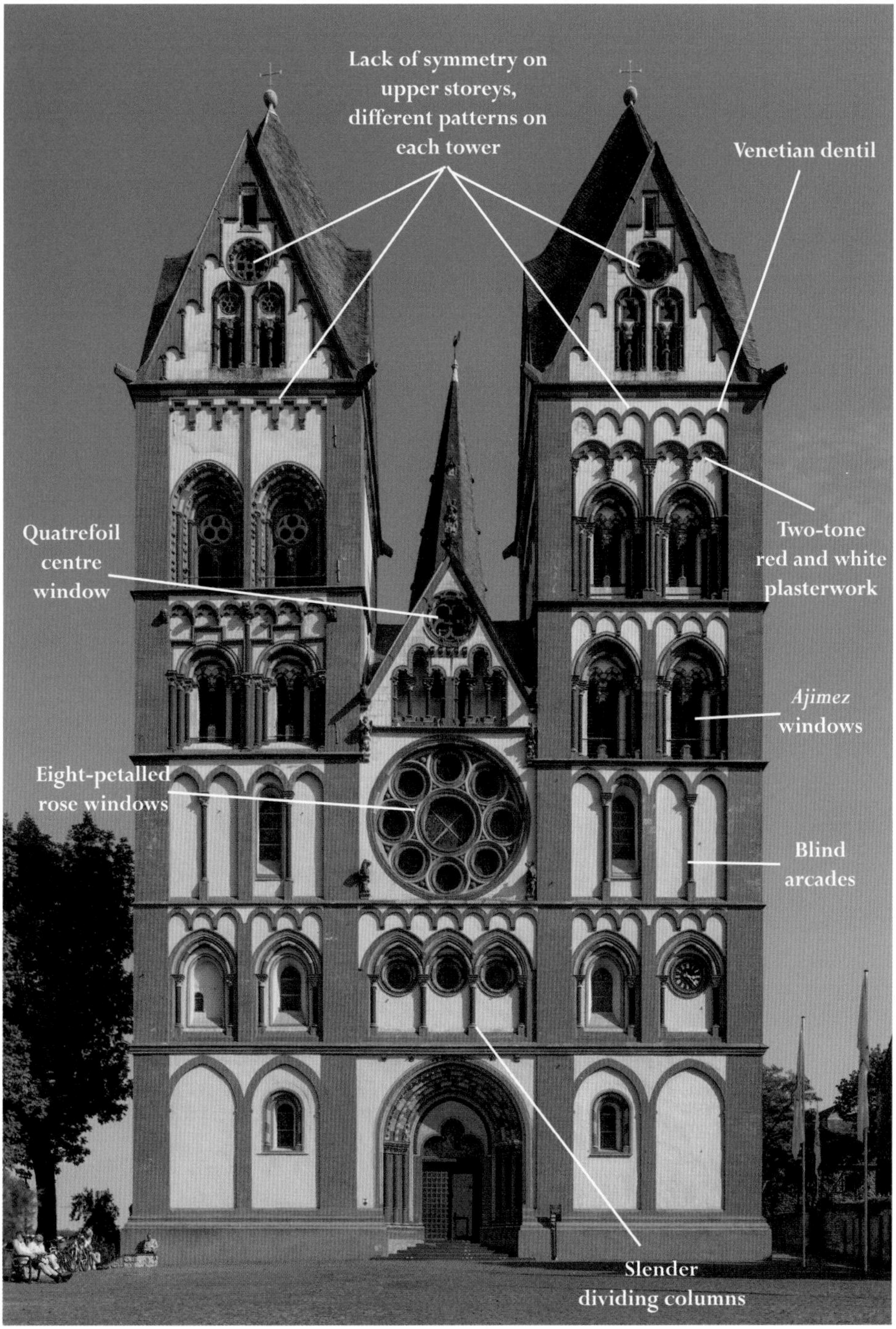

LIMBURG CATHEDRAL, GERMANY

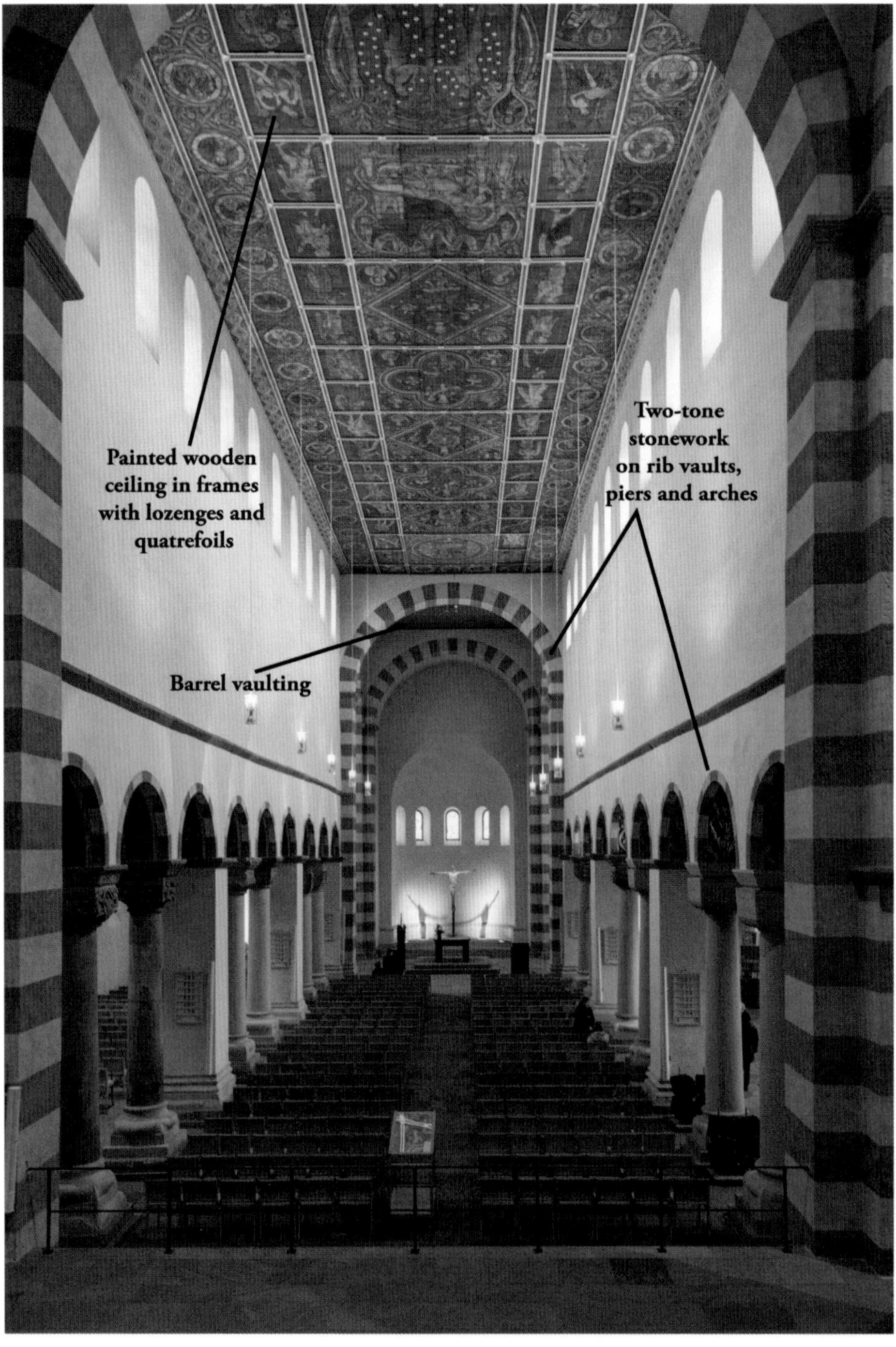

INTERIOR OF ST MICHAEL'S CHURCH, HILDESHEIM, GERMANY

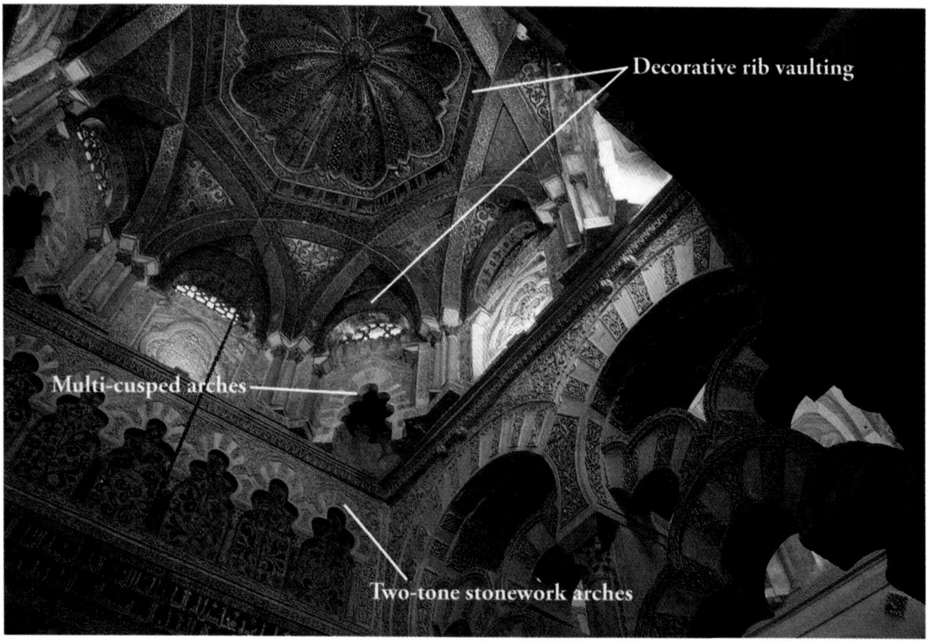

VAULTING ABOVE MIHRAB AT CÓRDOBA MEZQUITA, SPAIN

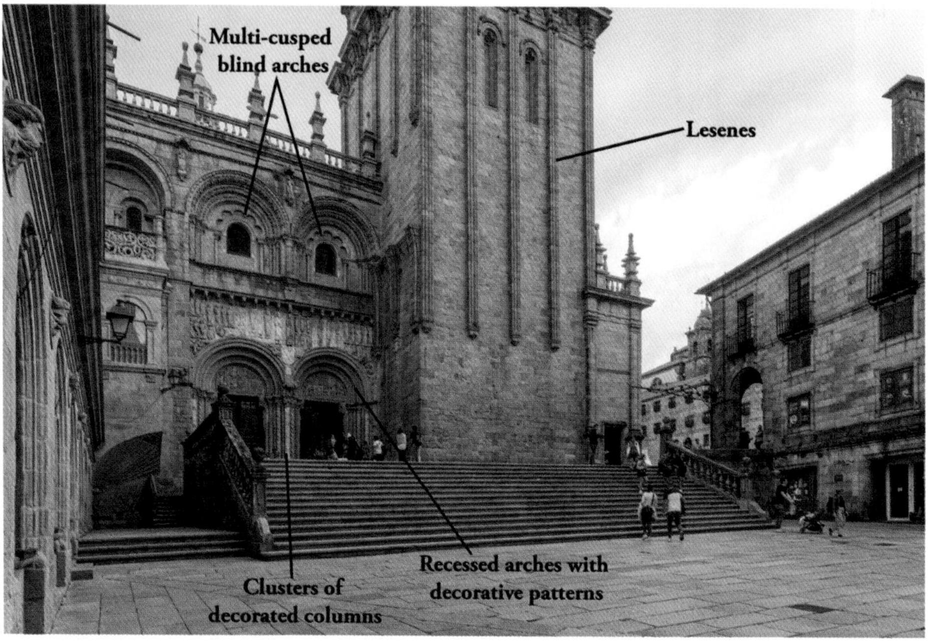

LAS PLATERIAS FACADE OF SANTIAGO DE COMPOSTELA CATHEDRAL, SPAIN

TOWER AND APSE AT SAINT-MARTIN DU CANIGOU MONASTERY, FRENCH CATALONIA

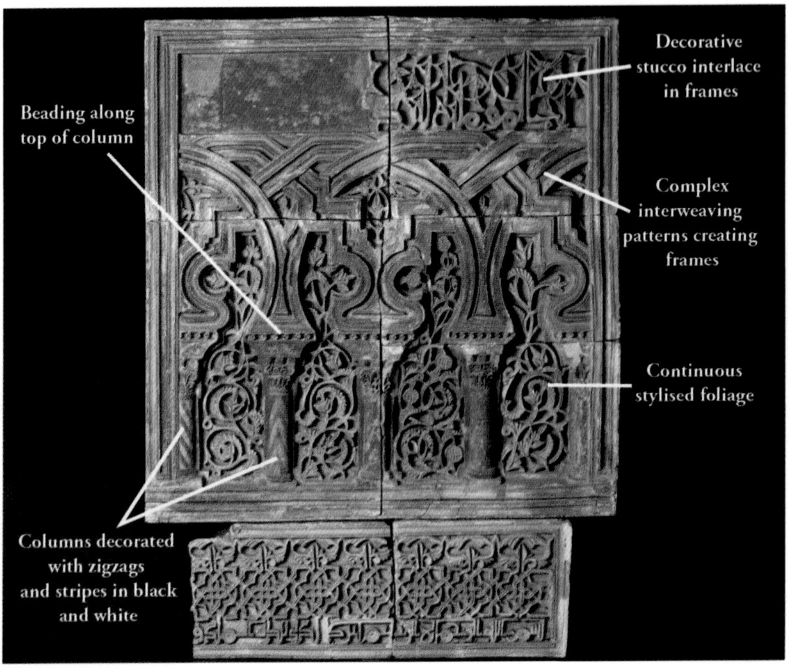

DETAIL OF FRIEZE FROM GOLDEN HALL OF AL-JAFERIA PALACE, ZARAGOZA, SPAIN

WEST FRONT OF COIMBRA CATHEDRAL, PORTUGAL

WEST FRONT OF LISBON CATHEDRAL, PORTUGAL

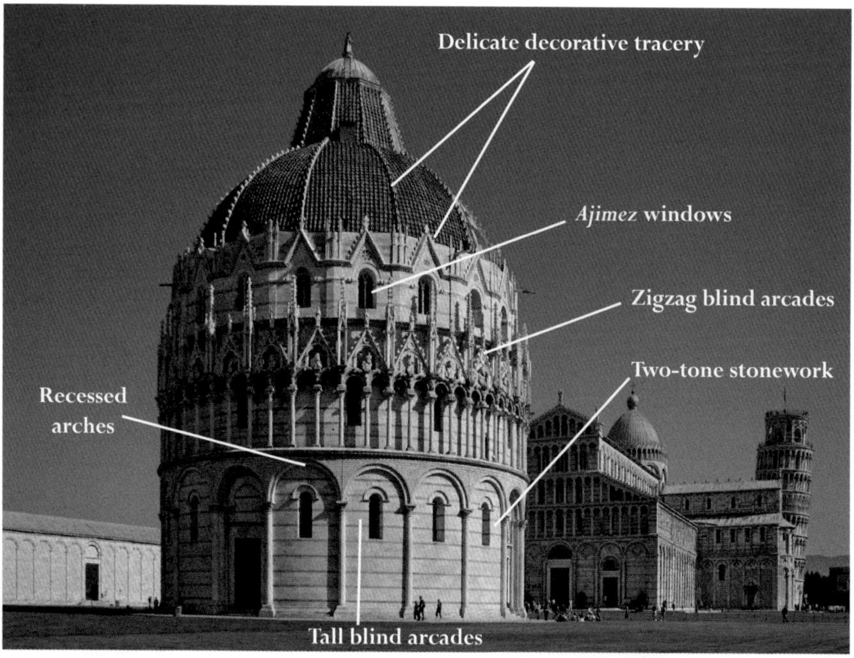

BAPTISTERY WITH CATHEDRAL AND LEANING TOWER, PISA, ITALY

WEST FRONT OF SAN MINIATO AL MONTE BASILICA, FLORENCE, ITALY

TOWER AT SAN FREDIANO BASILICA, LUCCA, ITALY

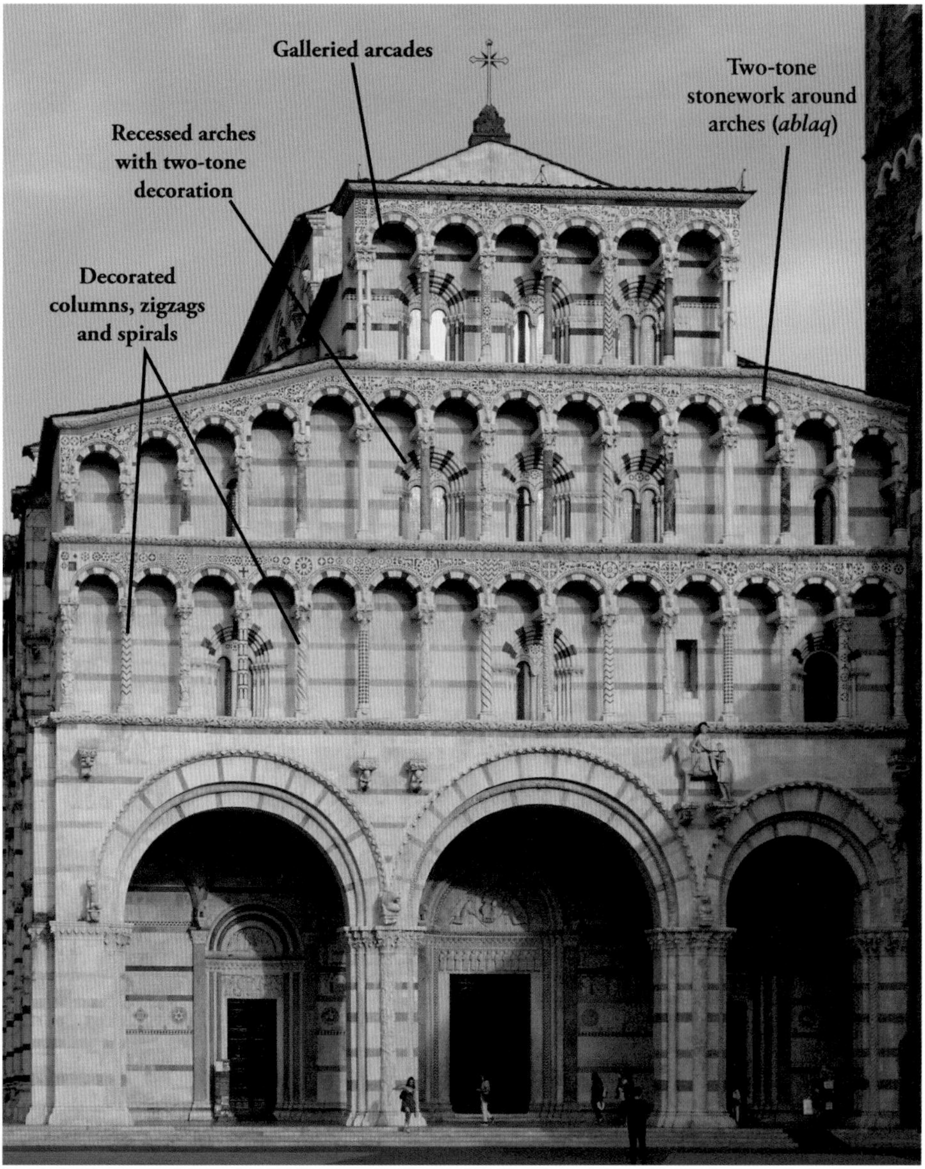

WEST FRONT OF LUCCA CATHEDRAL, ITALY

EASTERN APSE OF PARMA CATHEDRAL, ITALY

WEST FRONT OF GENOA CATHEDRAL, ITALY

WEST FRONT OF THE BASILICA OF SAN ZENO MAGGIORE, VERONA, ITALY

EASTERN APSE OF MONREALE CATHEDRAL, SICILY

LA CUBA PALACE, PALERMO, SICILY

CONCLUSION

There is so much to be learnt from architecture. Each monument is a silent witness to the events that shaped its times, bringing back the past in a unique way. No new style just pops out of nowhere. It always grows organically out of an earlier one, building on what came before, sometimes quite literally, like churches built on temples, mosques built on churches, or vice versa, often recycling spolia from elsewhere. It is all part of the picture that can be pieced together by learning how to decipher a building, how to analyse its components and how to understand the influences at play within its structure. Everything is a clue to hidden connections that lurk just beneath the surface.

The received wisdom is that Romanesque emerged between the years 1000 and 1250 nearly simultaneously in multiple countries across Europe, especially in Italy, Spain, Germany, France and Britain, making it the first pan-European architectural style since Imperial Roman architecture. But why should that be? What was it that happened in those critical years in the eleventh and twelfth centuries that could account for such a phenomenon and, despite a few regional variations, for its remarkably shared characteristics?

What happened, in my view, is that a highly skilled new workforce entered Latin Christendom over the course of those two centuries, bringing with them a knowledge of advanced building techniques, like vaulting and the pointed arch, that had not been seen before. They also introduced a repertoire of ornamental detailing, archetypes from their own cultural heritage, which they passed across into new settings. Christian Europe was becoming ever wealthier, especially the Church, at precisely this time, so could afford prestigious new building projects. During that crucial period from 1000 to 1250, their star was on the rise while the Islamic world's was in freefall. And here is the biggest irony of all—Christian wealth was made on the back of its conquests in Spain, Sicily and the Holy Land, but the conquered craftsmen of those lands then built a whole new architecture for their Christian masters, thereby enabling the gradual transfer of their construction skills into the

European workforce forever. They gave Europe the essential foundation and springboard for all future architectural styles from the Gothic onwards.

'It's arguable that Western civilisation was saved by its craftsmen',[1] states Kenneth Clark in the opening episode of *Civilisation*, where he focuses on Europe after the so-called 'Dark Ages'. But where did these craftsmen come from? Later in the episode, against a backdrop of Charlemagne's Aachen Chapel, seen as the first spark of a new, rising Christian culture, he casually mentions as an aside: 'Of course, the craftsmen may have come from the East.'[2] In Episode Two, while sitting in the Moissac cloisters, he marvels at the sudden appearance of Romanesque around the year 1100, and how the Crusaders 'brought back from the East, Persian decorative motifs which were combined with the rhythms of northern ornament to make the Romanesque style'. He wonders about the origins of the concept of 'Romance', musing: 'I suppose that, as the word suggests, it was Romanesque and grew up in those southern districts of France where the memories of Roman civilisation had not been quite obliterated when they were overlaid by the more fantastic imagery of the Saracens.' His language, talking loosely of 'the East' and 'Saracens', is of his time, but once again, it is as if he is inadvertently making my argument for me.

There is much evidence presented in this book to show that it was precisely these 'Saracens', Muslim masons and craftsmen, who worked on monasteries and churches for their new Christian masters carrying out prestige commissions, in demand because of their high skill levels. They were the best, and rulers or wealthy abbots and bishops could afford to pay them accordingly. The same was true in previous centuries, of course, in ways we do not generally question, when, for example, Christian mosaicists, the best in that particular field, were summoned to work on the magnificent facade of the Damascus Umayyad Mosque. Instead of the saints and biblical scenes they were familiar with, they created scenes of the Islamic Paradise, with fantasised palaces, gardens, rivers and trees, following the new iconography of their Muslim masters. The designer of Cairo's Ibn Tulun Mosque is also recorded as being an Orthodox Christian, probably a Copt.

Just as Christians were familiar with Muslim iconography, so too were Muslims equally familiar with the requirements of Christian iconography. Both religions are monotheistic, worshipping the same God, and both are Abrahamic. The Virgin Mary is mentioned more times in the Quran than in the Bible, seventy times to be precise. She is the only woman to be named in the Muslim holy book and is venerated as the greatest woman that ever lived. Jesus is seen as the Messiah in Islam and venerated as a prophet. The Gospel was seen as revealed to Jesus in the same way that the Quran was revealed to the Prophet Muhammad. Many Old Testament stories are also narrated in the Quran, like Noah and the Ark, Abraham's near sacrifice of his son, Adam and Eve in the Garden of Eden, Cain and Abel, Moses, Joseph, David and Solomon, and Jonah and the Whale. All are very much part of Muslim tradition. Muslim sculptors would have had no problem, therefore, with sculpting images like Christ in Majesty, surrounded by angels—images that were in any case already similiar in their own decorative vocabulary to those of the caliph surrounded by his courtiers—and other biblical scenes, especially in a setting that was not a mosque. Figural imagery in secular settings was common in Islam, especially in caliphal palaces where the top craftsmen worked. The boundaries were far more blurred in medieval times and a rich cultural interchange took place between Muslims and Christians (and Jews), especially in Muslim Spain and Sicily.

In our media age, obsessed with Muslim–Christian conflict, it is ever more important to understand the realities of how closely connected both communities were, especially during the turbulent period between 1000 and 1250. There were constant Muslim–Christian military alliances in both directions. The Castilians and the Catalonians, for example, regularly allied themselves with Muslim leaders in order to fight against their own Christian neighbours; King Alfonso VI of León and Castile, nicknamed the Brave and known as the Emperor of Two Religions, made an alliance in 1074 with al-Ma'mun, ruler of the Taifa kingdom of Toledo, against the Zirid ruler of Granada. Yet despite the political turmoil of those times, with much displacement on both sides, cultural links flourished. Art and architecture thrived through this cultural interaction, as both communities were buffeted with new ideas. It was in the seeds of this cross-fertilisation that the style we now call 'Romanesque', in my view, was born.

In Notre-Dame de Paris's super-fast five-year restoration, triggered by the accidental fire in 2019, the decision was taken to use only traditional medieval methods of craftsmanship. Much work had to be subcontracted to smaller specialist firms, since the big French companies no longer had the right level of expertise. All such companies were required to sign an agreement to keep a low profile.

Among those smaller firms was the traditional carpentry company Atelier de la Grande Oye, founded by Paul Muhsin Zahnd, chosen to build twelve out of the forty-six wooden frames of Notre-Dame's nave frames supporting the roof. 'As French Muslims', he explained to me by email,

> we are very happy and proud to participate in that work, and we are looking for the best way to communicate our beautiful crafts and our faith, which are

> of course perfectly compatible, feeding one another... we prayed all along the work, to bless the trees, our craft, our friendship, the Almighty who allowed us to be part of the project, to bless all the people who work with us, to celebrate the beauty and majesty of our creator... some of us are affirmed Muslims claiming our faith and our joy to rebuild a cathedrale!

What an irony that across Europe, at the time of writing, there are increasingly loud calls from far-right parties to rid their country of immigrants, especially Muslims, in order to save the 'purity' of their own race and culture, who are unaware that their very civilisation was built on the superior skill of immigrants.

If this is a difficult thought for European arch-nationalists to digest, it may help if they remember that most of Europe has only been Christian for about 1,000 years, while Arabs were Christian at least 600 years before the English. Some Europeans were Muslim, as in Spain, before they ever became Catholic.

All the evidence has shown that it is not necessary to be a Christian in order to create Christian art, just as people of all faiths and none can enjoy and appreciate church music, church architecture, Islamic decorative styles and mosque architecture. Muslims could put their skills to use in churches, just as Christians could build mosques, and indeed have done, throughout history. The important consideration was not their religion but their skill.

It is the same today, where the graceful 'green' Cambridge Central Mosque, built in 2019, was conceived by a British architect who had never designed a mosque in his life and had no knowledge of the Islamic world. But his design was the best, and the wood mimicking the curved branches of the abstract palm trees of the prayer hall was prepared by a Swiss company, the only one in the world capable of bending the wood to the required level of precision. Similarly, in Saudi Arabia, at the Prophet's Mosque in Medina, the delicate hi-tech photo-sensitive umbrella shades in the courtyard which open up into mock palm trees were engineered by a German company, judged to be the best qualified by the Saudi paymasters.

* * *

There has been a tendency among architectural historians to credit Byzantium with any unexplained 'oriental' features that suddenly appeared in the medieval buildings of Latin Christendom. Byzantium is often misunderstood to be 'Greek' and therefore closer to home. But if that were true, why did these advances not happen sooner, or within Byzantium itself? Medieval architecture from 1000 onwards represented a major advance on Roman building techniques, and its techniques conflict with what already existed in Byzantium, where the arch remained round and passive, as it had been under the Romans. In fact, Byzantium, from the eighth century onwards, gradually adopted new skills from the Islamic world, with Emperor Theophilos (d.842 CE) even modelling his own palace on the caliph's residence in Baghdad. Careful analysis of the Romanesque style shows that its evolution in Western Christendom coincides with the time of closest contacts with Islam, not with Byzantium. It is no coincidence that Durham's vaulted ceiling, the first in Europe, was built just five years after the First Crusade, using know-how and skilled manpower brought back from the Holy Land; just as it is no accident that in both England and Italy the first rib vaulting began within ten years of the fall of Toledo in 1085, where Islamic Spain had been experimenting and developing the technique for well over a century beforehand.

Beyond the vaulting and the pointed arch, other clues embedded in the structure are more subtle, revealed not only in the ornamentation, but also in the way motifs are carved. It is like handwriting. The subject matter of the carving can vary, just as what the writing says will vary, but what will not vary are the unconscious, deeply embedded signs, like pressure, stroke, spacing, type of movement and continuity. The principles are the same in carving. The blank stone comes to reveal the artist's own unique style through how spacing is approached, the amount of fluidity and the elegance of the flow. On top of that, we have seen throughout this book again and again how carving styles fall into patterns, using certain distinctive motifs like pearl-beaded frames, beaded interlace, zigzag bands and endlessly scrolling abstract foliage. Taken altogether, these are the signatures that reveal the identity of the artists.

In the Iberian Peninsula and in Sicily Muslims exercised a near monopoly in the field of high-level construction, including masonry, brickwork, carpentry, stucco carving, painting and engineering, from the eighth to the twelfth centuries, readily applying their skills and techniques to produce Christian styles in Christian settings as power moved from the Muslim to the Christian world. Even as late as the Renaissance there are clear cases of Arab or North African craftsmen and artisans working for Christian masters in Europe, exactly as illustrated on the front cover of this book.

Titled *St Benedict Founds Twelve Monasteries*, the scene depicts the saint himself, accompanied by a retinue of monks, inspecting the works in progress, while the craftsmen are busily engaged in their various tasks. A sculptor in the foreground shapes a capital base, two men in the rafters look as if they are conferring over the plans, a man appears to measure the height of the ceiling and a turbaned man sits in the rafters. My stonemason friend Andrew

Ziminski says he can tell the fresco was drawn from a real building site because of the way the capitals are scaffolded and the way the trowel is being handled. The workmen too, therefore, must have been 'as seen' by the artist. All appear to be Arab or African, from their features and skin colour, apart from the one monk labourer kneeling on the floor.

What is striking in this High Renaissance fresco—apart from St Benedict obligingly pointing to the word *Islamesque* with his stick—is that nothing I can find even sees fit to comment on it, which suggests that the scene was entirely normal for the time, rather like the appearance of a few Black maids or manservants waiting on white masters in other Renaissance paintings. Five hundred years ago, there was not, it seems, any attempt to disguise the identities of the craftsmen. At the time of writing, by contrast, because of European societal problems resulting from negative perceptions of Islam and Muslim immigration, there seems to be a palpable determination to distance Europe, and France in particular, from its Muslim legacy.

In researching this book, I could not fail to notice how souvenir shops of medieval monasteries, abbeys, churches, palaces and castles all over Europe, especially in France and Spain, sell colourful children's booklets filled with cartoon pictures of young European-looking lads—with the occasional girl thrown in for political correctness—up ladders and dangling from scaffolding at imagined medieval construction sites. Even at Lérida Old Cathedral, recorded as having been built by a Muslim workforce who stayed on after the Christian Reconquista, the children's *Little Story of the Seu Vella in Lleida* shows a sea of uniformly white faces, perpetuating in young readers' minds a subtle narrative of European cultural superiority.

Yet, all the key innovations of Romanesque—new vaulting techniques, ornamental blind arches, Lombard bands (blind arcades), pearl-beaded frames and interlace, lesenes, decorative patterns like Venetian dentil and the use of fantastical beasts and foliage in sculpture—found their way onto European soil via the Islamic world. In that key period from 1000 to 1250, local Christian craftsmen simply did not have the repertoire or skill set to handle such challenges. Of course, Islamic art and architecture had already inherited much of its own repertoire from Coptic Egypt, Byzantine Syria and Sassanian Iran, absorbed it and developed it further over hundreds of years.

Cultural developments never prosper in isolation, but invariably benefit from a wide range of stimuli. Political rivalry does not necessarily preclude the infusion of new ideas, brought in by various avenues like commerce and pilgrimage. Sometimes feuds and wars stimulate the most dramatic of creative impulses, the human spirit's way of coping with adversity. A top craftsman at the peak of his abilities would be most unlikely to be satisfied with routine local employment, but, like any artist, would be constantly seeking new challenges under new patrons, at the highest rates of pay.

The many centuries of Christian warfare against the Muslims in Spain did not mean the end of Islamic society and culture in Europe. Muslim craftsmen were still in demand for top prestige commissions from new Christian masters, as were top musicians, singers and entertainers. Papa Luna (1328–1423), who ruled as Benedict XIII, one of the Avignon Antipopes, was an owner of Muslim slaves and a patron of Muslim artists and artisans. He was a great *aficionado* of Mudéjar styles and contracted Muslim architects and carpenters to build and furnish his churches and palaces. Peoples around the medieval Mediterranean were, it seems, as fluid as the sea itself, unlike today, where much narrower identities, both ethnic and religious, seem to have come to the fore.

It is clear from the pre-existing examples of Islamic architecture in Spain, Sicily, southern Italy, Egypt and North Africa covered in this book that buildings in those regions were already using the techniques and styles found in Romanesque architecture well before the Romanesque period 'began' around the year 1000. It is therefore also evident, from the proof evidenced in the buildings themselves, that the source of these innovations can only have been Islamic architecture.

The deep undercurrents of Islamic skill and knowledge that can be detected by the trained eye across the Romanesque cathedrals and churches of Europe are then directly responsible for the subsequent development towards Gothic. The masons and artisans who created these magnificent medieval monuments, schooled in skills perfected over many centuries across the Islamic world, have never been acknowledged as individuals, but their massive contribution can at least be acknowledged collectively here, albeit a thousand years late. It may be no exaggeration to conclude, as Kenneth Clark suggested, that Western civilisation was saved by its craftsmen—just not, perhaps, the ones he had in mind.

ACKNOWLEDGEMENTS

This book has grown out of a twenty-year fascination with zigzags, an interest that first developed in my house in Damascus, where the pattern runs in triplicate round the walls of the courtyard. My original publishing contract gives the title as *The Secret History of Zigzags*. Not many publishers would have believed in such a bizarre project, but Michael Dwyer of Hurst not only did so, but even, as my research evolved and a much bigger picture began to emerge, gave me free rein to develop the book way beyond zigzags, into a book that challenges the very concept of 'Romanesque' architecture. I will be forever grateful to him for trusting in my ideas and for investing in such a lavishly illustrated volume to accompany *Stealing from the Saracens* (2020). That book was the Islamic backstory of Gothic architecture, while this is the Islamic backstory of Romanesque. The team at Hurst have done an excellent job, especially my editor Alice Clarke, copy-editor Rose Bell and production director Daisy Leitch.

Most of my clues in this voyage of discovery were embedded in the buildings themselves, but two people in particular provided me with what turned out to be very significant steers. Rosie Llewellyn-Jones, a fellow Hurst author whom I had never met, emailed me out of the blue to tell me about the dendrochronology reports that had been conducted by Professor Dan Miles of Oxford University, funded by English Heritage, into the roof timbers of Salisbury Cathedral. An accidental discovery during his work had been Arabic numerals carved as assembly marks into the timbers in the 1220s, a date far too early for English carpenters, who were at that time and until the 1500s still using Roman numerals. Thanks to Rosie, and her friend John Doble, I was then able to see for myself other Arabic numerals carved into the roof timbers of a medieval manor house now in use as a bed-and-breakfast, and another set of Arabic numerals in the roof timbers of the Priory of St John, now a private house in Wells. My thanks are due to Jonathan and Rozzie Buxton, the owners of Westcourt Farm in Shalbourne, the Wiltshire B&B, for allowing their Arabic numerals to be examined for the first time by an Arabist, and for kindly showing me all the newspaper cuttings they have saved about the Arabic numerals found at Salisbury Cathedral, and to Anne Mackay, owner of the Priory of St John, who let me clamber round her loft examining Arabic numerals carved into her roof timbers.

My thanks are also due to another lady whom I have never met, known to me only as @convivencia on Twitter (now X). She alerted me to the *History Cold Case* episode 'Ipswich Man' on BBC Two, discussed in Chapter 2 of this book, and also recalled seeing another TV programme where Arabic numerals were found high up in a cathedral nave, out of public sight.

The archivist at Wells Cathedral, Veronica Howe, went above and beyond the call of duty to send me snippets of archived handwritten notes about the Arabic numerals in the sculpture of the Resurrection Tier of the Wells West Front whenever she came across them, and then prepared a whole file of notes for me, quite possibly not seen since they were first written over a century ago, and then suggested I make a special visit to study them. On that same visit, she also alerted me to Jerry Sampson's book on the Wells West Front, which turned out to be a goldmine of detailed information. At Wells, the volunteer guide Austin Bennett was also extremely helpful, giving me a tour of the Tracing Room in the North Porch and the roof areas above the nave.

At Canterbury Cathedral, I am grateful to the archivist Daniel Korachi-Alaoui, who prepared all the notebooks, diagrams and plans for me to examine, which showed the thousands of masons' marks documented between 1960 and 1964 by the two teenage Horsfall Turner brothers from The King's School, located within the precincts of the cathedral. To this day, it is the only study of the masons' marks at the cathedral that has ever been undertaken, conducted with the permission of the Dean, after dark by torchlight, when the cathedral was closed to visitors. Their remarkable, unpaid, painstaking labour, born of nothing more than pure curiosity, deserves to be more widely known.

At Domfront in Normandy, where Richard the Lionheart is recorded as keeping 'his Saracens', French local historian Jean-Philippe Cormier provided helpful details by email after his daughter at the Tourist Office informed him of my interest.

Within academia I am particularly indebted to the pioneering studies on society in medieval Spain by Thomas Glick (*Islamic and Christian Spain in the Early Middle Ages (711–1250)*, 2005) and Brian Catlos (*Muslims of Medieval Latin Christendom, c. 1050–1614*, 2014); and in medieval Sicily to the books by Giuseppe Bellafiore (*The Cathedral of Palermo*, 1976), Adele Cilento and Alessandro Vanoli (*Arabs and Normans in Sicily and the South of Italy*, 2022) and Ernst Grube and Jeremy Johns (*The Painted Ceilings of the Cappella Palatina*, 2005). Brian Catlos in particular gave me several helpful pointers by email from the US. Gawdat Gabra's many books on Coptic art and culture have been invaluable, as have Jonathan Bloom's and Assadullah Souren Melikian-Chirvani's books on the Fatimids and their culture. Meyer Schapiro's work on Moissac and Silos also provided me with many important clues. Tony Denny kindly shared with me his father Thomas Denny's Architecture PhD on Moorish Spain, which also had useful pointers. The London Library has, as ever, served as an excellent resource, giving me access to an astonishing range of books and articles which I could never have found elsewhere.

Stonemason and author Andrew Ziminski lent me more books, in one of which I first saw the picture which now forms the cover of this book, and was always happy to discuss ideas and answer questions about craftsmen's tools. Syrian jurist Bachar Adnan al-Jamali contributed constructive feedback on cover options and design, while also giving philosophical advice which helped me through the final month of writing as my deadline approached. American academic and Crusades expert Paul Chevedden was, as ever, a boundless source of information on learned books and articles, giving helpful steers and suggestions. Syrian sculptor Zahed Tajeddin was always willing to discuss artists' techniques, and to accompany me to exhibitions and museums where we examined works of sculpture from both the ancient and medieval Middle East.

I owe my brother, Mark Taylor, a huge debt of gratitude. When I was struggling to marshal the vast amount of material in my manuscript, he cut through my first draft like a razor, speedily bringing it within sight of the contractually agreed length. It was also at his recommendation that I first watched *The Secret History of Writing*, the TV documentary which unexpectedly sparked my zigzag eureka moment. I am grateful also to my sister-in-law, Deborah Taylor, for sending me many helpful photos of churches taken on their travels.

My husband, John McHugo, has been, as always, an invaluable support and fount of knowledge on all things historical and political in the Arab world, sharing my interests, acting as a sounding board and accompanying me on many research trips which masqueraded as holidays, across Europe and the Middle East.

My children, Chloe Darke and Max Darke, both born in Cairo, have also been a vital part of the picture. Carried in backpacks up the Sinai mountains to the pharaonic turquoise mines of Serabit al-Khadim, round the Coptic monasteries of the Wadi Natrun and the mosques and *madrasas* of Islamic Cairo, they deserve credit for their remarkable resilience. Chloe's eye for colour and design helped finalise the cover, while Max's eye for zigzags, on a recent trip to Sicily, was better than my own.

It has been a privilege and a joy.

GLOSSARY

Abbasids	Arab-Islamic dynasty who ousted the Umayyads from the caliphate in 750, retaining it till 1250. The Abbasid Islamic empire was centred on Iraq and the Abbasid caliphs resided mainly in Baghdad which they founded in 762.
Ablaq	striped masonry
Ajimez	double arched windows (rounded or pointed) separated by a slender column, sometimes also called mullioned windows, from Arabic *ash-shammis* meaning 'exposed to the sun', common in Islamic architecture from the tenth century onwards
Alfiz	Spanish; a rectangular frame for an arch, probably derived from the Arabic *al-hayyiz*, a container
Ambulatory	covered walkway encircling a temple or shrine
Andalusia	the area of Spain under Muslim rule, also al-Andalus
Apse	semicircular structure at the east end of a church nave
Arabesque	an ornamental design found in early Islamic art where stylised foliage and/or flowers intertwine in intricate patterns of continuous, rhythmic interlaced lines
Archivolt	decorative mouldings running round the face of an arched window or door
Ayyubid	dynasty founded by Saladin that ruled from 1169 to 1258. Ayyubid rule was marked by economic prosperity and a period of Sunni revival, with Damascus turned into a city of fine schools and *hammams*, many of which are still extant.
Bab	door, gate
Barrel vault	vault in the shape of a half-cylinder, superseded by groin or cross vault

Basilica	building of Roman origins in the form of a central nave flanked by two aisles
Bema	raised platform with seating arranged in a horseshoe shape, found in the main nave of a Byzantine church
Blind arcade	row of continuous blind arches used as a decorative feature, also called Lombard band
Blind arch	arch built against a wall as a decorative feature, not as a window or door
Boss	ornamental knob on a ceiling, especially at the intersection of rib vaults
Caliph	from the Arabic *khalifa* meaning successor, used as the title for Muslim leaders who succeeded the Prophet Muhammad
Cavetto	a concave, overhanging cornice first seen in ancient Egyptian temples and common in the ancient Near East, occurring only rarely in Western classical architecture
Chancel	area, often raised by steps, in front of the altar
Chevet	semicircular structure at the east end of a church nave
Clerestory	upper storey of windows flanking the nave of a church, to let in more light
Continuous order	a pattern that runs in unbroken fashion round arches, arcades and portals
Corbel	stone supports for an overhanging cornice/lintel, often decorated with animal or human heads
Cross vault	see Groin vault
Cupola	rounded dome
Deir	monastery
Double dome	dome where the exterior and interior profile are different, creating two shells with a hollow space in between, enabling much higher, stronger dome profiles from the outside
Emir	commander, prince
Foliated	ornamented like a leaf, in a leaf shape
Green Man	a term invented in England in 1939 for an ornamental foliate head used as decoration, especially in sculpture, that first appeared in England in the twelfth century

Groin vault — the use in stone roofing of two barrel vaults intersecting at right angles, also known as cross vaulting. The 'groins' are where the four diagonal edges intersect or cross, meaning that the vault only needs support in those four places where the weight and thrust is concentrated. The arches of a groin vault can be round, as was the case in early Roman architecture, or pointed, as developed in the Islamic world.

Hammam — public bathhouse with steam room, adapted from the Roman baths but with no pool

Imam — spiritual and general leader

Intarsia — the use of inlaid stone (or wood) in a different colour to create decorative patterns, a technique that originated in Egypt and was widely adopted in Islamic art from the seventh century onwards

Ismaili — sect within Shia Islam and religion of the Fatimid dynasty. Since the Fatimids, Ismailism has split into many offshoots, including Druze and Nizari Ismailism, which was followed by the medieval Order of Assassins. Today Nizari Ismailis are the largest branch of Ismaili Muslims; their titular head is the Aga Khan

Iwan — roofed but open reception area, often north-facing and thus the coolest place in summer, with an arch giving directly onto the courtyard

Keel arch — pointed, keel-shaped arch, same as ogee arch or Tudor arch

Kufic — type of Arabic script used in the early Arab period, with square-shaped lettering

Lombard band — decorative blind arcade with no structural function, usually on the exterior of a building

Madrasa — school for teaching Islamic law, often endowed by a prominent citizen, usually alongside a mosque

Mamluk — Arabic meaning 'owned'; the Mamluk Sultanate of Egypt and Syria which lasted from 1250 to 1517 was based on 'slave' soldiers, trained to be part of a military elite and therefore free from family feuds because succession could not pass on in hereditary fashion

Mandorla	almond-shaped oval frame used to enclose holy figures like Christ in Majesty, especially in early medieval art. The word means 'almond' in Italian.
Maronite	the dominant sect of Christianity in Lebanon, named after a fifth-century saint called Maron. Some claim descent from the Phoenicians.
Medallion	shaped frame used decoratively on walls to enclose a special scene or design
Melkites	Syrian Catholics, sometimes confusingly also called the Greek Catholics. Today they are in full communion with Rome and belong to the Patriarchate of Antioch.
Merlon	step-sided triangle used as an ancient Mesopotamian architectural decoration, found throughout modern Syria (including crowning the walls of the Damascus Umayyad Mosque), and even in Petra
Mezquita	Spanish for mosque
Mihrab	prayer niche in a mosque indicating the direction of Mecca
Minaret	tower of a mosque used to call the faithful to prayer
Minbar	pulpit in a mosque used by the imam during Friday sermons
Modillion	decorative carved stone bracket supporting an overhanging cornice
Moors	from the Greek *mauros*, dark; used by the Greeks for the aboriginal inhabitants of northwest Africa. In English usage, the Islamic inhabitants of medieval Spain, whether of African or Near Eastern or mixed descent.
Morisco	Muslims living in the Iberian Peninsula who were forced to convert to Christianity by the Catholic Church or else face compulsory exile. 'Morisco' means Moorish in Spanish.
Mozarabs	from Arabic *musta'ribun*, 'Arabised'; Christian communities in Islamic Spain
Mudéjar	from Arabic *mudajjan*, domesticated. Term used for Muslims who stayed in Spain after the Spanish Reconquista, paying tribute to the Christian rulers.

Multifoil arch	(also called poly-lobed or multi-cusped arch); an arch that has been divided into more than three leaves/foils/lobes/cusps, such as cinquefoil for five, up to thirteen, always an odd number spreading out from the arch centre
Muqarnas	honeycomb-like decorative motif in wood or stone consisting of numerous geometric niches first seen in the Islamic world in the eleventh century, used in transitional zones between domes and their supports, conveying a sense of infinity
Ogee arch	curved, pointed, four-centred arch, introduced to Europe via Venice where it became the defining feature of Venetian Gothic; also called keel arch or the Tudor arch in England
Opus sectile	an inlay technique where different coloured stones are cut into different shapes to make patterns, unlike mosaics where all the pieces (tesserae) are the same size. In Islamic art the patterns are always geometric.
Orthodox	indigenous Syrian Christians of the Eastern Church (as opposed to the later Catholic arrivals who first came to the region at the time of the Crusades). They are not in communion with Rome and do not follow the Pope, but follow Constantinople and their own patriarchs.
Pendentive	triangular segment of a sphere, used to carry the transition between a square base and a round dome
Quran	literally meaning 'Recitation', the collected revelations made to the Prophet Muhammad orally by God over a twenty-three-year period, written down after his death to form the Muslim holy text, the main source for Sharia or Islamic Law. Considered 'the word of God', so only ever recited in Arabic, the language in which it was 'revealed'.
Qibla	direction of prayer towards Mecca
Reconquista	Spanish; the Christian reconquest of the parts of Spain controlled by the Moors
Rib vaulting	structural and decorative roof support system achieved by geometric division into a framework of diagonal arched ribs

Rose window	circular stone window decorated with stained glass held in place by elaborate stone tracery
Saracens	Muslims in Syria, Palestine and Egypt during the period from the First Crusade (1095) till the Ottoman conquest (1453)
Shi'i	follower of Shia Islam, the second largest Muslim sect, which accounts for under 10 per cent of Muslims worldwide. The sect split off from the Sunni orthodoxy, believing that Ali was the rightful successor to the Prophet Muhammad. Syria has some small pockets of Shi'i Muslims (who are not Alawi), such as the villages of Fou'a and Kefraya in the northern province of Idlib.
Spandrel	the roughly triangular area between two arches
Squinch	small arch or niche placed across a corner to carry the transition to a domed or octagonal structure, first invented by the Iranian Sassanians (224–651)
Stilted arch	an arch that springs from a point higher than the capital, as if 'on stilts', often slightly horseshoe in shape, commonly used in Islamic architecture, as at the ninth-century Great Mosque of Kairouan and the tenth-century palatial city of Madinat al-Zahra in Córdoba
Sufi	Muslim mystic
Sunni	Sunnis are the orthodox, mainstream Muslim grouping who follow the Prophet Muhammad's 'path' (Arabic *sunna*, meaning custom or wont) and who account for nearly 90 per cent of Muslims worldwide. Syria's population is estimated at 70 per cent Sunni.
Syriac	ancient Semitic language related to Aramaic, language of Christ, used as the liturgical language of the indigenous Syriac Christians (also called Assyrians), much smaller in number than the Syrian Orthodox today, who use Arabic as their liturgical language. Syriac was once the lingua franca of the region.
Tracery	elaborate decorative stonework supporting stained glass in a Gothic window
Transept	section of the church that crosses the nave, forming a cross, usually in front of the altar

Trefoil arch	three-foiled cusped arch widely used in church architecture on windows to represent the Trinity
Umayyads	the first Islamic dynasty of caliphs reigning from 660 to 750 from their capital Damascus. They were largely wiped out by the Abbasids in 750, but one of them, Abd al-Rahman, fled across North Africa and into Spain where he founded the Umayyad dynasty which ruled from their capital of Córdoba from 756 to 1031.
Vaulting	arch system that supports a roof or ceiling
Venetian dentil	a continuous arcade of rounded arches decorating the top of the walls beneath the roofline to form an ornamental frieze, first seen in North African mosques and fortifications of the ninth century like the Ribat of Sousse in Tunisia
Voussoir	wedge-shaped stone used to form the components of an arch; alternately coloured voussoirs are an important motif in Islamic architectural decoration, usually black and white, or red and white

NOTES

INTRODUCTION

1. Khaled Diab, 'When a Christian Emperor Courted a Muslim Caliph', *New Lines Magazine*, 15 July 2022, last accessed 22 May 2024, https://newlinesmag.com/essays/when-a-christian-emperor-courted-a-muslim-caliph/
2. Thomas Graham Jackson, *Byzantine and Romanesque Architecture*, 2 vols., Cambridge: Cambridge University Press, 1913, Vol. 1, p. 11.
3. Ibid., p. 12.
4. Paul Lacroix, *Science and Literature in the Middle Ages and the Renaissance*, New York: Frederick Ungar, 1964, p. 77.
5. From an interview with Andrew Garrad on BBC Radio 4 *Today* programme, 7 February 2024. See also Jonathan Amos, 'Climate Change: "Godfathers of Wind" Share Engineering's QEPrize', BBC News, 7 February 2024, last accessed 22 May 2024, https://www.bbc.co.uk/news/science-environment-68207881
6. George Gordon Coulton, *Art and the Reformation*, Cambridge: Cambridge University Press, 1953, p. 70.
7. Brian A. Catlos, *Muslims of Medieval Latin Christendom, c. 1050–1614*, Cambridge: Cambridge University Press, 2014, p. 450.
8. G. A. Loud & A. Metcalfe (eds.), *The Society of Norman Italy*, Leiden: E. J. Brill, 2002, pp. 299, 311.
9. Jean Bony, *French Gothic Architecture of the 12th and 13th Centuries*, Berkeley: University of California Press, 1983, pp. 358–9.

1. THE ZIGZAG CLUE

1. BBC Four, Episode 1, *The Secret History of Writing*, September 2020, last accessed 22 May 2024, https://www.bbc.co.uk/programmes/m000mtml
2. Adele Cilento & Alessandro Vanoli, *Arabs and Normans in Sicily and the South of Italy*, Bologna: Magnus Edizioni, 2022, p. 47.
3. UNESCO World Heritage Convention, 'Arab-Norman Palermo and the Cathedral Churches of Cefalú and Monreale', 2015, last accessed 22 May 2024, https://whc.unesco.org/en/list/1487/
4. H. E. J. Cowdrey, 'Pope Urban II's Preaching of the First Crusade', *History*, Vol. 55, No. 184 (1970), pp. 177–88, last accessed 22 May 2024, https://www.jstor.org/stable/24406851

5. Andrew Ziminski, *The Stonemason: A History of Building Britain*, London: John Murray, 2020, p. 126.
6. This material was first published in a *New Lines* article I wrote in 2022 for Lydia Wilson, the presenter of *The Secret History of Writing* documentary. See Diana Darke, 'A New Theory: European Cathedrals Show Traces of Ancient Egypt', *New Lines Magazine*, 18 November 2022, last accessed 29 June 2024, https://newlinesmag.com/essays/a-new-theory-european-cathedrals-show-traces-of-ancient-egypt/

2. FANTASTICAL BEASTS, FRAMES, FOLIAGE AND FACES: EXPLORING THE ANCIENT ARCHETYPES

1. Often quoted by historians of the Romanesque, the original source is Bernard's *Apologia ad Guillelmum*, written in 1125 in a letter to fellow abbot William of Saint-Thierry.
2. Jennifer Miyuki Babcock, *Ancient Egyptian Animal Fables: Tree Climbing Hippos and Ennobled Mice*, Leiden: E. J. Brill, 2022, p. 83.
3. Bernard Bruyère (1879–1971) began excavating in 1922 and continued till 1951. It was he who suggested the dig location to Howard Carter that resulted in the discovery of the Tomb of Tutankhamun.
4. Babcock, *Ancient Egyptian Animal Fables*, p. 92.
5. Eva R. Hoffman, 'The Beginnings of the Illustrated Arabic Book: An Intersection between Art and Scholarship', *Muqarnas*, Vol. 17 (2000), pp. 37–52.
6. Georges Marçais, *Mélanges d'histoire et d'archéologie de l'occident musulman*, Tome 1 et 2, Algiers: Gouvernement Géneral de l'Algérie, 1957, Vol. 1, p. 77.
7. John Doyle, *Canterbury Cathedral: A Walk Round Guide*, Hastings: Print2Demand, 2018, p. 9.
8. Alessandra Avanzini, 'Some Thoughts on Ibex on Plinths in Early South Arabian Art', *Arabian Archaeology and Epigraphy*, Vol. 16, No. 2 (2005), pp. 144–53.
9. Janet Newson, 'Beakhead Decoration on Romanesque Arches in the Upper Thames Valley', *Oxoniensia* (2013), Oxfordshire Architectural and Historical Society, p. 73, https://www.oxoniensia.org/volumes/2013/Newson.pdf
10. Georges Marçais, *L'Art musulman*, Paris: Quadrige, 1981, p. 115; my translation.
11. Ibid., p. 108; my translation.
12. Ibid., p. 112; my translation.

3. COPTIC AND FATIMID FORERUNNERS

1. Gertrud J. M. van Loon, 'Decoration of Coptic Churches', in Gawdat Gabra (ed.), *Coptic Civilization: Two Thousand Years of Christianity in Egypt*, Cairo: American University in Cairo Press, 2014, p. 207.
2. Ibid., p. 208.
3. Youhanna Nessim Youssef, 'Coptic Literature', in Gawdat Gabra (ed.), *Coptic Civilization: Two Thousand Years of Christianity in Egypt*, Cairo: American University in Cairo Press, 2014, pp. 123–9.

4. Kees Veelenturf, 'Osiris Once Again: A Pharaonic Motif on Irish High Crosses', in Conor Newman, Mags Mannion & Fiona Gavin (eds.), *Islands in a Global Context: Proceedings of the Seventh International Conference on Insular Art, held at the National University of Ireland, Galway, 16–20 July 2017*, Dublin–Portland: Four Courts Press, 2017, pp. 222–32, plate 27.
5. Martin Werner, 'On the Origin of the Form of the Irish High Cross', *Gesta*, Vol. 29, No. 1 (1990), pp. 98–110.
6. Naser-e Khosrow, 'Alavi-e Qobadiyani', *Safar-Nameh*, Berlin, November/December 1922, p. 14.
7. Jonathan Bloom, *Arts of the City Victorious: Islamic Art and Architecture in Fatimid North Africa and Egypt*, New Haven & London: Yale University Press, 2007, p. 65.
8. Annie Labatt & Charlotte Appleyard, 'Byzantine Art under Islam', Metropolitan Museum of Art, October 2004, last accessed 22 May 2022, Byzantine Art under Islam | Essay | The Metropolitan Museum of Art | Heilbrunn Timeline of Art History (metmuseum.org).
9. Philip K. Hitti, *History of the Arabs*, London: Macmillan, 1970, p. 445.
10. Bloom, *Arts of the City Victorious*, p. 69.
11. Assadullah Souren Melikian-Chirvani, 'Fatimid Art and its Unresolved Enigmas', in Assadullah Souren Melikian-Chirvani (ed.), *The World of the Fatimids*, Toronto: Aga Khan Museum; London: Institute of Ismaili Studies; Munich: Hirmer Verlag, 2018, p. 130.
12. Bloom, *Arts of the City Victorious*, p. 94.
13. Ibid., p. 167.
14. Ibid., p. 81.
15. Melikian-Chirvani, 'Fatimid Art and its Unresolved Enigmas', p. 87.
16. Ibid., p. 78.
17. Ibid., p. 100.
18. Bloom, *Arts of the City Victorious*, p. 160.
19. Ibid., p. 170.
20. A. Camiz, 'Morphology of Roman, Islamic and Medieval Seismic Design: Pointed Arch and Ablaq', *Key Engineering Materials*, Vol. 628 (2014), pp. 12–13; Final International Conference of SMART BUILD (Structural Monitoring of Artistic and Historical Building Testimonies), ed. Dora Foti, Pfaffikon, Switzerland: Trans Tech Publications Ltd.
21. Bloom, *Arts of the City Victorious*, p. 128.
22. Doris Behrens-Abouseif, 'The Fatimid Dream of a New Capital', in Assadullah Souren Melikian-Chirvani (ed.), *The World of the Fatimids*, Toronto: Aga Khan Museum; London: Institute of Ismaili Studies; Munich: Hirmer Verlag, 2018, p. 56.
23. Ibid., p. 57.
24. Felix Arnold, *Islamic Palace Architecture in the Western Mediterranean*, Oxford: Oxford University Press, 2017, p. 1.
25. Leonard G. Chiarelli, *A History of Muslim Sicily*, Malta: Midsea Books, 2011, p. 257.

26. Ibid., p. 255.
27. Karen Rose Mathews, 'Pisan Bacini and the Churches of Pisa', in *A Companion to Medieval Pisa*, Leiden: E. J. Brill, 2022, p. 456.
28. Lamia Hadda, 'Zirid and Hammadid Palaces in North Africa and their Influence on Norman Architecture in Sicily', in C. Gambardella (ed.), *World Heritage and Knowledge, Le Vie dei Mercanti—XVI Forum International di Studi*, Rome: Gangemi Editore, 2018, pp. 323–32.

4. SARACEN CRAFTSMEN ACROSS EUROPE

1. Catlos, *Muslims of Medieval Latin Christendom*, p. 434.
2. Juan A. Souto, 'Documents of Christian Workers in the Great Mosque of Cordoba', *Al-Qantara*, Vol. 31, No. 1 (June 2010), pp. 31–75.
3. Catlos, *Muslims of Medieval Latin Christendom*, p. 399.
4. Thomas F. Glick, *Islamic and Christian Spain in the Early Middle Ages (711–1250)*, Leiden: E. J. Brill, 2005, p. 152.
5. Ibid., p. 222.
6. Leo A. Mayer, *Islamic Woodcarvers and their Works*, Geneva: A. Kundig, 1958, p. 13.
7. Glick, *Islamic and Christian Spain in the Early Middle Ages*, pp. 12–13.
8. Catlos, *Muslims of Medieval Latin Christendom*, p. 303.
9. Ibid., p. 44.
10. John Harvey, 'The Development of Architecture', in J. Evans (ed.), *The Flowering of the Middle Ages*, London: Thames & Hudson, 1985, p. 85.
11. Catlos, *Muslims of Medieval Latin Christendom*, p. 50.
12. Ibid., p. 47.
13. Ibid., p. 88.
14. Ibid., p. 39.
15. H. C. Lea, *A History of the Inquisition of Spain*, 4 vols., New York: Macmillan, 1907, Vol. 3., p. 317.
16. Catlos, *Muslims of Medieval Latin Christendom*, p. 187.
17. Ibid., p. 188.
18. Ibid., p. 270.
19. Ibid., p. 203.
20. John Gillingham, *Richard I*, New Haven & London: Yale University Press, 1999, p. 295.
21. Ibid., p. 295.
22. William Chester Jordan, *The Apple of His Eye: Converts from Islam in the Reign of Louis IX*, Princeton, NJ: Princeton University Press, 2019, p. 43.
23. J. Bourchier, Lord Berners (trans.), *The Chronicles of Froissart*, London: D. Nutt, 1903, Vol. 1, pp. 269–74.
24. Catlos, *Muslims of Medieval Latin Christendom*, p. 527.
25. Ibid., p. 132.
26. Ibid., p. 133.

27. Ibid., p. 270.
28. Ibid., p. 142.
29. Bernard Lewis, 'The Islamic Guilds', *The Economic History Review*, Vol. 8, No. 1 (1937), p. 25.
30. Ibid., p. 34.
31. Catlos, *Muslims of Medieval Latin Christendom*, p. 443.
32. Ibid., pp. 442–3.
33. Leo A. Mayer, *Islamic Architects and their Works*, Geneva: A. Kundig, 1956, p. 14.
34. Ibid.
35. Peter Kidson, 'Panofsky, Suger and St Denis', *Journal of the Warburg and Courtauld Institutes*, Vol. 50, No. 1 (1987), p. 17.
36. Bony, *French Gothic Architecture of the 12th and 13th Centuries*, p. 68.
37. Ibid., p. 72.
38. Idries Trevathan, *Colour, Light and Wonder in Islamic Art*, London: Saqi Books, 2024, p. 84.
39. 'Civilisation, by Kenneth Clark [1969], Ch. 02: The Great Thaw' [video], YouTube, last accessed 22 May 2024, https://www.youtube.com/watch?v=z8R_Hyi5XK4, 24 minutes onwards.
40. Dominique Clévenot, *Ornament and Decoration in Islamic Architecture*, London: Thames & Hudson, 2000, p. 67.
41. Margot E. Fassler, *The Virgin of Chartres: Making History through Liturgy and the Arts*, New Haven & London: Yale University Press, 2010, pp. vii–ix.
42. Annette Münchmeyer, 'The Masons' Marks in the Western Part of the Cathedral of Santiago de Compostela: An Approach to its Construction History', *Construction History*, Vol. 28, No. 2 (2013), p. 4.
43. Ibid., p. 4.

5. SARACEN CRAFTSMEN IN BRITAIN

1. Kathryn Hurlock, 'Family, Faith, and Knights of the Holy Sepulchre in Late and Post-Medieval Wales', in Kathryn Hurlock & Laura J. Whatley (eds.), *Crusading and Ideas of the Holy Land in Medieval Britain*, Medieval Texts and Cultures of Northern Europe 34, Turnhout, Belgium: Brepols, 2022, p. 154.
2. Catlos, *Muslims of Medieval Latin Christendom*, p. 266.
3. Eric Fernie, *The Architecture of Norman England*, Oxford: Oxford University Press, 2002, p. 283.
4. Catlos, *Muslims of Medieval Latin Christendom*, p. 278.
5. Katie Martin, 'History of St Chad's Church', BBC Local History Radio Series, Stoke & Staffordshire, 24 September 2014, last accessed 22 May 2024, https://www.bbc.co.uk/stoke/content/articles/2008/06/11/st_chads_stafford_feature.shtml
6. John Sleigh, *A History of the Ancient Parish of Leek, in Staffordshire*, Leek: Robert Nall, 1862, p. 161.
7. The Journey Man [Johnny Gillett], *Staffordshire Folk Tales*, Cheltenham: The History Press, 2012, p. 114.

8. Ibid., pp. 115, 116.
9. Ibid., p. 116.
10. Münchmeyer, 'The Masons' Marks in the Western Part of the Cathedral of Santiago de Compostela', p. 8.
11. Norman Hammond, 'Study Reveals French and Irish Secrets of Cathedral', *The Times*, 14 December 2003. For the report discussed by Hammond, see Daniel Miles, 'The Tree-Ring Dating of the Roof Carpentry of the Eastern Chapels, North Nave Triforium, and North Porch, Salisbury Cathedral, Wiltshire', Historic England Report, 22 November 2022. Miles also wrote another report, 'The Tree-ring Dating of the Nave Roof at Salisbury Cathedral, Wiltshire', Centre for Archaeology Report 58/2005, English Heritage, 2005.
12. Duncan James, 'Carpenters' Assembly Marks in Timber-Framed Buildings', *Vernacular Architecture*, Vol. 49, No. 1 (2018), p. 11.
13. Arnold Pacey, 'Some Carpenters' Marks in Arabic Numerals', *Vernacular Architecture*, Vol. 36, No. 1 (2005), p. 69.
14. Ibid., p. 69.
15. Charles Robert Cockerell, *Iconography of the West Front of Wells Cathedral, with an Appendix on the Sculptures of other Medieval Churches in England*, London: John Henry Parker, 1851, p. v.
16. Rev. Percy Dearmer, *The Cathedral Church of Wells: A Description of its Fabric and a Brief History of the Episcopal See with an Appendix on the Sculptures of Other Medieval Churches in England*, 1898; London: George Bell & Sons, 1915, p. 31.
17. Ibid., p. 33.
18. From the archived notes of Wells Cathedral historian Linzee Sparrow Colchester (1914–1989).
19. Raffaele Danna, 'The Spread of Hindu-Arabic Numerals in the European Tradition of Practical Arithmetic: A Socio-Economic Perspective (13th–16th Centuries)', PhD thesis, University of Cambridge, 15 December 2020.
20. Mr Irvine, 'Memorandum relative to the Arabic Numerals found on certain of the carved groups in the West Front of Wells Cathedral', *Proceedings of the Somersetshire Archaeological and Natural History Society*, Vol. 34 (1888), pp. 62; table between pp. 62 and 63. Also online, last accessed 22 May 2024, https://sanhs.org/wp-content/uploads/2019/09/05ThirdExcursion-13.pdf
21. Ibid., p. 56.
22. Dearmer, *The Cathedral Church of Wells*, p. 31.
23. Ibid., p. 31.
24. Jerry Sampson, *Wells Cathedral West Front: Construction, Sculpture and Conservation*, Stroud: Sutton Publishing Ltd, 1998, p. 192.
25. Ibid., p. 193.
26. Ibid., p. 191.
27. Charles Burnett, 'Introduction', in Charles Burnett (ed.), *Adelard of Bath: An English Scientist and Arabist of the Early Twelfth Century*, London: The Warburg Institute, University of London, 1987, p. 9.

28. Margaret Gibson, 'Adelard of Bath', in Charles Burnett (ed.), *Adelard of Bath: An English Scientist and Arabist of the Early Twelfth Century*, London: The Warburg Institute, University of London, 1987, p. 14.
29. Dafydd Evans, 'Adelard on Falconry', in Charles Burnett (ed.), *Adelard of Bath: An English Scientist and Arabist of the Early Twelfth Century*, The Warburg Institute, University of London, 1987, p. 25.
30. Burnett, 'Introduction', pp. 4–5.
31. Matthew Reeve, 'The Capital Sculpture of Wells Cathedral: Masons, Patrons and the Margins of English Gothic Architecture', *JBAA*, Vol. 163 (2010), p. 72.
32. Ibid., p. 72.
33. Ibid., p. 82.
34. Ibid., p. 90.
35. John Weever, *Antient funeral monuments, of Great-Britain, Ireland, and the islands adjacent: With the dissolved monasteries therein contained; Their Founders, and what eminent Persons have been therein interred. As also, the Death and Burial of certain of the Blood-Royal, nobility and gentry of these kingdoms, entombed in foreign nations*, London: Printed by W. Tooke, for the editor, and sold by J. Wilkie, 1767, p. 751.
36. Geoffrey of Beaulieu, 'Vita Sancti Ludovici Auctore Gaufrido de Belloloci', *Recueil des Historiens des Gaules et de la France* [RHGF], Vol. 20 (1840), pp. 16–17.
37. Henry Richards Luard (ed.), *Matthaei Parisiensis, Monachi Sancti Albani, Chronica Majora*, 7 vols., London: Longman, 1872, Vol. 5, p. 425 (Chronicle).
38. 'Tabulae Ceratae Johannis Sarraceni', RHGF, Vol. 21 (1855), pp. 365–6.
39. Jordan, *The Apple of His Eye*.
40. Ibid., p. 127.
41. Jackson, *Byzantine and Romanesque Architecture*, Vol. 2, p. 167.
42. BBC Two, 'Ipswich Man', *History Cold Case*, 27 July 2010, last accessed 22 May 2024, https://www.bbc.co.uk/programmes/b00sbjp7

6. SICILY: THE ARAB-NORMAN SYNTHESIS

1. Charles E. Nicklies, 'Builders, Patrons, and Identity: The Domed Basilicas of Sicily and Calabria', *Gesta*, Vol. 43, No. 2 (2004), pp. 99–114.
2. Chiarelli, *A History of Muslim Sicily*, p. 255.
3. Jeremy Johns, 'Muslim Artists and Christian Models in the Painted Ceilings of the Cappella Palatina', in Rosa Bacile (ed.), *Romanesque and the Mediterranean*, London: Routledge, 2015, pp. 59–89.
4. Kenneth Baxter Wolf, *Making History: The Normans and their Historians in Eleventh-Century Italy*, Philadelphia: University of Pennsylvania Press, 1995, pp. 126–8.
5. Cilento & Vanoli, *Arabs and Normans in Sicily and the South of Italy*, p. 142.
6. UNESCO World Heritage Convention, 'Arab-Norman Palermo and the Cathedral Churches of Cefalù and Monreale', 2015, last accessed 22 May 2024, https://whc.unesco.org/en/list/1487
7. Hadda, 'Zirid and Hammadid Palaces in North Africa', pp. 323–32.

8. Chiarelli, *A History of Muslim Sicily*, p. 313.
9. Ibid., p. 314.
10. Ibid., p. 314.
11. F. Basile, 'Le nuove ricerche sull'architettura del periodo normanno in Sicilia', in *Atti del VII Congresso nazionale di storia dell'architettura*, Palermo: Comitato presso la Soprintendenza ai monumenti, 1956, p. 261; M. Amari, *Storia dei musulmani di Sicilia*, Vol. 3, Firenze: Successori le Monnier, 1854, p. 880.
12. Bellafiore, *The Cathedral of Palermo*, p. 283.
13. Ibid., p. 60.
14. Ibid., p. 293.
15. Novairo (an-Nuwayri), 'Storia d'Africa', in [M. Amari], *Nuova raccolta di scritture e documenti intorno alla dominazione degli arabi in Sicilia*, Palermo: Giuseppe Meli, 1851, p. 297.
16. Amari, *Storia dei musulmani*, Vol. 3, p. 430; H. R. Idris, *La Berbérie orientale sous les Zirides*, Paris: Librairie d'Amérique et d'Orient, 1962, p. 374.
17. Amari, *Storia dei musulmani*, Vol. 3, p. 430.
18. G. Marçais, *L'Architecture musulmane d'Occident*, Paris: Arts et métiers graphiques, 1954, pp. 125–7; L. Golvin, *Le Maghrib Central à l'époque des Zirides*, Algiers: Arts et métiers graphiques, 1957, pp. 213–18.
19. Bellafiore, *The Cathedral of Palermo*, p. 24; Giuseppe Bellafiore, *Dall'Islam alla maniera: Profilo dell' architettura dal IX al XVI secolo*, Palermo, S. F. Flaccovio, 1975.
20. Bellafiore, *The Cathedral of Palermo*, p. 289.
21. Ibid., p. 132.
22. Ibid., p. 143.
23. Ibid., p. 210.
24. Ibid., p. 211.
25. Cilento & Vanoli, *Arabs and Normans in Sicily and the South of Italy*, p. 208.
26. Bellafiore, *The Cathedral of Palermo*, p. 252.
27. Ibid., p. 258.
28. Ibid., p. 262.
29. Ibid., p. 256.
30. Ibid., p. 262.
31. Ibid., p. 267.
32. Ibid., p. 269.
33. Trevathan, *Colour, Light and Wonder in Islamic Art*, pp. 122–3.
34. Bellafiore, *The Cathedral of Palermo*, p. 273.
35. Ibid., p. 293.
36. Ibid., p. 295.
37. Ibid., p. 299.
38. Ibid., p. 303.
39. Ibid., p. 273–4.
40. Ibid., p. 274.

41. Johns, 'Muslim Artists and Christian Models', pp. 59–89.
42. Ibid., p. 64.
43. Hitti, *History of the Arabs*, p. 664.
44. Ernst J. Grube & Jeremy Johns, *The Painted Ceilings of the Cappella Palatina*, Islamic Art Supplement 1, Genova: Bruschettini Foundation for Islamic and Asian Art; New York: East-West Foundation, 2005, p. 25.
45. Johns, 'Muslim Artists and Christian Models', p. 51.
46. Ibid., p. 51.
47. Bellafiore, *The Cathedral of Palermo*, Palermo, p. 289.
48. Ibid., p. 290.
49. Chiarelli, *A History of Muslim Sicily*, p. 322.
50. Loud & Metcalfe, *The Society of Norman Italy*, pp. 313–15.
51. Ibid., pp. 315, 294.
52. Ibid., p. 315.
53. Maria Antonietta Spadaro, Sergio Troisi & Bruno Carusa, *The Arab-Norman Itinerary: The UNESCO Heritage in Palermo, Monreale and Cefalù*, Palermo: Edizioni d'arte Kalós, 2018, p. 126.
54. Ibid., p. 126.
55. D. M. Hayes & J. P. Hayes, 'The Norman Sicily Project: A Digital Portal to Sicily's Norman Past', *Digital Medievalist*, Vol. 12, No. 1 (2019), last accessed 22 May 2024, https://journal.digitalmedievalist.org/article/id/7021/
56. Cristian Capelli et al., 'Moors and Saracens in Europe: Estimating the Medieval North African Male Legacy in Southern Europe', *European Journal of Human Genetics*, Vol. 17, No. 6 (2009), pp. 848–52.

7. ITALIAN ISLAMESQUE

1. Randle Cotgrave, *A Dictionarie of the French and English Tongues*, London: Adam Islip, 1611.
2. This hypothesis of the unbroken tradition from Late Roman times was set forth in Giovanni Teresio Rivoira's *Le origini dell'architettura lombarda*, Roma: E. Loescher, 1901, Vol. 1, and has been incorporated into the lore of Freemasonry.
3. Géza De Francovich, 'La corrente comasca nella scultura romanica europea', Part I and II, *Rivista del Reale Istituto di Archeologia e Storia dell'Arte*, Vol. 5 (1935), pp. 267–305; Vol. 6 (1937–8), pp. 47–129. Géza De Francovich, *Benedetto Antelami*, Milan-Florence: Electa, 1952, p. 8; De Francovich, 'La corrente comasca', Part I, p. 287.
4. Diana Luber, *Islam in Europe*, Sam Fogg Exhibition Catalogue, London: Paul Holberton Publishing, 2023, pp. 38, 42.
5. Ibid., p. 150.
6. Cilento & Vanoli, *Arabs and Normans in Sicily and the South of Italy*, p. 33.
7. Joselita Raspi Serra, 'English Decorative Sculpture of the Early Twelfth Century and the Como-Pavian Tradition', *The Art Bulletin*, Vol. 51, No. 4 (1969), pp. 352–62.
8. Ibid., pp. 352–3.

9. Wolf, *Making History*, pp. 126–8.
10. Jackson, *Byzantine and Romanesque Architecture*, Vol. 1, p. 263.
11. Ibid., p. 265.
12. Ibid., p. 273.
13. Deborah Howard, *Venice and the East*, New Haven & London, Yale University Press, 2000, p. 148.
14. Jackson, *Byzantine and Romanesque Architecture*, Vol. 1, p. 235.
15. Nicklies, 'Builders, Patrons, and Identity', pp. 99–114.
16. Ibid., p. 107.
17. UNESCO World Heritage Convention, 'Cattolica Monastery in Stilo and Basilian-Byzantine Complexes', 1 June 2006, last accessed 23 May 2024, https://whc.unesco.org/en/tentativelists/1150/
18. Jackson, *Byzantine and Romanesque Architecture*, Vol. 1, p. 242.
19. Isa Belli Barsali, 'Buscheto (Busketus, Buschetto, Boschetto)', in *Dizionario biografico degli italiani*, Vol. 15: *Buffoli–Caccianemici*, Rome: Istituto dell'Enciclopedia Italiana, 1972.
20. Ibid.
21. Ibid.
22. 'Buschetto [Boschetto; Busketus]', in Colum Hourihane (ed.), *The Grove Encyclopedia of Medieval Art and Architecture*, 6 vols., Oxford University Press, 2012, Vol. 1, pp. 472–3.
23. Paul Moses, *The Saint and the Sultan: The Crusades, Islam, and Francis of Assisi's Mission of Peace*, New York: Doubleday, 2009.
24. Jill Caskey, 'Stuccoes from the Early Norman Period in Sicily: Figuration, Fabrication and Integration', *Medieval Encounters*, Vol. 17, No. 1–2 (2011), pp. 80–119.
25. UNESCO World Heritage Convention, 'Longobards in Italy: Places of the Power (568–774 A.D.)', 2011, last accessed 23 May 2024, https://whc.unesco.org/en/list/1318/
26. Jackson, *Byzantine and Romanesque Architecture*, Vol. 1, p. 215.
27. Ibid., pp. 215–16.
28. Stefan Goodwin, 'Islam and Realignments', in *Malta, Mediterranean Bridge*, Westport, CT: Bergin & Garvey, 2002, chapter 2, pp. 23–4.
29. Catlos, *Muslims of Medieval Latin Christendom*, p. 126.

8. SPANISH ISLAMESQUE

1. Ian Almond, *Two Faiths, One Banner: When Muslims Marched with Christians across Europe's Battlegrounds*, London: I. B. Tauris, 2009, p. 14.
2. E. R. Truitt, 'Celestial Divination and Arabic Science in Twelfth-century England: The History of Gerbert of Aurillac's Talking Head', *Journal of the History of Ideas*, Vol. 73, No. 2 (2012), pp. 201–22.
3. T. J. Denny, 'Moorish Architecture in Spain', PhD thesis, University of Oxford, 1936.

4. Isidora González Fernández, *The Priory of Escalada*, Barcelonia: Escudo de Oro, 2000, p. 11.
5. Ibid., pp. 11–12.
6. Trevathan, *Colour, Light and Wonder in Islamic Art*, p. 128.
7. Alan Greenlees, 'To Beard or Not to Beard', Blog, The Burrell Collection, 30 March 2021, last accessed 23 May 2024, https://burrellcollection.com/the-burrell-blog-insights-from-the-project-team/to-beard-or-not-to-beard/#:~:text=In%20art%20of%20this%20period,angels%20are%20invariably%20clean%2Dshaven
8. UNESCO World Heritage Convention, 'Poblet Monastery', 1991, last accessed 23 May 2024, https://whc.unesco.org/en/list/518/
9. Peter Strafford, *Romanesque Churches of Spain: A Traveller's Guide*, London: Giles de la Mare Publishers, 2010, p. 60.
10. UNESCO World Heritage Site, 'Durham Castle and Cathedral', last accessed 23 May 2024, https://www.durhamworldheritagesite.com/learn/architecture/romanesque/display/santo-domingo-panel
11. The Monks of Santo Domingo de Silos, *The Monastery of Silos*, León, 2015, pp. 19, 22.
12. Strafford, *Romanesque Churches of Spain*, p. 260.
13. Meyer Schapiro, 'From Mozarabic to Romanesque in Silos', *The Art Bulletin*, Vol. 21, No. 4 (December 1939), p. 321.
14. Elizabeth Valdez del Álamo, *Palace of the Mind: The Cloister of Silos and Spanish Sculpture of the Twelfth Century*, Turnhout, Belgium: Brepols, 2012, p. 143.
15. Ibid., p. 148
16. Ibid., p. 155.
17. Ibid., p. 170.
18. Ibid., p. 170.
19. Strafford, *Romanesque Churches of Spain*, p. 311.
20. Isidora González Fernández, *The Priory of Escalada*, Barcelona: Escudo de Oro, 2000, p. 14.
21. Ibid., p. 25.
22. UNESCO World Heritage Convention, 'Monuments of Oviedo and the Kingdom of the Asturias', 1985, last accessed 23 May 2024, https://whc.unesco.org/en/list/312/
23. Ramón Yzquierdo Peiró, *Museo Catedral de Santiago*, Santiago Cathedral Foundation, 2018, p. 2.
24. UNESCO World Heritage Convention, 'Santiago de Compostela (Old Town), 1985, last accessed 24 June 2024, https://whc.unesco.org/en/list/347/; J. H. Harvey, *English Medieval Architects: A Biographical Dictionary Down to 1550, Including Master Masons, Carpenters, Carvers, Building Contractors, and Others Responsible for Design*, London: Batsford, 1984.
25. Münchmeyer, 'The Masons' Marks in the Western Part of the Cathedral of Santiago de Compostela', p. 8.

26. Catlos, *Muslims of Medieval Latin Christendom*, p. 491.
27. Denny, 'Moorish Architecture in Spain'.
28. Manuel Expósito Sebastián, José Luis Pano Gracia & Isabel Sepùlveda Sauras, *The Aljafería of Zaragoza: A Historical, Artistic and Literary Guide*, Zaragoza: Cortes de Aragón, 2020, p. 36.
29. Ibid., p. 48.
30. UNESCO World Heritage Convention, 'Mudejar Architecture of Aragon', Criterion (iv), 1986, last accessed 23 May 2024, https://whc.unesco.org/en/list/378/#:~:text=Criterion%20(iv)%3A%20The%20Mud%C3%A9jar,building%20methods%20employed%20by%20Christians%2C

9. GERMANIC ISLAMESQUE

1. Manfred W. Wenner, 'The Arab/Muslim Presence in Medieval Central Europe', *International Journal of Middle East Studies*, Vol. 12, No. 1 (1980), pp. 59–79.
2. Ibid., pp. 59–79.
3. Ibid., p. 70.
4. Ibid., pp. 59–79.
5. Ibid., p. 71.
6. Ariel David, 'Third Time's the Charm: Sapiens from the Levant Made Three Attempts to Settle in Europe, Study Shows', *Haaretz*, 3 May 2023, last accessed 23 May 2024, https://www.haaretz.com/archaeology/2023–05–03/ty-article/sapiens-from-the-levant-made-three-attempts-to-settle-in-europe-study-shows/00000187-e0cd-d9b4-abaf-e8ff431d0000
7. Peter Joseph Ruppen, *Die Chronik des Thales Saas fur die Thalbewohner*, Sitten: Buchdruckerei von Calpini-Albertazzi, I85I, pp. 11–14.
8. Jackson, *Byzantine and Romanesque Architecture*, Vol. 2, p. 1.
9. Ibid., p. 2.
10. Stuart Cristo, 'The Art of Ravenna in Late Antiquity', *The Classical Journal*, Vol. 70, No. 3 (February–March 1975), p. 17.
11. Riccardo Belcari & Giulia Marrucchi, *Art of the Middle Ages: Masterpieces in Painting, Sculpture and Architecture*, New York: Barnes & Noble, 2007, p. 56.
12. Maxime K. Yevadian, 'Ermittlung über die Widmungsinschrift von Dombaumeister Odo im Aachener Dom', *Karlsverein-Dombauverein*, Vol. 22 (2020), pp. 63–73.
13. Jean Abélanet, *Lieux et légendes du Roussillon et des Pyrénées catalanes*, Perpignan: Editorial Trabucaire, 2000, p. 155.
14. Oleg Grabar, 'Islamic Architecture and the West: Influences and Parallels', in *Islamic Visual Culture, 1100–1800: Constructing the Study of Islamic Art*, Vol. 2, Aldershot, Hampshire: Ashgate Publishing, 2006, p. 384.
15. UNESCO World Heritage Convention, 'Aachen Cathedral', 1978, last accessed 23 May 2024, https://whc.unesco.org/en/list/3/#:~:text=It%20is%20Emperor%20Charlemagne%C2%B4,under%20the%20aegis%20of%20Charlemagne
16. Hitti, *History of the Arabs*, p. 315.

17. Daniel Nathan Hickman, 'Ibn Hazm: An Islamic Source of Courtly Love', PhD thesis, University of Tennessee, Knoxville, 2014.
18. 'Civilisation, by Kenneth Clark [1969], Ch. 03: Romance and Reality' [video], YouTube, last accessed 23 May 2024, https://www.youtube.com/watch?v=_lpZFKUbO8, 7.27 minutes in.
19. Grabar, 'Islamic Architecture and the West', p. 381.
20. Jackson, *Byzantine and Romanesque Architecture*, Vol. 2, p. 7.
21. Peter Schappert & Mario Colletto, *Der Dom zu Speyer: Gebaut für Gott und Kaiser*, Annweiler: Pilger Verlag, 2012, p. 79.
22. Johannes Fritz & Jirí Janák, 'How Human Intervention and Climate Change Shaped the Fate of the Northern Bald Ibis from Ancient Egypt to the Present', *BioRxiv*, 26 November 2020, last accessed 23 May 2024, https://www.biorxiv.org/content/10.1101/2020.11.25.397570v1.full
23. Bloom, *Arts of the City Victorious*, p. 69.
24. Jackson, *Byzantine and Romanesque Architecture*, Vol. 2, p. 22.

10. FRENCH ISLAMESQUE

1. Xavier Darcos, *Prosper Mérimée*, Paris: Flammarion, 1998, p. 118.
2. Jackson, *Byzantine and Romanesque Architecture*, Vol. 2, pp. 267–8.
3. Bony, *French Gothic Architecture of the 12th and 13th Centuries*, pp. 14, 15.
4. Ibid., p. 17.
5. Jackson, *Byzantine and Romanesque Architecture*, Vol. 2, p. 91.
6. UNESCO World Heritage Convention, 'Routes of Santiago de Compostela: *Camino Francés* and Routes of Northern Spain', 1993, last accessed 23 May 2024, https://whc.unesco.org/en/list/669/
7. Bony, *French Gothic Architecture of the 12th and 13th Centuries*, p. 18.
8. Ibid., p. 13.
9. Jackson, *Byzantine and Romanesque Architecture*, Vol. 2, p. 88.
10. Meyer Schapiro, 'The Romanesque Sculpture of Moissac', *The Art Bulletin*, Vol. 13, No. 3 (September 1931), p. 280.
11. Ibid., p. 291.
12. Ibid., p. 255.
13. Ibid., p. 269.
14. Ibid., p. 270.
15. Ibid., p. 251.
16. Ibid., p. 251.
17. Ibid., p. 273.
18. Ibid., p. 274.
19. Jackson, *Byzantine and Romanesque Architecture*, Vol. 2, p. 98.
20. Ibid., p. 108.
21. Ibid., p. 42.
22. Ibid., p. 36.

23. Ibid., p. 43.
24. Bony, *French Gothic Architecture of the 12th and 13th Centuries*, p. 74.
25. UNESCO World Heritage Convention, 'Abbey Church of Saint-Savin sur Gartempe', 1983, 2007, 2015, last accessed 23 May 2024, https://whc.unesco.org/en/list/230/
26. Luber, *Islam in Europe*, p. 18.
27. Jackson, *Byzantine and Romanesque Architecture*, Vol. 2, p. 144.
28. Ibid., p. 145.
29. UNESCO World Heritage Convention, 'Routes of Santiago de Compostela in France', 1998, last accessed 23 May 2024, https://whc.unesco.org/en/list/868/
30. Marçais, *Mélanges d'histoire et d'archéologie de l'occident musulman*, p. 208.
31. Ibid., p. 210.
32. Jackson, *Byzantine and Romanesque Architecture*, Vol. 2, p. 82.
33. James McDonald, 'Cathars and Cathar Beliefs in the Languedoc', February 2017, last accessed 23 May 2023, http://www.cathar.info/
34. Jackson, *Byzantine and Romanesque Architecture*, Vol. 2, p. 83.
35. Ibid., p. 103.
36. Ibid., p. 103.
37. Ibid., p. 104.
38. Ibid., p. 240.
39. Bony, *French Gothic Architecture of the 12th and 13th Centuries*, p. 85.
40. Luber, *Islam in Europe* (many examples feature in this catalogue).
41. Bloom, *Arts of the City Victorious*, p. 71.
42. Jean Pierre Sarrasin, *Lettres françaises du XIIIe siècle*, ed. Alfred Foulet, Paris: H. Champion, 1924.
43. Hitti, *History of the Arabs*, p. 664.
44. Amelia Soth, 'The Medieval Castle that Pranked its Visitors', JSTOR Daily, 5 July 2018, last accessed 23 May 2024, https://daily.jstor.org/the-medieval-castle-that-pranked-its-visitors/

11. ISLAMESQUE IN THE BRITISH ISLES

1. 'Civilisation, by Kenneth Clark [1969], Ch. 01: By the Skin of Our Teeth' [video], YouTube, last accessed 23 May 2024, https://www.youtube.com/watch?v=UiqDG7rEp1k, 21 minutes onwards.
2. BBC History Magazine, 'Long Read: The Man at Sutton Hoo', *History Extra*, 19 March 2021, last accessed 23 May 2024, https://www.historyextra.com/period/anglo-saxon/sutton-hoo-burial-who-long-read-professor-james-campbell/
3. Katy Prickett, 'Viking Replica Arabic Coin Brooch Found at Watton by Detectorist', BBC News, 29 July 2023, last accessed 23 May 2024, https://www.bbc.co.uk/news/uk-england-norfolk-66320409
4. Werner, 'On the Origin of the Form of the Irish High Cross', pp. 98–110.

5. Zehava Jacoby, 'The Beard Pullers in Romanesque Art: An Islamic Motif and its Evolution in the West', *Arte Medievale*, Vol. 1 (1987), pp. 65–85, https://dn790005.ca.archive.org/0/items/Jacoby/Jacoby_text.pdf
6. Hector McDonnell, 'Irish Round Towers: Origins and Purposes', *Ulster Journal of Archaeology*, Vol. 74, (2017–18), p. 131.
7. Ali Ibrahim Moghawi, 'Basic Principles of Construction of Houssounes (Houses, Fortresses)', in *Rojal: Memory of an Arab Village*, trans. Ghania Ahmed Jerrar, Jeddah: King Fahd National Library, 2010, chapter 4, pp. 78–88.
8. Jackson, *Byzantine and Romanesque Architecture*, Vol. 2, p. 181.
9. Ibid., p. 182.
10. Ibid., p. 197.
11. Ibid., p. 197.
12. Ibid., p. 203.
13. Ibid., p. 256.
14. Ibid., p. 256.
15. Richard Foster, *Patterns of Thought: The Hidden Meaning of the Great Pavement of Westminster Abbey*, London: Jonathan Cape, 1991, p. 4.
16. George Zarnecki, Janet Holt & Tristram Holland (eds.), *English Romanesque Art, 1066–1200*, catalogue of an exhibition at the Hayward Gallery, London, 5 April–8 July 1984, London: Arts Council/Weidenfeld & Nicolson, 1984, pp. 33–4.
17. Canterbury Historical and Archaeological Society, 'Capitals in Western Crypt', last accessed 23 May 2024, https://www.canterbury-archaeology.org.uk/capitals-in-western-crypt#:~:text=The%20western%20section%20(completed%20under,%2C%20dragons%2C%20monsters%20and%20men
18. Cockerell, *Iconography of the West Front of Wells Cathedral*, p. 50.
19. Allan Brodie, 'Old Sarum Cathedral, Old Sarum, Wiltshire', *The Corpus of Romanesque Sculture in Britain & Ireland*, 2010, last accessed 23 May 2024, https://www.crsbi.ac.uk/view-item?i=111398
20. Cockerell, *Iconography of the West Front of Wells Cathedral*, 'Appendix F: Rochester Cathedral', p. 58.
21. Jacob Scott, 'Masons' Marks: 12th Century', Rochester Cathedral, 3 October 2021, last accessed 23 May 2024, https://www.rochestercathedral.org/research/masons
22. T. Hearne (ed.), *Textus Roffensis*, Oxford, 1720, pp. 145–8.
23. Sampson, *Wells Cathedral West Front*.
24. Ibid., p. 75.
25. Ibid., p. 83.
26. Ibid., caption on plate 2, between pp. 172–3.
27. Ibid., p. 85.
28. Ibid., p. 85.
29. Ibid., p. 266.
30. Ibid., p. 86.
31. Ibid., p. 92.

32. Ibid., p. 96.
33. Ibid., p. 99.
34. Ibid., p. 100.
35. Dearmer, *The Cathedral Church of Wells*, p. 48.
36. Laura Slater, 'Bodies or Buildings? Visual Translations of Jerusalem and Dynastic Memories in Medieval England', in Kathryn Hurlock & Laura J. Whatley (eds.), *Crusading and Ideas of the Holy Land in Medieval Britain*, Medieval Texts and Cultures of Northern Europe 34, Turnhout, Belgium: Brepols, 2022, p. 139.
37. Anon., 'Castle Rising', King's Lynn, Norfolk, on-site booklet.
38. Jackson, *Byzantine and Romanesque Architecture*, Vol. 1, p. 252.
39. Christian Jacq, *Le Message des constructeurs de cathédrales: La Symbolique des edifices*, Paris: Éditions J'ai Lu, 2022, p. 63.
40. Jackie Hall & Susan M. Wright (eds.), *Conservation and Discovery: Peterborough Cathedral Nave Ceiling and Related Structures*, London: Museum of London Archaeology (MOLA), 2015, pp. 67–71.
41. Ibid., p. 71.
42. Edgar De Bruyne, *The Esthetics of the Middle Ages*, trans. Eileen B. Hennessy, New York: Frederick Ungar Publishing, 1969, p. 59.
43. Paul Bush, *The Painted Ceiling of Peterborough Cathedral*, n.p.: Paul Bush, 2001, p. 5.
44. Peter Lowis, *Carvings at Durham Cathedral*, p. 5.
45. UNESCO World Heritage Site, 'Durham Castle and Cathedral', last accessed 23 May 2024, https://www.durhamworldheritagesite.com/learn/architecture/cathedral/intro/galilee-chapel/andalusian-influences
46. Fernie, *The Architecture of Norman England*, p. 273.

CONCLUSION

1. 'Civilisation, by Kenneth Clark [1969], Ch. 01: By the Skin of Our Teeth' [video], YouTube, https://www.youtube.com/watch?v=UiqDG7rEp1k, 18.20 minutes in.
2. Ibid., 39.35 minutes in.

LIST OF ILLUSTRATIONS

SELECT BIBLIOGRAPHY

Abulafia, David, *The Two Italies: Economic Relations between the Kingdom of Sicily and the Northern Communes*, Cambridge: Cambridge University Press, 1977.

———, *Frederick II: A Medieval Emperor*, London: Allen Lane, 1988.

———, *The Western Mediterranean Kingdoms, 1200–1500: The Struggle for Dominion*, Abingdon: Longman, 1997.

Agnelli, Fabrizio, 'The Painted Ceiling of the Nave of the Cappella Palatina in Palermo: An Essay on its Geometric and Constructive Features', *Muqarnas*, Vol. 27 (2010), pp. 407–47 (online, 2011).

Al-Hassani, Salim, *1001 Inventions: Muslim Heritage in Our World*, Manchester: FSTC, 2007.

Alkhateeb, Firas, *Lost Islamic History: Reclaiming Muslim Civilisation from the Past*, London: Hurst, 2017.

Almond, Ian, *Two Faiths, One Banner: When Muslims Marched with Christians across Europe's Battlegrounds*, London: I. B. Tauris, 2009.

Arnold, Felix, *Islamic Palace Architecture in the Western Mediterranean*, Oxford: Oxford University Press, 2017.

Babcock, Jennifer Miyuki, *Ancient Egyptian Animal Fables: Tree Climbing Hippos and Ennobled Mice*, Leiden: E. J. Brill, 2022.

Behrens-Abouseif, Doris, *Islamic Architecture in Cairo: An Introduction*, Leiden: E. J. Brill, 1989.

———, *The Minarets of Cairo*, London: I. B. Tauris, 2010.

Belcari, Riccardo, & Giulia Marrucchi, *Art of the Middle Ages: Masterpieces in Painting, Sculpture and Architecture*, New York: Barnes & Noble, 2007.

Bellafiore, Giuseppe, *The Cathedral of Palermo*, Palermo: S. F. Flaccovio, 1976.

Birk, Joshua C., *Norman Kings of Sicily and the Rise of the Anti-Islamic Critique: Baptized Sultans*, London: Palgrave Macmillan, 2016.

Bloom, Jonathan, *Arts of the City Victorious: Islamic Art and Architecture in Fatimid North Africa and Egypt*, New Haven & London: Yale University Press, 2007.

———, *Architecture of the Islamic West: North Africa and the Iberian Peninsula, 700–1800*, New Haven & London: Yale University Press, 2020.

Bony, Jean, *French Gothic Architecture of the 12th and 13th Centuries*, Berkeley: University of California Press, 1983.

Bridgeford, Andrew, *The Hidden History of the Bayeux Tapestry*, New York: Harper Perennial, 2005.

Brown, Nancy Marie, *The Abacus and the Cross: The Story of the Pope who Brought the Light of Science to the Dark Ages*, New York: Basic Books, 2011.

Burnett, Charles (ed.), *Adelard of Bath: An English Scientist and Arabist of the Early Twelfth Century*, London: The Warburg Institute, University of London, 1987.

Bush, Paul, *The Painted Ceiling of Peterborough Cathedral*, Paul Bush, 2001.

Camiz, A., 'Morphology of Roman, Islamic and Medieval Seismic Design: Pointed Arch and Ablaq', *Key Engineering Materials*, Vol. 628 (2014), pp. 9–14; Final International Conference of SMART BUILD (Structural Monitoring of Artistic and Historical Building Testimonies), ed. Dora Foti, Pfaffikon, Switzerland: Trans Tech Publications Ltd.

Caskey, Jill, 'Stuccoes from the Early Norman Period in Sicily: Figuration, Fabrication and Integration', *Medieval Encounters*, Vol. 17, No. 1–2 (2011), pp. 80–119.

Catlos, Brian A., *Muslims of Medieval Latin Christendom, c. 1050–1614*, Cambridge: Cambridge University Press, 2014.

Chiarelli, Leonard G., *A History of Muslim Sicily*, Malta: Midsea Books, 2011.

Cilento, Adele, & Alessandro Vanoli, *Arabs and Normans in Sicily and the South of Italy*, Bologna: Magnus Edizioni, 2022.

Clapham, Alfred W., F.S.A., *English Romanesque Architecture*, Vol. 1: *Before the Conquest*, Oxford: Clarendon Press, 1930.

———, *English Romanesque Architecture*, Vol. 2: *After the Conquest*, Oxford: Clarendon Press, 1934.

Clévenot, Dominique, *Ornament and Decoration in Islamic Architecture*, London: Thames & Hudson, 2000.

Cockerell, Charles Robert, *Iconography of the West Front of Wells Cathedral, with an Appendix on the Sculptures of other Medieval Churches in England*, London: John Henry Parker, 1851.

Conant, Kenneth John, *The Early Architectural History of the Cathedral of Santiago de Compostela*, Cambridge, MA: Harvard University Press, 1926.

———, *Carolingian and Romanesque Architecture, 800–1200*, New Haven: Yale University Press, 1978.

Coulton, G. G., *Art and the Reformation*, Cambridge: Cambridge University Press, 1953.

Critchlow, Keith, *Islamic Patterns: An Analytical and Cosmological Approach*, London: Thames & Hudson, 2011.

Dalrymple, William, *From the Holy Mountain: A Journey among the Christians of the Middle East*, London: Owl Books, 1999.

de Vogüé, Melchior, *Syrie centrale: Architecture civile et religieuse du Ier au VII siècle*, Paris: J. Baudry, 1865–77.

Dearmer, Percy, Rev., *The Cathedral Church of Wells: A Description of its Fabric and a Brief History of the Episcopal See with an Appendix on the Sculptures of Other Medieval Churches in England*, London: George Bell & Sons, 1898.

Doyle, John, *Canterbury Cathedral: A Walk Round Guide*, Hastings: Print2Demand, 2018.
Draper, Peter, 'Islam and the West: The Early Use of the Pointed Arch Revisited', *Architectural History*, Vol. 48 (2005), pp. 1–20.
Expósito Sebastián, Manuel, José Luis Pano Gracia & María Isabel Sepúlveda Sauras, *La Aljafería de Zaragoza: Guía histórico-artística y literaria* [The *Aljaferia of Zaragoza: A Historical, Artistic and Literary Guide*], Zaragoza: Cortes de Aragón, 2020.
Fassler, Margot E., *The Virgin of Chartres: Making History through Liturgy and the Arts*, New Haven & London: Yale University Press, 2010.
Fernie, Eric, *The Architecture of Norman England*, Oxford: Oxford University Press, 2002.
———, *Romanesque Architecture: The First Style of the European Age*, New Haven & London: Yale University Press, 2014.
Fontaine, Jacques, *L'Art préroman hispanique*, Vol. 2: *L'Art mozarabe*, Paris: Zodiaque, 1977.
Foster, Richard, *Patterns of Thought: The Hidden Meaning of the Great Pavement of Westminster Abbey*, London: Jonathan Cape, 1991.
Gabra, Gawdat, *Cairo: The Coptic Museum and Old Churches*, Cairo: Egyptian International Publishing Co., Longman, 2019.
Gabra, Gawdat (ed.), *Coptic Civilization: Two Thousand Years of Christianity in Egypt*, Cairo: American University in Cairo Press, 2014.
Gabra, Gawdat, & Marianne Eaton-Krauss, *The Treasures of Coptic Art in the Coptic Museum and Churches of Old Cairo*, Cairo: American University in Cairo Press, 2006.
Gabra, Gawdat, Gertrud J. M. van Loon, Stefan C. Reif & Tarek Swelim, *The History and Religious Heritage of Old Cairo: Its Fortress, Churches, Synagogue, and Mosque*, Cairo: American University in Cairo Press, 2016.
Garrett, Simon, & Anne Crawford, *The People Who Made Wells Cathedral: More than Stone and Glass*, Wells: Heritage Films & Publications Ltd, 2013.
Gies, Francis, & Joseph Gies, *Cathedral, Forge and Waterwheel: Technology and Invention in the Middle Ages*, 60th edition, New York: HarperCollins, 2010.
Gillingham, John, *Richard I*, New Haven & London: Yale University Press, 1999.
Glick, Thomas F., *Islamic and Christian Spain in the Early Middle Ages (711–1250)*, Leiden: E. J. Brill, 2005.
Grabar, Oleg, 'Islamic Architecture and the West: Influences and Parallels', in S. Ferber (ed.), *Islamic Visual Culture, 1100–1800: Constructing the Study of Islamic Art*, Vol. 2, Aldershot: Ashgate Publishing, 2006, pp. 381–8.
Grube, Ernst J., & Jeremy Johns, *The Painted Ceilings of the Cappella Palatina*, Islamic Art Supplement 1, Genova: Bruschettini Foundation for Islamic and Asian Art; New York: East-West Foundation, 2005.
Guilmain, Jacques, 'The Geometry of the Cross-Carpet Pages in the Lindisfarne Gospels', *Speculum*, Vol. 62, No. 1 (1987), pp. 21–52.
Hall, Jackie, & Susan Wright (eds.), *Conservation and Discovery: Peterborough Cathedral Nave Ceiling and Related Structures*, London: Museum of London Archaeology (MOLA), 2015.

Harte, Jeremy, *The Green Man*, London: Pitkin Publishing, 2017.

Harvey, J., *The Master Builders*, London: Thames & Hudson, 1973.

———, *English Mediaeval Architects: A Biographical Dictionary Down to 1550, Including Master Masons, Carpenters, Carvers, Building Contractors, and Others Responsible for Design*, London: Batsford, 1984.

Hennessy, Kathryn (ed.), *Signs and Symbols*, London: DK Penguin Random House, 2019.

Hess, Catherine (ed.), *The Arts of Fire: Islamic Influences on Glass and Ceramics of the Italian Renaissance*, Los Angeles: J. Paul Getty Trust, 2004.

Hessing, Edward, Rev., *A Walk-around Guide to the Church of St Nicholas, Barfrestone*, ed. Richard Hoskin, The Friends of Barfreston Church, 2017.

Hewett, Cecil A., *English Historic Carpentry*, Chichester: Phillimore, 1980.

Hill, G. F., *The Development of Arabic Numerals in Europe Exhibited in Sixty-Four Tables*, Oxford: Clarendon Press, 1915.

Hitti, Philip K., *History of the Arabs*, London: Macmillan, 1970.

Hoffman, Eva R., 'The Beginnings of the Illustrated Arabic Book: An Intersection between Art and Scholarship', *Muqarnas*, Vol. 17 (2000), pp. 37–52.

Hourihane, Colum, *The Mason and His Mark: Masons' Marks in the Medieval Irish Archbishoprics of Cashel and Dublin*, Oxford: British Archaeological Reports, 2000.

Howard, Deborah, *Venice and the East*, New Haven & London: Yale University Press, 2000.

Hurlock, Kathryn, & Laura J. Whatley (eds.), *Crusading and Ideas of the Holy Land in Medieval Britain*, Medieval Texts and Cultures of Northern Europe 34, Turnhout, Belgium: Brepols, 2022.

Iversen, Margaret, *Alois Riegl, Art History and Theory*, Cambridge, MA: MIT Press, 1993.

Jackson, Thomas Graham, *Byzantine and Romanesque Architecture*, 2 vols., Cambridge: Cambridge University Press, 1913.

Jacq, Christian, *Le Message des constructeurs de cathédrales: La Symbolique des edifices*, Paris: Éditions J'ai Lu, 2022.

Jenkins, Simon, *Europe's 100 Best Cathedrals*, London: Penguin Random House, 2021.

Johns, Jeremy, *Arabic Administration in Norman Sicily: The Royal Diwan*, Cambridge: Cambridge University Press, 2002.

———, 'Muslim Artists and Christian Models in the Painted Ceilings of the Cappella Palatina', in Rosa Bacile (ed.), *Romanesque and the Mediterranean*, London: Routledge, 2015, pp. 59–89.

Jordan, William Chester, *The Apple of His Eye: Converts from Islam in the Reign of Louis IX*, Princeton, NJ: Princeton University Press, 2019.

Keates, Jonathan, & Angelo Hornak, *Canterbury Cathedral*, London: Scala Arts & Heritage Publishers, 2021.

Kidson, Peter, 'Panofsky, Suger and St Denis', *Journal of the Warburg and Courtauld Institutes*, Vol. 50, No. 1 (1987), pp. 1–17.

Krautheimer, Richard, *Early Christian and Byzantine Architecture*, London: Penguin, 1965.

Lambert, Élie, *Art musulman et art chrétien dans la péninsule ibérique*, Paris: Editions Privat, 1958.

Lewis, Bernard, 'The Islamic Guilds', *The Economic History Review*, Vol. 8, No. 1 (1937), pp. 20–37.

Loud, G. A., & A. Metcalfe (eds.), *The Society of Norman Italy*, Leiden: Brill, 2002.

Luber, Diana, *Islam in Europe*, Sam Fogg Exhibition Catalogue, London: Paul Holberton Publishing, 2023.

Luyster, Amanda (ed.), *Bringing the Holy Land Home: The Crusades, Chertsey Abbey, and the Reconstruction of a Medieval Masterpiece*, Studies in Medieval and Early Renaissance Art History 3, Turnhout, Belgium: Brepols, 2022.

MacEvitt, Christopher, *The Crusades and the Christian World of the East: Rough Tolerance*, Philadelphia: University of Pennsylvania Press, 2008.

Mackay, Jamie, *The Invention of Sicily*, London: Verso, 2021.

Mâle, Emile, *Religious Art in France: The Twelfth Century: A Study of the Origins of Medieval Iconography*, Princeton, NJ: Princeton University Press, 1978.

Marçais, Georges, *Mélanges d'histoire et d'archéologie de l'occident musulman*, Tome 1 et 2, Algiers: Gouvernment Géneral de l'Algérie, 1957.

———, *L'Art musulman*, Paris: Quadrige, 1981.

Mayer, Leo A., *Islamic Architects and their Works*, Geneva: A. Kundig, 1956.

———, *Islamic Woodcarvers and their Works*, Geneva: A. Kundig, 1958.

Meinecke, Michael, *Patterns of Stylistic Changes in Islamic Architecture: Local Traditions versus Migrating Artists*, New York: New York University Press, 1996.

Melikian-Chirvani, Assadullah Souren (ed.), *The World of the Fatimids*, Toronto: Aga Khan Museum; London: Institute of Ismaili Studies; Munich: Hirmer Verlag, 2018.

Metcalfe, Alex, *Muslims and Christians in Norman Italy: Arabic Speakers and the End of Islam*, London: Routledge, 2003.

———, *The Muslims of Medieval Italy*, Edinburgh: Edinburgh University Press, 2009.

Moses, Paul, *The Saint and the Sultan: The Crusades, Islam, and Francis of Assisi's Mission of Peace*, New York: Doubleday Religion, 2009.

Münchmeyer, Annette, 'The Masons' Marks in the Western Part of the Cathedral of Santiago de Compostela: An Approach to its Construction History', *Construction History*, Vol. 28, No. 2 (2013), pp. 1–22.

Newson, Janet, 'Beakhead Decoration on Romanesque Arches in the Upper Thames Valley', *Oxoniensia* (2013), Oxfordshire Architectural and Historical Society, https://www.oxoniensia.org/volumes/2013/Newson.pdf.

Nicklies, Charles, E., 'Builders, Patrons, and Identity: The Domed Basilicas of Sicily and Calabria', *Gesta*, Vol. 43, No. 2 (2004), pp. 99–114.

O'Kane, Bernard, *The Illustrated Guide to the Museum of Islamic Art in Cairo*, Cairo: American University in Cairo Press, 2012.

Parker, Philip, *History of World Trade in Maps*, London: HarperCollins, 2020.

Peña, Ignacio, *The Christian Art of Byzantine Syria*, Reading: Garnet Publishing, 1997.

Phythian-Adams, Mark, & Geoffrey Tyack, *St Mary's Iffley, History, Design & Symbolism: An Introduction*, Oxford, 2018.

Richardson, Ruth, *Dore Abbey, The Parish Church of Holy Trinity and St Mary*, Much Wenlock: RJI Smith & Associates, 1999.

Riegl, Alois, *Stilfragen: Grundlegungen zu einer Geschichte der Ornamentik*, Berlin: G. Siemens, 1893.

Rogers, Byron, *The Last Englishman: The Life of J. L. Carr*, London: Aurum Press, 2003.

Russell, Josiah Cox, 'The Many-sided Career of Master Elias of Dereham', *Speculum*, Vol. 5, No. 4 (October 1930), pp. 378–87.

Sampson, Jerry, *Wells Cathedral West Front: Construction, Sculpture and Conservation*, Stroud: Sutton Publishing Ltd, 1998.

Scarfe Beckett, Katharine, *Anglo-Saxon Perceptions of the Islamic World*, Cambridge: Cambridge University Press, 2003.

Schapiro, Meyer, 'The Romanesque Sculpture of Moissac', *The Art Bulletin*, Vol. 13, No. 3 (September 1931), pp. 249–351.

———, 'From Mozarabic to Romanesque in Silos', *The Art Bulletin*, Vol. 21, No. 4 (December 1939), pp. 313–74.

Schappert, Peter, & Mario Colletto, *Der Dom zu Speyer: Gebaut für Gott und Kaiser*, Annweiler: Pilger Verlag, 2012.

Serra, Joselita Raspi, 'English Decorative Sculpture of the Early Twelfth Century and the Como-Pavian Tradition', *The Art Bulletin*, Vol. 51, No. 4 (1969), pp. 352–62.

Spadaro, Maria Antonietta, Sergio Troisi & Bruno Carusa, *The Arab-Norman Itinerary: The UNESCO Heritage in Palermo, Monreale and Cefalù*, Palermo: Edizioni d'arte Kalós, 2018.

Stalley, Roger, *Early Irish Sculpture and the Art of the High Crosses*, London: Paul Mellon, 2020.

Strafford, Peter, *Romanesque Churches of France: A Traveller's Guide*, London: Giles de la Mare Publishers, 2005.

———, *Romanesque Churches of Spain: A Traveller's Guide*, London: Giles de la Mare Publishers, 2010.

Sugden, Keith, *Saints, Shrines and Pilgrims*, London: Pitkin Publishing, 2018.

Thurlby, Malcolm, *The Herefordshire School of Romanesque Sculpture*, Eardisley, Herefordshire: Logaston Press, 2016.

Valdez del Álamo, Elizabeth, *Palace of the Mind: The Cloister of Silos and Spanish Sculpture of the Twelfth Century*, Turnhout, Belgium: Brepols, 2012.

Van der Zee, Elsa, *Wells Cathedral: An Architectural and Historical Guide*, Wells: Close Publications, 2017.

Verner, Miroslav, *Temple of the World: Sanctuaries, Cults, and Mysteries of Ancient Egypt*, Cairo: American University in Cairo Press, 2012.

Wenner, Manfred W., 'The Arab/Muslim Presence in Medieval Central Europe', *International Journal of Middle East Studies*, Vol. 12, No. 1 (1980), pp. 59–79.

Werner, Martin, 'On the Origin of the Form of the Irish High Cross', *Gesta*, Vol. 29, No. 1 (1990), pp. 98–110.

Wickham, Chris, *The Donkey and the Boat: Reinterpreting the Mediterranean Economy, 950–1180*, Oxford: Oxford University Press, 2023.

Wilson, Eva, *Islamic Designs*, British Museum Pattern Books, London: British Museum Press, 2008.

Wright, George R. H., *Ancient Building Technology*, Vol I: *Historical Background*, Technology and Change in History, Leiden: E. J. Brill, 2000.

Zarnecki, George, Janet Holt & Tristram Holland (eds.), *English Romanesque Art, 1066–1200*, catalogue of an exhibition at the Hayward Gallery, London, 5 April–8 July 1984, London: Arts Council/Weidenfeld & Nicolson, 1984.

Ziminski, Andrew, *The Stonemason: A History of Building Britain*, London: John Murray, 2020.

INDEX

[**BOLD** = major entry, ***BOLD ITALICS*** = photo/image]

INDEX